D1617345

ETHICS, GOVERNMENT, AND PUBLIC POLICY

A Reference Guide

Edited by
James S. Bowman
and
Frederick A. Elliston

JA
79
.E824
1988
West

Greenwood Press

New York · Westport, Connecticut · London

Copyright Acknowledgments

The editor and publisher gratefully acknowledge
permission to use the following copyrighted materials:

The Code of Ethics of the American Society for
Public Administration, 1120 G Street NW,
Washington, D.C. 20005.

The Code of Ethics of the International City
Management Association.

Excerpts from O. P. Dwivedi, "Ethics, the Public Service and Public Policy,"
International Journal of Public Administration 10, no. 1 (1987): 32–37. Reprinted
by courtesy of Marcel Dekker, Inc.

Library of Congress Cataloging-in-Publication Data

Ethics, government, and public policy : a reference guide / edited by
   James S. Bowman and Frederick A. Elliston.
      p. cm.
   Includes bibliographies and index.
   ISBN 0–313–25192–4 (lib. bdg. : alk. paper)
    1. Political ethics. 2. Political ethics—United States.
I. Bowman, James S., 1945–   II. Elliston, Frederick.
JA79.E824   1988
172—dc19   88–3110

British Library Cataloguing in Publication Data is available.

Copyright © 1988 by James S. Bowman and the Estate of Frederick A. Elliston

All rights reserved. No portion of this book may be
reproduced, by any process or technique, without the
express written consent of the publisher.

Library of Congress Catalog Card Number: 88-3110
ISBN: 0–313–25192–4

First published in 1988

Greenwood Press, Inc.
88 Post Road West, Westport, Connecticut 06881

Printed in the United States of America

The paper used in this book complies with the
Permanent Paper Standard issued by the National
Information Standards Organization (Z39.48–1984).

10 9 8 7 6 5 4 3 2 1

In Memoriam

Frederick Allen Elliston

1944–1987

scholar, teacher, colleague

Contents

Ethics,
Government,
and Public
Policy

Introduction

James S. Bowman

Popular interest in ethics has fluctuated—and steadily increased—in contemporary times. Governmental officials, as repositories of the public trust, can play an important role in nurturing ethical conduct in American democracy. Indeed, as Chester Barnard noted years ago, the real role of the executive is to manage the values of the organization.[1] Values, those ideas that allow for distinctions between right and wrong, form the core of management. If public policy decisions are statements that action ought to be taken, then management is the maximization of values. The study of ethics, or the way that values are practiced, therefore is critical in a democracy, since representative government rests in large part on public officials and the trust they engender.

Yet the daily practice of ethics is close to a nontopic among managers because there are few institutional structures in American organizations that accord a public character to ethical concerns.[2] Undergirded by the celebrated, if discredited, politics–administration dichotomy, public administration advocated an apolitical civil service and embraced science in its quest for universal management principles. The divorce of politics and administration 100 years ago elevated the value of efficiency to a position of preeminence in public management at the expense of other values in American democracy.[3] Organizations were seen as economic and legal entities, not as arenas in which multiple competing values reside. This legacy remains; one recent study, for example, revealed that few administrators see ethical considerations as crucial to decision-making. This is not to say that they are unethical but rather that "the average manager is amoral most of the time."[4]

Employees may make decisions based on personal standards, but organizations define and control the situations in which decisions are made. Executives can create policy "more consistently and with a greater assurance of support in organizations where core values have been clearly articulated and practiced over time."[5] Affirmative control systems that address key variables in organizational decision-making—such as opportunity, incentive, and risk—are needed to deter, rather than merely detect, ethical problems.

Humankind may never resolve the global ethical problems of our age—nuclear terror, world hunger, environmental degradation, racial conflict—without coming to terms with the impact of organizations on people. This may be the lasting contribution of the so-called excellence literature of the early 1980s.[6] More than a catchy phrase of popular writers, the search for excellence begins with bringing into sharper focus shared values and by reconciling bureaucracy with democracy. A perennial task of humanity is to work for a wiser morality, and the authors in this work seek to contribute to that goal.

As a result of a nationwide call for proposals and the subsequent refereeing process, this book gathers together scholars concerned with the processes of government administration.[7] It, most certainly, will not produce easy answers to contemporary ethical questions. Yet while we cannot "solve" ethical issues in government, this does not mean that they are unimportant or that progress is impossible. The fact that decisions are hard to make does not stop them from being made, and ignoring moral problems will not make them go away.

James Thurber once remarked that "it is better to know some of the questions than to know all of the answers." In that spirit, the authors have sought to explore the middle ground between the naive view that one person can change the world and the cynical approach that everyone is a helpless victim of "the system." In this way they hope to assist in a better understanding of the ethical questions that affect government policy and administration.

This volume consists of four sections: (1) Analytical Approaches; (2) Ethical Dilemmas and Standards for Public Servants; (3) Techniques and Methods in Ethical Policy-Making; and (4) Studies of Systemic Issues in Government. The book concludes with an essay that places the American experience in a comparative perspective.

Part one introduces the study of ethics and differing approaches to the subject. Anthony G. Cahill and E. Sam Overman, in "Contemporary Perspectives on Ethics and Values in Public Affairs," briefly trace important historical periods of concern for ethics in government. They contend that the challenge today is to devise ways to gain a "comprehensive understanding of seemingly diverse perspectives on ethics." As an initial step, the authors canvass current approaches: social philosophy and political theory, ethical issues and social morality, professional and administrative ethics, and metaethics and ethical analysis. These schools of thought find expression in subsequent chapters, although the second and third approaches receive the most attention. Cahill and Overman conclude that, because of the uncertain future in the study and practice of government ethics, the need to synthesize these conceptions has never been greater.

The second chapter, "Ethics in Government: A Framework for Analysis,"

by Gerald M. Pops, integrates several approaches to ethics: personal, professional, organizational, and policy, each of which is also examined in further
detail by the other contributors. Following a historical overview and an investigation of the literature, Pops provides a conceptual design to analyze the key
components of administrative decisions. Issues of responsibility, competing obligations, decision choice, and implementation strategies are then scrutinized.
This inquiry promotes understanding of ethical issues and, as such, assists in
the search for legitimizing principles to support the role of administrators in
policy-making.

The selections in part two emphasize ethical dilemmas that appointed and
elected officials may confront in the public service. Sociologists Myron Glazer
and Penina Glazer, in "Individual Ethics and Organizational Morality," explore how some employees deal with these dilemmas by "blowing the whistle." Case studies illustrate the mechanisms used to affect the fate of these
"ethical resisters": blacklisting, transfer, and harassment—techniques that often
result in dismissal. The individual profiles are particularly interesting since they
coincide with many of the ideal requirements of justifiable dissent: appropriate
motives, use of internal procedures, and reasonable evidence. They maintain
that the case histories are not isolated instances and that organizational morality—efforts to protect conscientious employees against reprisals—is little more
than a "porous shield."

Larry A. Bakken and Vera Vogelsang-Coombs examine ethical concerns with
respect to congresspeople in "The Conduct of Legislators." They contend that
extant standards for behavior are too narrowly drawn to be meaningful. Seeking
ways to promote a more ethical environment in Congress, they analyze the
International City Management Association and the American Society for Public Administration codes of conduct. Based on this examination, recent corruption, financial misconduct, and life-style controversies are considered. The writers,
a lawyer and a social scientist, suggest that "legislative codes have important
political and organizational consequences, even though they may not be the
ones expected by reformers." These consequences constitute the argument for
change delineated in their chapter.

Part three presents studies that take stock of several techniques and methods
that may enhance the role of ethics in decision-making: risk analysis and management, negotiated settlements, the office of the ombudsman, and equal employment opportunity laws. In "Controversies in Risk Analysis in Public Management," philosopher Albert Flores and political scientist Michael E. Kraft
examine the determination of technological risk in policy development. They
clarify the types of value issues in risk analysis and consider ways in which
such choices may be made more explicit. "Risk management policies are enormously consequential for important public values such as health, occupational
safety, and environmental quality," and "because of the necessity of making
such judgments, a lively debate has arisen over . . . how objective or scientific
the process is or can be." Critical questions, such as "How are human rights

and individual moral interests considered in risk evaluation?'' may not have definitive answers but decision-making techniques to deal with them are considered. The authors find that although risk analysis is unlikely to be ''a panacea for dealing with the multiple risks of a technological society . . . if it is employed carefully . . . and if the value issues surveyed here are more widely acknowledged, it can be a useful tool in regulatory policy analysis.''

Recognizing the central importance, indeed severity, of such issues, attorney Lloyd Burton, in ''The Legitimacy of Negotiating Rules and Standards,'' advocates the adoption of a consensually oriented, negotiation-based strategy for policy implementation in toxic waste regulation. The central concern of this movement away from adversarial, legalistic rule-making to negotiated settlements hinges on the legitimate use of government agency power. A review of California cases leads to the identification of evaluative ethical criteria as well as to recommendations for enhancing negotiated settlements. These settlements are seen as a ''cheaper, simpler, faster way'' to fulfill policy implementation goals than that afforded by the traditional due process model.

Jonathan P. West continues the decision-making theme in ''The Role of the Ombudsman in Resolving Conflicts.'' This contribution, like others in part three, evaluates a decision-making tool and its implications for augmenting the role of ethics in the policy process. West first reviews the experience of the ombudsman and the accompanying literature. A framework for analyzing four case studies of ombudsman programs—two successes and two failures—is then posited and implemented. Finally, the ombudsman, as one method to encourage administrative responsibility, is assessed.

The last selection in part three probes the kinds of ethical and legal choices that public officials make in public service recruitment and termination actions. Since government employers are expected by many to serve as exemplars, their employment selections play an important role in the pursuit of equal opportunity in American society. The focus of Gary Bryner's chapter, ''The Use of Equal Opportunity and Affirmative Action in Employment Decisions,'' is on preferential treatment and the difficult issues it raises. Like the other contributors, Bryner traces the evolution of his topic and synthesizes pertinent, earlier work on the subject. He then sketches the legal requirements for preferential treatment and turns this analysis to the case of race-conscious reductions in the workforce.

Part four consists of four contributions that deal with systemic issues in ethics and public policy. Political scientists John P. Burke and Richard Pattenaude consider the implications of the professionalization of bureaucracies as well as the bureaucratization of professionals in ''Professional Expertise in Politics and Administration.'' They explore the place of expert knowledge in public policy and the tensions that arise between democratic government and professional competence. Following a discussion of the background to the problem and the appropriate scholarly literature, they present three doctrines—the separatist, the ''ordinary morality,'' and the political—used to address the problem of professions in a democracy. These theses are then employed in the study of a local government problem. It is through their interaction, the authors conclude, that professional expertise can find its proper place in the policy process.

One aspect of the professionalization of the governance process in the twentieth century has been the increasing use of statistics and probabilistic reasoning, a topic probed by Jeremy F. Plant in "The Use of Quantitative Analysis in the Public Sector." An examination of the intellectual heritage of ethics and the relevant published work precedes a discussion of the politicization of bureaucracy and its information services. The tensions that arise between the probabilistic worldview of the statistician and the action-oriented politician may be eased through the understanding and use of the canons of science, legal doctrines of statistical proof, and monitoring activities. The author believes, however, that unless scientists "are free to search for knowledge that informs the processes of public decision-making . . . we will choose between a politics of ideology that refuses to look at the facts or a politics of control that uses information only to maintain centers of power. The result may be a politics of confusion."

Jerome B. McKinney, an expert in public management, examines the pervasiveness of fraud, waste, and abuse in domestic policies and ways to deal with it in "Fraud, Waste and Abuse in Government." He describes the importance of the issue, offers an overview of the literature, and outlines the major schools of thought—personalistic, institutional, and systemic—used to comprehend the problem. These viewpoints are then put into play by assessing contemporary responses to ethical issues. The author concludes that such perspectives are helpful, albeit in different ways, but the absence of a public service philosophy is a significant impediment in the fight against corruption.

In the final chapter in part four, "Morality in the Making of Foreign Policy," Ralph G. Carter argues that the difficulties of making moral choices in government are magnified in the foreign policy arena. His analysis of the literature identifies these convictions about ethics in international affairs: realist, idealist, and proceduralist. They are then used to interpret three controversies: the Nicaraguan *contras,* the Panama Canal treaties, and military aid to Turkey. Like McKinney, he finds that no approach or combination of approaches will make policy-making any easier given the lack of a public consensus about American goals.

The concluding selection, "A Comparative Analysis of Ethics, Public Policy, and the Public Services," furnishes an overview of ethics and public policy. O. P. Dwivedi discusses prominent ethical issues confronting government examined in this book and elsewhere, offers an international perspective on the American experience, and makes a plea for an "administrative theology" as a means to improve public service ethics. He finds that a model public servant is not simply one who obeys laws but also one who strives to strengthen conditions for a moral government. By fulfilling that duty, he or she can inspire public confidence, the hallmark of democratic government.

Clearly, no single reference guide to an interdisciplinary pursuit like ethics can or should be complete, and readers are encouraged to inspect complementary works.[8] Yet a timely study of the management implications of ethics in government by social scientists, management scholars, attorneys, and philosophers can be found in these pages. The chapters should be beneficial to all with a serious interest in the topic—scholars, students, and practitioners alike. Their effective use is facilitated by the manner in which the selections were prepared; most chapters proceed by introducing the subject matter, sketching its historical background, reviewing the body of relevant literature, developing an analytical framework, and examining a key issue using that design. The concluding section of most contributions is followed by a bibliography that not only directs readers to past efforts but also may suggest future research directions.

The study of ethics in government is an important, if a fledgling enterprise. Yet it is precisely because fundamental problems have not been fully addressed that thoughtful reflection is needed. As an introduction to significant ethical issues in governing, this volume seeks to foster such reflection in the years ahead.

NOTES

1. Chester Barnard, *Functions of the Executive* (Cambridge, Mass.: Harvard University Press, 1968).

2. James A. Waters, "The Moral Dimension of Organizational Culture," *Journal of Business Ethics* 6 (1987): 18.

3. *See* Jack Rabin and James S. Bowman, eds., *Politics and Administration: Woodrow Wilson and American Public Administration* (New York: Dekker, 1984), chapter one; Richard A. Bush, "Democracy and Public Ethics: A Second Century Revival of an Alternative Base for Ethics in Public Administration" (Paper presented at the Annual Meeting of the American Society for Public Administration, Boston, March 28–April 1, 1987).

4. Archie B. Caroll, "In Search of the Moral Manager," *Business Horizons* 30 (March–April 1987): 12; Sami M. Abbasi and Kenneth W. Hollman, "An Exploratory Study of the Personal Value Systems of City Managers," *Journal of Business Ethics* 6 (1987): 52.

5. Barry Z. Posner and Warren H. Schmidt, "Ethics in American Companies," *Journal of Business Ethics* 6 (1987): 390.

6. *See,* for example, Thomas J. Peters and Robert H. Waterman, Jr., *In Search of Excellence: Lessons from America's Best Run Companies* (New York: Harper and Row, 1982); Craig R. Hickman and Michael A. Silva, *Creating Excellence: Managing Corporate Culture: Strategy and Change in the New Age* (New York: New American Library, 1984); Rosabeth Moss Kanter, *The Changemasters: Innovation for Productivity in the American Corporation* (New York: Simon and Schuster, 1983); Terrence E. Deal and Allan A. Kennedy, *Corporate Cultures: The Rights and Rituals of Corporate Life* (Reading, Mass.: Addison-Wesley, 1982).

7. The referees who participated in the blind review process of the draft chapters are Kenneth Kernaghan, Robert Jackall, Walter A. Rosenbaum, John Rohr, Henry Kass,

Kathryn G. Denhardt, Gerald Caiden, Terry L. Cooper, Stuart S. Nagel, Robert K. Fullinwider, Lloyd Musolf, Elliot Kline, and Robert D. Miewald, as well as a number of scholars who asked to remain anonymous.

Appreciation is also expressed to the numerous people who responded to the call for proposals but whose interests could not be accommodated within the confines of this book. Finally, the editors are glad to acknowledge professional publications in philosophy, ethics, and public administration for listing the initial announcement of this project.

8. *See,* for example, Amy Gutmann and Dennis Thompson, eds., *Ethics and Politics: Cases and Comments* (Chicago: Nelson Hall, 1984); W. Michael Hoffman and Jennifer Mills Moore, eds., *Business Ethics: Readings and Cases in Corporate Morality* (New York: McGraw-Hill, 1984); Peter A. French, *Ethics in Government* (Englewood Cliffs, N.J.: Prentice-Hall, 1983); James R. Glenn, Jr., *Ethics in Decision Making* (New York: Wiley, 1986); Mark Pastin, *The Hard Problems of Management* (San Francisco: Jossey-Bass, 1986); Joel L. Fleishman, Lance Liebman, and Mark H. Moore, eds., *Public Duties: the Moral Obligations of Government Officials* (Cambridge, Mass.: Harvard University Press, 1981); John A. Rohr, *Ethics for Bureaucrats,* 2d ed.. (New York: Dekker, 1986); Terry Cooper, *The Responsible Administrator,* 2d ed. (Port Washington, N.Y.: Associated Faculty Press, 1986); Kathryn Denhardt, *Toward a More Ethical Public Administration* (Westport, Conn.: Greenwood Press, 1988); Rosemarie Tong, *Ethics in Policy Analysis* (Englewood Cliffs, N.J.: Prentice-Hall, 1986); Suresh Srivastva et al., *Executive Integrity: The Search for High Human Values in Organizational Life* (San Francisco: Jossey-Bass, 1988).

PART ONE

ANALYTICAL APPROACHES

1

Contemporary Perspectives on Ethics and Values in Public Affairs

Anthony G. Cahill and E. Sam Overman

For some observers of contemporary public affairs, increased attention to issues of ethics in government appears to be a new phenomenon, but this is not the case. Thus despite calls for a new political morality, the study and practice of public administration have experienced cyclical waves of interest in ethics. Indeed, as Mark Lilla argued in 1981, the origins of the discipline of public administration "in American colleges and universities was itself the result of an 'ethics' movement." [1]

The ethics movement in late nineteenth-century public administration was in large measure a response to the excesses of the highly visible spoils system and a desire for "good government." The resulting wave of concern embodied the ethos that administration and politics could be separated and that beneath the democratic process one could find politically responsive, incorruptible public administrators inculcated with the moral imperatives of the democratic ethos.

The same themes were evident in the next major wave of concern for ethics during the New Deal. The growth and complexity of government, the importance of administrative action, and the increasing social and political pluralism raised new questions about administrative discretion. [2] This second wave included an issue orientation in which specific public policy problems such as national defense, school integration, or education became arenas for ethical debate. Also introduced at this time was what Dennis Thompson called the "possibility of administrative ethics," which emphasized a focus on individual administrative ethics and moral judgment. [3]

The third and most recent wave of interest in ethics was dominated not by the field of public administration but by students of public policy. As the public policy movement gained strength in the 1960s, many of its adherents approached ethics in government as if it were a new phenomenon. Peter Brown, writing in 1986, suggested that the 1960s, and the then-new policy perspective, represented the historical and disciplinary origins of public sector ethical studies.[4] Nothing, however, could be further from the truth. The study of ethics within the policy perspective, like other elements of the policy perspective, represented not a beginning but a highly specialized and valuable addition. Policy ethicists, since the beginning of the movement, concentrated not on the democratic administrative ethos, the content of policies, or the moral judgments of individual administrators but instead on rational scientific methods of ethical analyses and moral reasoning.[5] Some even claim that in schools of public policy and public affairs the analytic study of ethics has to a large degree replaced moral education.[6]

The problem confronting both practitioners and academics today is not one of making a choice among divergent perspectives such as moral education, issues debates, individual ethics, or ethical analysis; rather it is to discover ways in which a more comprehensive understanding of seemingly diverse perspectives on ethics in public affairs can be discerned.

Of what utility is such a comprehensive understanding to those who engage in the practice and study of government? The answer lies in the increasingly complex and qualitatively different types of issues that government is now being asked to address. Quantum advances in technology and the ever more rapid rate of these advances have combined to present society with issues for which current ethical and philosophical systems seem at least partially and frustratingly inadequate.

Only twenty years ago, for instance, the first hesitant attempts at organ transplantations were made. In 1987, we were asked to consider the ethical dimensions of multiple transplants of scarce organs for one individual in relation to others needing a first transplant. Furthermore, the Supreme Court has ruled that new forms of life artificially created in the laboratory may be patented as "inventions." What ethical system will guide future actions about the implications of this for human life—particularly in light of the position of the Catholic church that the creation of human life outside the womb is immoral? To take yet a third example, with technology now available, nearly limitless information can be and is collected on the daily activities of citizens. What ethical principles should shape and guide the new relationship between citizen and government caused by this new capacity?

These examples and numerous others are harbingers of things to come. Although different in many respects, they share one critical element: each places significant strains on societal expectations concerning ethical systems to guide governmental action. Each requires that we extend ethical systems to assess events and developments that only a few years ago were considered to be in the realm of science fantasy. Set against these new demands, a critical examination of contemporary perspectives on ethics and values is a much needed, overdue first step in developing ethical and philosophical systems for a radically different future.

BACKGROUND

Although the historical development of ethics in government has received attention in the past, little has been done to provide a systematic synthesis and critical examination of larger issues of concern. Those studies that do attempt to provide such an overview rely primarily on information concerning the teaching of ethics in schools of public affairs and administration.

The most comprehensive studies in higher education were undertaken by the Hastings Center. Joel Fleishman and Bruce Payne, writing in 1980 about schools of public affairs, found that fewer than one-quarter of the 134 programs responding to their survey offered courses in government ethics. Moreover, in almost every instance it was a specific individual's conviction that sustained that emphasis in the curriculum. The majority of the courses focused on potential ethical conflicts faced by individuals working in government, and the rest were primarily oriented toward the study of larger moral issues confronting society as a whole. Fleishman and Payne advocated sustaining this dual character of the study of ethics in public affairs by emphasizing to students the "dilemmas of responsibility" (ethical problems of administrative and political office) and the "dilemmas of choice" (ethical problems of conflicting values and social priorities).[7] Another Hastings-sponsored study revealed even less emphasis on ethics in social science curricula. Donald Warwick estimated in 1977 that no more than ten courses dealing with ethics in the social sciences existed across the United States. In 1980 the number was not over fifteen.[8]

Major professional associations have also studied ethics in government. A recent conference of the Association for Public Policy Analysis and Management (APPAM) on curricula design assembled ethics syllabi from major policy schools.[9] Most courses can be characterized in one of three ways: (1) framework courses, (2) topics or issues courses, and (3) problems of ethics-in-the-workplace courses. The APPAM materials have a clear policy perspective, one that is biased toward ethical analyses and less attentive to the democratic–administrative ethos, individual ethics, or issue debates.[10]

PERSPECTIVES ON ETHICS IN GOVERNMENT

Although valuable, curricula-based assessments are necessarily limited in perspective. Syntheses of ethics in government must go beyond how ethics are taught to include perspectives or approaches that guide *both* ethical action and research on ethics. A careful examination of previous literature as well as research and teaching materials reveals four primary conceptual approaches: (1) social philosophy and political theory, (2) ethical issues and social morality, (3) professional and administrative ethics, and (4) metaethics and ethical analysis.

Social Philosophy and Political Theory

Questions of ethics and values have their most deep-seated applications within the traditions of social philosophy and political theory. These traditions examine the volatile and ambiguous relationship between the individual and the social and political system of which he or she is a part. Thus theories of social contract, including those defined by Locke, Rousseau, Kant, and Rawls, are central to this approach. Debate over basic rationalities—economic, political, social and legal—and defining criteria for social choice also dominate this literature.

Such concerns are distinctive as a vehicle for ethical issues to move from abstract and ambiguous statements of like, dislike, and preference to more prescribed definitions of ethics as abstract beliefs. That is, they allow individuals to draw distinctions between what "is" and what "ought" to be. These distinctions in turn lead to "dispositions to behave in certain ways."[11] They also lead to the belief that an action "is in some way right; it is not merely what is done, it is also what is to be done."[12]

The application of this tendency in public affairs education is evidenced by available curricula information. One-third of the public administration courses surveyed in 1980 by the Hastings Center were based on ethical principles of social and political theory.[13] Not surprisingly, the most frequently cited work in these courses is John Rawls's 1971 *Theory of Justice*.[14] His argument that "distributive justice" and natural rights should replace a dominant utilitarian system of ethics is central in discussions of the changing nature of the social contract.

Utilitarianism, communitarianism, and liberalism are the most cited examples of moral theory in the course descriptions using a social philosophy motif. Most posit utilitarianism or the pragmatic efficiency orientation of public choice of public goods as the dominant theme in moral theory. Communitarianism is a minority view, emphasizing doing "good" in addition to the utilitarian norms of doing "well." Liberalism, in contrast, is a debate between liberty and equality in the distribution (or redistribution) of scarce resources. What is the ethical role of the state in managing equity or preserving the rights and liberties of individuals? The core issues of the moral-philosophy approach, then, are the relative primacy of liberty and equality in the determination of distributive justice and how rights might be justified in the design of social and political institutions.

Other frequently cited authors are William Frankena, who undertook primarily metaethical analyses; Wayne Leys, who addressed the role of ethics and values within the context of democratic theory; and contemporary philosophers such as Hannah Arendt. Finally, the classic works of Plato, Aristotle, Kant, and others frequently serve as material for those using this school of thought.[15]

A second theme addresses the difficulties, or impossibility, of aggregating preferences into a common social welfare function. Arrow's impossibility theo-

rem, Pareto's optimality, Kaldor-Hicks's criterion, and the social welfare cal-
culus of economics serve to demonstrate the problems inherent in reaching
consensus on which ethical systems are to dominate in a given society or group.
Within this approach, the central question concerns definitions of "good" government, that is, what criteria are to be used to assess a government as good
or bad?

A third theme debates the fundamental nature of humankind and the political
structure of the social contract. Hobbes assumed the worst of the human race
and championed a strictly codified and enforced public morality, a theory reflected in many contemporary codes of ethics. Conversely, Rousseau argued
that in light of the innate goodness of the species, many of the socially organized relationships between individuals and political authority structures could
remain unspecified.[16]

Beyond these general themes are a host of other more specific issues particularly germane to social philosophy and political theory. They include civil
disobedience, liberty and equity, public interest, civil duty, and political obligation. They are most often discussed in reference to diverse systems of governance (democratic or socialist theories) and within the context of philosophies
such as evolutionism, existentialism, humanism, historical materialism, phenomenology, pragmatism, and utilitarianism.[17]

Ethical Issues and Social Morality

One distinguishing characteristic of the first current of thought is its broad
philosophic nature. The consequence of such an approach, however, is the lack
of a topical focus. It is difficult to apply abstract ethical and moral theories
without the specific context provided by policy issues. The second approach to
the study of ethics initiates discourse on specific topics through consideration
of contemporary issues. A distinctive characteristic here is addressing issues
that individuals both in and outside public service are forced to confront and
make judgments about on a regular basis.

These concerns are placed within the context of an aggregate or group level
of policy-making. Using contemporary problems as a starting point, a conscious effort is made to recognize the evolution of social interest groups and
policy networks that create and are created by popular opinion. Political debates concerning issues that stem from moral positions are generally intense,
as deep-rooted beliefs are subjected to the compromises of the political system
in allocating values. What is at the heart of the issue-oriented school, then, is
the dynamic process of creating shared interests and values in which individuals
acknowledge the public nature of a particular issue by organizing in an attempt
to influence public policy and popular opinion.

Specific issues change to reflect contemporary debate in the political arena.
In 1964 Harry Girvetz emphasized, in *Contemporary Moral Issues,* the problems of national security, civil rights, and war.[18] By 1975 Tom Beauchamp's

Ethics and Public Policy reflected changing public priorities in its treatment of concerns such as abortion, capital punishment, and sexual discrimination in the workplace.[19] In 1984 Amy Gutmann and Dennis Thompson examined violence, deception, official disobedience, equal opportunity, and liberty and life as major areas of ethical conflict.[20]

Two chapters in this volume emphasize the issue approach to ethics in government. Jerome McKinney, in his examination of fraud, waste, and abuse in government, found that it is the absence of a public service philosophy, perhaps the democratic administrative ethos, that impedes the fight against corruption. Ralph Carter, in his foreign policy cases, concluded that despite some anomalies, Americans prefer moral foreign policy goals pursued by ethical means.

Studies in this school are grounded in an explicit recognition of pluralistic ethical systems that create and sustain public debate. Many works are centrally concerned with *descriptive ethics* (descriptions of sets of observed behavior with an explicit attempt to be nonjudgmental), whereas others focus on *normative ethics* (sets of value-based judgments taken by individuals and groups on social issues).

These positions, grounded in particular moral belief structures and ethical theories, are principles for guidance in complex and ambiguous social settings.[21] Issues used as teaching tools are frequently crafted to force individuals to make and defend value judgments—the "values clarification" method. Although few institutions offer ethics courses, the vast majority of those that do focus on "ethical conflicts" or "moral issues."[22]

One of the major difficulties encountered in placing social and political theory in an issue-oriented approach is that the distinctions drawn between descriptive and normative ethics may be mooted as they are applied to the theory and practice of public affairs. Proponents of "value relativism" argue that rational examination of essentially nonrational value beliefs is counterproductive. Efforts to undertake a "value-free" examination of ethics and to distinguish between the detached analysis called for in descriptive ethics and the prescriptive nature of normative ethics may be creating what are, in effect, distinctions without real differences. Descriptive ethics can all too easily become normative ethics when introduced into the pluralistic setting of policy-making.

It is difficult in practice to conceive of ethics and values that are not applied, since ethics inevitably carry with them some referent in a social context. Whose ethics and values are being examined or advocated and for what means and ends? Encouraging distinctions between descriptive and normative ethics may serve as a smokescreen that blurs issues surrounding divergent social groups as they compete in the process of the authoritative allocation of values.

Professional and Administrative Ethics

A characteristic of the issue-oriented approach is its applied policy specificity. It is often criticized for lack of attention to administrative implementation and bureaucratic control in the resolution of ethical conflicts, for ignoring, as Gary Bryner says elsewhere in this volume, the "kinds of ethical and legal choices that public employees must make every day." A third approach to ethics and value, then, consciously focuses on the norms and standards of professional groups, in particular public officials and bureaucrats as discussed in the chapter by John P. Burke and Richard Pattenaude. The perspective explicitly defines the relationship between the individual, the public organization, and the larger political system as an ongoing conflict between "public duty, personal morality, and private interest."[23] This school of thought receives the most attention from authors whose concern leads not only to questions of public rights but also to an explicit emphasis on public duties.[24]

Frequently lumped under the aggregate term *applied ethics*, this motif distinguishes between personal- and system-level value systems. Potential conflicts between these two levels of value systems are frequently used by the professions to highlight ethical issues in organizations. The distinction was clearly drawn by Paul Appleby in 1959 when he proposed a normative theory of democratic government and moral systems within which bureaucrats must operate; he saw politics and hierarchy as institutional variables that guide the ethical behavior of agency personnel.[25] As pointed out by Jeremy Plant in this book, a decade later Stephen Bailey used Appleby's work to develop a contrasting normative theory of personal ethics. Instead of systemic sets of ethical codes affecting the behavior of public officials, Bailey argued, the individual affects the organization through personal conviction: "the essential moral qualities of the ethical public servant are: (1) optimism; (2) courage; and (3) fairness tempered by charity."[26]

The impact of ethical issues in professional and agency settings was further developed by John Rohr in the 1970s in his *Ethics for Bureaucrats: An Essay on Law and Values*. Rohr drew a distinction between a "low-road" approach, which addresses ethical issues almost exclusively in terms of "adherence to agency rules" (e.g., use of agency vehicles, allocation of time off) and a "high-road" approach associated with the "new" public administration, which suggests that "social equity be added to the classical norms of efficient, economical and coordinated management as criteria for evaluating the performance of new public administrators."[27]

Advocates of the new public administration such as Frank Marini and H. George Frederickson argued that social equity transcended all other value systems in considering the "good of humankind" as a criterion for administrative judgment and behavior.[28] This is echoed in Rohr's "equitable administrator" who "actively intervenes to enhance the political power and economic well-being of disadvantaged minorities in order to address the neglect suffered by such minorities at the hands of customary procedures of representative democracy."[29]

Principles of social equity, in turn, are based on and derived from political philosophy and humanistic psychology. What Rohr termed *regime values*—the values of the polity as expressed in basic documents such as the Constitution and legislation—can be used to discuss ethics by reviewing major Supreme Court cases as an expression of social values.

Using strategic court decisions and national legislation, however, assumes that public law and social values are explicitly linked and that disputes over law in the courts are an accurate expression of current ethical debates in government and society as a whole. Although certain recurring issues (e.g., abortion) may indeed reflect this linkage, court cases are just as frequently static and artificially structured representations of dynamic social ethics that occur well after issues have been raised in the policy-making process. Discussion of *Brown vs. Board of Education,* for example, has limited utility to current issues of discrimination when set against more broadly defined groups of minorities, including handicapped individuals and gay-rights organizations.

Moreover, a "regime values" theme can have the unfortunate effect of narrowing the range of debates to those that occur at a level of abstraction that has proven difficult to connect to concrete policy actions (e.g., methods to prevent discrimination in various organizational settings). One answer to this criticism is to undertake a comprehensive assessment of all relevant levels of policy. This would permit the examination of the interplay between strategic legislative and judicial decisions on the one hand and the implementation of those decisions through regulatory and procedural actions on the other hand. Gary Bryner, for example, uses this tact in this book to outline the role of ethics in redressing long-standing inequities in employment policy.

Other writers have used different approaches. Louis C. Gawthrop, in *Public Sector Management, Systems, and Ethics,* confirmed the centrality of individual administrative responsibility toward social ethics.[30] He described two forms of administrative ethics. There predominates, Gawthrop maintained, an ethics of civility that is mechanistic, procedural, pragmatic, quantitative, and ultimately reductionistic. The ethics of civility is oriented toward administrative and political self-preservation. Gawthrop, however, disagreed with the process of the ethics of civility: "The incremental allocation of the limited governmental resources among the pluralist groups by professional political participants on the basis of bargained agreements is the epitome of an ethics of civility."[31]

In place of an ethics of civility, Gawthrop argued for a systems ethics that includes an ethics of consciousness and an ethics of maturity. An ethics of consciousness requires that all administrators become aware of the total system context in which they operate; an ethics of maturity provides the sense of purpose in an individual's life. A creative ethics, or the "faithfulness to being critically honest about one's self to one's self," is the final guarantor of ethical administrative behavior. Yet the reliance on individual ethical decisions and self-enlightenment may be criticized for ignoring the larger social and political context that can provide situational ethics. The tension, once again, is between individual ethical analyses and more transcendent ethical principles of the public administration ethos.

Gawthrop's work, like that of Appleby, Bailey, and Rohr, as well as books such as Terry Cooper's *Responsible Administrator: An Approach to Ethics for the Administrative Role* are excellent examples of applied administrative or professional ethics.[32] Recognizing the power and ambiguity of professional life and practice, each author developed a prescription for ethical behavior based on an individual's sense of duty and responsibility. This is both their strength and weakness. The strength is the procedural prescriptions (i.e., become more critically self-conscious and mature); the weakness remains a substantive relativism or an opposite absolutism as the ultimate source of ethical behavior. For Gawthrop, it is absolutism, that is, a reliance on some ultimate, transcendent ethical purposefulness and a rejection of pluralities of ethical behaviors, that weakens his case for systems ethics.

A popular method used within this field is to illustrate ethical dilemmas faced by administrators. Frequently cited published works include R. Golembiewski and M. White's *Cases in Public Management,* William Frankena and John Granrose's *Introductory Readings in Ethics,* and material prepared by the Standards and Ethics Committee of the American Society for Public Administration. In the material prepared by the committee readers are asked a series of "self-diagnostic" questions on topics such as responsibility and accountability, commitment, citizenship and the political process, conflicts of interest and public disclosure, and confidentiality.[33]

Three chapters in this volume, in addition to those already mentioned, use the administrative and personal dilemmas approach, and a fourth chapter takes a broader, more comparative view. Chapter three by Myron Glazer and Penina Glazer chronicles the consequences of "whistleblowing" in government and industry. Jonathan West, in chapter seven, examines the ombudsman as a mitigating force in the sometimes stormy relationship between citizens and their government. Chapter four by Larry Bakken and Vera Vogelsang-Coombs analyzes ethical conflict encountered by elected officials through an examination of professional codes of ethics. Finally, Gerald Pops, in chapter two assesses multiple conceptual frameworks for viewing the relationship between administrators and ethical systems.

Metaethics and Ethical Analysis

A fourth and final approach is one centrally concerned with the role of ethics and values in the process of analytical inquiry. This school, which is closely identified with the policy science and policy analysis movements of the 1960s and 1970s, has extended its influence into public administration and management.

As a topic of concern, metaethics focuses attention on the role of values and analysis in two ways. The first is a normative issue of the relative worth of ethical and valuative concerns as an object of study (i.e., should we study those concerns?). The second, and more far reaching, issue is primarily methodological and addresses effective ways of uncovering and assessing value positions (i.e., how can we discover those concerns?).

These problems, perhaps because of their long history in most of the social sciences, are more frequently dismissed as dead issues by numerous contemporary analysts and practitioners. In fact, however, the debate continues to take new forms and heightens in intensity as it does so. This controversy is entirely appropriate; during the past twenty years, the policy science and policy analysis movements have fostered a strong emphasis on analysis and rigorous scientific research as a basis for decisions. Schools of public administration, policy, and management, which train future officials and engage in scientific inquiry, emphasize research and analysis. Ignoring the focus that such methodological skills place on ethical and valuative concerns would be a dangerous oversight indeed.

The debate concerning whether or not values are an appropriate issue for study is reminiscent in many ways of the earlier one over "value-neutral" administration. This debate, however, focuses not on the existence of a value-neutral way of administering policies but on the extent to which the process of social inquiry allows value-neutral methods to solve public problems.

An increasingly large group of writers, including Laurence Tribe, Martin Rein, Duncan MacRae, and Fred Dallmayr, reject the claim that social inquiry is or ought to be confined to observational analysis and subsequent generalization as well as the similar claim made by Edith Stokey and Richard Zeckhauser in 1978 that the study of policy "should concentrate on differences in prediction as opposed to differences in values."[34]

Nevertheless, an equally wide body of literature supports the position that ethical and valuative concerns are outside the analyst's realm. Operating on such an assumption, this mode of inquiry presumes that the "evaluative premises of policy arguments are given" and that the role of social inquiry is therefore the "technical matter of what works."[35] With such a role assigned to inquiry, the analyst should take "goals as givens and then [attempt] to determine what policies will maximize or optimize them.[36]

Those who reject the claims of value-neutral research do so on a number of grounds. Erve Chambers synthesized well the dangers inherent in ignoring values by pointing out the possibility of missing the "common exceptions" whereby people act in essentially similar ways but on the basis of strikingly different values or act in dissimilar ways but on the basis of quite similar values.[37]

The continuing controversy over *how* values can best be elicited hinges on what type of value is being sought. Increasingly, *values* are defined not as normative judgments concerning relative preferences but as what has been called "value-as-criterion."[38] This is concerned with "not only how an object is rated, ranked or otherwise appraised, but with the criteria employed to make such evaluations. [This] meaning of values incorporates assumptions, decision rules, and other standards of assessment in terms of which evaluative and advocative claims are made."[39]

The concept of value-as-criterion is consistent with and extends Kurt Baier's principle of value as a normative base for action and may also be addressed as alternative conceptions of validity in research methodology. Here, the continuing debate over how values can best be elicited frequently takes the form of a "bifurcative fallacy" in which only two extreme solutions to a problem are considered. On one extreme are those who advocate "thick," "rich," or "deep" investigations to lead to a subjective understanding or "verstehen" of individual or collective values. Correspondingly, they believe that the search for empirical generalizations about values "never made much sense as far as the social sciences are concerned."[40] On the other extreme are those who define *validity* as "in general [as] being accurate" and in particular as "the external consistency with empirical reality"; in doing so they define validity as consistency and generalizability.[41]

From what sources does the overzealous focus on value-neutral inquiry arise? One source is the tension between the needs of practitioners and analysts: "It is difficult to escape the temptation of [investigating] gross indicators such as race or social class. This is especially true in practical applications to policy problems where, for example, racial and ethnic differences are often the important high visibility criteria for the policy decisionmaker."[42]

A second source lies in the rigidity of much basic and applied research. The need to replicate and generalize findings is often expressed in the tendency to regard measurement issues surrounding values as merely inconvenient in otherwise controllable research procedures. Expressions of value are thus viewed as outside the scope of what can be constituted as a variable for research purposes.

Donald Campbell referred to this tendency as "definitional operationalism"—the "advice to employ designated operational definitions for theoretical terms"—which he viewed as an "unmitigated disaster."[43] At the crux of the issue, then, is the problem of content validation.

An attempt to resolve this dilemma and provide the means to investigate ethical hypotheses has been suggested by Duncan MacRae in *The Social Function of Social Science*.[44] As described by one of the leading proponents of empirical investigation of valuative principles, MacRae's three "metaethical rules" are:

Specification of Ethical Hypotheses: Systems of ethical hypotheses put forth shall be specified in writing in advance. This specification is intended to support the norm of clarity and can include definitions specified in ways other than those of ordinary usage, statements of principles set off from context, and logical or mathematical symbols.

Application of Common Standards of Assessment: Proponents of competing systems of ethical hypotheses shall apply common standards for assessing normative disputes. Common standards of assessment include generality (scope of application), internal consistency (absence of contradictions within a system of ethical hypotheses) and external consistency (absence of contradictions betweeen a system of ethical hypotheses and other convictions about morally justifiable actions)

Assessment of Situational Adequacy: Proponents of competing systems of ethical hypotheses shall suggest different conflict situations designed to elicit inconsistencies in opposing arguments. After each such opportunity to present conflict situations, the proponent of the ethical system under criticism shall decide whether he wishes to alter his ethical system or make the choice dictated by it.[45]

The extent to which such a system will produce more studies with an explicit valuative orientation—as well as the extent to which the concept of value-defined-as-criteria will influence the choice of social science researchers to include valuative concerns as a focus of research—is unclear. The middle ground that such a stand represents between proponents of a reborn logical positivism and a reliance on subjective verstehen as the legitimate means of discovery, however, provides a mostly unrecognized opportunity for advancing the study of ethics and values in public sector research. Albert Flores and Michael Kraft, in chapter five, use this integrative approach as they assess the role of quantitative risk analysis techniques in regulatory policy.

CONCLUSION

As even this brief review has demonstrated, there is an evolutionary character to perspectives on values in public affairs. The examination of ethics from the vantage point of moral philosophy and political theory evolved in the early part of the century to one that addressed ethics from the standpoint of discrete issues. In the middle of the century, attention turned toward administrative ethics and more individual concerns over responsibility and accountability. The most recent wave of scholarly interest concerns both ethical analysis and the ethics of analysis.

The cyclical nature of attention to ethics makes clear the uncertain future with which students of ethics are confronted. In government as well as in academe, we have for better or worse abandoned a "transcendent moral imperative" that served to inform governmental action in an earlier era.[46] Society has likewise abandoned the early precepts of "moral education" and replaced them with what might be described as "analytic ethics." Given the pluralism of contemporary society, it is unlikely that a new moral imperative will emerge in the near future to serve as an unequivocal guide to governmental action.

Perhaps the most telling evidence of this is the fact that as a profession, those who teach ethics have moved beyond a plurality of divergent ethical principles to a plurality of competing approaches with which to study ethics. In such a setting (which has been called by one observer an era of "posttheological" ethics), what can we expect? Clearly, a heightened expectation exists that educational institutions (especially professional schools of public policy and administration, law, public health, and business) will not only mirror increasing ethical concerns in society as a whole but also will take a proactive role in both assessing and setting professional standards.

At the same time, we share with John Rohr a concern about the utility of much contemporary ethical debate in public affairs education: "current discussions of ethics and values, though interesting in themselves, offer little guidance to those concerned with questions about . . . curriculum."[47] Key findings of Fleishman and Payne's 1980 survey include the fact that the majority of courses concerned issues of philosophy and political theory and that most professors were trained in political theory.

Their remedy—to bring into the classroom instructors trained in social ethics, history, and law—could well serve to encourage an increasingly abstract approach to what must be grounded in some social context of professional experience and common understanding. Placing the study of ethics and values squarely within the domain of philosophy and political theory—or alternatively placing such work within the domain of an archetypal analytic framework— may fail to prepare future practitioners and researchers alike to confront successfully the valuative aspects of dramatically and qualitatively new issues that stretch the boundaries of contemporary perspectives on ethics. The challenge of arriving at ethical and philosophical systems that will adequately serve such a rapidly evolving society lies with our educational institutions and those who teach in them. A first and most pressing task for those accepting the challenge is to arrive at a synthesis that imposes at least a partial conceptual order on the competing and divergent approaches to the practice and study of ethics.

NOTES

1. Mark T. Lilla, "Ethos, 'Ethics,' and Public Service," *Public Interest*, no. 63 (Spring 1981): 4.
2. Ibid., pp. 4–7.
3. Dennis F. Thompson, "The Possibility of Administrative Ethics," *Public Administration Review* 45, no. 5 (September–October 1985): 555–561.
4. Peter Brown, "Ethics and Education for Public Service in a Liberal State," *Journal of Policy Analysis and Management* 6, no. 1 (Fall 1986): 62.
5. Ibid., pp. 56–68.
6. Lilla, "Ethos," pp. 7–11.
7. Joel L. Fleishman and Bruce L. Payne, *Ethical Dilemmas and the Education of Policymakers* (Hastings-on-Hudson, N.Y.: Hastings Center, 1980).
8. Donald P. Warwick, *The Teaching of Ethics in the Social Sciences* (Hastings-on-Hudson, N.Y.: Hastings Center, 1980).
9. Conference Proceedings of the Association of Public Policy Analysis and Management Conference on the Policy Curriculum, *Ethics, Political and Organizational Analysis, Public Management* (Hilton Head, S.C., April 16–19, 1986).
10. Brown, "Ethics and Education," pp. 56–68.
11. Kurt Baier, "What Is Value? An Analysis of the Concept," in Kurt Baier and Nicholas Rescher, eds., *Values and the Future* (New York: Free Press, 1969), p. 40.
12. Alan Gewirth, *Reason and Morality* (Chicago: University of Chicago Press, 1978), p. 977.
13. Fleishman and Payne, *Ethical Dilemmas*, pp. 1–4.

14. John Rawls, *A Theory of Justice* (Cambridge, Mass.: Belknap Press of Harvard University, 1971), p. 154.

15. *See* William Frankena and John Granrose, eds., *Introductory Readings in Ethics* (Englewood Cliffs, N.J.: Prentice-Hall, 1974); Wayne Leys, *Ethics and Social Policy: The Art of Asking Deliberative Questions* (New York: Prentice-Hall, 1941); Hannah Arendt, *The Life of the Mind: Willing,* vol. 2 (New York: Harcourt Brace Jovanovich, 1978).

16. William Scott and David Hart, "The Moral Nature of Man in Organizations: A Comparative Analysis," *Academy of Management Review* 14, no. 2 (1971): 241–255.

17. Ethel Albert and Clyde Kluckholm, *A Selected Bibliography on Values, Ethics and Esthetics in the Behavioral Sciences and Philosophy: 1920–1958* (Bloomington: University of Indiana Press, 1959).

18. Harry Girvetz, *Contemporary Moral Issues* (Belmont, Calif: Wadsworth, 1964), *passim.*

19. Tom Beauchamp, *Ethics and Public Policy* (Englewood Cliffs, N.J.: Prentice-Hall, 1975), *passim.*

20. Amy Gutmann and Dennis Thompson, eds., *Ethics and Politics: Cases and Comments* (Chicago: Nelson Hall, 1984).

21. Baier, "What Is Value?" p. 54.

22. Fleishman and Payne, "Ethical Dilemmas."

23. Ibid., p. iii.

24. Joel Fleishman, Lance Liebman, and Mark Moore, *Public Duties: The Moral Obligation of Public Officials* (Cambridge, Mass.: Harvard University Press, 1981).

25. Paul Appleby, *Morality and Administration in Democratic Government* (Baton Rouge: Louisiana State University Press, 1959).

26. Stephen K. Bailey, "Ethics and the Public Service," *Public Administration Review* 24 (December 1964): 235–236.

27. John Rohr, *Ethics for Bureaucrats: An Essay on Law and Values* (New York: Dekker, 1978), p. 55. *See also* John Rohr, "The Study of Ethics in the P.A. Curriculum," *Public Administration Review* 36 (July–August 1976): 398–406.

28. Frank Marini, ed., *Toward a New Public Administration: The Minnowbrook Perspective* (New York: Harper and Row, 1971); H. George Frederickson, ed., "Symposium on Social Equity and Public Administration," *Public Administration Review* 34 (1974): 1–51.

29. Rohr, *Ethics for Bureaucrats,* p. 55.

30. Louis C. Gawthrop, *Public Sector Management, Systems, and Ethics* (Bloomington: Indiana University Press, 1984), p. 141.

31. Ibid.

32. Terry Cooper, *The Responsible Administrator: An Approach to Ethics for the Administrative Role* (Port Washington, N.Y.: Kennikat Press, 1982).

33. Herman Mertins, Jr., and Patrick J. Hennigan, eds., *Applying Professional Standards and Ethics in the 1980's: A Workbook and Study Guide for Public Administrators,* 2d ed. (Washington, D.C.: American Society for Public Administration, 1982).

34. *See* Laurence Tribe, "Policy Science: Analysis or Ideology," *Philosophy and Public Affairs* 2, no. 1 (Fall 1972): 66–110; Martin Rein, *Social Science and Public Policy* (New York: Penguin Books, 1976); Duncan MacRae, *The Social Function of Social Science* (New Haven: Yale University Press, 1976); Fred Dallmayr, "Critical Theory and Public Policy," in William N. Dunn, ed., *Policy Analysis: Perspectives,*

Concepts, and Methods (Greenwich, Conn.: JAI Press, 1986), pp. 158–174; Edith Stokey and Richard Zeckhauser, *A Primer for Policy Analysis* (New York: Norton, 1978), p. 261.

35. David Paris and James Reynolds, *The Logic of Policy Inquiry* (New York: Longman, 1983), p. 70.

36. Stuart Nagel, "The Means May Be a Goal," in William N. Dunn, ed., *Symposium on Social Values and Public Policy, Policy Studies Journal* 9, no. 4 (1980–1981): 4. Special issue.

37. Erve Chambers, "The Cultures of Science and Policy," in William N. Dunn, ed., *Policy Analysis: Perspectives, Concepts and Methods* (Greenwich, Conn.: JAI Press, 1986), p. 101.

38. Robert Williams, *American Society: A Sociological Perspective* (New York: Knopf, 1960), p. 401.

39. William N. Dunn, ed., *Symposium on Social Values and Public Policy, Policy Studies Journal* 9, no. 4 (1980–1981): 87.

40. Clifford Geertz, *The Interpretation of Cultures* (New York: Basic Books, 1973), p. 5.

41. Stuart Nagel, "Conceptualizing Public Policy Analysis," in William N. Dunn, ed., *Policy Analysis: Perspectives, Concepts, and Methods* (Greenwich, Conn.: JAI Press, 1986) p. 258.

42. Chambers, "The Cultures of Science and Policy," p. 99.

43. Donald Campbell, "Can We Be Scientific in Applied Social Science?" in Ross Conner, David G. Altman, and Christine Jackson, eds., *Evaluation Studies Review Annual*, vol. 9 (Beverly Hills, Calif.: Sage, 1984), p. 3.

44. Duncan MacRae, *The Social Function of Social Science*, pp. 92–93.

45. William N. Dunn, "Values, Ethics, and Standards in Policy Analysis," in Stuart Nagel, ed., *Encyclopedia of Policy Studies* (New York: Dekker, 1983), pp. 342–343.

46. This phrase was suggested to us by a referee of an early draft of this chapter.

47. Rohr, *Ethics for Bureaucrats*, p. 51.

SELECTED BIBLIOGRAPHY

Albert, Ethel, and Clyde Kluckholm. *A Selected Bibliography on Values, Ethics, and Esthetics in the Behavioral Sciences and Philosophy: 1920–1985*. Bloomington: University of Indiana Press, 1959.

Appleby, Paul. *Morality and Administration in Democratic Government*. Baton Rouge: Louisiana State University Press, 1959.

Arendt, Hannah. *The Life of the Mind: Willing*. Vol. 2. New York: Harcourt Brace Jovanovich, 1978.

Baier, Kurt. "What Is Value? An Analysis of the Concept." In Kurt Baier and Nicholas Rescher, *Values and the Future*. New York: Free Press, 1969.

Bailey, Stephen K. "Ethics and the Public Service." *Public Administration Review* 24 (December 1964): 234–243.

Beauchamp, Tom. *Ethics and Public Policy*. Englewood Cliffs, N.J.: Prentice-Hall, 1975.

Brown, Peter. "Ethics and Education for Public Service in a Liberal State." *Journal of Policy Analysis and Management*, 6, no. 1 (Fall 1986): 56–68.

Brunner, Ron. "The Policy Science as Science." *Policy Sciences* 15 (1985): 115–135.

Campbell, Donald. "Can We Be Scientific in Applied Social Science?" In Ross Conner, David G. Altman, and Christine Jackson, eds., *Evaluation Studies Review
Annual.* Vol. 9. Beverly Hills, Calif.: Sage, 1984.

Chambers, Erve. "The Cultures of Science and Policy." In William N. Dunn, ed.,
Policy Analysis: Perspectives, Concepts, and Methods. Greenwich, Conn.: JAI
Press, 1985, pp. 41–67.

Cooper, Terry. *The Responsible Administrator: An Approach to Ethics for the Administrative Role.* Port Washington, N.Y.: Kennikat Press, 1982.

Dallmayr, Fred. "Critical Theory and Public Policy." In William N. Dunn, ed., *Policy
Analysis: Perspectives, Concepts and Methods.* Greenwich, Conn.: JAI Press,
1985, pp. 102–113.

Dunn, William N., ed. *Symposium on Social Values and Public Policy. Policy Studies
Journal* 9, no. 4 (1981). Special issue.

———. "Values, Ethics, and Standards in Policy Analysis." In Stuart Nagel, ed.,
Encyclopedia of Policy Studies. New York: Dekker, 1983, pp. 432–445.

Fleishman, Joel, and Bruce L. Payne. *Ethical Dilemmas and the Education of Policymakers.* Hastings-on-Hudson, N.Y.: Hastings Center, 1980.

Fleishman, Joel, Lance Liebman, and Mark Moore. *Public Duties: The Moral Obligation of Public Officials.* Cambridge, Mass.: Harvard University Press, 1981.

Frankena, William, and John Granrose, eds. *Introductory Readings in Ethics.* Englewood Cliffs, N.J.: Prentice-Hall, 1974.

Frederickson, H. George, ed. "Symposium on Social Equity and Public Administration." *Public Administration Review* 34 (January–February 1974): 1–51.

Friedman, Milton. *Essays in Positive Economics.* Chicago: University of Chicago Press,
1953.

Ganz, Carol. "Research in Progress." *Knowledge: Creation, Diffusion, Utilization* 1,
no. 4 (June 1980): 613–623.

Gawthrop, Louis. *Public Sector Management, Systems, and Ethics.* Bloomington: Indiana University Press, 1984.

Geertz, Clifford. *The Interpretation of Cultures.* New York: Basic Books, 1973.

Gewirth, Alan. *Reason and Morality.* Chicago: University of Chicago Press, 1978.

Girvetz, Harry. *Contemporary Moral Issues.* Belmont, Calif.: Wadsworth, 1964.

Golembiewski, Robert, and Michael White, eds., *Cases in Public Management.* Chicago: Rand McNally, 1976.

Gutmann, Amy, and Dennis Thompson, eds., *Ethics and Politics: Cases and Comments.* Chicago: Nelson Hall, 1984.

Kaplan, Abraham. *American Ethics and Public Policy.* New York: Oxford University
Press, 1963.

Leys, Wayne. *Ethics and Social Policy: The Art of Asking Deliberative Questions.* New
York: Prentice-Hall, 1941.

———. *Ethics for Policy Decisions.* New York: Prentice-Hall, 1952.

Lilla, Mark T. "Ethos, 'Ethics,' and Public Service." *Public Interest,* no. 63 (Spring
1981): 3–17.

MacRae, Duncan. *The Social Function of Social Science.* New Haven: Yale University
Press, 1976.

Marini, Frank, ed. *Toward a New Public Administration.* New York: Harper and Row,
1971.

Mertins, Herman, Jr., and Patrick J. Hennigan, eds. *Applying Professional Standards and Ethics in the 1980's: A Workbook and Study Guide for Public Administrators.* 2d ed. Washington, D.C.: American Society for Public Administration, 1982.

Nagel, Stuart. "The Means May Be a Goal." In William N. Dunn, ed., *Symposium on Social Values and Public Policy. Policy Studies Journal* 9, no. 4 (1980–1981): 567–579,

Paris, David, and James Reynolds. *The Logic of Policy Inquiry.* New York: Longman, 1983.

Pepper, Stephen. *The Source of Value.* Berkeley: University of California Press, 1958.

Rawls, John. *A Theory of Justice.* Cambridge, Mass.: Belknap Press of Harvard University, 1971.

Rein, Martin. *Social Science and Public Policy.* New York: Penguin Books, 1976.

Rohr, John. *Ethics for Bureaucrats: An Essay on Law and Values.* New York: Dekker, 1978.

Scott, William, and David Hart. "The Moral Nature of Man in Organizations: A Comparative Analysis." *Academy of Management Review* 14, no. 2 (June 1971): 241–255.

Steinfels, Peter. *The Place of Ethics in Schools of Public Policy.* Hastings-on-Hudson, N.Y.: Hastings Center, 1977.

Stokey, Edith, and Richard Zeckhauser. *A Primer for Policy Analysis.* New York: Norton, 1978.

Thompson, Dennis. "The Possibility of Administrative Ethics." *Public Administration Review,* 45, no. 5 (September–October 1985): 555–561.

Tribe, Laurence. "Policy Science: Analysis or Ideology." *Philosophy and Public Affairs* 2, no. 1 (Fall 1972): 66–110.

————. "Ways Not to Think about Plastic Trees." In Laurance Tribe, Corinne Schelling, and John Voss, eds., *When Values Conflict.* Cambridge, Mass.: Ballinger, 1976.

Warwick, Donald P. *The Teaching of Ethics in the Social Sciences.* Hastings-on-Hudson, N.Y.: Hastings Center, 1980.

Williams, Robert. *American Society: A Sociological Interpretation.* New York: Knopf, 1960.

Wollgar, Stephen. "The Identification and Definition of Scientific Collectivities." In Gerard Lemaine, ed., *Perspectives on the Emergence of Scientific Disciplines.* Chicago: Aldine, 1976, pp. 47–69.

2

Ethics in Government:
A Framework for Analysis

Gerald M. Pops

The subject of ethics in public administration has attracted great attention in the past decade. Public administration scholars have been actively reengaged in self-conscious study of the ethical and normative dimensions of their craft.[1] For convenience, the subject may be seen from the viewpoint of (1) personal ethics, (2) professional ethics, (3) organizational ethics, and (4) policy ethics.[2] All are visible in this volume. This chapter attempts to be integrative; it begins with a broad policy ethics perspective and proceeds by incorporating the other three levels of analysis.

The policy perspective has been chosen as a point of departure because it is the basis upon which ethics in government can be distinguished from ethics in organizations, in the professions, or in our personal lives. Special obligations distinguish government decision-making from other kinds of decision-making. Values are allocated among competing groups and individuals in society in a way that intentionally benefits the whole community, that is, which serves the public interest. The fact that government action often falls short of this goal and that there is great disagreement over what constitutes the public interest do not detract from this general expectation about the goals and methods of official action characteristic of the policy perspective. Personal, professional, and organizational ethics enter into administrative decisions and are very important, but focusing separately upon them is not desirable, since to do so would make this chapter unmanageable. Furthermore, exploring all of these perspectives is unnecessary since they are given thorough treatment in the other chapters of this book.

Past contributions to the public administration ethics literature, as reviewed in the next section, are rich and probative. However, as pointed out by Anthony Cahill and E. Sam Overman in chapter one, the need to address the normative aspects of administrative decision-making continues and may be increasing. A conceptual framework is needed that will help scholars and practitioners to understand the normative dimensions of their role in the policy process. For public administrators, the framework should not be geared to prescribing rules to apply in decision situations.[3] Nor should it lead to a set of "correct" values for approaching the performance of public duties. Rather, a framework should assist the decisionmaker first in identifying the variety of ethical problem situations that may be confronted in the policy process and second in guiding the administrator in analyzing those situations and raising the right kinds of questions in the effort to make thoughtful, responsible, and workable choices.[4] After tracing the intellectual heritage of this field in the next section, such a framework is presented.

BACKGROUND AND LITERATURE REVIEW

It has long and frequently been asserted by scholars that discretionary powers of public administrators are necessary and inevitably lead to an important, often critical, role for public administrators in the policy process.[5] Indeed, the assertion is so unchallenged that its validity stands as a central tenet of administrative ethics.[6] In a work sponsored and endorsed by the American Society for Public Administration, the premise of discretionary power is used to underscore the need for public administrators to raise and systematically consider ethical questions.[7]

Public administration writers were once prominent in treating the normative dimensions of policy-making. The debate between Carl Friedrich and Herman Finer remains the classic dialogue on the subject of administrative discretion and responsibility.[8] Herbert Simon saw clearly that administrative decision premises are essentially value laden or normative at higher-level and initial phases of decision-making but become less so at the implementation and technical levels of the "ends–means chain."[9] Wayne Leys, in his far too seldomly cited book *Ethics for Policy Decisions: The Art of Asking Deliberative Questions,* carefully analyzed philosophical prescriptions for ethical choice, a high point in the early administrative-ethics literature.[10] Paul Appleby and Emmette Redford vigorously defended bureaucratic policy-making as an institution, arguing that hierarchy and public service ideals combined to keep administrative discretion in bounds and consistent with notions of democracy and morality.[11] However, when Redford approached the subject in his later work, *Democracy in the Administrative State,* he was less optimistic that system forces could insure democratic morality and therefore presented an agenda for reform.[12] The principal new ingredient was participation.

Although very rich, this outpouring of insights concerning normative dimensions of administrative decision-making was essentially scattered and unorganized. Public interest theory attempted to fill the vacuum in the 1960s. Glendon Schubert's *The Public Interest* collected and classified the work of many scholars, particularly political scientists, using a typology of theories formulating how the interests of the polity could best be served by public administrators.[13] The concept itself was defended, assaulted, clarified, and qualified by a number of leading scholars in political science and public administration (Frank Sorauf, Schubert, Stephen Bailey, Harold Lasswell, and others) in *NOMOS V: The Public Interest.*[14] Michael Harmon usefully summarized the public interest concept as individualistic (not unitary), descriptive (not prescriptive), procedural (not substantive), and dynamic (not static) and argued that public administrators should seek roles in which they could be both responsive to the public and advocates for needed policy change.[15] Public interest theory will play an essential role in the framework for analysis to be presented in this chapter, particularly to shed light on the problem of when and how to exercise discretion.

According to Dwight Waldo, this impressive normative enterprise in decision theory was abandoned in the 1970s to the policy analysts.[16] This was due, at least in part, to the elegant methodological tools being developed in policy analysis, which were seemingly able to address "values" more systematically. This seems a great pity, as the earlier insights of the writers already cited, and other public administrationists, on authority, role, responsibility, citizenship, rule, and discretion were largely neglected.[17] Policy analysis has systematically underused these normative principles, favoring instead efficiency as its standard of choice to evaluate policy outcomes and the policy process itself.[18]

Antiauthoritarian sentiment associated with the antiwar movement and civil rights activity in the late 1960s stimulated a new wave of normative literature concerning the workings of government that broke upon the field in the Watergate era, presaged by Albert Hirschman's *Exit, Voice, and Loyalty* in 1970.[19] This is a brilliant study of internal advocacy, loyalty, and power relationships. Lying by government officials came under the intense scrutiny of Sissela Bok.[20] A considerable literature also has developed on whistleblowing.[21] The new wave blended with a continuing stream of writing inspired by postbureaucracy, humanistic perspectives on organizational theory and behavior.[22] Perhaps the mood of the times is best summarized in Eugene Dvorin and Robert Simmons's concept of "radical humanism," which "calls for the ultimate capitulation of operational mechanics and political strategies to a concept of the public interest based on man as *the* most important concern of bureaucratic power."[23]

Writing on the subject of administrative discretion also reemerged with the work of the eminent legal scholar Kenneth Culp Davis in 1969.[24] Davis challenged the traditonal legal profession view that administrative discretion should be minimized and held in check by the judiciary. He saw justice as being promoted by an increased use of discretion in areas not amenable to rule-making, as long as administrators took care to structure, check, and contain its use, primarily through formal and fair procedure and openness. Joel Handler applied Davis's analysis to social program administration.[25] Eugene Bardach and Robert Kagan went further and explored the general problem of balancing rule and discretion in a variety of administrative settings.[26] This literature gives an operational and technical force to the general theme of administrative discretion that has been a constant feature of theory in public administration. John Rohr's *Ethics for Bureaucrats* probably owes something to Davis but focuses on core or "regime" values, as articulated by the courts, rather than upon procedure.[27]

More recent literature has moved from an emphasis upon the choices to be made by administrators to one of pressures and obligations imposed upon administrative policymakers in the exercise of their discretionary powers.[28] In particular, judicial and legislative actions enlarging public official liability and forcing the disclosure of government information have helped to focus attention and make administrators more vulnerable to criticism for their policy judgments. Perhaps it is the law's fixing of responsibility upon the individual public administrator that has brought to the forefront the question of whether individuals are capable of exercising moral judgment within public organization and ought to be held morally responsible for their acts.[29] The answer has been affirmative. Thus if administrative decisionmakers are to be seen as more entrusted with discretion and less rulebound, they should be held both legally and morally responsible for their acts.

This outpouring of writing begs for synthesis and clarification. The occasion of the bicentennial of the nation's Constitution generated an interest in bringing about an approach to administrative ethics that fits into a political and constitutional rubric. Together, political influence (the result of discretion) plus personal moral and legal responsibility provide a pathway for the theory of public policy ethics focused on the administrator as a critical partner in the constitutional order. Appropriately, John Rohr accepted this challenge in his book *To Run a Constitution*.[30] Rohr reexamined the administrative experience of the United States in light of the political framework created by the Constitution. This chapter seeks to contribute to the literature by bringing together many of the concepts reviewed above within a unified perspective of ethical choice.

ETHICAL JUDGMENTS IN ADMINISTRATIVE POLICY-MAKING: A CONCEPTUAL FRAMEWORK

Any framework for the analysis of ethical decisions within the policy setting must take account of the entire policy process, from problem identification through policy evaluation. Administrators not only choose in ways that allocate values among individuals and groups, but they also participate in creating the very policies under which such decisions are made and participate in determining whether a past course of implementation was successful or failed.

Ethical judgments and issues occur throughout the administrative policy process. In broad terms, they are of four kinds, exercised in the following sequence:

1. Determining whether one has *responsibility*, that is, the legal discretion and willingness to act or not to act upon policy, and thus the opportunity to make an ethical policy judgment

2. Sorting out *pressures and obligations* that bear upon the decisionmaker, determining the values attaching to them, and determining whether an ethical dilemma exists

3. Choosing among *decision alternatives* and thus among the values implicit in them (i.e., resolving the dilemma)

4. Designing and selecting *strategies* to facilitate acceptance of or resistance to the decision taken and to reduce the opportunity costs attached to values not embraced in the decision

PHASE I: THE PROBLEM OF RESPONSIBILITY

Logically, the first occasion to consider ethical problems in the policy process has to do with the administrator's decision representing any role that he or she ought to play in the process. Taking responsibility for policy action or inaction is probably the core ethical dilemma for public administrators.[31] The problem is two part: the opportunity to be involved (discretion) and the will to act.

Law plays a premier role in the traditional constitutional–republican approach to policy formulation and execution. It must be given primary weight in determining whether discretion to make decisions (whether such decisions have an ethical content or not) exists at all. As important as law is, however, it is not the only dimension of discretion. Not all of the discretionary authority of administrators is handed to them by the lawmakers. Much results from active seeking. Whether an administrator should seek or not seek discretionary authority in the making of public policy and a specific kind of constitutional role are ethical issues.

Stating the matter more dramatically, who should rule? Rohr argued eloquently that "administrators should use their discretionary power in order to maintain the constitutional balance of powers in support of individual rights."[32] He saw public administration as a subordinate agent picking and choosing among constitutional masters, seeking cooperation, and "softening the harsh logic of separation of powers."[33] Recent controversy has focused on whether executive political leadership should attempt to narrow the role career bureaucrats play in influencing policy formulation.[34] Regardless of how clear the authority to act may be, discretion is not achieved unless and until the administrator accepts and acts upon the authority that is conferred. Thus role perception, the strength of personal values, and political courage are all important. Nonetheless, law remains the starting point for analysis of responsibility.

Legal Discretion

American public administrators acquire most decision-making authority through the delegating act of a legitimate political body (electorate, constitutional convention, court, or legislature) and through subdelegation within the administrative hierarchy. These delegations of authority may be either sweeping and general or specific and detailed, expressed or implied, and clear or vague and ambiguous.

This truism moves public officials who seek legitimacy in policy discretion to (1) identify, consult, and understand the delegating and subdelegating provisions; (2) be able to argue that a lawful delegation has occurred when guidelines do not clearly support their claim of authority to act; and (3) consider extralegal sources of discretion as a last resort. An alternative response is possible; officials not wishing to acquire discretion may consult the law to justify inaction. Either response follows from the making of an ethical judgement.

The law, when it is clear, either expressly delegates discretionary powers to the administrator to make or to participate in decisions or directs the administrator to act in such a specific and detailed way as to permit him or her no effective discretion.[35] In a sense, every new express delegation is unclear until it is applied in practice, regardless of its clarity or lack of it. To a very important degree, the language will take on meaning according to the will and imagination of the administrator to whom authority is delegated.

Managerial Discretion

Administrators also possess a type of implied authority to act as policymakers that is inherent in their roles as managers. They possess the authority to direct employees in their task accomplishments, to plan organizational strategy, to influence personnel hiring, to discipline employees, to allocate funds among organizational activities, to advocate for law change, to evaluate the agency's effectiveness in goal achievement, to coordinate the various agency programs both internally and with those of other agencies, and so forth.

The discretion rooted in this authority is often not "legal" in that authority is spelled out by statute, rule, or order.[36] Even those who hold no official leadership position, owing to circumstances thrusting them into advantageous locations or by dint of their personalities, often have the capacity to contribute to major decisions. It is said that such persons are acting in an informal leadership role and from this acquire a type of de facto discretionary authority.

The implied authority derived from the management function may be limited in various ways. Collective bargaining clearly reduces the degree of managerial discretion. Contract provisions often restrict management rights to act unilaterally, as when management consultation with union officials is required before certain types of actions are taken. Negotiated grievance procedures go beyond traditional civil service appeal systems in providing counsel and procedural protection.

Discretion through Inaction or Illegal Action

Two other, closely related sources of administrative discretion are inaction and action that are in violation of law. Circumstances often afford an administrator, who has the will to do so, the opportunity either to ignore or to violate a clear and specific legal command. Enforcement machinery may be too weak to compel compliance of the administrator. When it is lacking, administrators are left free to pursue their personally preferred courses of action. Unless the judiciary, legislature, or executive intervenes to correct the nonfeasance or misfeasance, the discretion continues. For example, when a housing administrator routinely overlooks housing-code violations and the local court is unwilling to intervene, code leniency becomes the policy in effect.

The issue of whether to exercise this type of discretion presents a major ethical dilemma. Inaction or illegal action is normally wrong from an ethical perspective, but occasionally circumstances arise in which the effect of following the law is so repugnant and so productive of mischief that an administrator rightly shrinks from the act.[37] Still, action in disregard or violation of law is not to be undertaken lightly. Indeed, this concept is so basic in our constitutional–legal polity that it could be argued to be an ethical tenet on the ground that if administrators were free to ignore law on whim or preference, democratic government would be impossible.[38]

Significance of Phase I Analysis

Self-determination by administrators that they have discretion to make or influence a policy decision, and the responsibility to do it, is the first step and a necessary precondition to normative decision-making. To reach for discretion when it is not legally the actor's is to invite reprisal from a number of quarters: a court's injunction, a superior's reprimand, a client's complaint. Conversely, to know one has legal discretion affords a valuable opportunity to structure the decision process in a way that protects against disabling criticism, enhances legitimacy and the morality of the action, and promotes the effectiveness of the decision once it is made.

Strategies become especially important when the legal basis of discretion is in question. For example, protection can be obtained by securing review of the decision by peers or superiors, by eliciting input from an advisory group, or by seeking a legal opinion. The administrator often has the option to choose among competing decision modes—rule-making, adjudication, bargaining, or edict—in either or both the predecision and final decision phases. The legal status of the problem may dictate the proper choice. In justifying or implementing a decision already taken, being able to refer to a legal basis for action is a powerful tool critical to the policy's acceptance or rejection.

Phase I ethical problems in administrative policy-making, in sum, involve the question of whether or not to take responsibility to act. A substantial part of this decision depends upon the analysis of whether legal or extralegal discretion exists, but the final decision rests upon perceptions of one's role in the political system, personal values, and courage. Additionally, it may hinge upon a glance forward into the ethical problems associated with Phase II. The larger those problems loom, the more cautious the administrator may be in assuming responsibility.

PHASE II: DEALING WITH COMPETING PRESSURES AND OBLIGATIONS

Discretion defines the opportunity for administrative decision-making. Discretion opens the door and lets the administrator into the inner sanctum of tough, normative choice. Once inside, the administrator must somehow come to grips with the decision to be made. Where do we begin? What elements are involved in the decision? To whom are we responsible for our decisions? What pressures and obligations that bear upon us are proper to consider, and which should be excluded? Whom do we allow to participate in the formulation and implementation phases of the policy process?

Administrators first seek to discover what elements are involved in the decision: parties and values, pressures and obligations.[39] One way to approach this is to identify the actors in the administrator's environment and then to associate these actors with the types of obligations and pressures they carry. It is useful to imagine a policy-making administrator as being at the center of a field of forces and interacting with many actors. Critical decisionmakers may not be, and usually are not, at the top of the administrative hierarchy. They are, as Emmette Redford told us, administrators and specialists holding strategic positions with important links to legislative staff, interest-group lobbyists and spokespersons, and professional organizations within their policy subsystems.[40]

Figure 2.1 points to the parties with whom the pressures for allegiance and attention originate. Influence is not necessarily exerted directly upon the critical position holder (referred to as "administrator") by the originator. For instance, a legislator interested in having an input into the administrator's decision may make his interest known to the agency head trusting that the message will be delivered through the chain of command (which may amplify the input). The chain of command would also be the natural conduit for many of the messages originating with other parties. Influence also may be silent; that is, the administrator may sense the presence of an interested party without receiving a message.

Four sets of actors—administrative superiors, administrator peers, subordinates, and political interest groups (shown at 12, 3, 6, and 9 o'clock of figure 2.1, respectively) are linked to the target administrator in a more direct way (shown by double lines) than the other actors depicted because of their constant communication and involvement in virtually every public decision process. Each of these sources carries unique obligations, pressures, and values. Agency superiors work upon the administrator's career aspirations, need for approval, job-security fears, authority-response patterns, and day-to-day work climate. Administrative peers, who may be participating through reviewing, checking, coordinating, or sharing in the same decision, exert the pressure of professional

Figure 2.1
Pressures, Parties, and Obligations Affecting the Administrative Policymaker

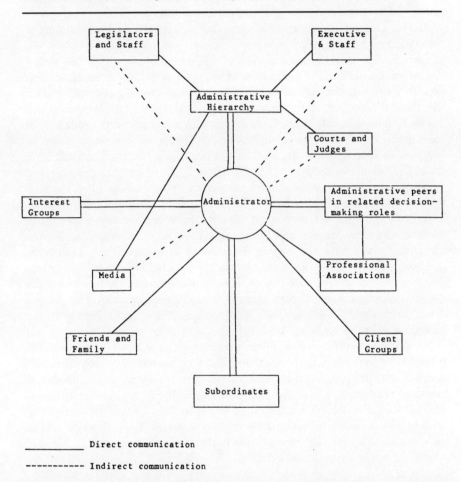

norms and peer approval. Subordinates hope for leadership, courage, protection, and a decision that is competent in terms of the organizational realities. Political interest groups seek outcomes, substantive or procedural, that will confer advantages upon their membership. Other actors can exert considerable force in selected cases—a legislative staff member, trusted friend, family member, client, news reporter, judge—and so these sources are included and linked by single lines.

The question of which actors and pressures to include or exclude from the policy process is a major ethical question, one going directly to the problem of democracy in the administrative state.[41] To what extent does the administrator promote participation of persons with her professional orientation or of persons not having the support of organized associations, especially the poor? Related ethical issues include deciding the degree of openness or secrecy attending the search and analysis stages, as well as the type of procedure to be employed.

Varying kinds of forums and decision rules are available to administrators in the making of policy choices. Choosing among them raises another set of ethical issues. The values implicit in each type of forum often work to the advantage of certain parties. For example, a hearing conducted before an administrative law judge that uses representation by counsel and courtlike rules of evidence will tend to favor parties that can afford highly competent legal counsel and discovery procedures. By associating values with advantages and disadvantages provided by the process, the administrator can manipulate competing claims in order to exclude or order them in such a way as to facilitate arriving at a desired decision outcome.

The professional or occupational association to which the deciding administrator belongs offers a special case. Normally powerless and not organized to act directly upon the decisionmaker, the association acts through a set of professional standards, norms and beliefs that have been inculcated within the administrator and often his peers as the result of an extended period of education and training. These standards, norms, or beliefs can be very strong. Or the profession may have gained some control over personnel policy within the deciding administrator's agency through its influence on hiring and promotion.[42] In this way, constancy with the prevailing norms and behaviors of the profession is encouraged.

Phase II ethical dilemmas, in review, focus upon an analysis of parties, competing claims and pressures, obligations, and their associated values. The most common and pressing of these items are those originated by or attributable to hierarchy, administrative or professional peers, subordinates, and political interest groups. Channeling and providing access to these forces introduces problems of ethical choice having directly to do with participation, democratic process, and due process as they may exist in the administrative arena.

PHASE III: CHOOSING AMONG COMPETING VALUES

Phase III, then, introduces the concept of an ethical policy dilemma and describes some of the more common of guidelines in resolving such problems. When two or more claims, representing competing values, press upon the deciding administrator simultaneously, and when these claims are both of significant weight, a decision dilemma arises. What gives the issue its special poignancy is the fact that in preferring one claim to another, the values attached to the losing claims are foregone. This is the opportunity cost of making an ethical judgment in a dilemma situation.

Decisions in such environments never present themselves as neat, clean choices among competing values. Rather, values are imbedded in alternatives available to or generated by the decisionmaker.[43] They exist side by side with other judgments that are not solely value based, namely, (a) an inquiry into the identity of the salient facts and (b) predicting the consequences that flow from policy choice. These observations must temper the discussion that follows and that is limited to values choice.

Systems of thought, which give formulas or guidelines for choice, are available for use as aids in resolving the value elements of ethical dilemmas. Some of these systems relate directly to standards used to test the quality of the policy.[44] Some relate only to the process through which decisions come and thus stress "process values." Four types of theory are introduced below: public interest, justice, efficiency, and moral codes.

Public Interest Theory

Public interest theory is one important canon of thought and is predominantly related to process, not substance or outcome.[45] It aids the administrator in determining personal responsibility in a given decision setting and is thus a valuable tool in Phase I analysis.[46] But it also helps to sort out and prioritize competing pressures and obligations. Since American society possesses a heterogeneous political culture, a variety of respectable public interest theories coexist. Although possessing a clear, personal definition of the public interest may not lead an administrator to make the "correct" choice among competing influences in a decision dilemma, it does lead to a more consistent choice in accord with personal values.[47]

No theory of public interest can realistically offer clear answers to the hard choices with which administrators and political leaders are confronted; nor does the theory presented here presume to do so. In fairness, all that can be reasonably demanded of such a theory is that it provide a framework within which administrative behavior may be tentatively, but productively, evaluated. . . . In behaving consistently with the theory of public interest offered here the proactive administrator is not assured correct answers. Perhaps it is not too presumptuous to suggest, however, that he will be aided in asking more of the right questions.[48]

Several varieties of public interest theory are discussed here because of their close relationship to administrative responsibility and role and for their value in pointing administrators toward process values leading to acceptable outcomes. They are overhead democracy, pluralism, organization loyalty, and professionalism.[49]

Overhead Democracy. Many believe that guidance to help resolve decision dilemmas must always be obtained from elected officials, both legislative and executive. This school of thought is founded upon the belief, familiar in American political theory, that legitimacy must originate and reside in those who are constitutionally authorized to make law and policy. This notion, often labeled "overhead democracy," is strongly supported by values of constitutionalism and the primacy of law. A holder of such a theory, finding himself in a dilemma situation, would look to the legislature, the executive, or the courts for a signal to determine the proper use of administrative discretion. This approach accepts the legitimacy of hierarchy, as long as the authority of hierarchial officials is clearly traceable to either legitimate political leaders or law. The traditional, ruling branches of government are seen as clearly establishing the policies and priorities of the public order. The performance of each descending level of bureaucracy is held accountable by comparing its actions with law or other policy directives from political superiors.

There are some problems with this theory in defining administrative responsibility. First, which is the most legitimate: the legislature, the executive, or the courts? Legislative bodies collectively contain the elected representatives of all of the people. The president is one of two public officials (the other is the vice-president) who is chosen by the entire electorate. The courts draw their legitimacy from the Supreme Court's self-declared exclusive right to interpret the Constitution. There is, moreover, the problem of delay. On the one hand, both legislatures and courts are inherently unable to respond quickly to problems of policy formulation or implementation. Executive officials, on the other hand, are in a better position to respond with some promptness to administrative pleas for direction.

Pluralism.   Power and discretion may be viewed as flowing into administrative agencies not only from the top through political leadership and law but from all directions—laterally and from the bottom as well.[50] Government is seen by such public interest theorists not as a legitimized set of official actors who are elected by "the people" but as a fragmented and wide-ranging set of actors, both official and unofficial, who have influence in areas of policymaking.

An administrator with such a view of the political system may well respond by listening to everybody having an interest, calculating each person's or group's strength, attempting to reconcile the various points of view, and issuing a decision (or designing a process) that maximizes the interests of the many. The administrator is in the center of a field of forces. His task is to find a line of decision as well as a procedure for making the decision and base it upon a utilitarian criterion. The administrator's preferred methodology becomes the exploration of positions, the presentation and discussion of alternatives, the development of a compromise, and the building of a broad consensus.

This approach to administrative responsibility is also fraught with difficulty. How is an administrator to balance varying interests? Groups vary in their intensity of interest in a particular issue as well as in their organizational skills in presenting their demands. How is the manager expected to weigh the interests of unorganized groups that do not effectively raise and press their claims? Presumably, if administrators do not hear from spokespersons for groups that have a legitimate stake in a decision, they will not properly weigh the collective demands of such groups. Administrators may give undue weight to more visibly represented groups because of their presumed political leverage while neglecting individuals of substance, insight, and creativity.[51] We may also question the decisionmaker's ability to judge political variables. Bureaucratic officials are not elected and thus may lack sensitivity to the political dimensions of the decision. For this reason alone, administrative decisionmakers may be critically deficient as carriers of democratic values.

Organizational Loyalty.   Many administrators who are faced with difficult dilemmas simply persuade themselves that they are not duty bound to look for the public interest beyond that which serves their organization's immediate interests. Managers are naturally attuned to what their agency superiors want in order to gain organization favor. They may also fear retribution if they vary from agency norms. Although not lofty, such an analysis is most realistic from the individual administrator's perspective.[52] It is at the bureaucratic level that administrators defend and promote their activities in the competition for scarce budget and political support. It is also the point at which most critical personnel decisions are made. Here, advocacy is expected and applauded.[53]

Such public interest theory is based upon the recognition of the existence of strong agency cultures and of clear organizational boundaries. These are undeniably realistic perceptions.[54] The strength and pervasiveness of these perceptions lead to one of the most profound ethical questions in American government. Do organizations indoctrinate their members to serve narrowly perceived organizational interests, leading to excessive growth and secrecy, unhealthy competition with other government organizations, sharp conflict between organizational norms and professional norms, and the occasional sacrifice of legitimated goals and required procedures? This is the central question raised and brilliantly analyzed by Frederick Mosher.[55]

Professionalism.   Professionalization offers some hope of leading individual administrators out of a sense of isolation and dependence upon their organization. Administrative responsibility can be seen as doing the job according to its description and the application of professional methods and norms involved in the position's duties, in short, the exercise of technical competence.[56] Administrators are observed by and therefore feel somewhat accountable to colleagues and knowledgeable persons in other organizations having similar professional backgrounds. Their professional societies help to induce in them a set of loyalties. Decisions based upon professional norms are reinforced by their professional peers. Furthermore, they may have the security of knowing that their services could be used by other agencies to which they might transfer their services. In sum, professionalism probably enhances the ability to operate upon a higher normative plane than that permitted by simple organizational subservience.

The case against professionalism as an approach to administrative choice is ably made by Mosher.[57] Professionalism promotes balkanization of agencies and the adoption of narrow points of view that stray from the interests of the whole public. Also, professions tend to be elitist and undemocratic in their entry practices and overly concerned with the protection of their members. Furthermore, they work through professional associations to create and control government programs while discouraging attempts by government generalists and other professions to contribute to problem resolution.

Justice Theory

The second theoretical package, after public interest theory, containing a rich trove of systematic thought capable of unlocking ethical dilemmas is justice theory. Theoretical formulations are voluminous and diverse, are drawn from all ages and from all social contexts, may purport to present universal principles, and are pertinent to the types of policy and personnel decisions facing modern administrators.[58] There exists no one generally accepted theory of justice, but as with public interest theory, there is great benefit to be gained from the study of alternate visions for both analyzing decision situations and for justifying hard choices once they are made.[59]

Contemporary literature offers the provocative theory of John Rawls, which offers formulaic principles of justice based upon an egalitarian philosophy.[60] Together with Rawls's serious and persuasive critics, this represents an intellectual advance in policy ethics potentially valuable to public administrators.[61]

Of special note is social equity theory. Inspired by Rawls and the literature of organizational humanism and participative management of the 1960s and 1970s, this called for vigorous analysis and action on the part of public administrators based on an egalitarian view of distributive justice.[62] Affirmative action and participative management norms are important features of a set of guidelines for administrative policy choice. It embodies a sympathetic response to demands for redistributive social policy.

Efficiency Theory

Third, much has been written both in support and condemnation of efficiency as the basis of decision-making in public administration.[63] Even during the late 1960s and early 1970s, when the New Left's critique demonstrated that the concept was value laden and woefully insufficient as a basis for policy-making, economic analysis and rational planning were making great strides in practice. The better view seems to be that the truth lies somewhere in between the views of efficiency as prime criterion and as false prophet.

It is not possible to derive a complete policy evaluation from any form of purely economic analysis. Efficiency is properly regarded as one ground of policy evaluation, a necessary one to be sure, but not as the exclusive consideration in policy appraisal. Efficiency is best regarded as an instrumental value, a tool for comparing policy options in terms of other values. In fact, in any cost–benefit analysis, we do not compare all alternatives but only those that have survived scrutiny on other evaluative grounds.[64]

Cost–benefit analysis is a fundamental methodology of much policy analysis. In this regard, it is overvalued and does not belong in a higher league than justice and responsibility criteria. Its attractiveness lies in its ability to reach conclusions and in the elegance of its presentation, but its science may be no better than the "scientism" of the scientific management movement. Charles Anderson would relegate cost–benefit analysis to the role of "tiebreaker" between policy options that are already acceptable on grounds of justice and authority.[65] Alternatively, it may be looked at as one formulation of justice theory—a brand of utilitarianism.

Moral Codes and Faith Systems

Public interest, justice, and efficiency theories are not the only guidelines for resolving ethical dilemmas. Many other formulas are found in theology, philosophy, science, and literature and find expression in other cultures and in some of the subcultures of America as well as in other times. Plato, Aristotle, Kant, Machiavelli, Hume, and Marx are but Western examples of seminal political philosophers who provide us with keys that help to unlock the riddles of difficult decision dilemmas. Some even find it possible to reduce all decision elements to logical symbols and quantitative relationships.[66]

Although all public administrators have social moral codes and thought systems, they differ in the threshold at which they are prepared to employ them. An administrator may feel that a particular decision is morally or logically correct but may refrain from acting upon that belief because of a judgment (actually, a public interest theory) that accepts a limited role in the policy process. Administrators who do take action on the basis of their thought systems may be the true "idealists."[67]

Perhaps the primary benefit of philosophical, moral, or logical thought systems is to cause the administrator to ask questions that bring an awareness of normative aspects of a problem that may otherwise escape attention.[68] Asking makes decision-making at once more difficult and easier. The difficulty lies in expanding the number of variables. But once the resolution process becomes complex and confusing, guidelines to thought and action consonant with personal values are brought into play to help clarify and resolve the dilemma. The result should be a richer, more complete decision process.

To summarize, in Phase III, various thought systems constructed for the purpose of resolving decision problems are brought to bear on policy dilemmas. They include public interest theories (which relate more to the process than to outcome) and justice theories (which relate both to preferred outcomes and process). These systems do not exhaust the possibilities. Efficiency criteria continue to be important in public administration but should not, according to the reasoning of most observers, be allowed to dominate. Finally, a variety of moral codes and faith systems may come into play.

PHASE IV: DEVISING STRATEGIES FOR EXECUTION AND EVALUATION

Analyzing a dilemma in its proper fullness and applying philosophically consistent and thoughtful reasoning does not exhaust the cycle of ethical judgment. Still to be considered are the strategic choices involved in the process of implementation and in the process of evaluation. Process is rarely, if ever, value neutral. In a society in which participation and democratic technology are highly valued, process can be at least as important as outcome. Elements within process are valued both as ends and as means to achieve valued outcomes.

Every decision is attended by a set of implementation procedures. The choice of a certain type of procedure is not value free; it often will influence outcome in a predictable direction.[69] Knowledge of the procedural dynamics constitutes a source of discretionary power. Procedural choices may lead to any of the following conditions: delay or hasten action upon the decision, spread or centralize the responsibility for it, politicize or depoliticize the decision, make the decision more or less expensive, open or close the implementation process to public view, and widen or narrow the support base for action. The ultimate result of such manipulation may be more or less political influence, more or less promotion of organization or professional objectives, or more or less influence of legal norms and judicial modes of action.

Skillfully selected strategies of implementation will often substantially reduce the opportunity costs of a normative decision. Cooptation, for example, is a strategy designed to blunt political opposition.[70] Secretiveness may significantly reduce, possibly eliminate, pressures coming from some external sources. Students of administration and public policy have much to learn about the value trade-offs inherent in procedural strategies. Whether to design and conduct policy evaluation to be self-serving or objective is another important ethical issue area. The potential for slanting evaluative research to support a policy direction or to salvage a program is great.[71]

The literature of strategic choice—communication, public disclosure and secrecy, rule-making and administrative adjudication, exit and voice, participative management, and collective bargaining—is waiting to be reexamined from the view of administrative policy ethics. Its consideration is likely to pay dividends to scholars and practitioners exploring public policy phenomena. Undoubtedly, there will be circumstances under which the availability of certain strategies may encourage the taking of responsibility, or expand participation, or suggest a route to resolution. Strategic choice, as a phase of ethical policy, is not the end of the chain but is integrally related to other phases.

CONCLUSION

This chapter argues that in their concern for promoting ethical choice and action in administrative decision-making, public administration academicians and practitioners should think more systematically about ethical problems faced in the policy process. This inquiry begins with the individual administrator's opportunity to become involved in policy matters (the issue of "responsibility") and proceeds through an analysis of competing values in policy-making settings, the recognition of ethical dilemmas, the review of coherent thought systems available to guide choice, and the calculation of the utilities and disutilities of alternative strategies attending implementation and evaluation strategies.

As a field of professional concern and intellectual endeavor, public administration enjoys a rich history of self-conscious inquiry into the proper role of government officials in policy-making. Since Woodrow Wilson's time, it has sought a respectable basis for action. The policy–administration dichotomy and the principle of efficiency sufficed for a time, but thoughtful men and women in the field have considered and rejected these notions and have searched for broader and more legitimizing principles. The study of "administrative ethics" is moving public administration in that direction but with somewhat less clarity than is desirable. This chapter attempts to bring together issues and concerns in a general framework to promote that understanding.

NOTES

1. John A. Rohr, "Ethics in Public Administration: A State of the Discipline Report" (Paper presented at the National Conference of the American Society for Public Administration, Anaheim, Calif., 1986). Rohr presented a report of activity in the public administration ethics field, summarizing much of the thinking and writing going on in this "chaotic" but vital literature.

2. Levels of administrative ethical analysis can be distinguished in the following manner. Personal and professional ethics are seen as guided by the criterion of "right conduct," what is right being determined by self, family, class, or religious sect in the former and by the norms of the professional group or society in the latter. Organizational ethics are guided by the criterion of "organizational effectiveness" or survival. Policy ethics are seen as guided by broad, social criteria such as justice, "regime values," and social equity. But the categories overlap. Ethical standards of persons, professions, and organizations may incorporate broad policy and social standards. Alternatively, the social ethic may draw its standards from personal norms (e.g., individual freedom embodied in a laissez-faire economic system) or professional or organizational norms (e.g., acceptance of the need for the "professional state").

3. James S. Bowman, ed., "Special Issue on Ethics in Government," *Public Personnel Management* 10, no. 1 (1981): 1.

4. Wayne A. R. Leys, *Ethics for Policy Decisions: The Art of Asking Deliberative Questions* (New York: Prentice-Hall, 1952).

5. John Dickinson, *Administrative Justice and the Supremacy of Law in the United*

States (New York: Russell & Russell, 1927); Ernst Freund, *Administrative Powers over Persons and Property: A Comparative Survey* (Chicago: University of Chicago, 1928); Wayne A. R. Leys, "Ethics and Administrative Discretion," *Public Administration Review* 3 (1943): 10–23; Dwight Waldo, *The Administrative State: A Study of the Political Theory of American Public Administration* (New York: Ronald Press, 1948); Kenneth Culp Davis, *Discretionary Justice: A Preliminary Inquiry* (Baton Rouge: Louisiana State University, 1969); John A. Rohr, *Ethics for Bureaucrats* (Chicago: Dekker, 1978); Philip J. Cooper, *Public Law and Public Administration* (Palo Alto, Calif.: Mayfield, 1983).

6. Rohr, "Ethics in Public Administration," pp. 53–55.

7. Herman Mertins, Jr., and Patrick J. Hennigan, *Applying Professional Standards and Ethics in 1980's: A Workbook and Study Guide for Public Administration,* 2d ed. (Washington, D.C.: American Society for Public Administration, 1982).

8. Carl J. Friedrich and E. S. Mason, eds., *Public Policy: A Yearbook of the Graduate School of Public Administration, Harvard University* (Cambridge, Mass.: Harvard University Press, 1940); Herman Finer, "Administrative Responsibility in Democratic Government," *Public Administration Review* 1 (1941): 335–350.

9. Herbert A. Simon, *Administrative Behavior: A Study of Decision-Making Processes in Administrative Organizations* (New York: Macmillan, 1947).

10. Leys, *Ethics for Policy Decisions.*

11. Paul Appleby, *Morality and Administration in Democratic Government* (Baton Rouge: Louisiana State University, 1952); Emmette S. Redford, *Ideal and Practice in Public Administration* (Tuscaloosa: University of Alabama, 1958).

12. Emmette S. Redford, *Democracy in the Administrative State* (New York: Oxford University Press, 1969).

13. Glendon Schubert, *The Public Interest* (Glencoe, Ill.: Free Press, 1960).

14. Carl J. Friedrich, ed., *NOMOS V: The Public Interest* (New York: Atherton Press, 1962).

15. Michael M. Harmon, "Administrative Policy Formulation and the Public Interest," *Public Administration Review* 29 (1969): 483–491.

16. Dwight Waldo, *The Enterprise of Public Administration* (Novato, Calif.: Chandler and Sharp, 1980).

17. Marshall E. Dimock, *A Philosophy of Administration: Toward Creative Growth* (New York: Harper, 1958); Roscoe C. Martin, *Public Administration and Democracy* (Syracuse, N.Y.: Syracuse University, 1965); Peter M. Blau and Marshall W. Meyer, *Bureaucracy in Modern Society,* 2d. ed. (New York: Random House, 1956); Frederick C. Mosher, *Democracy and the Public Service* (New York: Oxford University Press, 1968).

18. Charles W. Anderson, "The Place of Principles in Policy Analysis," *American Political Science Review* 73 (September 1979): 711–723.

19. Albert O. Hirschman, *Exit, Voice, and Loyalty* (Cambridge, Mass.: Harvard University Press, 1970).

20. Sissela Bok, *Lying: Moral Choice in Public and Private Life* (New York: Pantheon, 1978).

21. James S. Bowman, "Whistle-blowing in the Public Service: An Overview of the Issues," *Review of Public Personnel Administration* 1 (Fall 1980): 15–27.

22. Frank Marini, *Toward a New Public Administration? The Minnowbrook Perspective* (Scranton, Pa.: Chandler, 1971); H. George Frederickson, ed., "Symposium on

Social Equity and Public Administration," *Public Administration Review* 34 (1974): 1–51; Eugene P. Dvorin and Robert H. Simmons, *From Amoral to Humane Bureaucracy* (San Francisco: Canfield, 1972)

23. Dvorin and Simmons, *From Amoral to Humane Bureaucracy*, p. 61.

24. Davis, *Discretionary Justice.*

25. Joel F. Handler, *Protecting the Social Service Client: Legal and Structural Controls on Official Discretion* (New York: Academic Press, 1979). Davis also applied his thesis to police administration. *See* Kenneth Culp Davis, *Police Discretion* (St. Paul: West, 1975).

26. Eugene Bardach and Robert A. Kagan, *Going by the Book: The Problem of Regulatory Unreasonableness* (Philadelphia: Temple University, 1982).

27. Rohr, *Ethics for Bureaucrats.*

28. Waldo, *Enterprise;* Mark H. Moore, "Realms of Obligation and Virture," in Joel L. Fleishman, Lance Liebman, and Mark H. Moore, eds., *Public Duties: The Moral Obligations of Government Officials* (Cambridge, Mass.: Harvard University Press, 1981), pp. 3–31; Donald P. Warwick, "The Ethics of Administrative Discretion," in Joel L. Fleishman, Lance Liebman and Mark H. Moore, eds., *Public Duties: The Moral Obligations of Government Officials* (Cambridge, Mass.: Harvard University Press, 1981), pp. 93–127.

29. Dennis F. Thompson, "The Possibility of Administrative Ethics," *Public Administration Review* 45 (1985): 555–561; Debra Stewart, "Ethics and the Profession of Public Administration: The Moral Responsibility of Individuals in Public Sector Organizations," *Public Administration Quarterly* (Winter 1985): 487–495.

30. John A. Rohr, *To Run a Constitution: The Legitimacy of the Administrative State* (Lawrence: University Press of Kansas, 1986).

31. Rohr, "Ethics in Public Administration," pp. 54–55.

32. Rohr, *To Run a Constitution*, pp. 181–186, quotation at p. 184.

33. Ibid.

34. Michael Sanera, "Part 4: Implementing the Mandate," in Butler M. Stuart, Michael Sanera, and W. Bruce Weinrod, *Mandate for Leadership II: Continuing the Conservative Revolution* (Washington, D.C.: Heritage Foundation, 1984), pp. 459–560.

35. As early as 1943, Wayne A. R. Leys articulated the difference between the differing role of rules and principles in administrative discretion. In exercising the responsibility to make an indefinite standard of action precise and explicit, reference is made to use of the "general principle" to test what a rule of action requires. The general principle is philosophical, the rule a more or less detailed prescription for action. Leys, "Ethics and Administrative Discretion."

36. The exercise of managerial-derived administrative discretion is sharply circumscribed by law, nonetheless. Most of these restrictions upon action are procedural. For example, in taking an adverse action against an errant employee, the law normally requires that a grievance procedure be followed that includes a series of prescribed steps and the extension of certain protections to employees. Or when hiring an employee, explicit presentation must be made that justifies the manager's actions in conformity with regulatory guidelines on affirmative action and selection procedures.

37. H. George Frederickson and David K. Hart "The Public Service and the Paradigm of Benevolence," *Public Administration Review* 45 (1985): 547–553.

38. Five questions ought to be raised, and answered as shown in the parentheses, before an administrator violates law:

1. Can timely relief from applying the law be obtained through a higher authority with ability to change the law—legislature, executive, court, or administrative agency head? (no)
2. Is the law rationally related to an important and legitimate social purpose? (no)
3. Is the offending law in unavoidable conflict with a value the administrator holds dear? (yes)
4. Is the threatened value far dearer than the value implicit in the purpose to be effected by application of the law? (yes)
5. Are the consequences flowing from a decision to violate the law, relating either to the decision-maker's organization or to the decisionmaker personally, acceptable to the decision-maker? (yes)

39. Waldo, *Enterprise;* Moore, "Realms."

40. Redford, *Democracy,* pp. 41–42.

41. Ibid.

42. Frederick C. Mosher, *Democracy and the Public Service,* 2d ed. (New York: Oxford University Press, 1981), chapter five.

43. Joel L. Fleishman and Bruce L. Payne, *Ethical Dilemmas and the Education of Policy Makers* (Hastings-on-Hudson, N.Y.: Hastings Center, 1980).

44. An example of an "outcome" system is Rawls's principles of justice. John Rawls, *A Theory of Justice* (Cambridge, Mass.: Harvard University Press, 1971).

45. Michael M. Harmon, "Administrative Policy Formulation and the Public Interest," *Public Administration Review* 29 (1969): 483–491.

46. Fleishman and Payne, *Ethical Dilemmas;* Friedrich, *NOMOS V.*

47. To be "correct" one needs to act in conformity with a clear social consensus. In a dilemma, which usually is a situation in which reasonable persons in our society will differ, a consensus is likely to be lacking, and *right* and *wrong* become simply words of political preference. In a pluralistic society many "right" answers coexist.

48. Harmon, "Administrative Policy Formulation," p. 490.

49. A more complete discussion of the problem of overhead democracy as a public interest theory may be found under the heading of "rationalism," as treated by Schubert in *The Public Interest.* Pluralistic public interest theory is discussed under the heading of "realism" by Schubert in *The Public Interest.*

50. Norton E. Long, *The Polity* (Chicago: Rand McNally, 1962).

51. Redford, *Democracy.*

52. This picture of organizational fealty and the resulting isolation of members holding and asserting differing values may be accurate for many administrators but often does not preclude independent action by one faced with a particular decision dilemma. If it does not touch upon essential norms and goals or political support structures of the organization, the administrator's choice may be a matter of indifference to the agency leadership.

53. Anthony Downs, *Inside Bureaucracy* (Boston: Little, Brown, 1967), chapter nine.

54. Harold Seidman and Robert Gilmour, *Politics, Position, and Power: From the Positive to the Regulatory State,* 4th ed. (New York: Oxford University Press, 1986).

55. Mosher, *Democracy.*

56. Friedrich and Mason, *Public Policy.*

57. Mosher, *Democracy.*

58. Julius Stone, *Human Law and Human Justice* (Palo Alto, Calif.: Stanford University, 1965).

59. Leys, *Ethics for Policy Decisions*.

60. Rawls, *A Theory of Justice*.

61. Robert Nozick, *Anarchy, State, and Utopia* (New York: Basic Books, 1974).

62. Frederickson, "Symposium on Social Equity."

63. Waldo, *The Administrative State*.

64. Anderson, "The Place of Principles."

65. Ibid.

66. Robert Boguslaw, *The New Utopians: A Study of System Design and Social Change* (Englewood Cliffs, N.J.: Prentice-Hall, 1965); C. West Churchman, *The Systems Approach* (New York: Dell, 1968).

67. Schubert, *The Public Interest*.

68. Leys, *Ethics for Policy Decisions*.

69. Kenneth Culp Davis, *Administrative Law and Government*, 2d ed. (St. Paul: West, 1975).

70. Philip Selznick, *TVA and the Grass Roots* (Berkeley: University of California, 1949).

71. Martin Wachs, "Ethical Dilemmas in Forecasting for Public Policy," *Public Administration Review* 42 (1982): 562–567.

SELECTED BIBLIOGRAPHY

Anderson, Charles W. "The Place of Principles in Policy Analysis." *American Political Science Review* 73 (1979): 711–723.

Appleby, Paul. *Morality and Administration in Democratic Government*. Baton Rouge: Louisiana State University, 1952.

Bardach, Eugene, and Robert A. Kagan. *Going by the Book: The Problem of Regulatory Unreasonableness*. Philadelphia: Temple University, 1982.

Boguslaw, Robert. *The New Utopians: A Study of System Design and Social Change*. Englewood Cliffs, N.J.: Prentice-Hall, 1965.

Bok, Sissela. *Lying: Moral Choice in Public and Private Life*. New York: Pantheon, 1978.

Bowman, James S. "Whistle-blowing in the Public Service: An Overview of the Issues." *Review of Public Personnel Administration* 1 (Fall 1980): 15–27.

————, ed. "Special Issue on Ethics in Government." *Public Personnel Management* 10, no. 1 (1981).

Butler, Stuart M., Michael Sanera, and W. Bruce Weinrod. *Mandate for Leadership II: Continuing the Conservative Revolution*. Washington, D.C.: Heritage Foundation, 1984.

Churchman, C. West. *The Systems Approach*. New York: Dell, 1968.

Cooper, Philip J. *Public Law and Public Administration*. Palo Alto, Calif.: Mayfield, 1983.

Davis, Kenneth Culp. *Discretionary Justice: A Preliminary Inquiry*. Baton Rouge: Louisiana State University, 1969.

Dickinson, John. *Administrative Justice and the Supremacy of Law in the United States*. New York: Russell & Russell, 1927.

Dvorin, Eugene P., and Robert H. Simmons. *From Amoral to Humane Bureaucracy*. San Francisco: Canfield, 1972.

Finer, Herman. "Administrative Responsibility in Democratic Government." *Public Administration Review* 1 (1941): 335–350.

Fleishman, Joel L., and Bruce L. Payne. *Ethical Dilemmas and the Education of Policymakers*. Hastings-on-Hudson, N.Y.: Hastings Center, 1980.

Fleishman, Joel L., Lance Liebman, and Mark H. Moore, eds. *Public Duties: The Moral Obligations of Government Officials*. Cambridge, Mass.: Harvard University Press, 1981.

Frederickson, H. George, ed. "Symposium on Social Equity and Public Administration." *Public Administration Review* 34 (1974): 1–51.

Frederickson, H. George, and David K. Hart. "The Public Service and the Paradigm of Benevolence." *Public Administration Review* 45 (1985): 547–553.

Friedrich, Carl J., ed. *NOMOS V: The Public Interest*. New York: Atherton Press, 1962.

Friedrich, Carl J., and E. S. Mason, eds. *Public Policy: A Yearbook of the Graduate School of Public Administration, Harvard University*. Cambridge, Mass.: Harvard University Press, 1940.

Handler, Joel F. *Protecting the Social Service Client: Legal and Structural Controls on Official Discretion*. New York: Academic Press, 1979.

Harmon, Michael M. "Administrative Policy Formulation and The Public Interest." *Public Administration Review* 29 (1969): 483–491.

Hirschman, Albert O. *Exit, Voice, and Loyalty*. Cambridge, Mass.: Harvard University Press, 1970.

Leys, Wayne A. R. "Ethics and Administrative Discretion." *Public Administration Review* 3 (1943): 10–23.

———. *Ethics for Policy Decisions: The Art of Asking Deliberative Questions*. New York: Prentice-Hall, 1952.

Long, Norton E. *The Polity*. Chicago: Rand McNally, 1962.

Marini, Frank, ed. *Toward a New Public Administration: The Minnowbrook Perspective*. Scranton, Pa.: Chandler, 1971.

Martin, Roscoe C. *Public Administration and Democracy*. Syracuse, N.Y.: Syracuse University, 1965.

Mertins, Herman, Jr., and Patrick J. Hennigan. *Applying Professional Standards and Ethics in 1980's: A Workbook and Study Guide for Public Administrators*. Washington, D.C.: American Society for Public Administration, 1982.

Mosher, Frederick C. *Democracy and the Public Service*, 2nd ed. New York: Oxford University Press, 1981.

Nozick, Robert. *Anarchy, State, and Utopia*. New York: Basic Books, 1974.

Rawls, John. *A Theory of Justice*. Cambridge, Mass.: Harvard University Press, 1971.

Redford, Emmette S. *Ideal and Practice in Public Administration*. Tuscaloosa: University of Alabama, 1958.

———. *Democracy in the Administrative State*. New York: Oxford University Press, 1969.

Rohr, John A. *Ethics for Bureaucrats*. Chicago: Dekker, 1978.

———. *To Run a Constitution: The Legitimacy of the Administrative State*. Lawrence: University Press of Kansas, 1986.

Schubert, Glendon. *The Public Interest*. Glencoe, Ill.: Free Press, 1960.

Selznick, Philip. *TVA and the Grass Roots*. Berkeley: University of California, 1949.

Simon, Herbert A. *Administrative Behavior: A Study of Decision-Making Processes in Administrative Organizations*. New York: Macmillan, 1947.

Stewart, Debra. "Ethics and the Profession of Public Administration: The Moral Responsibility of Individuals in Public Sector Organizations." *Public Administration Quarterly* 8 (Winter 1985): 487–495.

Thompson, Dennis F. "The Possibility of Administrative Ethics." *Public Administration Review* 45 (1985): 555–561.

Wachs, Martin. "Ethical Dilemmas in Forecasting for Public Policy." *Public Administration Review* 42 (1982): 562–567.

Waldo, Dwight. *The Enterprise of Public Administration*. Novato, Calif.: Chandler and Sharp, 1980.

PART TWO

ETHICAL DILEMMAS AND STANDARDS FOR PUBLIC SERVANTS

3

Individual Ethics and
Organizational Morality

Myron Peretz Glazer and Penina Migdal Glazer

On January 28, 1986, millions of American citizens watched in horror as a presumably sophisticated and safe space shuttle exploded and destroyed the lives of six astronauts and the first teacher ever to fly in space. Until that time the National Aeronautics and Space Administration (NASA) enjoyed the reputation of an agency incorporating America's finest qualities. The best scientists, engineers, and managers had developed the world's most advanced technology to explore the new frontiers of space. Suddenly, the safety systems collapsed and the seemingly infallible technical expertise failed, leaving in its wake stunned citizens and political leaders searching for an explanation.

In the hearings held by the Rogers Commission, witnesses revealed that serious problems had been known to high-level administrators for years. Engineers had recognized defects in the crucial booster rockets as early as 1979.[1] On the night before the disaster, several engineers from the Morton Thiokol Company, a major contractor responsible for construction of the rockets, had clearly warned that the seals in the booster rocket could malfunction in the cold weather that was anticipated. Their recommendations to postpone the launch were overruled by their own managers and by NASA officials, all of whom were determined to go ahead.[2]

The decision to proceed under such dangerous flight conditions raised profound questions. Why had there been no public warning by those in a position to know about the potential disaster? It soon became apparent that employees who had disagreed with their superiors' decisions believed that voicing dissent from the official policy would put their careers in jeopardy. No one wanted to assume responsibility for halting a nationally publicized event.[3]

Nonetheless, by 1986 many Americans, including those in the commission, had come to expect that some courageous employees in both corporations and government would speak publicly in the face of lethal safety hazards. Models for such behavior had already surfaced among nuclear workers, big city police officers, Defense Department personnel, automobile design engineers, and many others. The term *whistle-blower* had entered America's vocabulary, and a few, such as Frank Serpico, Karen Silkwood, and Marie Rigghianti, had become household names after famous actors portrayed them as heroes in Hollywood films.[4] Yet many potential whistle-blowers are reluctant to step forward for fear of retaliation by their superiors. Their apprehension is grounded in the knowledge that virtually all of those who have done so have suffered severe consequences after protesting unethical and illegal behavior in the workplace. This chapter focuses on the career and emotional costs of public disclosure and the devastating impact on family life.

BACKGROUND

Whistle-blowers are a historically new group. Since the founding of the United States, there have been those who have demanded public attention to social injustice. Either acting individually or in organized efforts, they have dedicated themselves to political activity—speaking, writing, and protesting issues of unfair taxes, slavery, exploitation of workers, prostitution, war, and a myriad of other problems that have arisen in the rapidly growing, industrial society.

Like these earlier reformers, whistle-blowers proclaim their belief in individual responsibility and are willing to put themselves at risk for the well-being of their fellow citizens. But in other ways they embody a different type of protester—one who is actually employed by the organization and totally dedicated to its stated goals but who refuses to countenance a lack of accountability when employers bypass safety regulations, mishandle funds, or violate other laws. Moreover, unlike other dissenters in American history, most whistle-blowers do not initially have a strong interest in promoting large-scale social reform; nor do they define themselves as workers locked in an adversarial relationship with management. Rather, they turn to public disclosure only when they find that internal appeals to their superiors do not change objectionable practices, and they fear that they will become complicit in wrongdoing. Although often apolitical in conventional Left–Right ideological terms, these are people of strong convictions.[5] Their allegiance to their professions, churches, communities, and families are the sources of their commitment to the rights of patients and children, the protection of neighborhoods from chemical dumping, the shielding of women from sexual harassment, the marketing of safe products, and the guarding of public funds.

These internal protesters were dubbed "whistle-blowers" by Ralph Nader and others in the early 1970s to distinguish them from the informers who testified against their Mafia chieftains or from former Communists who "named names" for the FBI or congressional committees.[6] The whistle-blowers' admirers labeled them not as self-serving "snitches" but as valiant citizens of industrial society who cared deeply about responsible action and exposed significant corruption, despite risks to their careers or personal safety.

Several interrelated social and political factors allowed such individuals to surface as staunch defenders of legal and ethical standards. Among the most central were the struggle over the new government regulations of private industry in the 1960s and 1970s, widespread disillusionment with technology, and the increasing skepticism that industry could control the technological "monster" it had created. At the same time there was growing cynicism that government was effective or committed enough to monitor the potential hazards to public health and safety. Taken together, this created an environment in which the gap between ideal and actual standards widened. Increasingly, there was conflict between ethical employees and their managers over appropriate organizational behavior.

LITERATURE REVIEW

During the past fifteen years a burgeoning literature has developed on whistleblowing. As in many new fields of inquiry, the initial works in the early 1970s were compendia of individual case studies of whistle-blowers in diverse settings.[7] Building on this material, several authors have begun to analyze more systematically the significance of individual characteristics and of the organizational context and culture.

Substantial agreement exists on the characteristics of whistle-blowers and the paths they follow to public disclosure. Employee critics generally come on the job with great enthusiasm for their work. There is little in their background that would lead to a prediction that they would become alienated or marginal employees. On the contrary, virtually all have successful work histories and have been rewarded for their loyalty to their organizations. According to Frederick Elliston and his associates, "whistleblowing is more likely to occur if individuals are a) committed to the formal goals of the organization or to the successful completion of the project, b) identify with the organization, and c) have a strong sense of professional responsibility."[8] Similarly, in summarizing his analysis of ten cases, Alan Westin succinctly captured this point: "None of these persons was a 'poor performer' or had previously experienced difficulty in getting along with coworkers, supervisors, or customers. All were receiving good or superior ratings on the job before the issue arose that eventually led to their blowing the whistle."[9]

The employees' optimistic view of their work environment slowly became transformed when they observed illegal or unethical conduct that they believed jeopardized the goals of their organization and the well-being of others. Despite severe pressure from superiors and sometimes peers, employees refused to remain silent.

Elliston and his colleagues asserted that whistle-blowers are usually strong-minded and strong-willed individuals with high ideals and moral principles.[10]

James Bowman found that the majority were neither "malcontents, misfits, neurotics, nor radicals." Instead, he argued that most whistle-blowers were middle managers who observed problems and had no "vested interest in ensuring that they are never made public." [11] David Ewing corroborated this in analyzing more than twenty cases in which employees were concerned about problems of health and safety violations, mismanagement of funds, and abuse of power. In introducing his study, Ewing emphasized the professional and occupational values that impelled dissidents to move forward in their disputes with managers. Several other studies, including those by Deena Weinstein and by Myron Peretz Glazer and Penina Glazer, have underscored the special responsibilities professionals assume as a result of their training and duties. These accounts reveal the sharp conflict of loyalties some professionals experience when employed in bureaucratic organizations. [12]

In her analysis of fifty-one cases, Lea Stuart found that virtually all of the twenty-five employees still working in their organizations presented their concerns to superiors before they went to outside agencies. [13] When these officials refused to remedy the problems or rectify their behavior, protesting employees suffered a profound breach of trust in the competence and integrity of management. Indeed, Westin, Stuart, Ewing, and Elliston and his coauthors all provided evidence that the breakdown of trust is a crucial ingredient propelling ethical resisters to protest further and to take their allegations outside the organization. Bernard Barber, in his analysis of trust, provided convincing evidence that the alienation of Americans from both government and business derives from substantial evidence of lawless behavior. [14]

When the employees pressed their protest, they threatened powerful superiors who sought to belittle their concerns and force them to participate in acts that these employees believed were illegal and dangerous. Kermit Vandivier, Frank Camps, Grace Pierce, and James Boyd, among many others, have described their own responses to commands from superiors to obey orders and to remain silent. [15] They did not succumb to the blandishments of their superiors who insisted that loyalty and "going along" were the keys to personal success. As Stanley Milgram observed in his classic studies of obedience, such defiance is extremely uncomfortable for most Americans who are socialized to conform to authority. [16] Among whistle-blowers, the necessity of disobedience was profoundly reinforced by a belief that the organization's mission required a sense of concern for potential victims of management's decisions. Westin, Greg Mitchell, Nader and his associates, and Leslie Freeman all presented instances of employee resistance that were propelled by such a strong sense of compassion. Their writings document the cases of scientists and engineers in the Environmental Protection Agency who feared that illegal dumping of toxic wastes could poison the waters, causing cancer to unknowing citizens living downstream from the dump site; of technicians in the nuclear industry who agonized over community catastrophe when safety regulations were being overlooked; and of physicians in industry who decried the consequences of testing unsafe drugs.[17] Whistle-blowers did not confront their management over some abstract principle; rather, they felt a keen and concrete responsibility to protect the public.

According to Weinstein, their "bureaucratic opposition" singled them out within their workplace. They were soon stigmatized as uncooperative or naive employees who could no longer be counted on. Although these employees assumed they were working for rational bureaucracies, they learned to their misfortune that they were employed in authoritarian hierarchies with little tolerance for dissent.[18] Marcia Parmerlee, Janet Near, and Tamila Jensen observed that whistle-blowers were likely to suffer retaliation whether or not their case had merit.[19] Studies by the Merit Systems Protection Board reveal that most government workers refuse to come forward precisely because they fear retaliation or doubt the efficacy of remedial action.[20]

Reprisals were initiated at two distinct junctures in the process of whistle-blowing. For some, retaliation began as soon as they embarked on internal protest. This rapid effort to silence the concerned employee often backfired and resulted in the worker moving to public disclosure.[21] In other instances the employees believed that their internal protests produced insufficient results, and they took their allegations to outside sources, such as the press, Congress, or regulatory agencies. In these cases the act of moving beyond the organization triggered severe retaliation to undermine the credibility of whistle-blowers and prevent them from acting as witnesses against the organization.

One whistle-blower tracked the fate of others in the federal government by clipping all relevant articles in the *Federal Times* (weekly newspaper for federal government employees) between May 1984 and November 1985. In addition, he supplemented these with reports of whistleblowing from the *Washington Post* and *Science* and *Time* magazines. He collected articles on the tribulations of thirty whistle-blowers and determined that twenty-two were judged to have had unfavorable outcomes, an assessment we concur with on the basis of the evidence presented. He concluded "that for every unscathed survivor, there are dozens of wrecked lives."[22] Even among those he counted as vindicated, there is evidence of severe suffering. In another study, Donald and Karen Soeken surveyed ninety whistle-blowers. Sixty percent were federal government employees and 40 percent worked in private industry. Almost three-fourths were male. The Soekens found that one out of five people in their sample was out of work. Even among federal employees, protected by civil service, half were no longer with the same agency. They also experienced harassment and isolation.[23]

The extensive retaliation reported by the whistle-blowers resulted in a high evidence of physical and emotional deterioration.[24] This outcome is substantiated by our own study of fifty-five dissenters in government and industry. Virtually every respondent reported some serious and prolonged form of retaliation. Furthermore, the eighteen spouses we interviewed all delineated extensive costs not only to the whistle-blower but also to members of the family. Most whistle-blowers suspected that there might be some form of retribution after their superior asked them to put aside the complaints, but they never realized how damaging and extensive it would be. The wife of one employee critic captured this disbelief: "I had no idea that they were not through with my husband when he was fired. It never would have occurred to me that there would have been the effort that was made to absolutely squash his career. I could not, did not, imagine the vindictiveness."

CONCEPTUAL FRAMEWORK:
THE REPERTOIRE OF PUNISHMENT

The spouse in the above example could not "imagine the vindictiveness" of her husband's former superiors because she could not fully comprehend that they were responding to a direct challenge to their competence and integrity. They were unwilling to allow an exposure of serious organizational problems they had sought to deny. Whistle-blowers are guilty of rupturing organizational illusions that everything is under control, that any violations are minor—something that occurs in all organizations—and will have no serious consequence. When employees oppose this organizational ideology and choose to stand as witnesses attesting to significant problems, they threaten the "mutual pretense" that order, control, and integrity exist.[25] Organizations can either respond to the complaints or act to destroy the credibility of the dissidents. If management decides to retaliate, it often moves with severity and ruthlessness to isolate and punish the offending employees. Managers want to demonstrate that public protest has great costs and that institutional goals, as defined by them, will prevail.

In this chapter we argue that despite the concerted efforts to force whistle-blowers to drop their charges, retaliation often has precisely the opposite effect. It often fuels intensified resistance by the dissidents who become increasingly committed to proving that they, and not their superiors, are telling the truth and that they have the staying power to survive a lengthy conflict.

This sequence of the rupture of "mutual pretense," evoking a repertoire of punishment and, in turn, stimulating a renewed determination by protesting employees to seek vindication, is exemplified in the following cases. Although the details differ, the responses to retaliation closely resemble those of the fifty-five subjects we have studied in our ongoing research.

The three case studies presented below illuminate several principal mechanisms used by superiors to silence and punish employees: blacklist, transfer, and personal harassment. Each resulted in eventual dismissal. Since the direct impact of whistleblowing on family life has been largely unexplored in previous studies, we also examine the effects of retaliation on marital relations. The family is particularly vulnerable because few whistle-blowers have independent incomes. The status, economic well being, and emotional equilibrium of the family thus depends almost entirely on success on the job.

All three cases meet Norman Bowie's ideal requirements of justifiable acts of whistleblowing: (1) that the act of whistleblowing stem from appropriate moral motives of preventing unnecessary harm to others; (2) that the employee use all available internal procedures for rectifying the problematic behavior before public disclosure (Bowie conceded that special circumstances may preclude this); (3) that the whistle-blower have "evidence that would persuade a reasonable person"; (4) that the whistle-blower perceive serious danger that can result from the violation; (5) that the individual act in accordance with his or her responsibilities for "avoiding and/or exposing moral violations"; and (6) that the action have some reasonable chance of success.[26]

CASE ANALYSES

Case 1: Blacklisting

Blacklisting is one of management's potent weapons.[27] If successful, it prevents dismissed workers from gaining employment in a comparable organization, excludes them from access to potentially sensitive information, and maintains a feeling of solidarity among managers who agree to forewarn each other of potential troublemakers.

The victims of the blacklist are often initially unaware of the conspiracy to isolate and deny them work. They hope that, with persistence, future job applications will result in suitable employment. As they unravel the pattern of their exclusion, their frustration often turns to rage and then to depression. At times, they develop fantasies of destroying those who have deprived them of their achievements and dreams.[28] These workers exhibit all of the symptoms of grief, mourning over a lost job and a future that once seemed so promising.[29]

This pattern of ostracism is graphically illustrated in the nuclear field, which ultimately produced a larger number of whistle-blowers than any other industry. The nuclear industry developed after 1954 when Congress revised the Atomic Energy Act to allow private companies to own nuclear power. Construction of power plants began almost immediately and accelerated in the 1970s when workers first began to speak out about major safety problems. Professionals with managerial credentials also issued clear warnings. In one important instance in 1976, three management-level engineers at General Electric and one from the Nuclear Regulatory Commission resigned and offered public testimony about the serious risks involved in operating the nuclear plants.[30]

After the 1979 accident at Three Mile Island resulted in a partial meltdown, public sensitivity soared and additional whistle-blowers came forward. In one case, a young detective hired by Cincinnati Gas and Electric discovered serious safety violations at the Zimmer power plant. When no official agencies would pay serious attention, he took his information to the Government Accountability Project (GAP), an organization that defends whistle-blowers. In 1980 GAP submitted twenty-six affidavits, based on interviews with seventy-five whistle-blowers, alleging poor quality control in the construction of the Ohio plant. After GAP forced a more thorough investigation, the Nuclear Regulatory Commission (NRC) found gross violations and imposed substantial fines for safety infractions. The plant subsequently lost its license to operate.[31]

Similar patterns surfaced at the Comanche Peak nuclear plant in Glenrose, Texas, in the early 1980s, when workers complained about improper welding, clerks recognized inadequate adherence to quality-control regulations, and engineers exposed poorly designed safety systems. All encountered an unwillingness on the part of their superiors to slow down production to attend to these potentially hazardous situations. The economic costs loomed too large. The fear of a deadly accident; the reports of increased cancer, leukemia, and birth defects in areas where there has been exposure to radiation; the support of environmental groups; and the existence of a public licensing procedure all served to motivate these workers who increasingly believed that the public should know the risks to which they would be exposed.[32]

The first to come forward was Chuck Atchison who had initially approached the NRC in confidence in 1980 when he believed that there were serious safety violations in the construction of the plant. He knew that the Energy Reorganization Act of 1974 guaranteed immunity and confidentiality to any employee who brought allegations of safety problems to the NRC. Without the existence of special legislation to protect employees who speak up against safety violations, Atchison, like many nuclear whistle-blowers, would probably not have gone to the NRC. For two years Atchison remained an anonymous whistle-blower, a role that often provides maximum protection.[33] Atchison's profile was not unlike other nuclear whistle-blowers. He fully believed in the goals of the organization and in nuclear power. He had been well rewarded and had done supervisory work and quality-control inspections. Yet fear of potential disaster to his community led him to approach the responsible government agency secretly.

Then in April 1982 Atchison was suddenly fired. As a quality-assurance inspector (QA), he had recently reported serious construction and welding problems that required the company to have the work redone and reinspected. Although dismissal for such actions was not uncommon at Comanche Peak, Atchison was shocked when he was let go. His superiors charged that he had overstepped the boundaries that concerned him as an inspector and maintained that he was incompetent in evaluating the welds in the plant construction. Atchison's charge of unfair dismissal was later sustained by subsequent investigations by a Department of Labor administrative law judge and the secretary of labor who both found that Atchison had acted within his area of responsibility and had performed duties that were protected by the Energy Reorganization Act. This decision was later reversed by a U.S. court of appeals, which ruled that his actual firing was not for whistleblowing but for filing an internal nonconformity report that was not a protected activity. Atchison is currently appealing that 1984 ruling.[34]

Immediately after his dismissal, Atchison contacted the NRC. This time officials informed him that his anonymity as a whistle-blower could not be protected since he was no longer employed at the plant. On the day of his termination, one of the NRC inspectors violated his confidentiality and identified him to plant officials.[35] Atchison's decision to file a suit with the Department of Labor for unfair firing escalated his difficulties in finding employment in the nuclear industry: "I was on unemployment for twenty-six weeks. Meanwhile I went to job fairs in Dallas, took subscriptions to a job shopper magazine that lists all the jobs in the nuclear industry. I updated my resume and started cranking them out through the mail." Atchison could not find a job, but he refused to accept such punishment passively. He struck back by testifying publicly against Brown and Root and the Texas Utilities: "I read they were going to have a hearing to license Comanche Peak and wrote a letter to the NRC. I walked into that hearing, and the people I knew from Texas Utilities just came unglued. They were just about ready to get their license granted."

Chuck Atchison challenged the company image that production was under control at Comanche Peak. As he became a major critic of the nuclear plant, his actions provoked an intensified retaliation that followed him to distant work sites. He was finally employed by a contractor at a Louisiana power plant who learned of his testimony and fired him after he had been on the job for only three days. As Atchison found that he was *persona non grata* in the nuclear industry and struggled to survive economically, he became increasingly depressed. His wife now provided the major family income but it was insufficient to cover their expenses:

Everything that wasn't nailed down with the mortgage was sold. We lost our Visa and Mastercard rights and our gasoline credit cards. Finally we lost the house in July 1983. My wife, Jeanne, has always been employed as a secretary–clerk bookkeeper. That was the only thing that really kept us going. We let someone take over the payments on the house and found a trailer we could take over the payments on.

The company's grip now seemed so pervasive that Atchison even feared physical assault. The image of Karen Silkwood hovered in the shadows.[36] Her unsolved automobile death symbolized the extremes of organizational revenge. "Silkwood hit the headlines again. I became paranoid if things happened like a car following me. I'd make several turns and the car would keep up with me. I knew that the company could hire killers for big dollars. The company had this kind of reputation in South Texas." Chuck Atchison had lost his job, his home, his credit rating, and his sense of personal safety. His self-esteem as a breadwinner was shattered. Forced to leave familiar surroundings and to live without possessions, the family no longer felt like respected members of the community. Atchison became a graphic reminder to other Comanche Peak nuclear whistle-blowers of the cost of resisting large corporations. The pressure and humiliation recoiled deeply into his sense of self. He fantasized that he could strike a major blow against his adversaries:

My emotions went the full gamut from deep depression to hostility. There were times that I wanted to paint my face black and wear a camouflage T-shirt and pants and take the carbine and try to find some explosives. I knew where they were kept down at Comanche Peak, and I knew they could blow the place up. It actually crossed my mind a time or two. Now most of that part is gone; the main emotion I still get is tickled to death if I see an article in the paper that makes them look a little bit worse as they go along.

Atchison did not act on his fantasies. Instead, to fight his case of illegal firing, he contacted the Department of Labor and the press, hired lawyers, and worked with the Government Accountability Project. The reprisals enacted against him for whistleblowing extracted a heavy toll but simultaneously resulted in his developing a new reference group of environmentalists organized to fight the plant. He became a principal witness in the campaign of a local grass-roots antinuclear group. Atchison also received national publicity and was subsequently recognized in 1984 when GAP and the Christic Foundation selected him among the first winners of the Karen Silkwood award for exposing dangerous working conditions. While organizational retaliation was personally costly, it catapulted Atchison into the midst of a national controversy about the safety of nuclear power. Atchison is an embodiment of the principle that punishment perceived as unjust and unwarranted generates sustained resistance. On the other hand, Atchison has not been able to replace the Comanche Peak position with one of comparable pay.

Although it is difficult to obtain definitive evidence of blacklisting, not one of the ten nuclear industry whistle-blowers that we interviewed ever worked in that field again. In addition, our sample of the blacklisted ethical resisters includes lawyers and physicians working in large corporations as well as employees of local, county, and federal agencies. Blacklisting extracts a heavy financial and emotional price. Paradoxically, it often keeps employees dedicated to the effort to expose their organization's behavior. Their actions, which begin as a dissent based upon the principle of concern for others, become overlaid with a determination to seek redress for personal abuse.

Case 2: Transfer

The blacklisting of Chuck Atchison occurred in private industry, although the NRC did play a major role in increasing his vulnerability and in failing to protect him. Despite the integral role of this federal agency in the Atchison case, the particular retaliation foisted on him could most readily occur in the private sector. Although recent labor law has developed a series of limitations on private enterprise's right to "employment at will," industry still has greater flexibility than government in firing and blacklisting a long-term employee, without notice or explanations.[37]

Since employees in the public sector are ostensibly protected against such precipitous and arbitrary dismissal, dissidents in government agencies are more frequently punished initially by demotion and transfer. They may be relegated to positions outside their areas of expertise or assigned tasks well below their level of competence. This is a painful reminder to the dissenters of their powerlessness in the hands of the bureaucracy and often serves as a first step in an extended process of retaliation culminating in dismissal or forced resignation. Protesters can accept the humiliation associated with the new position or fight back by contacting lawyers, the press, the Congress, public interest groups, and the Inspector General's office.[38] In our study the cases where transfer was used punitively included actions against employees in the Nuclear Regulatory Commission, the Veterans Administration, and the New York City Office of Special Services for Children. In all of these instances, the transfer or demotion of a dissenting employee transformed a protest into a full-scale public act of whistleblowing as the case of Jim Pope most clearly demonstrates.

Pope, a pilot and inventor, joined the Federal Aviation Administration (FAA) in the 1960s. A respected engineer, he had responsibility for the department in charge of both airport and air safety of private, noncommercial planes. In 1976 Pope became embroiled in a controversy about two systems designed to prevent midair collisions. Pope firmly believed that the evidence clearly pointed to the advisability of the Airborne Collision Avoidance System (ACAS), whereas most of the high-level FAA officials advocated the alternative Beacon Collision Avoidance Systems (later called TCAS). The Airborne system was located in the aircraft under the control of the pilots whereas the Beacon system would be controlled from the ground. Pope argued that the Airborne system was more effective, was cheaper, and could be more quickly operational. He believed his opponents were against it because it had been developed by a private company, Honeywell, in competition with the FAA's own system and further charged that there was a cover-up of an FAA-commissioned study by the Mitre Corporation that documented the superiority of the ACAS.[39] The FAA officials favoring the ground-based system insisted that it was less susceptible to false alarms.

The issue became particularly heated after a disastrous 1978 midair collision over San Diego in which 144 people died. Pope argued that the collision could have been avoided if the Airborne system had been used. Frustrated, he approached a congressional committee staff director in confidence, providing information on the report supporting an airborne system. The FAA's chief administrator later testified before Congress that neither he nor any member of his staff had knowledge of the Mitre Corporation report that had evaluated the Airborne system as superior and cheaper. The controversy over the crash-avoidance systems led to the decision to disband Pope's unit, the General Aviation Department, and to transfer him to Seattle. He was the only one in the unit who was not given a choice of location, although a number of colleagues believed that there were several appropriate positions available in the Washington, D.C., area.

Pope reluctantly accepted the transfer to Seattle and the promise that an exciting new job awaited him. Despite his wife's protests, he decided to go without her, convincing her that she should stay in Virginia with their recently completed home until he was settled in Seattle. Unfortunately, the new and challenging position never materialized. Pope was allocated office space, an impressive title, and maintained his $51,000 annual salary, but the job description was fictitious. He had virtually no work.

His new supervisors did not want him and warned colleagues to stay away from him if they valued their careers. For Jim Pope the transfer to Seattle was a trap, a dead-end position, a punishing form of dismissal with pay. He sat at an empty desk while his supervisors insisted that his relocation had no punitive intent. He became deeply bitter:

They separated me from my family and my kids. They made up all these stories about me in the hope that they could fire me. I didn't have any way of fighting back. I kept thinking that they would not get away with it. What they did was illegal and wrong. They are letting people get away with weekly collisions on airplanes. They are destroying everything I've worked for all my life.

Jim Pope was so furious that he thought of attacking those who had humiliated him. He purchased a gun, and his son was sufficiently concerned that he went to Seattle to try to offer him some support.

Now, of course, I backed off from some of that violent thinking. Boy, after a while, the pressure started coming on and I didn't know what I would do. I don't really care about guns but one was kind of neat looking and I thought, "Well, I ought to have one just in case." It never came about because I came home just about that time.

Florence Pope gave a poignant account of the two years of their separation. Like most spouses, she could testify to the emotional costs to her spouse when he was pushed aside and defined as an employee bereft of recognition or advancement. This was a second marriage for Jim, and they had been married only for a few years. Florence later realized that she did not fully understand how depressed he had been. Their marriage suffered from the strain of the separation. Despite some concerns about their new house, she did not agree with his decision that she should remain in Virginia.

In our separation he was isolated and I was isolated. I went to a psychiatrist wondering what I should do about our marriage. How do I get across the message that I needed to be with him? Jim couldn't hear me. His whole energy was in another direction and he was really suffering a lot. He was very depressed, and I was getting depressed.

Jim Pope could not fully admit his despair. He defined himself as someone tough enough to fight back, and in 1980, after a year and a half in Seattle, he contacted a local newspaper. Like many whistle-blowers, Pope went public when he had exhausted all of his agency's internal mechanisms. Again, as with Atchison, the effort to isolate him had resulted in his resolve to publicize his complaints. He received coverage and support in the Seattle press and in several professional aviation journals, and he appeared on "60 Minutes" in March 1981.[40] His public disclosure about airport safety problems and his claim that he was receiving $51,000 of government funds for a nonexistent job embarrassed the FAA. His superiors responded by inundating him with so much work that they could justify a flood of memos criticizing his work performance and set the stage to fire him. For the first time in his sixteen years of government service, Jim Pope was evaluated as an unsatisfactory employee.

The new effort to break him took a heavy toll. He was in great emotional turmoil and began to suffer from chest pains. His wife urged him to see a psychiatrist who recommended that he enter a hospital where the physicians suggested that he apply for a disability retirement from the FAA. When Pope began these proceedings, the FAA charged him with being AWOL and fired him. Under this provocation, Florence Pope later concluded that this country has characteristics that make it no different from Russia. Several of our respondents made comparable statements when they felt most desperate. It signified their lack of comprehension about what had befallen them and their belief that these retaliatory acts could not happen here to upstanding, hardworking American citizens.

Once again Jim Pope refused to back down in the face of reprisals and appealed his termination to the Merit Systems Protection Board. In August 1982 the FAA agreed to drop the dismissal action, to purge his personnel file of all charges and allegations, and to approve disability benefits for him. Despite this victory, Pope pressed his case, and in 1985 the Office of the Special Counsel (OSC) of the Merit Systems Protection Board found that there was a "substantial likelihood" that Pope's initial charges about the FAA mismanagement of air-safety issues were true. The Department of Transportation (DOT) was ordered to undertake an investigation of the failure of the FAA to certify collision-avoidance systems that had been found to be inexpensive and safe. When the DOT cleared the FAA of all charges without ever interviewing Pope, the OSC was not satisfied and took the unusual step of ordering a reinvestigation. The DOT reasserted its initial findings.[41] But a 1986 midair collision in California involving a commercial airliner and a private plane rekindled interest in the Airborne Collision Avoidance System.

The chairman of the National Transportation Safety Board recently complained about the FAA's inability to mount its own system. "The FAA told us in 1981 that it would be ready in 1985. Now it tells us we will have it by 1988. . . . if it's a voluntary program it's safe to assume that a majority of our fleet won't have a TCAS (traffic-alert collision avoidance system) by the end of the century."[42] Pope, who now works for NASA, reappeared on "60 Minutes" and the "McNeill-Lehrer" program to present his version of the controversy. His battle for public vindication took on new momentum.

The transfer and humiliation of Jim Pope is a prime example of high-level government officials exiling those who voice strong opposition to their policies. It is an ingenious bureaucratic device that transforms a conventional organizational procedure into a punishment that is accompanied by various symbols of humiliation. In some instances government whistle-blowers found themselves in offices with no windows and no heat controls. In other cases they were given less pay or no work to perform. Jim Pope was relocated 3,000 miles away when it was known that he wanted to stay in the Washington, D.C., area. Equally devastating was the decision to give him nothing to do, to rob him of his sense of expertise and productivity that came from his engagement with his work. Transfer may not always lead to termination, but it results in isolation and often serves to continue rather than deescalate the conflict.

The cases of Atchison and Pope both demonstrate that bureaucratic organizations caught in conflicts over serious policy issues often prefer to eliminate opposition through punitive acts and lengthy battles rather than disrupt entrenched patterns and threaten vested interests. By refusing to back down, whistle-blowers continue to challenge the organization's insistence that no major changes are necessary. The continued struggle can also serve to signal areas of major public concern.

Case 3: Personal Harassment

Destroying one's career, either through dismissal and blacklist or through transfer, is by far the most frequent form of retaliation. Although there are many variations in the applications of these punitive measures, in all cases the whistle-blowers receive the message that their career aspirations are no longer valid, that they have been cast aside.

There are less common, but by no means less devastating instances, in which these measures are not deemed effective, and other more personal forms of retaliation are invoked. No whistle-blower can forget the fate of Karen Silkwood, who may have been deliberately contaminated with plutonium and whose car mysteriously ran off the road as she was driving allegedly to give damaging information about her employer, Kerr McGee, to a *New York Times* reporter.[43] In another instance, when Marie Ragghiante exposed corruption in the governor's office in Tennessee, she faced fabricated charges of drunk driving, was subjected to false rumors about her sexual promiscuity, and feared for her personal safety.[44]

In both cases these whistle-blowers were intent on challenging powerful men in industry and government, which provoked immediate and severe reprisals that went far beyond a threat to their careers. Angry employers, seeking any possible means to retaliate against "difficult" workers, can easily resort to gender-specific attacks. These women were subjected to accusations about their morality and sexuality. To destroy their credibility as witnesses and to intimidate them further, there were threats of physical reprisals to them and their children. Once again the threats primarily served to exacerbate the conflict and to bring issues of worker safety and government fraud to public attention. The case of Billie Garde fits into this pattern.

Garde was raised in a traditional Lutheran family in Wisconsin. As a youth and young adult she was exposed to contemporary ideas about women and minority rights. Denied an opportunity to apply to West Point because it did not yet accept women, she had enlisted in the air force and served in Vietnam. By 1980 she was a divorced single mother living in Moskogee, Oklahoma. At that time she accepted the position of assistant director of the local Census Bureau to earn money both to support her two daughters and to enable her to leave teaching and to attend graduate school. She knew that a major issue in Moskogee had been the undercounting of the local Native American population in the previous census, which had cost the district substantial federal funds. She hoped to help remedy this problem.

The ideas about expanding opportunities for women and increasing attention to minority rights were not idiosyncratic. Although the equality revolution may not have been very popular in Moskogee, Oklahoma, it was a vital force in American society of the 1960s and 1970s and shaped many of Billie Garde's values and expectations. Nothing had prepared her, however, for her superior's attitude toward the census, for his plans to use the office for his own private political aggrandizement, and for his willingness to exploit others sexually for his own goals:

John Hudson wanted me to hire a harem of young women from among my former students who would sleep with visiting political officials. Now, he could not have been more explicit about what he wanted to do. I just thought he was nuts. I did not think he would ever try to implement that. As disgusting as it may seem, what he said was, "I know which politicians like little girls, and which ones like little boys, and which ones drink, and which ones run around, and which ones take bribes, and that's how you control them." He pretty much got away with it, and in the beginning he was searching for my Achilles heel.

After six weeks, Garde spoke with local political leaders and with the Census Bureau's regional director, but they did not want to get involved. When Hudson realized that she had complained of his activities to others, he escalated his attempts to intimidate her: "He called me in and said that my ex-husband wanted custody, and he was going to help him get it, if I didn't conform. I went home and I was absolutely terrified." Her superior began attacking her sex life and her fitness as a mother. Even though the accusations he made were not true, she felt increasingly vulnerable: "There would also be calls in the middle of the night saying things like 'I saw you screwing so-and-so.' And it terrified me—at every turn, there was something about my kids. I called his boss and then his boss's boss, and everyone said they would take care of it.''

Finally, several other workers in the office also complained of Hudson's sexual exploitation, use of drugs, and dereliction of duty. He was given three weeks to prepare for an inspection. He singled out Garde as the ringleader and immediately fired her.

Garde was outraged, yet relieved, and as a temporary employee decided not to fight the dismissal. She moved to Washington, D.C. Her children were spending the month with their father in Moskogee and were to join her on June 27, 1980. Within a few days Garde received a call from an Oklahoma newspaper reporter who wanted her to confirm the story he was writing on the Census Bureau scandal. She refused, still hoping that the investigation by the Denver office would result in a just solution. "So I called the director of the regional office, who had investigated and had heard the whole story from many others. He said that he was not going to do anything. He hoped Hudson would resign, but if not, the census office was going to close in a month anyway.''

Garde could not believe that the bureau would not take action despite such an abundance of evidence of gross misbehavior: "It was so outrageous. In the heat of my anger, without giving any thought to the fact that I didn't have my kids, I called back the newspaper and said, 'Let me tell you the story.' ''

Garde had immediate misgivings. Hudson had warned her that he would help her husband get custody of her children, but the reporter persuaded her that it was impossible. She was also reassured by earlier conversations with her former husband. "Larry said that he had heard through the grapevine that if he wanted to keep the kids, that Hudson had enough power to do that; but he said that I shouldn't think that he would do that . . . that he wanted what was best for the kids, and . . . I believed him.''

The newspaper story appeared the day the children were to leave Oklahoma for Washington. They never arrived:

Within a couple of hours, Larry and Hudson had gone to a lawyer in Muskogee. Then they went to the courthouse. The judge was getting off the elevator, and Larry's lawyer said to the judge, "This is Larry Garde; he's married to the woman involved in the Census scandal. He doesn't want to send the kids back." And the judge didn't say a word, and he signed the order and changed custody from me to him. No notice, no hearing, no nothing . . . just boom! And so then, when I called later that day to make sure everything was o.k., he said, "You're never going to see the kids again."

The initial shock was overwhelming. Garde finally managed to ask Larry what had happened.

He said that Hudson had told him that I was the one that was going to go to jail and I was guilty of all these sins and crimes and political abuse. He claimed that I had had an affair with Hudson and others and that I was using drugs. Everything Hudson had said that he was going to make sure people believed about me then came out of Larry's mouth. And I of course thought "He got to me."

Garde's worst fears were realized. Through the use of falsehood and political connections, John Hudson had inflicted the most painful punishment on her. In Garde's case the more typical work-related retaliation would have been ineffective. She had planned to leave the area and relocate more than 1,000 miles away and pursue a new career. Since this did not insure Hudson that she would not return as a witness against him, he stigmatized her as an unfit mother and hoped to destroy her credibility in the community.

As in the cases of Silkwood and Rigghiante, it is significant that Garde is a woman. When she came on the job, her superior made physical overtures toward her and attempted to involve her in a nefarious sexual arrangement. When this failed, he systematically tested to find where she was most vulnerable. As a woman and a single mother, he calculated that nothing could be more threatening than to separate her from her children.

Hudson's campaign against Garde backfired, for she became ever more ready to testify against him. Ultimately, he was sentenced to prison, and Larry Garde learned that all of the charges against his former wife had been a fabrication. After a year-long battle he agreed to return custody of their daughters. In her struggle for vindication Billie Garde received substantial assistance from the Government Accountability Project. In the ensuing years, she joined the staff of GAP, completed law school, and has become an advocate for embattled workers, particularly in the nuclear industry. She is among a small contingent of whistle-blowers who have drawn directly upon their ordeals to rebuild their careers.

CONCLUSION

The cases of Chuck Atchison, Jim Pope, and Billie Garde are not isolated instances of severe retaliation against whistle-blowers. The reprisals of blacklisting, transfer, and personal harassment represent three of the most commonly employed actions. Dismissal is the goal of most managers, and in the majority of the cases we studied, the protesting employees did indeed lose their jobs. Blacklisting is most likely to occur where there is a well-organized network of communication among employers. This is true not only in the nuclear industry but also in the federal government where references and personnel files can easily be forwarded from one agency to another, often resulting in a de facto blacklist against any whistle-blower defined as a "troublesome employee."[45] Whereas transfers do not necessarily involve a geographical relocation 3,000 miles away, other critics were reassigned to jobs where they had to commute long distances from their homes or found themselves demoted to positions with little or nothing to do. Although no other person we studied lost custody of her children, sexual and personal harassment were not uncommon to other women.[46]

All of the whistle-blowers learned just how vulnerable they actually were. Although many felt they had built a secure economic base over the years, they quickly found that, like most Americans, they lived from one paycheck to the next. Even a few months of unemployment left most virtually devoid of resources and unable to maintain their standard of living. Beyond the economic dislocation was the severe assault on self. When deprived of their identity as productive, knowledgeable, and respected employees, they could not maintain emotional equilibrium. Depression and withdrawal were common symptoms as whistle-blowers found that others in positions of power whom they had previously respected would no longer corroborate their definition of reality—of what was right and wrong.

Their sense of disbelief was exacerbated by their isolation. Although they drew upon professional ethics, religious beliefs, and community ties to reject lawless acts on the job, they seldom found that their professional organizations or unions, their churches or civic groups, were prepared to intervene against bureaucratic reprisals.[47]

As early as 1972 a survey of 800 members of the National Society of Professional Engineers (NSPE) revealed that most respondents favored the professional societies supporting engineers who had acted in the public interest by finding new jobs for them and by taking actions against firms that penalized such employees. The majority further believed that the professional society should condemn firms that do not act in the public interest by recommending that engineers not work for such companies. Despite these strong findings, the leadership of the NSPE, like that of most other professional associations, has rarely been willing to take its society into areas of employee–management controversy.[48] Groups that might have organized to shield the whistle-blower against onerous attack on their credibility often stood by while they were fired, blackballed, transferred, and harassed. They infrequently attempted to mediate between employer and employee, to censure those organizations engaged in unfair practices, or to strike or boycott on behalf of a worker's rights who spoke up on behalf of ethical practices.

The inability of local groups to facilitate a speedy resolution of disputes impelled employees either to accept defeat or to undertake a lengthy and expensive fight. When they chose to pursue their cases, they had to seek support from more remote authorities who might assist them in their quest for recognition and vindication. The media, congressional investigating committees, public service organizations, and the courts became the prime vehicles in individuals' struggles against intimidation and discharge. Although they often found sympathetic supporters there, the procedures they had to follow were prolonged and complex, often involving expensive legal assistance and years of intense involvement before reaching a settlement. Some never achieved the satisfaction of victory or reinstatement. For others no success could compensate for their sacrifice of prestige and income and especially for the assault on their belief in the primacy of our system.

As they worked for the achievement of their own personal vindication, they kept alive pressing issues such as nuclear and airline safety and the sexual harassment of women. The more personally costly the retaliation, the more determined they became to salvage their self-respect and reconstitute their careers. In this struggle, they and other whistle-blowers have come to represent an important voice of individual conscience and personal responsibility in large-scale bureaucratic organizations.

NOTES

This chapter is part of a larger work, *The Courage of Their Convictions: An Ethical Odyssey in Industry and Government*, to be published by Basic Books in 1989.

1. *Report of the Presidential Commission on the Space Shuttle Challenger Accident* (Washington, D.C.: U.S. Government Printing Office, 1986), chapter six, especially pp. 123–124.

2. "Burying the Truth at Morton-Thiokol," *New York Times*, 13 May 1986. For an excellent analysis of the entire issue, *see* Trudy E. Bell and Karl Esch, "The Fatal Flaw in Flight 51-L," *IEEE Spectrum* 24 (February 1987): 36–51.

3. David E. Sanger, "How See-No-Evil Doomed Challenger," *New York Times*, 29 June 1986; *Huntsville Times*, 28 February 1986.

4. The films were *Serpico, Silkwood,* and *Marie*.

5. Harry C. Boyte, *The Backyard Revolution* (Philadelphia: Temple University Press, 1980), chapter one.

6. Victor Navasky, *Naming Names* (New York: Viking, 1980).

7. Ralph Nader, Peter J. Petkas, and Kate Blackwell, eds., *Whistle Blowing* (New York: Bantam, 1972); Alan Westin, ed., *Whistle-Blowing! Loyalty and Dissent in the Corporation* (New York: McGraw-Hill, 1981); Charles Peters and Taylor Branch, *Blowing the Whistle: Dissent in the Public Interest* (New York: Praeger, 1972); Robert M. Anderson, Robert Perucci, Dan D. Schendel, and Leon E. Tractman, *Divided Loyalties: Whistle-Blowing at BART* (West Lafayette, Ind.: Purdue University, 1980); Greg Mitchell, *Truth and Consequences* (New York: Dembner Books, 1981).

8. Frederick Elliston, John Keenan, Paula Lockhart, and Jane Van Schaick, *Whistleblowing Research: Methodological and Moral Issues* (New York: Praeger, 1985), p. 26.

9. Westin, *Whistle-Blowing!* p. 132.

10. Elliston, Keenan, Lockhart, and Van Schaick, *Whistleblowing Research*, p. 26. *See also* Myron Peretz Glazer and Penina Migdal Glazer, "Pathways to Resistance," in Joann Miller and Michael Lewis, eds., *Social Problems and Public Policy*, vol. 4 (Greenwich, Conn.: JAI Press, 1987), pp. 193–219.

11. James S. Bowman, "Whistle-Blowing in the Public Service: An Overview of the Issues," *Review of Public Personnel Administration* 1 (Fall 1980): 17.

12. David W. Ewing, *"Do It My Way or You're Fired": Employee Rights and the Changing Role of Management Prerogatives* (New York: Wiley, 1983), pp. 11–14; Deena Weinstein, *Bureaucratic Opposition* (New York: Pergamon, 1979), p. 43; Glazer and Glazer, "Pathways," pp. 202–206; Frank von Hippel, "Protecting the Whistle-blowers," *Physics Today,* October 1977, p. 9.

13. Lea P. Stuart, " 'Whistle Blowing' Implications for Organizational Communication," *Journal of Communication* 30 (Autumn 1980): 90-101.

14. Bernard Barber, *The Logic and Limits of Trust* (New Brunswick, N.J.: Rutgers University Press, 1983), chapters five and six.

15. Kermit Vandivier, "The Aircraft Brake Scandal," *Harper's*, April 1972, pp. 45–52; Frank Camps "Warning an Auto Company about an Unsafe Design," in Alan Westin, ed., *Whistle-Blowing!* pp. 119–129; Grace Pierce, "Asserting Professional Ethics against Dangerous Drug Tests," in Alan Westin, ed., *Whistle-Blowing!* pp. 107–117; James Boyd, *Above the Law* (New York: New American Library, 1968).

16. Stanley Milgram, *Obedience to Authority: An Experimental View* (New York: Harper and Row, 1974), chapter twelve.

17. Mitchell, *Truth and Consequences;* Leslie J. Freeman, *Nuclear Witnesses* (New York: Norton, 1981), pp. 206–224; Westin, *Whistle-Blowing!* pp. 39–54; Nader, Petkas, and Blackwell, *Whistle Blowing,* pp. 118–125; Westin, *Whistle-Blowing!* pp. 107–117.

18. Weinstein, *Bureaucratic Opposition,* chapter four.

19. Marcia A. Parmerlee, Janet P. Near, and Tamila C. Jensen, "Correlates of Whistleblowers' Perceptions of Organizational Retaliation," *Administrative Science Quarterly* 27 (1982): 17–34.

20. U.S. Merit Systems Protection Board, *Whistle Blowing and the Federal Employee* (Washington, D.C.: U.S. Government Printing Office, October 1981).

21. Ewing, *"Do It My Way,"* pp. 142–152; Myron Glazer, "Ten Whistleblowers and How They Fared," *The Hastings Center Report* 13 (December 1983): 33–40.

22. Unpublished communication from Dr. Anthony Morris to authors, November 13, 1985.

23. Clyde Farnsworth, "Survey of Whistle Blowers Finds Retaliation but Few Regrets," *New York Times,* 22 February 1987.

24. Ibid.; Don Oldenburg, "Whistle Blower's Anguish," *Washington Post,* 31 March 1987.

25. For a discussion of how "mutual pretense" safeguards the social order, *see* Myra Bluebond-Langner, *The Private Worlds of Dying Children* (Princeton, N.J.: Princeton University Press, 1978), chapter six.

26. Norman Bowie, *Business Ethics* (Englewood Cliffs, N.J.: Prentice-Hall, 1982), p. 143.

27. Navasky, *Naming Names,* pp. 85–96, 423–424.

28. Willard Gaylin, *The Rage Within* (New York: Simon and Schuster, 1984).

29. David Peretz, "Reaction to Loss," in Bernard Schoenberg, Arthur C. Carr, David Peretz, and Austin H. Kutscher, eds., *Loss and Grief: Psychological Management in Medical Practice* (New York: Columbia University Press, 1970), pp. 20–35.

30. Freeman, *Nuclear Witnesses,* pp. 245–292.

31. *Time,* October 31, 1983, p. 96; *New York Times,* 13 November 1982.

32. Freeman, *Nuclear Witnesses.*

33. Frederick Elliston, "Anonymous Whistleblowing: An Ethical Analysis," *Business and Professional Ethics* 1 (Winter 1982): 39–59.

34. Charles A. Atchison vs. Brown and Root, Inc., Department of Labor Case No. 82-ELA-9, Recommended Decision (Dec. 3, 1982) and Decision and Final Order (June 10, 1983); Brown & Root, Inc. vs. Raymond J. Donovan, U.S. Court of Appeals, Fifth Circuit, No. 83-4486 (Dec. 10, 1984).

35. Deposition of Robert R. Taylor, Texas Utilities Electric et al., before The Atomic Safety & Licensing Board, Nuclear Regulatory Commission (July 17, 1984).

36. Richard Rashke, *The Killing of Karen Silkwood* (Boston: Houghton Mifflin, 1981).

37. Alfred G. Feliu, "Discharge of Professional Employees: Protecting against Dismissal for Acts within a Professional Code of Ethics," *Columbia Human Rights Law Review* 11 (1979–1980): 186–87; Elliston, Keenan, Lockhart, and Van Schaick, *Whistleblowing Research,* chapter seven.

38. Frederick Elliston, John Keenan, Paula Lockhart, and Jane Van Schaick, *Whistleblowing: Managing Dissent in the Workplace* (New York: Praeger, 1985), chapters seven to nine.

39. "Probe of TCAS," *Aviation Digest,* January 1986, Sec. B, pp. 5–7; Don Aplin and Tom Devine, "Is the FAA Perpetuating Jet Crashes?" *Sacramento Bee* 21 September 1986, pp. 1–2.

40. *See,* for example, "Portrait of a 'Whistle-Blower,' " *Aviation Consumer,* January 1, 1981, pp. 8–13; John Doherty, "Collision Course," *Reason,* June 1982, pp. 32–42; Jim Pope, "The FAA Collision Avoidance Sham," *Professional Pilot,* February 1981, pp. 8–9.

41. Aplin and Devine, "Is the FAA Perpetuating Jet Crashes?" p. 1; "Probe of TCAS," p. 5.

42. "Probe of TCAS," p. 6.

43. Rashke, *The Killing of Karen Silkwood,* chapters one to eight.

44. Peter Maas, *Marie* (New York: Random House, 1983).

45. Vivian Weil, "Moral Responsibility and Whistleblowing in the Nuclear Industry: Browns Ferry and Three Mile Island," in Frederick Elliston, ed., *Conflicting Loyalties in the Workplace* (South Bend, Ind.: Notre Dame University Press, 1986). Weil gives an excellent discussion of how this works for professionals in the nuclear industry and regulatory agency.

46. *See,* for example, Cristine Colt, "Protesting Sex Discrimination against Women"; Adrienne Tompkins, "Resisting Sexual Demands on the Jobs," in Alan Westin, ed., *Whistle-Blowing!* pp. 55–74.

47. *See* Weinstein, *Bureaucratic Opposition,* pp. 72, 119, 121; an exception can be found in Elliston, Keenan, Lockhart, and Van Schaick, *Whistleblowing,* chapter 6.

48. Von Hippel, "Protecting The Whistleblowers," p. 9.

SELECTED BIBLIOGRAPHY

Anderson, Robert M., Robert Perucci, Dan D. Schendel, and Leon E. Tractman. *Divided Loyalties: Whistle-Blowing at BART.* West Lafayette, Ind.: Purdue University, 1980.

Aplin, Don, and Devine, Tom. "Is the FAA Perpetuating Jet Crashes?" *Sacramento Bee.* 21 September 1986.

Aviation Consumer. January 1, 1981.

Aviation Digest. January 1986.

Barber, Bernard. *The Logic and Limits of Trust.* New Brunswick, N.J.: Rutgers University Press, 1983.

Bayles, Michael D. *Professional Ethics.* Belmont, Calif.: Wadsworth, 1981.

Bell, Trudy E., and Karl Esch. "The Fatal Flaw In Flight 51-L." *IEEE Spectrum* 24 (February 1987): 36–51.

Bellah, Robert N., Richard Madsen, William Sullivan, Ann Swidler, and Steven Tipton. *Habits of the Heart.* Berkeley: University of California Press, 1985.

Bluebond-Langner, Myra. *The Private Worlds of Dying Children*. Princeton, N.J.:
    Princeton University Press, 1978.
Bowie, Norman. *Business Ethics*. Englewood Cliffs, N.J.: Prentice-Hall, 1982.
Bowman, James S. "Whistle-Blowing in the Public Service: An Overview of the Is-
    sues." *Review of Public Personnel Administration* 1 (Fall 1980): 15–28.
Bowman, James S., Frederick A. Elliston, and Paula Lockhart. *Professional Dissent:
    An Annotated Bibliography and Resource Guide*. New York: Garland, 1984.
Boyd, James. *Above the Law*. New York: New American Library, 1968.
Boyte, Harry C. *The Backyard Revolution*. Philadelphia: Temple University Press, 1980.
Brodeur, Paul. *Outrageous Misconduct: The Asbestos Industry on Trial*. New York:
    Pantheon, 1985.
Brodsky, Carroll M. *The Harassed Worker*. Lexington, Mass.: Lexington Books, 1976.
Brown, Michael. *Laying Waste*. New York: Washington Square Press, 1981.
Clinard, Marshall. *Corporate Ethics and Crime*. Beverly Hills, Calif.: Sage, 1983.
Clinard, Marshall B., and Peter C. Yeager. *Corporate Crime*. New York: Free Press,
    1980.
Coleman, James W. *The Criminal Elite: The Sociology of White Collar Crime*. New
    York: St. Martin's Press, 1985.
Cullen, Francis T., William J. Maakestad, and Gary Cavender. "The Ford Pinto Case
    and Beyond: Corporate Crime, Moral Boundaries, and Criminal Sanction." In
    Ellen Hochstedler, ed., *Corporations as Criminals*. Beverly Hills, Calif.: Sage,
    1984, pp. 107–130.
Daly, Robert. *Prince of the City*. Boston: Houghton Mifflin, 1978.
Doherty, John. "Collision Course." *Reason*. June 1982, pp. 32–42.
Doig, Jameson W., Douglas E. Phillips, and Tycho Manson. "Deterring Illegal Behav-
    ior by Officials of Complex Organizations." *Criminal Justice Ethics* 3, no. 1
    (Winter–Spring 1984): 27–56.
Donaldson, Thomas. *Corporations and Morality*. Englewood Cliffs, N.J.: Prentice-Hall,
    1982.
Elliston, Frederick. "Anonymous Whistleblowing: An Ethical Analysis." *Business and
    Professional Ethics* 1 (Winter 1982): 39–59.
Elliston, Frederick, John Keenan, Paula Lockhart, and Jane Van Schaick. *Whistleblow-
    ing: Managing Dissent in the Workplace*. New York: Praeger, 1985.
———. *Whistleblowing Research: Methodological and Moral Issues*. New York: Prae-
    ger, 1985.
Erikson, Kai. *Everything in Its Path*. New York: Simon and Schuster, 1976.
Ewing, David W. *"Do It My Way or You're Fired": Employee Rights and the Chang-
    ing Role of Management Prerogatives*. New York: Wiley, 1983.
Feliu, Alfred G. "Discharge of Professional Employees: Protecting against Dismissal
    for Acts within a Professional Code of Ethics." *Columbia Human Rights Law
    Review* 11 (1979–1980): 149–187.
Fitzgerald, A. Ernest. *The High Priests of Waste*. New York: Norton, 1972.
Freeman, Leslie J. *Nuclear Witnesses*. New York: Norton, 1981.
Gamson, William, Bruce Fireman, and Steven Rytina. *Encounters with Unjust Author-
    ity*. Homewood, Ill.: Dorsey Press, 1982.
Garfinkel, Harold. "Conditions of Successful Degradation Ceremonies." *American Journal
    of Sociology* 61 (January 1956): 420–424.
Gaylin, Willard. *The Rage Within*. New York: Simon and Schuster, 1984.

Glazer, Myron. "Ten Whistleblowers and How They Fared." *The Hastings Center Report* 13 (December 1983): 33–40.

Glazer, Myron P., and Penina M. Glazer. "Whistleblowing." *Psychology Today,* August 1986, pp. 36–43.

Glazer, Penina M., and Miriam Slater. *Unequal Colleagues: The Entrance of Women into the Professions.* New Brunswick, N.J.: Rutgers University Press, 1986.

Goldman, Alan H. *The Moral Foundations of Professional Ethics.* Totowa, N.J.: Rowman and Littlefield, 1980.

Hirschman, Albert O. *Exit, Voice, and Loyalty.* Cambridge, Mass.: Harvard University Press, 1970.

Johnson, John M., and Jack D. Douglas, eds. *Crime at the Top: Deviance in Business and the Professions.* New York: Lippincott, 1978.

Levine, Adeline Gordon. *Love Canal: Science, Politics, and People.* Lexington, Mass.: D. C. Heath, 1982.

Maas, Peter. *Marie.* New York: Random House, 1983.

McGraw, Thomas K., ed. *Regulation in Perspective.* Cambridge, Mass.: Harvard University Press, 1981.

Milgram, Stanley. *Obedience to Authority: An Experimental View.* New York: Harper and Row, 1974.

Mitchell, Greg. *Truth and Consequences.* New York: Dembner Books, 1981.

Nader, Ralph, Peter J. Petkas, and Kate Blackwell, eds. *Whistle Blowing.* New York: Bantam, 1972.

Navasky, Victor. *Naming Names.* New York: Viking, 1980.

Near, Janet P., and Marcia P. Miceli. "Organizational Dissidence: The Case of Whistle-Blowing." *Journal of Business Ethics* 4 (1985): 1–16.

Parmerlee, Marcia A., Janet P. Near, and Tamila C. Jensen. "Correlates of Whistleblowers' Perceptions of Organizational Retaliation." *Administrative Science Quarterly* 27 (1982): 17–34.

Peretz, David. "Reaction to Loss." In Bernard Schoenberg, Arthur C. Carr, David Peretz, and Austin H. Kutscher, eds., *Loss and Grief: Psychological Management in Medical Practice.* New York: Columbia University Press, 1970.

Pertschuk, Michael. *Revolt against Regulation: The Rise and Pause of the Consumer Movement.* Berkeley: University of California Press, 1982.

Peters, Charles, and Branch, Taylor. *Blowing the Whistle: Dissent in the Public Interest.* New York: Praeger, 1972.

Pope, Jim. "The FAA Collision Avoidance Sham." *Professional Pilot,* February 1981, pp. 8–9.

Rashke, Richard. *The Killing of Karen Silkwood.* Boston: Houghton Mifflin, 1981.

Rasor, Dina. *The Pentagon Underground.* New York: Times Books, 1985.

Report of the Presidential Commission on the Space Shuttle Challenger Accident. Washington, D.C.: U.S. Government Printing Office, 1986.

Sabini, John, and Silver, Maury. *Moralities of Everyday Life.* New York: Oxford University Press, 1982.

Sheehan, Neil, Hedrick Smith, E. W. Kenworthy, and Fox Butterfield, eds. *The Pentagon Papers.* New York: Bantam, 1971.

Simon, David R., and D. Stanley Eitzen. *Elite Deviance.* Boston: Allyn and Bacon, 1982.

Sinclair, Upton. *The Jungle.* New York: Doubleday, Page & Co., 1906.

Stone, Alan. *Regulation and Its Alternatives.* Washington, D.C.: Congressional Quarterly Press, 1982.

Stuart, Lea P. " 'Whistle Blowing' Implications for Organizational Communication." *Journal of Communication* 30 (Autumn 1980): 90–101.

U.S. Merit Systems Protection Board. *Whistle Blowing and the Federal Employee.* Washington, D.C.: U.S. Government Printing Office, October 1981.

Vandivier, Kermit. "The Aircraft Brake Scandal." *Harper's,* April 1972, pp. 45–52.

Von Hippel, Frank. "Protecting the Whistleblowers." *Physics Today,* October 1977, pp. 8–13.

Weil, Vivian. "Moral Responsibility and Whistleblowing in the Nuclear Industry: Browns Ferry and Three Mile Island." In Frederick Elliston, ed., *Conflicting Loyalties in the Workplace.* South Bend, Ind.: University of Notre Dame Press, 1986.

Weinstein, Deena. *Bureaucratic Opposition.* New York: Pergamon, 1979.

Weisband, Edward, and Thomas M. Franck. *Resignation in Protest.* New York: Penguin Books, 1975.

Westin, Alan, ed. *Whistle-Blowing! Loyalty and Dissent in the Corporation.* New York: McGraw-Hill, 1981.

Wilcox, Fred A. *Waiting for an Army to Die: The Tragedy of Agent Orange.* New York: Vintage Books, 1983.

4

The Conduct of Legislators

Vera Vogelsang-Coombs and Larry A. Bakken

This chapter addresses the relationship between legislative ethics and the ethicality of elected officials by comparing actual congressional behavior with ideal behavior implied in selected ethical codes. It reviews selected recent cases of ethical violations by legislators and speculates on the prospect of promoting a more ethical environment in Congress, based on the professional codes for public administrators developed by the International City Management Association and the American Society for Public Administration. Central to this chapter is the question, "How can we effectively build an ethical environment in Congress?"

The issue of ethics in government has in recent years attracted interest beyond that of philosophers, ethicists, and a few political scientists. In the wake of Vietnam, Watergate, and, more recently, the Iran–Contra affair, policymakers and public administrators have been searching for mechanisms to promote effective policies and ethical behavior in government.

In monitoring its own behavior, the Congress, critics claim, protects its members from the outside world rather than enforcing its own ethical standards.[1] The seriousness of the matter regarding congressional ethics was documented by the Hastings Center; its 1985 report concluded that legislators "face a crisis of public confidence and a crisis of legitimacy that, if not historically unprecedented, is at least deep and persistent enough to provide ample cause for alarm."[2]

It is appropriate, for several reasons, to study cases of congressional wrongdoing. First, members of Congress are far more visible than public administrators who are often described in the popular literature as faceless bureaucrats. Second, the legislature contains only 535 members in contrast to the national civilian bureaucracy, which numbers approximately 2.7 million, a fact that makes

Congress relatively easy to study. Third, the national legislature is responsible for regulating the behavior of its members, in addition to that of federal judges and executive-branch officials. Fourth, incidents involving ethical violations by legislators are frequent topics for journalists, giving readers the impression that unethical conduct in Congress—and in government—is pervasive. For example, a recent public opinion poll showed that half of the respondents believe that government officials are corrupt.[3]

Since the behavior of individuals and institutions is observable and can be documented, this study focuses on the behavior of legislators (the alleged violations) and on Congress (the sanctions imposed). This is consistent with our intent to evaluate codes of ethics for government officials because such documents attempt to establish institutional standards of ethical behavior.

Our method uses a matching process: actual legislative behavior is identified and contrasted with behavior implied under extant codes of ethics. There is a limit to application of this method—it obviously involves an examination of fairly extreme legislative behavior, which make ours a highly selective sample. Although we would prefer a more representative sample incorporating a range of legislative behavior, it is not readily available to independent scholars. This approach, however, is more preferable than relying on the mass media, which is the primary source of information on ethics in government.

LITERATURE REVIEW

Legislative ethics involves the morality of public policies and collective decisions by legislators as well as the morality of their individual conduct. It encompasses personal morality based on individual conceptions of standards of right and wrong as well as institutional moral responsibilities based on individual conceptions of criteria of judgment for public policies. Ethical dilemmas in legislative life arise from: (1) the enormous discretion legislators have in choosing how they define and execute their array of official and, often conflicting, duties; and (2) the substantial impact their decisions have upon the lives of citizens.

Reviewing the literature, one finds that there is no consensus on the definition, scope, and standards related to legislative ethics. There exists conceptual ambiguity over what is and is not ethical behavior in the legislative context. Given the absence of universal ethical standards, the analytical task becomes one of grouping related ethical behavior along important theoretical dimensions. One of the most enduring discussions in the literature focuses on ''theories of representation.''

Two primary theories of representation are the trustee and delegate conceptions. Underpinning these two conceptions are different ethical values and legislative responsibilities. As John Saxon noted, these differences largely arise out of an absence of universal agreement on how to define ''publics'' and to which ''public interests'' legislators should respond.[4]

Legislators acting as trustees are, according to Edmund Burke, supposed to use their own judgment to serve the general interest rather than personal or narrowly based constituency interests.[5] The trustee notion is based on the assumption that "public office is a public trust." In contrast, there is the delegate theory, which is premised on the notion of a social contract between sovereign citizens and their representatives; legislators acting as delegates are expected to bind themselves to their community because of the inability of the citizens to perform the business of government themselves. According to James Mill, delegates must have an "identity of interest" with their constituency so that there is almost a one-to-one correspondence between their interests and the interests of those who elect them.[6] A paradox occurs because although citizens may admire the trustee type of public official, they appear to elect the delegate type of representative because of what the latter promises to do on behalf of the constituents in his or her district.

Both conceptions contain simplistic notions of representation. The trustee notion assumes an easily discernible, relatively fixed set of public interests. It also presupposes the existence of a political aristocracy whose moral superiority and "objective" approach are prerequisites for public office. The delegate notion, although more egalitarian, assumes that legislators have no choice but to follow the instructions of the organized interests of their districts. But as Burke pointed out, this notion of representation leaves out the "unattached interests" as well as underrepresented groups.

Not only is there a problem in how they are constructed, these theories lack explanatory power and are incapable of documenting empirical relationships. As Amy Gutmann and Dennis Thompson noted, such theories cannot tell legislators when it is best to act as a trustee or as a delegate, how to vote on issues, or which criteria of judgment to apply to policy choices.[7] In practice, legislators sometimes vote with their constituency against the "general interest" and at other times with the national interest, irrespective of constituent views. Saxon concluded that given the empirical evidence showing that legislators alternate between the trustee and delegate roles, uniformity may not be a necessary ingredient of legislative ethics.[8]

Other areas in the literature focus on the motives of legislators, legislative priorities, and the proper conduct of legislators. Joel Fleishman argued that the rise of self-interested candidates whose primary goal is reelection and political security has left citizens "famished" for bold and courageous leadership.[9] David E. Price argued that structural and normative changes in the "new Congress" have given rise to destructive particularism, in which legislators successfully "run for Congress" by running against the institution.[10] Furthermore, he said that the weakening of legislature's "folkways" or norms of specialization and apprenticeship, in combination with the pressures for self-promotion in the new Congress, have made "showhorse" behavior more profitable and less costly than in the past, thereby eroding the incentives for legislators to engage seriously in the work of the Congress.[11] Price saw these tendencies for legislative self-promotion and ''position taking'' without seriousness in purpose in making public policies as corrupting the representation function.[12]

Fleishman and Price separately suggested that electoral entrepreneurship, self-promotion, and showhorse behavior are more prevalent today than in the past. Are legislators really more self-interested or personally motivated than they were in the past? Firsthand observations of legislators at work by Richard Fenno in the sixties and David Mayhew in the seventies reveal that there were many legislators in the ''old Congress'' who ''constantly engage[d] in activities related to re-election.''[13]

Stephen Bailey went one step further by arguing that nonself-interested public officials would be antithetical to democracy. His view is that it is appropriate for government officials to seek personal and private goals because:

[I]t is in appreciating the reality of self-interest that public servants find some of the strongest forces for motivating behavior—public and private. Normally speaking, if a public interest is to be orbited, it must have as a part of its propulsive fuel a number of special and particular interests. A large part of the art of the public service is in the capacity to harness private and personal interests to the public interest causes. Those who will not traffic in personal and private interests (if such interests are themselves within the law) to the point of engaging their support on behalf of causes in which public and private interests are served are, in terms of moral temperament, unfit for public responsibility.[14]

Bailey can accept the personal motives of legislators, such as achieving reelection or higher office, or in amassing power and prestige within the Congress or with important constituencies, as long as they are directed toward legitimate public ends.[15]

Bailey's view is not necessarily an acceptance of moral relativism but is based on a recognition that ethics, organization, and politics intermingle. Public officials, including legislators, exercise discretion in an environment characterized by moral ambiguity and political conflict. ''To the morally sensitive public servant, the strains of establishing a general value framework for conducting the public business is nothing compared to the strains of re-sorting specific values in the light of changing contexts.''[16] Gaining agreement on what constitutes a public problem and public interests is part of the political process. Furthermore, Bailey recognized that public policies, like men, are ''morally ambiguous.''[17] Morally mature public officials, he said, will appreciate the inevitability of ''untoward and malignant effects'' of moral public policies.[18] An awareness of these ethical dilemmas and paradoxes inherent in the governmental setting creates humility in public officials. These paradoxes and dilemmas are worked out through the political process involving negotiation and compromise. In short, politics converts private interests and personal ambition into legitimate public interests.

The pursuit of private interests by legislators is often misunderstood and at times abused. Given the absence of universal ethical standards and the absence of agreement on the representation function, the variety of personal motives of legislators and discretion and dilemmas inherent in the congressional setting, how does Congress judge whether the behavior of legislators is ethical or unethical, and who should judge such conduct?

Historically, Congress has relied on ethics committees to render judgments on legislative conduct. The next section provides a brief history of the work of these committees.

HISTORICAL CASES

According to the federal Constitution, Congress has the authority to judge the qualifications of its members and to punish those members who behave improperly.[19] This carte blanche authority is, however, limited by the constitutionally prescribed "qualification requirements" and by the two-thirds majority needed for expulsion of congressional members.

Currently, each chamber disciplines its own members through a variety of sanctions including expulsion, censure, fines, loss of chairmanships, reprimand, or denial of a member's right to vote.[20] The right to punish, in addition to being implied in the U.S. Constitution, was confirmed in *Kilbourn vs. Thompson* when the Supreme Court initially upheld the right of Congress to punish its members.[21] The Court's ruling was reaffirmed in *In re Chapman* when it defined specific circumstances under which the House or Senate could expel one of its members.[22]

During the nation's early history, Congress was unwilling to discipline its members, recognizing that it has "its weak members and its weak moments."[23] In the twelve censure proceedings in the House conducted before the Civil War, only four resulted in the censure of a member.[24] Richard Baker reported that in the majority of these early incidents, Congress closed cases once an apology was extracted from those involved, relying on adverse public opinion to punish violators.

Since 1797 the Senate has heard approximately thirty cases concerning expulsion. Fifteen members were eventually expelled from the Senate for being involved in the support of rebellion or conspiracy.[25] Of these fifteen cases, fourteen occurred during the thirty-seventh Congress (1861–1862). During the same period the House also considered approximately thirty expulsion cases, but it expelled only four members, three for supporting rebellion and the fourth for corruption.

The U.S. House of Representatives, although apparently reluctant to expel its members, has censured twenty legislators and has considered thirty-three censure cases since 1789. The grounds for censure have varied but have included assault, insulting or offensive utterances, financial misconduct, abuse of authority, and corruption. The U.S. Senate, since 1811, has censured only eight senators and has heard only ten censure cases. Grounds relied on by the

Senate for censuring senators were breach of confidence, assault, bringing the Senate into disrepute, obstruction of legislative process, and financial misconduct.

When a member of the House of Representatives is censured, it usually means public admonishment by other members and no opportunity to speak on one's own behalf in the House, whereas in the Senate, the privilege of a personal defense is permitted during the consideration of a censure resolution. Because of the seriousness of expulsion and censure sanctions, other lesser disciplinary actions have been developed by the House and Senate to sanction legislators. In the past, reprimands, loss of committee chairmanships, and suspensions have been considered sufficient punishments to prevent congressional violators from running for reelection or to contribute significantly to negative public opinion causing their defeat at the next election.

Adverse public opinion was seen as insufficient punishment in the 1970s after two senators and fifteen house members (in addition to one president) were targets of congressional, judicial, or criminal proceedings for wrongdoing. As Baker noted, "Hostile public reaction to the apparent tendency within Congress to ignore these cases of wrong-doing led the [Congress] to toughen their codes of conduct."[26]

CONCEPTUAL FRAMEWORK:
LESSONS FROM PUBLIC ADMINISTRATION

The literature shows that attempts by scholars to develop precise definitions of legislative ethics are fraught with conceptual ambiguity. The historical cases reveal that, through the seventies, congressional ethics committees have been reluctant to render judgments or to apply criminal sanctions in cases of ethical wrongdoing. Instead, they have relied on adverse public opinion to discipline members.

More recently, efforts at operationalizing legislative ethics have focused on drafting and redrafting codes of conduct. Vanessa Merton noted that although the increasing professionalization of legislators is undeniable, legislators have largely ignored the ethical problems preoccupying other professionals.[27] Daniel Callahan argued that legislators are not professionals because the constitutional requirements to represent citizens are minimal and are not based on the possession of professional credentials.[28]

Whether or not legislators can be appropriately labeled as "professionals," ethics codes provide moral, professional, legal, and practical reasons for their establishment. In theory, legislative ethics provides standards of behavior that are, according to Amy Gutmann and Dennis Thompson, more restrictive than ordinary ethics. The justification, they said, is moral: legislative ethics gives legislators permission to serve as the advocate for particular interests without betraying the public interest. Legislative ethics is more restrictive because lawmakers are held to higher (legal) standards than ordinary citizens in order for them to serve in office.[29]

From a professional perspective, these codes provide simultaneously positive statements concerning the moral conduct of practitioners and negative exhortations outlining the minimum level of acceptable professional behavior. From a legal perspective, legislative ethics has advantages in that laws provide standards that are known in advance, promote fairness in application, and can be enforced. On a practical level, ethics codes often are far easier to construct than altering structural conditions underlying ethical misconduct.[30] Finally, they provide a "shortcut to professional prestige and status."[31]

The view prevailing in the literature is that extant legislative ethics codes are problematic. Codes, for instance, reduce complicated moral problems into a set of rigid procedures covering a narrow band of legislative behavior. Although couched in language of high moral principle, legal prohibitions provide the lowest common ethical denominator and produce narrow moral directives because they are the product of negotiation and compromise. There is also a problem with code enforcement. Enforcement of codes is not automatic. It is costly—politically, legally, and organizationally. Legislators, moreover, place low priority on oversight activities. The result, as Charles Levy aptly pointed out, is that the legislative codes become "the unrealistic, unimpressive, and widely unknown or ignored guides to wishful thinking."[32]

Both the House of Representatives and the Senate have codes of ethics that have been widely criticized as weak and that appear not to be taken seriously in their formulation, implementation, and enforcement.[33] Daniel Callahan, for example, is critical of the Senate code because it is narrow in scope, is short on aspirational standards, is long on legal prohibitions, and fails to cover the full range of official legislative duties.[34] Not only does the Senate code reduce ethical problems to eight topics related to financial conflicts of interest or the misuse of office for personal financial gain, its sole purpose is to curtail misbehavior through the imposition of disciplinary rules.[35] The House Code of Ethics for Government Service, adopted in 1958, contains ten principles, originally designed for all federal government employees.[36] This code expresses primarily a "sense of the Congress" because when it was established, it created no law, no penalties, no restraints, and was limited only to U.S. representatives.[37] After 1958 the Congress recognized the need for explicit legislation in the area of conflicts of interest. Common Cause and the National Conference of State Legislatures have formulated, in 1974 and 1977, respectively, models of legislative ethics.[38] These models, though lengthy and detailed, are specific proposals designed to regulate legislative behavior related to conflict of interests, disclosure, and compliance with open meeting laws. The difference between these model codes and those of Congress is a difference in magnitude, not in kind; hence the problems cited above remain.

Given the narrowness of extant legislative codes and given that legislators are public officials, it is useful to examine the professional codes of city managers and public administrators to see what lessons can be learned. In the next section, we examine these codes in terms of the behavior and values implied to be ethically ideal. Based on this examination, we have formulated an alternative conceptualization that will become a backdrop for an analysis of recent cases of congressional wrongdoing.

ETHICS CODES AND PUBLIC OFFICIALS

The International City Management Association (ICMA) and the American Society for Public Administration (ASPA) have separately adopted codes that embody the ethical norms considered ideal for public officials (*see* Appendices). The ICMA code is the oldest; the ASPA code, the newest. The former has been used by city managers to regulate behavior since 1924; the latter, adopted in 1984, is intended to apply to a variety of public administrators. The content of these codes appears to be derived from three sources of ethical values: personal morals, professional values, and legal prohibitions. For the sake of clarity, we analyze each dimension separately here, although they are substantively intertwined and are empirically inseparable.

Personal Morals

Both the ICMA and ASPA exhort members to act in their personal and professional relationships according to the highest standards of honor, virtue, equity, fairness, honesty, integrity, and courtesy. These standards not only bring individuals the respect and confidence of peers but also help inspire public confidence and trust in the institutions of government. These aspirational and inspirational standards, derived from Judeo–Christian principles, are the least restrictive in terms of standards of right and wrong and are the most difficult to enforce.

Professional Values

Professional values embody the principles associated with a profession. A profession (1) requires higher education to enable individuals to perform competently role-related tasks and (2) offers a lifetime career to its members.[39] The ASPA and ICMA require members to "serve the best interests of all the people" and to strive for professional excellence by conducting the "people's business" efficiently, effectively, responsively, and responsibly. Both codes embody the value of the "selfless" public official: the ASPA recognizes that "service to the public is beyond service to oneself"; the ICMA prohibits using office for personal aggrandizement, profit, or personal favors. Both include statements that public officials, in order to perform in a truly professional way, need to approach their day-to-day responsibilities with a "positive," "creative," and "constructive" attitude. It is through the exercise of professional values that public administrators and city managers can discipline self-interest and personal goals in favor of legitimate public ends. Instances concerning violations of standards discredit not only the individuals involved but the profession as well.

Legal Prohibitions

Legal prohibitions reflect very specific attempts to regulate action or activities of specified persons. It is believed that the ethical behavior of public officials can be controlled through specific regulations that hold officials to higher standards than those expected of ordinary citizens. The ICMA code addresses the issues of financial misconduct and corruption by directing its members to "seek no favor" and to "believe personal gain or profit secured by confidential information or by misuse of public time is dishonest." Direct or indirect solicitation of gifts is prohibited and acceptance of unsolicited gifts that appear to influence improperly are also prohibited. Likewise, personal investments, especially real estate investments, that create conflicts with official duties are considered inappropriate and are therefore discouraged. The ICMA code prohibits the use of confidential information and inappropriate private employment endorsements. It restricts city managers from participating in partisan political activities. The rationale for separating administration from politics is that "public office is a privilege, not a right."

The ASPA code, like the ICMA code, directly confronts the issues of financial misconduct and corruption by prohibiting undue personal gain from the performance of one's official duties and by avoiding any activity that conflicts with one's official duties. Unlike the ICMA code, it is not as specific in what is personal gain and what is the performance of official duties. The ASPA code also addresses the importance of upholding laws relating to civil rights, discrimination, employment, and whistleblowing.

These two codes are not presented here as panaceas. In fact, one can argue that the ASPA model is not an ethics code but rather a statement of individual grievances that have been recast in positive terms. In addition, one can contend that the problems the ASPA is addressing may be "corrected" better through changes in legislation than through an ethics code. The ICMA model, on the other hand, concentrates more on mechanical processes and places less emphasis on an aspirational standard. Neither document attempts to articulate fundamental moral principles and purposes.

Nonetheless, two important lessons can be drawn from this examination of the public administration codes. First, the ASPA and ICMA codes are drawn from multiple sources of ethical values—the personal, the professional, and the legal. By embodying values related to personal morality and professional responsibility, the ASPA and ICMA models are broader than the extant legislative ethics codes. Second, these codes blur the boundaries between the personal, the professional, and the legal. Rather than separating ethics into discrete domains, they integrate personal morality, professional responsibility, and legal directives into one domain. This integration is more consistent with reality: public officials operate along all three dimensions simultaneously. Professional codes that integrate these three ethical dimensions can more effectively cover the "gray areas" of public life than is presently the case.

SELECTED CONTEMPORARY CASES

The cases discussed here involve recurring problems such as financial misconduct, life-style issues, and corruption. We have excluded cases related to assault, disorderly conduct, treasonable utterances, insults, support of rebellion, and conspiracy because they have not been considered grounds for punishment since the Civil War. The following cases provide an opportunity to compare congressional action to ethical norms embodied in the ICMA and ASPA codes.

Corruption

The most notable example of corruption charges recently considered by Congress arose from the Abscam (Arab and Scam) investigation, which implicated seven members of Congress in criminal wrongdoing. In 1981 six House members—John Jenrette, Jr. (D–S.C.); Richard Kelly (R–Fla.); Raymond F. Lederer (D–Pa.); Frank Thompson, Jr. (D–N.J.); Michael Myers (D–Pa.); and John M. Murphy (D–N.Y.)—and one senator—Harrison A. Williams, Jr. (D–N.J.)—were convicted by juries for criminal activities.[40] The Abscam investigation was an undercover operation in which FBI agents acted as representatives of wealthy Arab individuals interested in seeking assistance from U.S. legislators. The indicted congressional members were asked to use their positions to help arrange real estate deals or to obtain U.S. residency, federal grants, or gambling licenses.

Large sums of cash and stock were provided to the accused, and five legislators (Williams, Kelly, Lederer, Myers, and Thompson) were actually videotaped accepting cash or stock. Jenrette was tape-recorded, and Murphy was accused of directing an associate to accept the payment of cash. The House Ethics Committee did not act on the corruption charges against these legislators until Myers and Jenrette were convicted in court for a variety of crimes, including bribery and conspiracy. Jenrette resigned before the House Standards Committee handed down a recommendation for his expulsion. The House Standards Committee recommended that Myers be expelled, and subsequently, the full House agreed, expelling him on October 2, 1980. Congress then adjourned before the committee could act on the remaining cases, and at the next election Kelly, Murphy, and Thompson were defeated. No congressional disciplinary actions were taken against them because they were no longer members of Congress. Lederer was reelected but subsequently resigned to avoid facing disciplinary measures by the House of Representatives.

At the time of their indictments, Murphy was chairman of the House Merchant Marine and Fisheries Committee and its Merchant Marine Subcommittee. Thompson was chairman of the House Administration Committee, the Education and Labor Committee's Subcommittee on Labor–Management Relations, and the Joint Committee on Printing. Once indicted, they were required by House rules to surrender their committee chairs until the resolution of the criminal proceedings. The only Republican legislator to be indicted and charged in the Abscam investigation was Kelly, and although he was not disciplined by the House, he was pressured by his fellow Republicans to resign from the House Republican Conference. The Democratic counterpart had not pressed for similar sanctions against its members accused of criminal wrongdoing.

The corruption charges against the legislators focused on acceptance of bribes or outside compensation for performing official duties, receiving unlawful gratuities, or promising to use their influence to obtain favorable government action.

Harrison Williams was also charged with criminal wrongdoing as the result of the Abscam investigation. He was indicted for promising to use his influence to help obtain favorable government contracts for a mining operation in which he was given undisclosed shares of ownership. The New Jersey senator was also charged with promising to introduce private immigration bills and for accepting bribes concerning that action. Finally, Williams was charged with receiving unlawful gratuities and for receiving illegal compensation of loans and stock certificates. The case of Williams was investigated by the Senate Ethics Committee, and on August 24, 1981, the ethics panel unanimously recommended that he be expelled. After various delays, Williams resigned when it became clear that more than two-thirds of the senators were willing to vote to expel him. By resigning before the end of his term and before the Senate could vote to expel him, Williams retained full pension rights and the right to enter the Senate chamber.[41]

Financial Misconduct

Financial misconduct is closely related to the general topic of congressional corruption. Much of the public is keenly aware of congressional wrongdoing when it relates to misuse of funds, misappropriation of public monies, or abuse of campaign contributions. Charges of financial misconduct are the most frequently recurring ethical problem in both the House and the Senate. However, neither chamber has expelled members in recent years for financial misconduct or misuse of congressional funds.

In 1979 Representative Charles C. Diggs (D–Mich.) was censured for diverting more than $60,000 of his clerk-hire funds to his personal use.[42] Initially, he was charged by the House Standards Committee of violating House rules. After successfully negotiating with the committee, Diggs accepted a censure motion. He admitted to certain wrongdoings, agreed to repay more than $40,000 of the disputed amount, and apologized for his actions to other House members. Diggs was convicted of a felony and later resigned from the U.S. House of Representatives after the Supreme Court denied his appeal regarding his previous conviction on twenty-nine felony counts.[43]

In 1980 the House censured Charles H. Hansen (D–Calif.) for financial misconduct. In this case, Hansen was sanctioned for improperly converting nearly $25,000 in campaign funds to his personal use and for accepting more than $10,000 in gifts from an individual who had a direct interest in pending legislation before Congress. The censure also resulted in Wilson's being removed from his chairmanship of the Subcommittee on Postal Operations of the House Post Office and Civil Service Committee. The loss of this chair resulted from the rules of the House Democratic Caucus, which required automatic deprivation of chairs if a member was censured by the full House of Representatives.

Most recently, three members of Congress faced similar investigations by congressional ethics panels. Representative George Hansen (R–Idaho) was reprimanded by the House for having violated the 1978 Ethics in Government Act.[44] The House, in handing down its mildest form of punishment, criticized Hansen for failing to reveal various financial dealings required to be disclosed under the Ethics Act. Hansen failed to report $334,000 in loans and profits between 1978 and 1981. He was not reelected in the campaign following his reprimand.

Representative Geraldine A. Ferraro (D–N.Y.) was also charged with financial misconduct. The House Committee on Standards of Official Conduct concluded there was a technical violation of the 1978 Ethics in Government Act when she failed to include information about her husband's finances on the congressional disclosure forms. She was charged with twelve financial disclosure violations for the period between 1978 and 1983, and the committee ultimately found her in violation of ten of the allegations. Ferraro gave up her seat to run for vice-president in 1984; therefore, she was not present when Congress reconvened in January 1985. As a result, the committee decided it could not act on the complaint concerning the former legislator.

During 1984 Senator Mark Hatfield (R–Oreg.) was charged with not fully reporting the source of his wife's income. Although some links existed between the work that Mrs. Hatfield performed and the senator's support for pipeline legislation, the Senate Ethics Committee voted unanimously that evidence was insufficient to warrant a full-scale investigation of Hatfield.

The most recent case in which the Senate found that financial misconduct had occurred was in 1979 when it denounced Herman E. Talmadge (D–Ga.).[45] At that time he was chairman of the Senate Agriculture Committee, a ranking member of the Finance Committee, and the fifth-ranking member in seniority of the entire Senate. Specifically, the Georgian was accused of collecting $24,000 in reimbursement for Senate expenses not incurred, collecting $13,000 for expenses that were not reimbursable, receiving $27,000 in campaign committee reimbursements for unreported campaign expenses, and participating in the purchase of land valued at $600,000 where an interstate highway was to be built. The charges against Talmadge were hotly debated; the senator contended that he was merely negligent and that his staff had committed the transgressions. His staff refuted these allegations. Eventually, the Senate concluded that Talmadge had committed "gross neglect of his duty and had conducted himself in a reprehensible way," but the Senate never actually voted in favor of any specific sanction.

Life-style

During 1983 the House Committee on Standards of Official Conduct addressed several life-style issues regarding its members. The House censured Daniel Crane (R–Ill.) and Gerry E. Studds (D–Mass.) for sexual misconduct with teenage congressional pages.[46] The censure votes overturned the committee's recommendation of reprimand, which is the minimum sanction that can be approved by the House if wrongdoing is substantiated. The House Ethics Committee reported that both Crane and Studds had sexual relationships with seventeen-year-old pages and had committed a "serious breach of the duty owed by the House and its individual members to the young people who serve the House as its pages." Neither legislator was actually charged with a crime because the legal age of consent in the District of Columbia is sixteen. However, the House Democratic Caucus made Studds forfeit his chairmanship of the Subcommittee on the Coast Guard of the Committee on Merchant Marines and Fisheries when the House censured him. When Crane and Studds stood for reelection, Crane was defeated, but Studds was returned to Congress by his constituents.

During 1983 the House Ethics Committee ended a sixteen-month investigation into the life-styles of Ronald Dellums (D–Calif.) and Charles Wilson (D–Tex.) for allegations of drug use.[47] The House Ethics Committee found insufficient evidence to justify these allegations or to proceed further with its ethics investigation. Investigators concluded, however, that three former House members, John L. Burton (D–Calif.), Fred Richmond (D–N.Y.), and Barry Goldwater, Jr. (R–Calif.), had used or bought illegal drugs while in office.[48]

CONCLUSION

As shown, corruption, financial misconduct, and life-style cases have been recurring issues in congressional investigations during recent years. Charges of corruption generally include a variety of activities such as conspiracy, improper use of legislative influence, and receiving unlawful gratuities. When corruption charges are brought against members of Congress, severe consequences such as expulsion result if the charges are proved. Usually, however, proof is the result of a criminal conviction by the courts rather than a conclusion reached by the House or Senate investigating panels.

Financial misconduct, a narrower concept than corruption, is the most highly publicized ethical problem facing Congress today. Usually, when a charge of financial misconduct is brought against a member, Congress will impose sanctions such as censure, reprimand, and loss of committee leadership roles. In many cases, violations result from failure to comply with the Ethics in Government Act, which requires certain financial disclosures to be made by legislators and their immediate families.

Similar sanctions may also be applied to members of Congress if they fail to comply with the life-style standards of their colleagues. Currently, only specific sexual habits and the use of illegal drugs have caused members of Congress to be investigated or sanctioned.

The cases that have been examined indicate that Congress is willing to investigate and occasionally sanction its members. However, they also indicate that Congress is limited in its ability to sanction violators of existing standards. It appears to be reluctant to make recommendations and take action unless there is a sufficient case such as previous convictions to buttress its own investigation. Congress is also limited by its inability to sanction those who are no longer members of the House and Senate. These limitations prevent it from acting fully and encourage possible violators to resign if the pressure becomes too great. When considering the legislators involved in the previous cases, only a few were actually sanctioned by their specific chambers. Most were defeated when they stood for reelection, and several others resigned their congressional seats before sanctions could be applied against them.

Examination of the recent cases also shows that if one chooses to contest the sanction recommendation on the floor of the House or Senate, there is a chance that the recommended sanction will be reduced in severity. Likewise, if the legislator is popular with his constituents, congressional recommendations or sanctions may affect an incumbent's chances for reelection.

In this chapter, we have described ethical norms embodied in two public administration codes and congressional behavior in cases concerning ethical wrongdoing. The number of cases is relatively small, despite an increase in the number of ethical investigations and considering that Abscam was, in part, a setup. This suggests that the ethics of the average legislator may not be problematic, contrary to popular opinion. Our review of recent congressional action indicates that the ethicality of legislators is probably no better or worse than the earlier congressional behavior.

The Congress in recent years has not vigorously applied sanctions to members who have violated legislative rules concerning ethical behavior. The current system of enforcing sanctions against ethics violators requires a majority vote of the members in either chamber. Neither the Senate Select Committee on Ethics nor the House Committee on Standards of Official Conduct can alone enforce its decision or implement its sanctions. Each committee can only recommend action to the full House or Senate. Because each has only advisory authority, recommendations are subject to the political realities of either chamber.

The case analysis showed that the congressional response to the ethical violations studied has ranged from doing nothing and letting the voters decide to expelling members charged under criminal law. Adverse public opinion, coupled with reprimands, are still the primary actions taken by Congress, conveying to the public a "business-as-usual" attitude toward ethical wrongdoing.

The "business-as-usual" attitude of Congress is popularly viewed as a "cop-out." It also leaves Congress open to criticism that its reluctance to enforce ethical codes undermines professionalism and ethics in government. By not vigorously enforcing its code or by treating ethical violations as essentially internal matters, members (such as Ferraro or Talmadge) escaped harsher legal sanctions. The perverse outcome is that the ethics codes, although presented in the name of raising standards, end up lowering them by protecting violators from more severe sanctions. The legislators' reluctance to be the "national nanny" is often justified on the grounds that the electorate ought to serve as the final arbiter of an individual's ethical fitness to serve.[49]

The analysis of the life-style cases implies that it may be rational for Congress to use a "public" strategy in responding to allegations of ethical violations. The House reduced the sanctions from censure to reprimand in those cases because the two legislators had not violated any District of Columbia ordinances. However, by publicly censuring Studds and Crane, Congress changed the context in which their behavior was evaluated. By changing the context from the congressional chamber to the public arena, Studds and Crane's behavior was subjected to wider public scrutiny in which standards of personal morality were integrated. Although the electoral outcomes were different, the constituents and the press assessed the personal morality of both incumbents. Illinois voters failed to reelect a contrite Crane primarily because his behavior violated the standards of personal morality of his midwestern district. Studds offered no public apology and was reelected, implying that his behavior with the male page may not have been inconsistent with the prevailing standards of personal morality acceptable to the Cape Cod voters. The application of standards of morality by the electorate can reduce considerably the power of incumbency.

The life-style cases provide a concrete example that morality encompasses a behavior dimension. Dennis Thompson observed that the personal morality of public officials is often ignored in the literature.[50] The case analysis implies that standards of personal morality have high importance to citizens.[51] The Illinois voters were able to apply sanctions in the "gray areas of life," areas that legislative codes of ethics are unable to address. As a consequence, there may be some merit in having public participation on legislative ethics panels. This participation may be in the form of highly respected individuals appointed by the Congress to serve on a bipartisan legislative advisory commission to investigate and to recommend actions in cases of ethical wrongdoing.

Another way for Congress to improve its public image is to enforce vigorously its ethics codes. As James Bowman said, "any creed worth having is worth enforcing."[52] The case analysis showed that "tougher stances" were, in fact, taken by Congress when congressional party caucuses decided to apply sanctions, such as stripping party members of the chairs of committees and subcommittees. Given the fragmentation of power and authority in Congress, there seems to be an important role for the congressional parties in enforcing (and redesigning) legislative ethics codes. The integration of legislative politics and legislative organization offers the Congress institutional mechanisms for promoting legislative ethics.

The issue of code enforcement is closely linked to code content. In contrast to Daniel Callahan, we view the narrowness of existing legislative ethics codes as a rational organizational response to cut back the costs of code enforcement to the amount that a legislature can realistically afford to enforce.[53] Narrow (legalistic) ethics creeds reduce substantially the organizational and political costs of code enforcement. Codes that contain many broad appeals and aspirational standards produce costs (personal, financial, organizational, political) that may be higher than that which the Congress can afford to pay.

This examination of the ASPA and ICMA codes questions the conventional wisdom concerning the legitimacy of holding public officials to a higher standard of behavior than ordinary citizens. For example, Frederick Mosher argued that the ethical standards governing individuals and their private behavior are inadequate for government officials.[54] Because "government is different" and because "government employment is a privilege," an elaborate system of ethical rules has been constructed in which public officials are deprived of some rights and freedoms of ordinary citizens. These rules are supposed to protect government and citizens from the adverse effects of unethical individuals. An underlying assumption is that these special rules can convert unethical citizens into ethical legislators. When problems arise, they are attributed to faulty rules.

The problems are not in the rules per se but in the conceptualization of the three sources of ethical values. Contrary to the view of John Swanner, we argue that standards of personal morality cannot be separated from standards of professional responsibility and legal regulations.[55] Swanner argued that these three domains yield three separate sets of standards; we maintain that the domains and the standards are the same. This is consistent with Thompson's observation that "ascribing responsibility to public officials . . . attaches to persons, not offices."[56] The upshot is that the curtailment of moral deviance may be accomplished as effectively through the application of standards of personal morality through open government and free press (which reports on the lifestyles of incumbents) as by restricting the rights and freedom of government officials through legal prohibitions. The current practice that separates ethical standards into discrete codes of conduct ends up, as Wallace Sayre warned forty years ago, emphasizing procedures over goals and results.[57] Under the present system, Congress did not dismiss members engaged in questionable ethical practices. Furthermore, the elaborate system of rules, coupled with the deprivation of rights, may hinder government's ability to attract and retain "people of principle" in office.

A final issue concerns the success or effectiveness in using codes of ethics to change legislative behavior. Reformers interested in upgrading the ethicality of public officials emphasize the need to alter the content of ethics codes or legislation. The case analysis implies that legislative behavior may operate independent of ethics creeds; changes in the language of codes may not produce the ethicality of legislators demanded by the creeds. This does not imply that legislative behavior is unethical. Some is; most is not. Rather, it raises a question about faith in the effectiveness of using codes to alter behavior.

The success of ethics standards can be evaluated in terms of their symbolic political effects;[58] they contain powerful political symbols shared by individuals inside and outside government. The effectiveness of codes lies in their simultaneous ability to (1) reassure the general public that their top officials can provide moral leadership necessary for governance and (2) foster in government the moral leadership and political continuity necessary for political stability in spite of unrealized political promises and public expectations.[59] Legislative standards serve as "vehicles for expression" for legislators and the citizenry more than they are "instruments for changing behavior."[60] They not only simplify the complicated political world, they reduce the tension between government and its citizens by providing a mechanism to make possible "bold and courageous moral leadership." To view codes as part of a symbolic political process does not undermine their value or effectiveness. As Murray Edelman argued, the symbolic analysis of politics enhances traditional analysis of political phenomena.[61]

In conclusion, this chapter addressed legislative ethics and the ethicality of legislators by contrasting actual congressional behavior and ideal behavior embodied in selected public administration codes. Based on this examination, a set of implications were generated that integrate legislative ethics with congressional politics and organization. It showed that codes had important political and organizational consequences, even though they may not be the ones expected by reformers. The findings have applicability to the design, structure, and enforcement of legislative ethics codes at other levels of government as well as to public organizations in general.

APPENDIX A: THE ICMA CODE OF ETHICS (AS ADOPTED BY THE ICMA EXECUTIVE BOARD IN 1972)

1. Be dedicated to the concepts of effective and democratic local government by responsible elected officials and believe that professional general management is essential to the achievement of this objective.

2. Affirm the dignity and worth of the services rendered by government and maintain

a constructive, creative, and practical attitude toward urban affairs and a deep sense of social responsibility as a trusted public servant.

3. Be dedicated to the highest ideals of honor and integrity in all public and personal relationships in order that the member may merit the respect and confidence of the elected officials, of other officials and employees, and of the public.

4. Recognize that the chief function of local government at all times is to serve the best interests of all of the people.

5. Submit policy proposals to elected officials, provide them with facts and advice on matters of policy as a basis for making decisions and setting community goals, and uphold and implement municipal policies adopted by elected officials.

6. Recognize that elected representatives of the people are entitled to the credit for the establishment of municipal policies; responsibility for policy execution rests with the members.

7. Refrain from participation in the election of the members of the employing legislative body, and from all partisan political activities which would impair performance as a professional administrator.

8. Make it a duty continually to improve the member's professional ability and to develop the competence of associates in the use of management techniques.

9. Keep the community informed on municipal affairs; encourage communication between the citizens and all municipal officers; emphasize friendly and courteous service to the public; and seek to improve the quality and image of public service.

10. Resist any encroachment on professional responsibilities, believing the member should be free to carry out official policies without interference, and handle each problem without discrimination on the basis of principle and justice.

11. Handle all matters of personnel on the basis of merit so that fairness and impartiality govern a member's decisions, pertaining to appointments, pay adjustments, promotions, and discipline.

12. Seek no favor; believe that personal aggrandizement or profit secured by confidential information or by misuse of public time is dishonest.

APPENDIX B: CODE OF ETHICS, AMERICAN SOCIETY FOR PUBLIC ADMINISTRATION

We, the members of ASPA, recognizing the critical role of conscience in choosing, among courses of action and taking into account the moral ambiguities of life, commit ourselves to:

1. demonstrate the highest standards of personal integrity, truthfulness, honesty and fortitude in all our public activities in order to inspire public confidence and trust in public institutions.

2. serve the public with respect, concern, courtesy, and responsiveness, recognizing that service to the public is beyond service to oneself;

3. strive for personal professional excellence and encourage the professional develop-

ment of our associates and those seeking to enter the field of public administration;

4. approach our organization and operational duties with a positive attitude and constructively support open communication, creativity, dedication and compassion;

5. serve in such a way that we do not realize undue personal gain from the performance of our official duties;

6. avoid any interest or activity which is in conflict with the conduct of our official duties;

7. respect and protect the privileged information to which we have access in the course of official duties;

8. exercise whatever discretionary authority we have under law to promote the public interest;

9. accept as a personal duty the responsibility to keep up to date on emerging issues and to administer the public's business with professional competence, fairness, impartiality, efficiency and effectiveness;

10. support, implement, and promote merit employment and programs of affirmative action to assure equal opportunity by our recruitment, selection, and advancement of qualified persons from all elements of society;

11. eliminate all forms of illegal discrimination, fraud, and mismanagement of public funds, and support colleagues if they are in difficulty because of responsible efforts to correct such discrimination, fraud, mismanagement or abuse;

12. respect, support, study, and when necessary, work to improve federal and state constitutions, and other laws which define the relationships among public agencies, employees, clients and all citizens.

NOTES

The authors wish to acknowledge the assistance of Marvin Cummins, Charles Walcott, John Harrigan, William Swenson, Steven Coombs, as well as the editors of this volume, for helpful suggestions on the earlier drafts of this chapter.

1. Jacqueline Calmes, "The Ethics Committees: Shield or Sword?" *Congressional Quarterly Weekly,* April 4, 1987, pp. 591–597.

2. Ibid., p. 592.

3. Ibid.

4. John D. Saxon, "The Scope of Legislative Ethics," in Bruce Jennings and Daniel Callahan, eds., *Representation and Responsibility: Exploring Legislative Ethics* (New York: Plenum Press, 1985), pp. 200, 203.

5. Peter French, "Burking a Mill," in Norman E. Bowie, ed., *Ethical Issues in Government* (Philadelphia: Temple University Press, 1981), p. 11.

6. James Mill, cited in French, "Burking a Mill," p. 9.

7. Amy Gutmann and Dennis Thompson, "The Theory of Legislative Ethics," in Bruce Jennings and Daniel Callahan, eds., *Representation and Responsibility: Exploring Legislative Ethics* (New York: Plenum Press, 1985), pp. 167–195.

8. Saxon, "Scope," p. 204.

9. Joel D. Fleishman, "Self-Interest and Political Integrity," in Joel Fleishman, Lance Liebman, and Mark Moore, eds., *Public Duties: The Moral Obligations of Government Officials* (Cambridge, Mass.: Harvard University Press, 1981), p. 82.

10. David E. Price, "Legislative Ethics in the New Congress," in Bruce Jennings and Daniel Callahan, eds., *Representation and Responsibility: Exploring Legislative Ethics* (New York: Plenum Press, 1985), p. 143.

11. Ibid., p. 138.

12. Ibid., p. 140.

13. David Mayhew, *Congress: The Electoral Connection* (New Haven: Yale University Press, 1974), p. 49.

14. Stephen K. Bailey, "Ethics and the Public Service: The Concept of Moral Ambiguities of Public Choice," in Richard J. Stillman, ed., *Public Administration: Cases and Concepts* (Boston: Houghton Mifflin, 1980), p. 442.

15. These goals are ones that legislators reported to Richard Fenno. *See* Richard F. Fenno, Jr., *Congressmen in Committees* (Boston: Little, Brown, 1973), chapter one.

16. Bailey, "Ethics," p. 443.

17. Ibid.

18. Ibid., p. 442.

19. U.S. Const. art. I, Sec. 5, cl.1–2; amend. xvii.

20. "Seating and Disciplining" *How Congress Works* (Washington, D.C.: Congressional Quarterly, 1983), p. 181.

21. 103 U.S. 168 (1880).

22. 166 U.S. 66 (1897).

23. Richard Allen Baker, "The History of Congressional Ethics," in Bruce Jennings and Daniel Callahan, eds., *Representational Responsibility: Exploring Legislative Ethics* (New York: Plenum Press, 1985), pp. 5, 27.

24. *1983 Congressional Quarterly Almanac* (Washington, D.C.: Congressional Quarterly, 1984), p. 581.

25. "Seating and Disciplining," *How Congress Works* (Washington, D.C.: Congressional Quarterly, 1983), p. 181.

26. Baker, "History," p. 26.

27. Vanessa Merton, "Legislative Ethics and Professional Responsibility," in Bruce Jennings and Daniel Callahan, eds., *Representation and Responsibility: Exploring Legislative Ethics* (New York: Plenum Press, 1985), p. 307.

28. Daniel Callahan, "Legislative Codes of Ethics," in Bruce Jennings and Daniel Callahan, eds., *Representation and Responsibility: Exploring Legislative Ethics* (New York: Plenum Press, 1985), p. 225.

29. Gutmann and Thompson, "Theory," p. 168.

30. Callahan, "Legislative Codes," p. 221.

31. Charles Levy, "On the Development of a Code of Ethics," cited in Callahan, "Legislative Codes," p. 222.

32. Ibid.

33. *See* Committee on Standards of Official Conduct, *Ethics Manual for Members and Employees of the U.S. House of Representatives*, 98-2 (1984); *Senate Code of Official Conduct*, Report of the Special Committee on Official Conduct of the U.S. Senate, 95-1 (1977).

34. Callahan, "Legislative Codes," p. 225.

35. Ibid., p. 222.

36. Committee on Standards of Official Conduct, *Ethics Manual,* p. 10.

37. Robert S. Getz, *Congressional Ethics: The Conflict of Interest Issue* (Princeton, N.J.: Van Nostrand Co., 1966), pp. 28–50.

38. National Conference of State Legislatures and Common Cause, *State Legislative Ethics* (Denver: National Conference on State Legislatures, 1977). Common Cause Model Conflict of Interest Act.

39. Frederick Mosher, *Democracy and the Public Service* (New York: Oxford University Press, 1968), p. 106.

40. "Congress and Government," *1980 Congressional Quarterly Almanac* (Washington, D.C.: Congressional Quarterly, 1981), p. 513.

41. "Congress and Government," *1982 Congressional Quarterly Almanac* (Washington, D.C.: Congressional Quarterly, 1983), p. 509.

42. "Congress and Government," *1979 Congressional Quarterly Almanac* (Washington, D.C.: Congressional Quarterly, 1980), p. 561.

43. "Major Congressional Action," *1980 Congressional Quarterly Almanac* (Washington, D.C.: Congressional Quarterly, 1981), p. 524.

44. "Congress and Government," *1984 Congressional Quarterly Almanac* (Washington, D.C.: Congressional Quarterly 1985), pp. 210–211.

45. "Major Congressional Action," *1979 Congressional Quarterly Almanac* (Washington, D.C.: Congressional Quarterly, 1980), p. 566.

46. "Major Congressional Action," *1983 Congressional Quarterly Almanac* (Washington, D.C.: Congressional Quarterly, 1984), p. 580.

47. Ibid., p. 595.

48. Ibid.

49. Quote attributed to Senator Warren Rudman in Calmes, "The Ethics Committees," p. 592.

50. Dennis Thompson, "The Possibility of Administrative Ethics," *Public Administration Review* 45, no. 5 (September–October 1985), p. 560.

51. This view is supported by a recent public opinion poll indicating that 76 percent of respondents in a *U.S.A. Today* poll taken May 9, 1987, thought that a presidential candidate's personal life is "somewhat to very important" when deciding their vote. *See* James A. Barnes, "Lingering Hart-Breaking Doubts," *National Journal* 19, no. 19 (May 9, 1987): 1126.

52. James S. Bowman, "Ethical Issues for the Public Manager," in William B. Eddy, ed., *Handbook on Public Organizational Management* (New York: Dekker, 1983), p. 89.

53. Callahan, "Legislative Codes," p. 222.

54. Mosher, *Democracy,* p. 21–23.

55. John M. Swanner, "Enforceable Standards and Unenforceable Ethics," in Bruce Jennings and Daniel Callahan, eds., *Representation and Responsibility: Exploring Legislative Ethics* (New York: Plenum Press, 1985), pp. 237–240.

56. Thompson, "Possibility," p. 560.

57. Wallace Sayre, "The Triumph of Techniques Over Purposes," in Frank J. Thompson, ed., *Classics of Public Personnel Policy* (Oak Park, Ill.: Moore, 1979), pp. 30–35.

58. Murray Edelman, *The Symbolic Uses of Politics* (Chicago: University of Illinois Press, 1964). *See also* Vera Vogelsang-Coombs and Marvin J. Cummins, "'Reorganizations and Reforms: Promises, Promises," *Review of Public Personnel Administration*

2, no. 2 (Spring 1982): 21–34. For a conceptual framework and methodology for examining symbolic political processes, *see* Vera Vogelsang-Coombs, "'The Dialogues on Executive Reorganization" (Ph.D. diss., Washington University, 1985), chapters one, three.

59. Murray Edelman, *Politics as Symbolic Action: Mass Arousal and Quiescence* (New York: Academic Press, 1971), p. 83.

60. Edelman, *The Symbolic Uses of Politics*, p. 11.

61. Ibid., p. 4.

SELECTED BIBLIOGRAPHY

American Society for Public Administration. "Code of Ethics and Implementation Guidelines." Washington, D.C.: American Society for Public Administration, March 1985.

Appleby, Paul. *Morality and Administration in Democratic Government*. Baton Rouge: Louisiana State Press, 1952.

Bailey, Stephen K. "Ethics and the Public Service: The Concept of Moral Ambiguities of Public Choice." In Richard J. Stillman, ed., *Public Administration: Cases and Concepts*. Boston: Houghton Mifflin, 1980.

Baker, Richard Allen. "The History of Congressional Ethics." In Bruce Jennings and Daniel Callahan, eds., *Representation and Responsibility: Exploring Legislative Ethics*. New York: Plenum Press, 1985.

Barnes, James A. "Lingering, Hart-Breaking Doubts." *National Journal* 19, no. 19 (May 19, 1987): 1126.

Bowman, James S. "Ethical Issues for the Public Manager." In William B. Eddy, ed., *Handbook on Public Organizational Management*. New York: Dekker, 1983.

Brown, Peter. "Assessing Officials." In Joel D. Fleishman, Lance Liebman, and Mark H. Moore, eds., *Public Duties: The Moral Obligations of Government Officials*. Cambridge, Mass.: Harvard University Press, 1981.

Callahan, Daniel. "Legislative Codes of Ethics." In Bruce Jennings and Daniel Callahan, eds., *Representation and Responsibility: Exploring Legislative Ethics*. New York: Plenum Press, 1985.

Calmes, Jacqueline. "The Ethics Committees: Shield or Sword?" *Congressional Quarterly Weekly*, April 4, 1987, pp. 591–597.

Chandler, Ralph Clark. "The Problem of Moral Reasoning in American Public Administration: The Case for a Code of Ethics." *Public Administration Review* 43, no. 1 (January–February 1983): 32–39.

Chandler, Ralph C., and Jack C. Plano. *The Public Administration Dictionary*. New York: Wiley, 1982.

Congressional Quarterly. "Seating and Disciplining. *How Congress Works*. Washington, D.C.: Congressional Quarterly, 1983.

Congressional Quarterly. "Congress Approves Tough Ethics Codes." *Inside Congress*, 2d ed. Washington, D.C.: Congressional Quarterly, 1979.

Congressional Quarterly Almanac. Washington, D.C.: Congressional Quarterly, 1979–1986.

Dewey, John. *The Public and Its Problems*. Chicago: Swallow Press, 1954.

Edelman, Murray. *The Symbolic Uses of Politics*. Chicago: University of Illinois Press, 1964.

. *Politics as Symbolic Action: Mass Arousal and Quiescence.* New York: Academic Press, 1971.

Fenno, Richard F., Jr. *Congressmen in Committees.* Boston: Little, Brown, 1973.

Fleishman, Joel D. "Self-Interest and Political Integrity." In Joel Fleishman, Lance Liebman, and Mark Moore, eds., *Public Duties: The Moral Obligations of Government Officials.* Cambridge, Mass.: Harvard University Press, 1981.

French, Peter. "Burking a Mill." In Norman E. Bowie, ed., *Ethical Issues in Government.* Philadelphia: Temple University Press, 1981.

Getz, Robert. *Congressional Ethics: The Conflict of Interest Issue.* Princeton, N.J.: Van Nostrand Co., 1966.

Gutmann, Amy, and Dennis Thompson. "The Theory of Legislative Ethics." In Bruce Jennings and Daniel Callahan, eds., *Representation and Responsibility: Exploring Legislative Ethics.* New York: Plenum Press, 1985.

Hosmer, LaRue Tone. *The Ethics of Management.* Homewood, Ill.: Irwin, 1987.

International City Management Association. "ICMA Code of Ethics with Guidelines." *Public Management* 66, no. 2 (February 1984): 10–11.

. "Rules of Procedure for Enforcement of City Management Code of Ethics." *Public Management* 66, no. 2 (February 1984): 12–14.

Jennings, Bruce. "Legislative Ethics and Moral Minimalism." In Bruce Jennings and Daniel Callahan, eds., *Representation and Responsibility: Exploring Legislative Ethics.* New York: Plenum Press, 1985.

Jennings, Bruce, and Dennis Callahan, eds. *Representation and Responsibility: Exploring Legislative Ethics.* New York: Plenum Press, 1985.

Lilla, Mark T. "Ethos, 'Ethics,' and Public Service." *Public Interest* no. 63 (Spring 1981): 3–17.

Mertins, Herman, Jr., and Patrick Hennigan. *Applying Professional Standards and Ethics in the 1980's: A Workbook and Study Guide for Public Administrators,* 2d ed. Washington, D.C.: American Society for Public Administration, 1982.

Merton, Vanessa. "Legislative Ethics and Professional Responsibility." In Bruce Jennings and Daniel Callahan, eds., *Representation and Responsibility: Exploring Legislative Ethics.* New York: Plenum Press, 1985.

Mosher, Frederick. *Democracy and the Public Service.* New York: Oxford University Press, 1968.

National Conference of State Legislatures and Common Cause, *State Legislative Ethics.* Denver: National Conference on State Legislatures, 1977.

Niebuhr, H. Richard. "The Meaning of Responsibility." In H. Richard Niebuhr, ed., *The Responsible Self.* New York: Harper–Row, 1963, chapter one.

Price, David E. "Legislative Ethics in the New Congress." In Bruce Jennings and Daniel Callahan, eds., *Representation and Responsibility: Exploring Legislative Ethics.* New York: Plenum Press, 1985.

Saxon, John D. "The Scope of Legislative Ethics." In Bruce Jennings and Daniel Callahan, eds., *Representation and Responsibility.* New York: Plenum Press, 1985.

Sayre, Wallace. "The Triumph of Techniques Over Purposes." In Frank J. Thompson, ed., *Classics of Public Personnel Policy.* Oak Park, Ill.: Moore, 1975.

Swanner, John M. "Enforceable Standards and Unenforceable Ethics." In Bruce Jennings and Daniel Callahan, eds., *Representation and Responsibility: Exploring Legislative Ethics.* New York: Plenum Press, 1985.

Thompson, Dennis. "The Possibility of Administrative Ethics." *Public Administration Review* 45, no. 5 (September–October 1985): 555–561.

U.S. Congress. Ethics in Government Act Amendments of 1982, P.L. 97-409, 97th Congress, 51 *Law Week* 169.

U.S. Congress. House of Representatives. Committee on Standards of Official Conduct. *Rules of Procedure*. Washington, D.C.: U.S. Government Printing Office, 1985.

U.S. Congress. Senate. *Senate Code of Official Conduct*. Report of the Special Committee on Official Conduct. Washington, D.C.: U.S. Government Printing Office, 1977.

Van Riper, Paul. *History of the United States Civil Service*. Evanston, Ill.: Row, Peterson & Co., 1958.

Vogelsang-Coombs, Vera. "The Dialogues on Executive Reorganization." Ph.D. dissertation, Washington University, 1985.

Vogelsang-Coombs, Vera, and Marvin J. Cummins. "Reorganization and Reforms: Promises, Promises." *Review of Public Personnel Administration* 2, no. 2 (Spring 1982): 21–34.

Walter, J. Jackson. "The Ethics in Government Acts, Conflict of Interest Law, and Presidential Recruiting." *Public Administration Review* 41, no. 6 (November–December 1981): 659–665.

Willbern, York. "Types and Levels of Public Morality." *Public Administration Review* 44 (March–April 1984): 102–108.

PART THREE

TECHNIQUES AND METHODS IN ETHICAL POLICY-MAKING

5

Controversies in Risk Analysis in Public Management

Albert Flores and Michael E. Kraft

During the past two decades, public concern over a wide array of technological risks to health, safety, and the environment has risen sharply. As a result, governments have assumed extensive and complex responsibilities for assessing and balancing risks, costs, and benefits. To assist in meeting these responsibilities, public officials have turned increasingly to formal methods of risk analysis, which are attractive to some extent because they appear to offer a systematic and objective way to address some of the most difficult and contentious issues in social regulation. If, as many critics assert, regulation is often irrational, inefficient, or excessive, one should clearly be prepared to answer the question of how safe is safe enough; otherwise we cannot set reasonable regulatory standards and limit the growing burden and cost of government regulation.

But how can we best determine how safe is safe enough? What particular methods are most appropriate? How good are the data and methods used for estimating risks? How should analysts and decisionmakers deal with the limitations in data and methods, including significant uncertainties? To what extent should risk analysis influence regulatory decision-making? There are no easy answers to these questions. Indeed, despite the persuasive case for improving our capacity to anticipate, prevent, or reduce technological risks in modern society, considerable controversy surrounds the conduct and use of these methods in regulatory decision-making. The reasons are clear. Risk-management policies are enormously consequential for important public values, such as health, occupational safety, and environmental quality. Yet the methods and data employed are insufficiently developed, risk analysis is poorly understood and viewed with suspicion by many policymakers and the general public, and reform of these policies has become highly politicized in recent years, creating additional concern about the impact of such approaches on the process of regulatory reform.

The probability that we will see greater rather than less reliance on risk analysis in the future impels us to inquire into some relatively neglected aspects of the debate over these methods and their use. There is a voluminous literature on the methodological aspects of *risk assessment,* which is an activity that is mainly technical (*see* "Literature Review"). But there has been much less attention paid to *risk evaluation,* which is essentially a normative activity—"a matter of personal and social value judgment," as William Lowrance said.[1] This neglect is, in part, due to a kind of unintentional blindness to complex value issues, particularly when values are unclear and controversial, making consensus difficult. It may also be a result of a broad lack of agreement on the proper methodological approach to, and the significance of, problems common to risk evaluation. Indeed, "value neutrality" has generally been the watchword, a throwback to logical positivism, hence the lack of attention to normative concerns inherent in risk analysis.

In this chapter, we focus largely on risk-evaluation methods and explore, in particular, ethical and political issues involved in risk-evaluation processes. Since risk analysis (composed of risk assessment and risk evaluation) is essentially a form of policy analysis, our concerns are similar to those raised in more general treatments of ethics and policy analysis.[2] We attempt to clarify the different kinds of value issues in risk analysis, especially in risk evaluation, and to consider ways in which value choices may be made more explicit and consistent with appropriate ethical criteria. Doing so should indicate how policy analysts, public officials, and the general public might better cope with these new demands and may help guide further inquiry into the dimly lit intersection of risk analysis, ethics, and politics.

There is considerable variation in the use of terminology. *Risk analysis* is used here to refer to the combination of two activities: risk assessment and risk evaluation. *Risk assessment* includes both the identification of risks and the estimation of the probability and severity of harm associated with them. Estimates of the probability of occurrence of certain events and the severity of negative consequences of those events are normally stated in terms of injury, disease, or premature death to persons or in economic terms of property loss or damage to environmental quality. In this usage, risk itself is the magnitude of adverse consequences of an event or exposure. On the other hand, *risk evaluation* refers to the process of determining the acceptability of risks or what constitutes "safety." As Lowrance puts it, "a thing is safe if its risks are judged to be acceptable."[3] Who participates in this judgment process is of special importance. Finally, many commentators, following the lead of the National Research Council (1983), refer to the determination of actions needed to control risk as *risk management.*[4] Thus risk management includes all of the actions taken by government to reduce a given risk. The process of risk management extends from legislative specification of policy goals, means, and guidelines to administrative activities associated with policy implementation.

The actual processes of risk assessment and evaluation are complex. Figure 5.1, compiled by Lester Lave, depicts the sequence of decisions involved.[5] Typically, a risk assessment (e.g., of a carcinogenic substance) is performed by scientific and technical staff and is then sent to an office of regulatory analysis, where some form of economic and policy evaluation is completed. In some cases these are iterative processes, with repeated discussions among regulatory officials and scientific staff, involving multiple studies and draft reports. The 1982 report of the Committee on Risk and Decision Making of the National Research Council succinctly describes the process:

After the various uncertainties are assessed, the policy choices may still be far from obvious. The policy maker has to consider, formally or informally, the alternative actions he or she might pursue, the intellectual and political constraints, value and ideological judgments, and so on. This is risk evaluation. It can be viewed as a subset of what some people call policy evaluation or policy analysis.[6]

The model portrays the process as one in which "facts and data" are separate from "judgments" at each step, from hazard identification through implementation and monitoring, and in which risk assessment precedes "decision analysis" and the regulatory decision itself. Although the separation of facts and data from judgments is not always distinct, Lave made clear that even in the early stages, where science is presumed to dominate and politics plays a very limited role, there are necessary judgments about how to identify and measure a given risk, how adequate existing data bases are, and how to deal with problems of uncertainty that are not susceptible to purely objective analysis. Indeed, by one count there are some fifty decision points of this kind in a typical risk assessment.[7]

Because of the necessity of making such judgments, a lively debate has arisen over not only just how objective or scientific the process of risk assessment is or can be but also as to the extent that one can separate risk assessment from risk evaluation. Some people worry that, especially when scientific consensus is lacking, the risk-assessment process may be politicized by making certain kinds of methodological assumptions that err consistently in a risk tolerent or risk-aversive direction.[8] Commonly, such observations are followed by strong recommendations for maintaining accountability for such agency decisions or for having Congress write more precise laws detailing the guidelines for determining appropriate procedures for risk assessments and the criteria for risk-acceptability decisions. Still other observers disagree strongly with Lowrance that one can separate the two kinds of activities in a risk analysis, the technical risk assessment and the normative risk evaluation. These critics see the two

Figure 5.1
Conceptual Steps in Risk Management

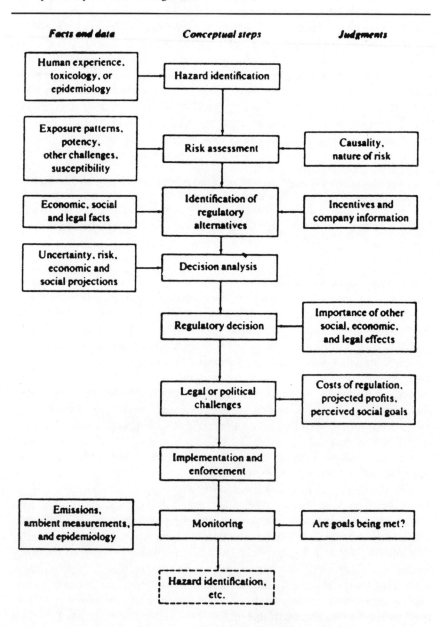

Source: Lester B. Lave, ed., *Quantitative Risk Assessment in Regulation* (Washington, D.C.: Brookings Institution, 1982), p. 6. Reprinted with permission.

activities as inevitably intertwined, with important implications for the conduct and use of risk analysis in regulatory decision-making.[9]

Here we view the distinction as useful. There is much to be said for separating scientific judgments from politics and values while appreciating the extent to which the scientific evidence may be soft or uncertain. It suggests that decisionmakers must be prepared to deal knowledgeably and frankly with scientific uncertainty as well as with the administrative, legal, and political challenges of risk management.

Our task here is to identify and analyze the various value issues associated with determining the acceptability of technological risks. In particular, we proceed from the premise that greater clarity and explicitness in considering value issues is desirable and a prerequisite for promoting the integration of ethics and risk analysis. Hence, following a brief review of the evolution of risk policies and a survey of the extant literature on risk assessment and evaluation, we examine the major value issues, both ethical and political. We conclude by suggesting how the policy-making process may be made more hospitable to risk evaluation that includes explicit attention to the ethical concerns raised below.

BACKGROUND

Risk-analysis activities take place at all levels of government in the United States and involve numerous governmental bodies at each level. Yet the most systematic analysis takes place in the federal government, particularly within administrative agencies such as the Environmental Protection Agency (EPA), the Food and Drug Administration (FDA), and the Nuclear Regulatory Commission (NRC). As might be expected, the extent and type of use of risk analysis varies significantly from agency to agency, reflecting the different kinds of policy problems dealt with, statutory differences, and differences in agency characteristics.[10] However, for our purposes these distinctions are not critical. Table 5.1 lists the sixty-one major statutes that set the general direction and characteristics of current federal risk-management operations. Even this list only begins to indicate the enormous range of federal activities that are intended to affect health, safety, and environmental risks.[11]

Examination of the most important of these federal statutes suggests a simple but useful typology.[12] Each statute may be classified in terms of whether it calls for consideration of only the technical or economic feasibility of regulating the risk (*technology only,* as in some provisions of the Clean Air Act and Clean Water Act) or the nature and extent of the risk (*risk only,* as in the Federal Aviation Act and the Dangerous Cargo Act), or whether it requires or permits a balancing of risks, costs, and benefits (*balancing,* which is most evident in the National Environmental Policy Act and the Toxic Substances Control Act). These policies incorporate different standards or guidelines for risk analysis in part because they address different public problems and in part

Table 5.1
Major Federal Risk Management Statutes

YEAR OF ENACTMENT	STATUTE
1877	DANGEROUS CARGO ACT
1893	SAFETY APPLIANCE ACTS
1906	FOOD, DRUG, AND COSMETICS ACT
1906	FEDERAL MEAT INSPECTION ACT
1936	FLOOD CONTROL ACT OF 1936
1938	FOOD, DRUG, AND COSMETICS ACTS AMENDMENTS
1946	ADMINISTRATIVE PROCEDURES ACT
1954	FOOD, DRUG, AND COSMETICS AMENDMENTS (PESTICIDE CHEMICAL RESIDUES)
1954	ATOMIC ENERGY ACT
1957	POULTRY PRODUCTS INSPECTION ACT
1958	FEDERAL AVIATION ACT
1958	FOOD, DRUG, AND COSMETICS ACT AMENDMENTS: FOOD ADDITIVES AMENDMENT ACT ("DELANEY CLAUSE")
1960	FEDERAL HAZARDOUS SUBSTANCES ACT
1960	FOOD, DRUG, AND COSMETIC ACT AMENDMENTS: COLOR ADDITIVE AMENDMENT ACT
1965	WATER RESOURCES PLANNING ACT OF 1965
1966	NATIONAL TRAFFIC AND MOTOR VEHICLE SAFETY ACT
1968	RADIATION CONTROL FOR HEALTH AND SAFETY ACT
1968	FOOD, DRUG, AND COSMETICS ACT AMENDMENTS: ANIMAL DRUG AMENDMENT ACT
1968	NATIONAL FLOOD INSURANCE ACT
1968	FIRE RESEARCH AND SAFETY ACT
1969	FEDERAL MINE SAFETY AND HEALTH ACT
1969	NATIONAL ENVIRONMENTAL POLICY ACT
1970	POISON PREVENTION PACKAGING ACT
1970	OCCUPATIONAL SAFETY AND HEALTH ACT
1970	CLEAN AIR ACT
1970	FEDERAL RAILROAD SAFETY ACT
1971	LEAD BASED PAINTPOISONING PREVENTION ACT
1971	NATIONAL CANCER ACT
1972	FEDERAL INSECTICIDE, FUNGICIDE, AND RODENTICIDE ACT
1972	CONSUMER PRODUCT SAFETY ACT
1972	MARINE PROTECTION, RESEARCH, AND CONSERVATION ACT
1972	PORTS AND WATERWAYS SAFETY AND HEALTH ACT
1972	FEDERAL WATER POLLUTION CONTROL ACT
1972	MARINE PROTECTION RESEARCH AND SANCTUARIES ACT
1972	NOISE CONTROL ACT
1972	COASTAL ZONE MANAGEMENT ACT
1972	NATIONAL DAM INSPECTION ACT
1973	ENDANGERED SPECIES ACT
1973	FLOOD DISASTER PROTECTION ACT
1974	MOBILE HOME CONSTRUCTION AND SAFETY STANDARDS ACT
1974	SAFE DRINKING WATER ACT

because the policies reflect changing circumstances at the time of enactment and the perspectives and influence of different clusters of policy actors in each problem area. Yet all but a few of the policies call for some kind of balancing, and they give considerable discretion to agency administrators to determine acceptable levels of risk, even when major differences exist in specification of the factors to be considered, assignment of the burden of proof, and costs associated with providing risk-assessment information. It is precisely the delegation by Congress of such administrative authority and the widespread belief

Table 5.1 *(continued)*

YEAR OF ENACTMENT	STATUTE
1974	NATIONAL TRAFFIC AND MOTOR VEHICLE SAFETY ACT AMENDMENTS: MOTOR VEHICLE SCHOOL BUS SAFETY AMENDMENTS
1974	HEALTH PLANNING AND RESOURCE DEVELOPMENT ACT
1974	FEDERAL FIRE PREVENTION AND CONTROL ACT OF 1974
1974	TECHNOLOGY ASSESSMENT ACT OF 1974
1974	HEALTH SERVICES RESEARCH, HEALTH STATISTICS, AND MEDICAL LIBRARIES ACT
1974	DISASTER RELIEF ACT OF 1974
1975	RAIL SAFETY IMPROVEMENT ACT
1975	HAZARDOUS MATERIALS TRANSPORTATION ACT
1976	TOXIC SUBSTANCES CONTROL ACT
1976	NATIONAL SCIENCE AND TECHNOLOGY POLICY ORGANIZATION AND PRIORITIES ACT OF 1976
1976	SOLID WASTE DISPOSAL ACT
1976	RESOURCE CONSERVATION AND RECOVERY ACT
1976	MEDICAL DEVICES AMENDMENTS ACT
1977	SURFACE MINING CONTROL AND RECLAMATION ACT
1977	FEDERAL WATER POLLUTION CONTROL ACT AMENDMENTS: CLEAN WATER ACT
1978	HEALTH SERVICES RESEARCH, HEALTH STATISTICS, AND HEALTH CASE TECHNOLOGY ACT OF 1973
1978	URANIUM MILL TAILINGS RADIATION CONTROL ACT OF 1978
1979	HAZARDOUS LIQUID PIPELINE SAFETY ACT
1980	COMPREHENSIVE ENVIRONMENTAL RESPONSE, COMPENSATION AND LIABILITY ACT
1980	REGULATORY FLEXIBILITY ACT

Source: Arthur A. Atkisson, Michael E. Kraft, and Lloyd L. Philipson, *Risk Analysis Methods and Their Employment in Governmental Risk Management,* Final report prepared for the National Science Foundation (Redondo Beach, Calif.: J. H. Wiggins, 1985), pp. 88–89.

that policy decisions are often arbitrary, biased, or unprofessional that provokes so much interest in and dissent over governmental regulation in the 1980s.

As Table 5.1 indicates, most of these statutes are of recent origin; forty-seven of the sixty-one statutes were enacted between 1965 and 1980. The activist period was even shorter than this, for most of the legislative activity that created these statutes took place between 1968 and 1976, before the Carter administration. Given the obvious and growing need for these regulatory mandates and their continuing popularity (evident in a large number of public opinion surveys), how is one to account for the apparent decline in enthusiasm for regulation among policymakers and the consequent attraction in the 1980s of methodologies like cost–benefit analysis?[13] There is no simple explanation for this change in the policy agenda. Indeed, the extent of the change itself varies by policy area; there has been more support for maintaining social regulation than economic regulation, and deregulation seems to have worked best in areas like banking, transportation, and communication. Perhaps the most appropriate explanation for increasing skepticism over the virtues of social regulation (e.g., environmental protection) is that a number of economic and political conditions changed significantly between the mid-1970s and the early 1980s that altered the regulatory policy agenda and in turn increased the visibility and attractiveness of analytic methodologies that promised some relief from what many critics considered to be burdensome and costly regulatory policies.

Economic, social, and political conditions in the 1960s and 1970s provided fertile ground for the growth of social regulation. Public concern for newly discovered risks and optimism over governmental capabilities and sustained economic growth were sufficient to support strengthening of existing regulatory policies (e.g., the Clean Air Act Amendments of 1970) and expansion of federal regulation into new areas such as toxic-substances control. These conditions facilitated the development of ambitious policies that some critics later asserted were often enacted with little understanding of the technical difficulties of implementation, the capability of governmental agencies at all levels to meet statutory mandates, and the costs that would be imposed on regulated parties. By the late 1970s, regulatory reform had become fashionable in Washington, evident in the sharp increase in commentary on the subject (especially in journals like *Regulation* and *The Public Interest*) and in publications of the American Enterprise Institute, the Brookings Institution, and other policy institutes on both the Left and the Right.

This new attitude toward regulation began emerging before the Carter administration, as can be seen in major studies of federal regulatory policies initiated by the Senate Committee on Government Affairs and the House Committee on Interstate and Foreign Commerce in the mid-1970s.[14] It became far more visible between 1976 and 1980 as critics complained of the cost of compliance with federal regulations and their overall impact on the nation's economy. The call for regulatory reform was further fueled by a growing perception critical of the complexity and inflexibility of regulations, the capability of agencies to implement policies effectively, the inconsistency of statutory guidelines, and the adequacy of scientific knowledge to establish regulatory standards. Policy goals themselves were often questioned in light of competing social and economic values, although most policies survived critical legislative scrutiny relatively unscathed.[15]

By the beginning of the Reagan administration, however, there appeared to be something of a consensus among regulatory advocates and critics alike that regulatory reform could improve the efficiency of health, safety, and environmental policies, among others. Risk analysis emerged as a major methodological approach that could be used to streamline governmental regulation and set policy priorities in an era of lowered expectations and increasingly scarce budgetary resources.

The apparent unanimity of support for regulatory reform was, nonetheless, deceptive. Frequent endorsement of the general concept implied no consensus on the methods to be used or especially on how particular federal policies or their implementation should be altered. Prescriptions ranged from extensive deregulation and greater reliance on the free market to proposals that enhanced the authority of regulatory agencies and improved their accountability to the public. During the Reagan administration the former approach attracted more support, and it reached its most visible and controversial expression in the Reagan administration's Task Force on Regulatory Relief and in the expanded role of the Office of Management and Budget (OMB) in regulatory review.[16]

LITERATURE REVIEW

A new and impressively large literature on regulation and its reform testifies to the growing importance of these concerns.[17] Along with the more general literature on regulatory reform that developed in the late 1970s and early 1980s, there has been an explosion of interest in the technical and methodological issues of risk administration. Basic treatments of risk assessment of this kind included David Okrent's *Risk–Benefit Methodology and Applications*, William Rowe's *Anatomy of Risk*, R. W. Kates's *Risk Assessment of Environmental Hazards*, Edmund Crouch and Richard Wilson's *Risk/Benefit Analysis*, and Lester Lave's *Quantitative Risk Assessment in Regulation*.[18]

Occasionally, a volume that dealt substantially with technical issues also included at least some discussion of political and ethical issues; William Lowrance's book *Of Acceptable Risk* is the most notable example. One was more likely to find such discussion in those works that were pointedly critical of risk assessment and its use as, for example, Dorothy Nelkin's *Technological Decisions and Democracy* and Kristin Shrader–Frechette's *Nuclear Power and Public Policy*.[19] Yet for the most part one searches in vain for extended treatments of either the ethical or political dimensions of risk assessment. The few exceptions—such as the collection *Risk Analysis, Institutions, and Public Policy*, edited by Susan Hadden; *Acceptable Risk* by Baruch Fischhoff and his associates on risk-acceptance criteria, and recent works on the epistemological and ethical assumptions plaguing science policy and risk evaluation by Shrader–Frechette—all illustrate the extent to which public debate over these methods and their use in regulatory decision-making has been shaped by methodologically oriented approaches that are frequently insensitive to ethical and political issues.[20]

Despite these omissions, however, the literature on risk analysis reveals a sharp division among scholars and other commentators, such as policy analysts and legislative staff, concerning the overall utility and proper use of these methods.[21] Proponents of risk analysis argued that such an approach was necessitated by the wide range of technological risks of varying magnitude to which society is exposed and the numerous and often burdensome risk-reduction policies that had been enacted (with no indication of priority) since the mid-1960s.[22] They believed that these methodologies were sound enough to contribute to what they regarded as a rational improvement in such decision-making; they assumed that reliable scientific data on risks could be compiled and that the costs of risk reduction could be calculated, thereby allowing for comparative risk analysis and priority setting. On the other hand, critics of these methodologies, including spokespersons for many environmental and consumer groups, legislative staff members, and a number of academics, argued that risk analysis was still too much of an inexact science, burdened by numerous methodological limitations, to be of any value in these kinds of decisions. They were skeptical that risks could be estimated accurately, that benefits could be identified and measured as thoroughly as the costs, and that the risks, benefits, and costs could be fairly evaluated by all agencies.[23] Some critics, including philosophers such as Shrader-Frechette and Rosemarie Tong, focused particularly on the ethical implications of using such underdeveloped and, in their judgment, overly quantitative methods.[24] Many others, such as Mark Rushefsky and Richard Andrews, pointed to the politicization of risk decisions in the Reagan administration as evidence that their concerns were warranted.[25]

Understanding how risk evaluations are performed is essential to appreciate the role of value issues in this process. According to Shrader-Frechette, the methods for evaluating risk fall into three basic types:[26] (1) *analytical* methods that depend upon the use of formal analytical tools that model and rationally analyze the risk situation under evaluation, such as computer simulation or fault-tree analysis;[27] (2) *empirical* methods that depend primarily upon data gathering of actual or evolving risk scenarios, as illustrated by unanalyzed accident and mortality statistics, toxicological data, and the like; and (3) *synthetic* methods that employ a combination of these methods within some prescribed interpretive framework, such as risk–cost–benefit analysis and revealed preferences. Synthetic approaches are generally preferred because of their comprehensiveness, flexibility, efficiency, and practicality. In addition, they are well suited to ill-structured situations affected by the problem of uncertainty and effectively take into account the lessons learned through a history of trial and error. For these reasons, we concentrate here on describing a variety of commonly used synthetic methods to evaluate risk: (1) risk–cost–benefit analysis, (2) revealed preferences, (3) expressed preferences, and (4) natural standards.

Among the most well-known and widely used methods of risk evaluation is *risk–cost–benefit analysis,* a process of evaluating risk in relation to whether the benefits derived from pursuing a hazardous activity outweigh the risks, or costs, that are involved. In general, this method involves several interrelated steps, beginning with a definition of the risk problem and the set of proposed solutions under consideration. Next, for each alternative, a series of consequences is identified; in particular, they include the anticipated risks for each proposal, as well as the associated direct and indirect costs and benefits that it is reasonable to expect will result. Risks are then compared with the expected costs and benefits, for each alternative solution, where the alternative with the greater balance of benefits against risk–costs is to be preferred. Since risks and benefits are normally incommensurable quantities, these comparisons must be done in terms of some common denominator; the usual standard is in monetary terms. Once each alternative is assessed in terms of its economic costs, we have, at last, a presumed common basis for evaluating risk and deciding what risks are acceptable. In sum, risk–cost–benefit analysis is intended to lead to the conclusion that a hazardous activity is acceptable if the benefits exceed the risks by a suitably defined margin.[28]

There are a number of reasons for favoring this approach to risk evaluation. The most obvious is that intrinsic to any deliberative situation that involves the weighing of alternatives is the evident need to decide whether the benefits to be derived from pursuing an activity are worth the risks involved, both in terms of the consequences to our well being and to our pocketbooks. Moreover, because decision problems regarding the acceptability of risk are normally complex and ill-structured problems, this is a desirable approach because it can reasonably and effectively deal with incommensurate variables. Environmental impact statements, for example, normally employ risk–cost–benefit analysis as their primary evidentiary base. Because the economic cost of controlling risk is typically the most critical factor affecting policy choices, risk–cost–benefit analysis is naturally favored, both by government and business.[29] Indeed, as noted above, most federal risk-control legislation mandates "the balanced weighing of costs and benefits" as a rational way of controlling the expenditure of tax dollars.

Another widely recognized method of risk evaluation is the method of *revealed preferences*. This method uses past risk-acceptance decisions as a comparative basis for evaluating the acceptability of a new hazardous activity. The results are often stated in terms of the comparative probabilities of a fatality, or a reduction in life expectancy, as a consequence of either engaging in different activities or tolerating a variety of exposure levels. New risks can then be judged acceptable to the degree that they provide similar benefits and do not exceed the levels of risk that have been historically (voluntarily or involuntarily) tolerated.

For example, Chauncy Starr has compiled data by which one can compare the ambient risk of death associated with a variety of natural disasters or the mortality rates associated with activities such as traveling by car or commercial airlines.[30] The preferences revealed here provide a basis against which the risks associated with a novel activity can be assessed. (See Figure 5.2.) Others, such as Bernard L. Cohen and I. Sing Lee, and Richard Wilson, have developed a variety of risk compendiums in which a series of hazardous activities are catalogued relative to their impact on life and longevity that serve as prescriptions of prevailing attitudes toward risk.[31] A few examples are given in Table 5.2.

On the basis of such data, Starr has advanced several useful hypotheses regarding the acceptance of risk: For example, (1) the public is willing to accept voluntary risks roughly 1,000 times greater than involuntary risks having the same benefits, and (2) the statistical risk of death from disease provides a

Figure 5.2
Relationship between Statistically Measured Risk of Death and Economic Benefit

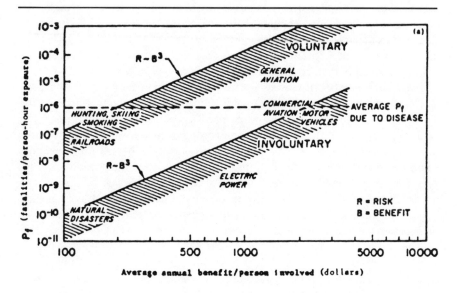

Source: Baruch Fischhoff, Sarah Lichtenstein, Paul Slovic, Steven L. Derby, and Ralph L. Keeney, *Acceptable Risk* (New York: Cambridge University Press, 1981), p. 84. Reprinted with permission.

benchmark for determining the acceptability of risks due to other activities.[32] Decisionmakers who are armed with information of this kind are more likely to be better suited to establishing policies and regulations that are informed and consistent with prevailing values.

Whereas the previous methods assume that prevailing risk-acceptance decisions can be inferred, the method of *expressed preferences* aims at determining some of the underlying consistencies regarding existing attitudes toward risk by directly sampling public and expert opinion. These preference surveys have become the basis of a growing field of research called "psychometrics" that attempts to identify and explain the kinds of risks that are explicitly regarded as acceptable. The resulting analysis of expressed preferences can yield useful information about how risk–benefit trade-offs are perceived when, for example, risks are voluntarily accepted or imposed, proximate or distant, long term or short lived, and so forth.

For example, Fischhoff concluded that there is a tendency to tolerate a wide variety of hazardous activities, such as smoking, drinking, or skiing, when they result in perceived benefits, even when the risks are high and the benefits are relatively low.[33] Moreover, voluntary risks are more readily accepted than those involuntarily imposed, and there is a greater aversion to activities when the

Table 5.2
Risks Estimated to Increase Chance of Death in Any Year by 0.000001 (One Part in One Million)

Activity	Cause of Death
Smoking 1.4 cigarettes	Cancer, heart disease
Living two days in New York or Boston	Air pollution
Traveling 150 miles by car	Accident
Eating 40 tablespoons of peanut butter	Liver cancer caused by aflatoxin
Drinking 30 12 oz. cans of diet soda	Cancer caused by saccharin
Living 150 years within 20 miles of a nuclear power plant	Cancer caused by radiation

Source: R. Wilson (1979), as cited in Baruch Fischhoff, Sarah Lichtenstein, Paul Slovic, Steven L. Derby, and Ralph L. Keeney, *Acceptable Risk* (New York: Cambridge University Press, 1981), p. 81.

risks are believed to be catastrophic, as compared to similar noncatastrophic risks. Indeed, the method of expressed preferences has tended to reinforce the results derived by the method of revealed preferences, thereby enhancing the assurance of decisionmakers that risk-acceptance decisions will be consistent with public expectations. Additionally, it provides decisionmakers with an index as to the public's expectations regarding acceptable standards of risk and safety.

In contrast to the methods previously described, the method of *natural standards* avoids the potential bias built into attempts to assess risk-acceptance decisions based on current social practices, relying instead on an appeal to

Figure 5.3
Comparison of Pollutant Standards, Background Levels, Exposures of Human
Origin, and Health Effects for Radiation, Sulfur Dioxide, and Nitrogen Dioxide

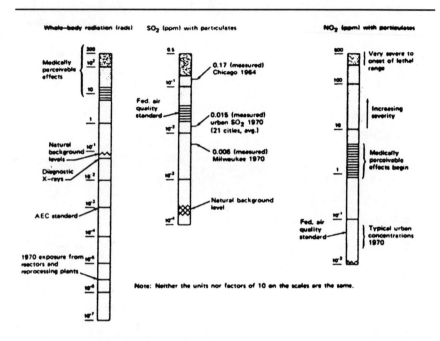

Source: WASH-1224, U.S. Atomic Energy Commission, as cited in Baruch Fischhoff, Sarah Lichtenstein, Paul Slovic, Steven L. Derby, and Ralph L. Keeney, *Acceptable Risk* (New
York: Cambridge University Press, 1981), p. 87. Reprinted with permission.

background geologic and biological risk factors present during the evolution of
the species. The natural risks tolerated through evolutionary time are said to
provide a more accurate measure of the level of risk to which human beings
have become accustomed. The risk levels defined as acceptable by reference to
natural standards can thus be used to determine the level of risk it is reasonable
to accept when nonnatural risks are to be evaluated; hence those risks that
exceed natural standards may be considered unacceptable.

   As Figure 5.3 shows, by using this approach the Atomic Energy Commission
established exposure standards for radiation, sulfur dioxide, and nitrogen dioxide that are regarded as consistent with exposure levels existing naturally. Similarly, it is on the basis of an appeal to natural standards that federal regulations
mandate that annual radiation-exposure levels should not exceed 500 millirems,
a level about the same as levels of background radiation occurring naturally.
Fischhoff and his associates claimed that such an approach to risk evaluation is
to be preferred because it avoids the problems associated with converting risk-

acceptance measures into a common unit, like dollars per life cost, and it allows the setting of standards without the need to resolve uncertainties about precise dose-response relationships.[34]

Although this brief review does not exhaust the variety of methods that can be used to evaluate risk, these are the most common synthetic methods presently used by policymakers. Given these approaches to risk evaluation, what are the most important ethical and political issues raised by the use of these methods? Before turning to this question, in the section below we set forth a perspective that is useful in helping to identify and understand the kinds of value dilemmas existing here.

TYPES OF VALUE ISSUES AND THE PROBLEM OF UNCERTAINTY

Given the development of health, safety, and environmental policies created by the legislative mandates discussed earlier and the increased demand for use of some methods for comparing risks and setting priorities for governmental regulation, what risk-evaluation methods should we adopt? In particular, how can ethical and political analysis be used to resolve some of the difficult and obviously consequential choices facing policymakers and administrators who must evaluate risk? In view of the need for social responsibility, can we determine how safe is safe enough? We believe that attention should focus far more than has been the case on risk-acceptability or risk-evaluation decisions and that explicit consideration of value issues (both ethical and political) inherent in such decisions should be used to help clarify acceptable courses of action.

The value issues generated by the process of risk evaluation may be conceptually distinguished into two generic types: substantive and procedural. Value questions that are *substantive* are those generated by a wide range of choices already made, including decisions about the methods to be used to evaluate risk, as well as the laws, policies, values, moral principles, or other rational constraints and desires that define the framework within which the process of risk evaluation occurs. Lowrance, for example, defined an array of factors, illustrated in Figure 5.4, that summarize some of the substantive value constraints affecting risk-evaluation methods, including whether a risk is accepted voluntarily or is borne involuntarily, whether the effects are immediate or delayed, and whether the consequences are reversible or irreversible.

These factors may be distinguished from procedural value issues that are associated with the various methods used to identify, assess, or evaluate risk. The latter concerns entail a unique set of technical-value problems of their own, such as those related to interpreting data that are statistically averaged or are based on computer models or public surveys of risk.

For example, what is the quality and duration of life that a worker in the nuclear industry can expect? Acknowledging appeals to human and legal rights, equity, due process, or existing regulatory policies are examples of substantive

Figure 5.4
An Array of Considerations Influencing Safety Judgments

Risk assumed voluntarily	———————	Risk borne involuntarily
Effect immediate	———————	Effect delayed
No alternatives available	———————	Many alternatives available
Risk known with certainty	———————	Risk not known
Exposure is an essential	———————	Exposure is a luxury
Encountered occupationally	———————	Encountered non-occupationally
Common hazard	———————	"Dread" hazard
Affects average people	———————	Affects especially sensitive people
Will be used as intended	———————	Likely to be misused
Consequences reversible	———————	Consequences irreversible

Source: Reproduced, with permission, from *Of Acceptable Risk,* by William W. Lowrance. Copyright © 1976 by William Kaufman, Inc., 95 First Street, Los Altos, California 94022. All rights reserved.

concerns that define the parameters for identifying and interpreting the value questions that a hazardous activity of this kind may entail. On the other hand, questions regarding the validity of data, or methods used in assessing the long-term health hazards of exposure to radiation, raise value issues regarding the interpretation of data that are technical and are introduced as a consequence of the kinds of evaluation techniques used. Although the latter questions are interesting in themselves, our immediate focus is limited to examining the broader and more demanding substantive value concerns central to the process of risk evaluation.

As this example illustrates, it may not always be possible to distinguish clearly the substantive value concerns that structure thinking about risk from those that are purely procedural. Historical data concerning the long-term health effects on workers in the nuclear industry, for instance, are generally poor and unreliable. Although this is primarily a procedural concern, the fact that very little negative data exist can, nonetheless, influence perceptions of the relative safety of employment in the nuclear industry. The result may be a failure to recognize substantive value concerns regarding the desirability of this type of employment. Conversely, this lack of data may mistakenly persuade us that existing procedures for determining the health effects of radiation exposure are fundamentally adequate. Thus although value concerns of either type may influence how we approach the evaluation of a hazardous activity, it is important to try to keep these concerns distinct.

The present discussion concentrates on examining only the substantive value concerns that generally structure the process of risk evaluation, specifically, the ethical and political value issues implicit in risk evaluation. In particular, the substantive concerns we are most concerned with are those based on moral and political rights, respect for the common good, and considerations of justice and political legitimacy.

Implicit in the entire process of risk analysis is the problem of uncertainty. It affects risk analysis at various stages, from the initial point of defining the nature of the risks to be regulated through measurement of the probability that such risks will occur to decisions on risk acceptability. The varying degrees of uncertainty that surround risk evaluation make the process of establishing rational public policy extremely difficult.[35]

These uncertainties are further compounded when decisionmakers must decide on the values that are to form the basis for evaluating risk, involving answers to questions such as what should be valued and why, how contradictory values are to be reconciled, and how to treat values that are as yet unconscious or not fully evolved. Because of these uncertainties the confidence we can have in the process of risk evaluation will necessarily vary, and when these uncertainties are ignored, or unacknowledged, they can seriously prejudice risk-acceptance decisions. In short, the process of risk evaluation is not a science but at best a rationally based art form that may in some cases lead to situations wherein alternative and incommensurable policy options may be regarded as equally acceptable, depending upon how the various problems of uncertainty are handled.

RISK EVALUATION: ETHICAL ISSUES

There are three basic types of ethical issues that are of primary concern when one is faced with acceptable-risk decision problems: (1) How are human rights and individual moral interests considered when risk is evaluated? (2) What are the expected consequences to social utility and the common good of acceptable risk decisions? (3) How are questions of fairness or equity in the distribution of risk considered? In each case, the methods used to evaluate risk involve making assumptions that can have serious consequences for the moral concerns expressed in each of these questions.

Consider the ethical issues raised by the duty to respect basic *human rights* such as life, liberty, and property.[36] The method of risk–cost–benefit analysis has been criticized by Michael Baram, Edmond Crouch and Richard Wilson, and others for failing to identify adequately, measure, and take into account the effects on *individual* rights involving life, health, and safety, for example, when risk and benefits are compared.[37] Because the focus of the risk–cost–benefit approach is on balancing aggregate quantities affecting society as a whole, the effects on individual rights are frequently ignored or discounted. More importantly, the ethical problem that is most obvious is the assumption that there are objective measures of what constitutes a morally permissible impact on these basic rights. The well-known controversies regarding the "value of life" and the morally proper limits of our natural rights present real difficulties whenever threats to these rights arise. This is particularly true when risks and benefits have to be translated into a common economic unit. Does anyone really suppose that we can determine how much human life, liberty, or physical well being are worth, in dollars and cents? Will these economic costs be freely chosen, or will they be imposed? What about the real harm to health and other valued interests that can develop? How much are these moral concerns worth? Are the social and economic costs associated with accepting restrictions on human rights and other legitimate moral interests rationally determinable? Will these costs be serious or minor, incapacitating or temporary, frequent or intermittent, wide ranging or isolated, to mention only a few of the questions that may arise whenever consequences are assessed?

But the moral difficulties existing here are more fundamental than this. For the entire enterprise of comparing risks against benefits for the sake of selecting the most advantageous option presupposes that moral rights can be traded against expected utilities. Can it be ethical to trade basic human rights for other nonmoral goods? Indeed, serious questions about the correctness of trading individual rights against the benefits of a risky activity, which are implied by risk–cost–benefit analysis, also exist for each of the other methods of risk evaluation discussed above. That is, each of these approaches assume that should the beneficial utilities of accepting a risky technology or activity be sufficiently great, this will permit pursuing it despite the fact that it may result in the violation of fundamental rights. Although all human rights may be overriden in special circumstances, the lack of widespread agreement as to when this is reasonable or ethically appropriate makes the process of evaluating risk, from the point of view of respecting basic rights, extremely problematic. In short, regardless of the methods used, it must be recognized that the process of risk evaluation assumes that human rights and other moral goods can be limited and justifiably compared with aggregated benefits.

Intimately related to rights-based concerns are the perplexing consequential-ist or utilitarian concerns affecting the *common good* that are raised whenever a choice must be made between alternative social goods. The establishment of social policy based on the use of risk-evaluation methods presupposes basic agreement on what kinds of things are good and what activities will contribute to achieving the common good. Among the goods most widely recognized as desirable are knowledge, pleasure, happiness, wealth, security, health, effi-ciency, and environmental quality. Since this is obviously not an exhaustive list, what additional goods ought to be considered in the process of formulating regulatory policy? Assuming that these goods are the focus of primary concern, how are they to be ordered and to what degree should they each be considered whenever risks are evaluated? More often than not, there will be unavoidable trade-offs required between health and wealth, for example; in these cases, policy analysts must take some position on the relative value of each and define the limits of acceptable restrictions of these goods when evaluating competing risk-reduction practices, if we are to avoid trading valued social goods for a pig in a poke.

For each of the risk-evaluation methods outlined earlier, careful considera-tion of the substantive value issues implicit in assessing competing social goods is a necessary part of evaluating and, ultimately, making acceptable risk deci-sions. Here the question is not what risks are acceptable but rather how much do the various benefits deriving from a hazardous activity contribute to the common good? The recent public controversies regarding, for example, the desirability of genetic engineering, artificial hearts, and nuclear power suggest the degree to which agreement is lacking, and difficult to achieve, when it comes to *new* technologies. These questions are further complicated whenever competing activities generate incommensurate goods, such as the debate over mass transportation versus the use of private autos in urban centers. Indeed, it may be unreasonable in a democratic society to expect that consensus should be reached on every issue. But if by the process of risk evaluation we hope to develop viable public policy intended to minimize risk, decisionmakers must make assumptions about social goals and values that can serve as background standards for judging the acceptability of risks.

Finally, the process of risk evaluation requires making decisions directly af-fecting issues of distributive *justice* and *equity* that cannot be ignored. Consider the following questions:

• How should society distribute risks that will result? Should risks be distributed equally or should the burden of societal risks be borne most heavily by those who benefit the most?

• What principles should inform risk-acceptance decisions, for example, equity, merit or need, and what should be done when there are conflicts among these principles?

• Will certain groups or localities be forced to bear a greater proportion of the most serious risks, as in Bhopal, India?

- Is it fair to impose risks upon society that directly limit personal freedom or should public policy tolerate only those risks that are voluntarily accepted?
- If we cannot avoid imposing some risks on individuals, to what degree should they be informed of the potential hazards to health and safety? What precautions ought to be included in policy decisions to mitigate the harmful consequences of these decisions?
- Will provisions be made to provide for due process and appropriate compensation should individuals be injured?
- By what means and according to what standards will those suffering the hardships of risk be compensated?
- What about future generations? In what way do their prospective interests and aspirations dictate a need to restrict or avoid transgenerational risk activities? To what extent is it fair for us to use, and perhaps exhaust, dwindling resources as a means of reducing the burden of present and future risks we create?

For each of the methods of risk evaluation used, answers to questions based on justice and equity must be formulated if we are to develop policies that responsibly address the question of how safe is safe enough. In short, we need to decide how to make the burdens of societal risk fair and equitable whenever we employ methods of risk evaluation.

Among the few proposals that have been suggested to deal with some of the substantive ethical value questions posed here, two deserve brief attention: the technology tribunal and weighted risk evaluations. The *technology tribunal*, based loosely on the "science court" idea that was prominent in the late 1970s, is an approach that attempts to deal directly with the moral conflicts over rights, social goods, and justice that arise whenever risk policy decisions must be made. Shrader–Frechette, who defended a version of this approach, offered a key rationale:

Pursuing the insight that several current methods of risk assessment have failed because analysts ignored the value components in their work, I believe that any fruitful method of risk analysis must explicitly address controversies over values. One of the best ways to do this is to pursue an adversary method of assessment, a method premised on the fact that desirable risk analyses are likely to be a product of rational interaction and compromise among those who disagree about how to evaluate a given risk. . . . I maintain that citizens, informed by scientists' participation in the proceedings, ought to join the experts in helping to evaluate risks and to provide a democratic basis for subsequent public policymaking.[38]

Thus the technology tribunal would be composed of anywhere from several dozen to several thousand informed scientists and citizens, who would be responsible for identifying the major ethical problems underlying policy issues for which risks to life, health, or safety are involved. Adversarial hearings similar to legal proceedings would be conducted in which spokespersons for competing perspectives on these issues could present their cases. Advocates would debate the issues, call and cross-examine witnesses, and defend specific policy recommendations. Once the "evidence and testimony" had been presented, the tribunal would render a formal decision that would attempt to create a rational balance among competing moral considerations implicit in policy alternatives. The result, based on a democratic consensus, would provide decisionmakers with a more reliable information base upon which to establish social policy regulating hazardous technology. As we shall see when we turn to an examination of the political issues implicit in risk evaluation, this is a crucial consideration.

Another viable approach to giving proper attention to the ethical inquiries raised above involves evaluating risks, costs, and benefits in a manner that puts a weight on each relative to the impact each has on human rights, the common good, and social justice. The use of *weighted risk evaluations* might compare favorably with the accepted practice in economic theory of putting different weights on utilities so as to discount increases in the rate of return gained as a result of inflation, for example. By analogy, as William Rowe and others have argued, by modifying our methods of risk evaluation in ways that permit the use of discounting procedures for weighing risks differently, depending on their effect on a variety of moral considerations, including rights, social utility, equity, privacy, and liberty, the resulting evaluation might reflect more effectively the real value of risk.[39]

One recent study advocating this approach showed how it may alter the decision outcome. The costs of nuclear power have been claimed as justified by its benefits; yet the use of an ethically weighted evaluation technique in this case resulted in just the opposite conclusion.[40] As this and numerous other examples illustrate, failure to take into account the ethically relevant aspects of risk can result in seriously misguided evaluations of risk and ultimately bad policy-making.

Both of these proposals, and especially the technology tribunal, underscore the close affiliation between ethics and politics. Certain political conditions must be met if ethically justifiable policy decisions are to be made.

RISK EVALUATION: POLITICAL ISSUES

Our review of the ethical issues in risk evaluation focused on important substantive value questions facing policy actors. In general, we suggested a range of ethical concerns that policy analysts, risk analysts, and decisionmakers should be prepared to address if risk-acceptability decisions are to be considered morally acceptable. This approach is consistent with the American Society for Public Administration's position that there should be self-analysis of ethical issues on the part of individual administrators.[41] (Chapter 2 in this volume explores in detail how individual administrators might deal with ethical issues.) To these ethical considerations we must add one additional substantive concern, that of *political legitimacy*. It helps to clarify one of the most important questions of where risk evaluation should take place, who should participate in the decisions, and how they should be conducted.

Generally, political legitimacy, or the process of policy legitimation, refers to decision-making that is constitutional and legal and that yields policy choices that are broadly acceptable to relevant political actors.[42] These actors may be the general public, regulated groups and other stakeholders (e.g., environmental and public health groups), legislators, and various officials in the administrative agencies. Because there is no agreed-upon way to resolve the classic question of what governmental actions are in the "public interest," the concept of policy legitimation is helpful for suggesting procedural criteria against which particular decisions or individual actions might be weighed.

For example, consider the following questions:

- Did the proposal receive majority approval in the legislature?
- Were significant minority perspectives on the issues considered?
- Did legislative consideration take place in an informed, open, and deliberative manner that helped to identify and reconcile conflicting values?
- Within an administrative agency, was the risk-acceptability decision process sufficiently open to a variety of interested parties? For example, was there sufficient opportunity for the general public to learn of the proceedings and to participate meaningfully in them?
- Was there an opportunity for interaction among participants and an effort to search for compromises?
- Was sufficient technical information available to officials and other participants to enable them to resolve differences in values?

As these questions illustrate, policy legitimation is important in part because the processes involved facilitate consideration of value conflicts and promote conflict resolution. Moreover, ethical issues are more likely to be addressed under these conditions, and the substantive decisions are more likely to reflect public preferences and needs, as expected in a democratic polity.

Most risk-acceptance decisions take place in administrative agencies, which raises some difficult questions of how norms of democratic accountability as well as policy legitimation can be maintained. In terms of democratic theory, administrative officials are acting as surrogates for elected officials who may be presumed (even if not confidently) to be acting in the interests of the public. For elected officials there is at least a direct process of political accountability provided for in the conduct of elections. For administrative officials, we have less assurance that acceptable risk decisions have fully met expectations for policy legitimation even when conventional mechanisms for accountability are present.

The standard model of risk management, for example, emphasizes the role of expertise; scientists, economists, and policy analysts in the bureaucracy play the major roles, typically using one or more of the methods of risk evaluation we described above. Yet, however well they do their job, questions of political legitimacy arise if, for example, the standards developed are not subject to a sufficient process of review and public comment. It is interesting to note that the Committee on Risk and Decision Making of the National Research Council rejected this model of policy-making as "both unattainable and incompatible with democratic principles."[43] It specified several reasons, including the inability of analysts to resolve conflicts of interest among parties; the fact that some problems are for all practical purposes unanalyzable and are in need of "political as well as intellectual contributions to their solution"; that professional analysis is fallible and often inconclusive; and finally, that it is frequently expensive and time consuming.[44]

The committee's position is important in at least two respects. First, it endorses a common perspective on the use of policy analysis in decision-making that is often ignored by the scientific community, namely, that analysis can inform but should not determine the outcome of a decision that is better left to political interaction and resolution.[45] Its view that the use of risk analysis "should be subject to the control of the electorate and political officials" parallels our own position on the importance of processes of policy legitimation. Obviously, many decisions require substantial technical expertise; we are concerned, however, when decisions that involve value judgments are presented as largely technical, thereby justifying excluding or downgrading the contribution of nonexpert public officials and the general public. Chapter nine in this volume about the role of professional expertise very nicely elaborates on these kinds of conflicts. Given our emphasis, we believe that risk analysts should be encouraged to incorporate substantive value issues into their analyses, as we suggest above. But that alone will be insufficient to provide for accountability to the public, which is, in effect, another ethical consideration. Thus additional measures must be taken.

The second implication of the committee's position is that risk-evaluation analyses can be made more useful for the diverse audiences and purposes for which they are conducted when public participation is encouraged. Given expectations for a pluralistic process of policy legitimation, this argument flows from the first. For policy legitimation to work properly, nonexpert decision-makers and other relevant parties must understand, at least minimally, both the technical and sociopolitical aspects of risk-acceptance decisions. One way of increasing their capacity to do so is for risk analysts to prepare reports that clearly describe the methods used, the major assumptions and uncertainties, and the bases for evaluating policy alternatives. In short, the manner in which risk analyses are prepared and reported is a significant and often disguised variable in risk-acceptance decisions.

It must be said, however, that the potential audience for risk analysis is so diverse that preparation of such reports will be a major challenge. For example, the audience includes the following: governmental administrators and their staffs, members of Congress and their staffs, industry officials, labor leaders, public health and safety organizations and their leaders, the academic community, and the general public. Each has distinct interests and needs. Thus Arthur Atkisson, Michael Kraft, and Lloyd Philipson argued that risk analysis (both assessment and formal evaluation) must concurrently serve five purposes:

(1) assist public and private managers and policymakers in designing and executing risk management decisions which more appropriately conform to relevant criteria of effectiveness, equity, economic efficiency, timeliness, and social relevance; (2) facilitate review of the "factual" components of risk management decisions by appropriate elements of the scientific community; (3) stimulate and enable relevant institutional entities and societal groups to engage in the informed review and legitimizing of those same decisions; (4) serve as a vehicle for equipping the general public with the knowledge necessary for improved participation in the framing and review of community and societal risk management decisions; and (5) reduce the socially divisive and economically expensive conflicts now associated with numerous risk management decisions.[46]

As great as the challenge of serving those five purposes is, nothing less will suffice given the implications for public health and safety, and the economic consequences of policy decisions such as hazardous-waste-facility siting, nuclear-waste disposal, air- and water-pollution control, and regulation of occupational health and safety.

Some serious effort to improve public understanding of risk and risk analysis has been made in the past few years that may facilitate policy legitimation in administrative agencies. Among the more notable of these educational efforts is the EPA's attempt, in 1985, to explain its new procedures for risk assessment to various groups, including congressional staff, journalists, environmentalists, industry representatives, and public administrators.[47] The sponsorship by the Conservation Foundation in 1986 of a National Conference on Risk Communication is another example illustrating a move to improve the effectiveness of public communication on risk management. Over time, such conferences and agency efforts to explain their procedures will doubtless improve public understanding of risks and may foster increased consideration of the value conflicts and ethical issues in risk-acceptance decisions. They are not, however, substitutes for building effective procedures within the administrative process that can increase accountability in decision-making and hence contribute to policy legitimation. Several of the approaches of this kind that merit attention are open and interactive decision-making processes, public participation programs, and congressional oversight.

Open and interactive decision-making refers to two characteristics of administrative procedures. The first concerns matters such as conducting open meetings, maintaining detailed records of meetings, insuring public access to records, and providing for external review and legal challenge to agency decisionmaking (which varies by statute). The importance of these guarantees is obvious in terms of democratic accountability. Numerous critics objected, for example, that the Reagan administration's OMB failed to meet such expectations under its program of regulatory review, and as a result, in 1986 Congress forced the administration to alter the process significantly to meet the need for greater accountability.[48]

The second characteristic concerns the manner of interaction among agency staff and officials. Agency personnel have different roles, values, interests, and perspectives that may lead to either conflict or cooperation among technical, legal, administrative, and political staffs. Extensive cooperative interaction among the staff, especially scientists and regulatory officials, may contribute to sound and responsive decision-making (e.g., by minimizing the use of poor data and by subjecting risk estimates and economic analyses to scrutiny by a diverse set of participants). One study of the use of risk analysis in regulatory agencies found, for example, that collaborative, cooperative efforts between scientists and consumer-safety officers in the FDA facilitated consistent decision-making on standards, whereas, as one official put it, if the technical people are left to their own devices "they can, unwittingly, be quite capricious."[49]

The meaning of *public participation* programs is self-explanatory. Some administrative decisions require the creation of opportunities for direct citizen participation, for example, through the conduct of public hearings, by providing compensation to public interest groups for their participation, or by creating certain provisions for litigation to enforce legislative mandates. Some argue that only such direct public participation allows adequate consideration of public preferences on risk acceptance.[50] Others object that public hearings and similar devices merely encourage the expression of uninformed or prejudiced opinions and hinder sound professional judgment on dealing with risks such as nuclear wastes or hazardous chemicals.[51] Under some conditions (e.g., when public feelings are intense, the risks affect large numbers of people, and they are involuntary, highly uncertain, and possibly irreversible), public participation seems essential. Under other conditions, indirect representation of the public's interest may suffice. In either case, administrative agencies may need to develop different approaches to public participation that more effectively facilitate public understanding of risks and contribute to the making of risk-acceptance decisions.

Finally, *congressional oversight,* one of the most traditional mechanisms of administrative accountability, might be relied upon more in the future to facilitate contentious risk-acceptance decisions. Unfortunately, the record of congressional oversight of administrative agencies has been weak to nonexistent and open to frequent criticism. Members of Congress are said to be poorly informed on the technical issues and insufficiently motivated to conduct oversight investigations and hearings except under unusual conditions (e.g., when controversy is exceptional and media attention extensive, as in inquiries over the handling of the toxic-waste program in the early 1980s). Yet Congress is well equipped with the resources necessary (e.g., committee staff, the

Congressional Research Service, and the Office of Technology Assessment) to supervise risk-acceptability decisions made by regulatory agencies. Its participation in such decisions could bring a more democratic perspective to what might otherwise be an excessive reliance on experts or political appointees of the president. Such participation may be especially important when partisan control over Congress and the presidency is divided; under that condition, increased congressional scrutiny of agency decisions creates access to a public forum for individuals and interest groups, thereby increasing the representativeness of the final policy decision. Given its constitutional and political independence from the executive branch, Congress also serves to keep executive agencies from overstepping their authority and violating due process. Congressional intervention in OMB's regulatory review powers is a case in point.

CONCLUSION

As a result of decisions made in the late 1960s and early 1970s, government regulation of risk-generating activities is now pervasive. Despite recent criticism of the new social regulation and the emergence of a new conservative political agenda, extensive deregulation in the established areas of risk management is unlikely. Survey data indicate that whatever general sentiment is expressed for reducing regulation and the intrusiveness of the federal bureaucracy, the public continues to support regulation of hazardous activities that impact on health, safety, and environmental quality. Congressional support for most social regulation also remains firm. Thus one can expect continuation in the near future of the full range of risk-management activities associated with these public policies, including the necessity of making risk-acceptance decisions.

Given the political controversies over attempts at deregulation in the early to mid-1980s, these decisions will remain as contentious as they are consequential for public safety and environmental quality. Although there has been little systematic effort to analyze either the ethical or political issues in risk-acceptance decisions, or to propose practical ways for resolving them, our analysis has explored some of these often-ignored questions and has suggested how public officials and others concerned with these decisions might deal with the inevitable value conflicts that arise.[52]

In a more practical vein, what should be done to insure that risk-acceptance decisions reflect consideration of these substantive value issues? We believe that more open, pluralistic, and interactive decision-making within the agencies, enhanced programs of public participation, and more regular and informed congressional oversight of the regulatory agencies' risk-management practices offer some promise of increasing the attention given to ethical issues and insuring that value conflicts are resolved in a way that reflects public preferences and needs.

Few people think that risk analysis is now or ever will be a panacea for dealing with the multiple risks of a technological society. But if it is employed carefully and with sufficient regard for the uncertainty of current data and scientific knowledge, and if the value issues surveyed here are more widely acknowledged and adequately considered, it can be a useful tool of policy analysis and sound regulatory decision-making. Given the nature of risks faced in modern societies and the impact of public policy decisions, it is very much in our collective interest to increase the capacity of both policymakers and administrators to use risk analysis with the caution, intelligence, and sensitivity to the value issues that it demands.

NOTES

1. William Lowrance, *Of Acceptable Risk: Science and the Determination of Safety* (Los Altos, Calif.: Kaufman, 1976), p. 8.
2. *See* Charles W. Anderson, "The Place of Principles in Policy Analysis," *American Political Science Review* 73 (1979): 711–723; Rosemarie Tong, *Ethics in Policy Analysis* (Englewood Cliffs, N.J.: Prentice-Hall, 1986).
3. Lowrance, *Of Acceptable Risk,* p. 8.
4. National Research Council, *Risk Assessment in the Federal Government: Managing the Process* (Washington, D.C.: National Academy Press, 1983).
5. Lester B. Lave, ed., *Quantitative Risk Assessment in Regulation* (Washington, D.C.: Brookings Institution, 1981).
6. National Research Council, *Risk and Decision Making: Perspectives and Research* (Washington, D.C.: National Academy Press, 1982), p. 33.
7. The estimate by J. Clarence Davies is cited in Judith Havemann, "How Do You Estimate Cancer Risk?" *Washington Post National Weekly Edition,* 28 July 1986, pp. 31–32.
8. Mark E. Rushefsky, "Assuming the Conclusions: Risk Assessment in the Development of Cancer Policy," *Politics and the Life Sciences* 4 (August 1985): 31–66.
9. *See* the introduction by Susan G. Hadden in her edited collection *Risk Analysis, Institutions, and Public Policy* (Port Washington, N.Y.: Associated Faculty Press, 1984); Kristin Shrader-Frechette, *Science Policy, Ethics, and Economic Methodology* (Boston: Reidel, 1985).
10. *See* Michael E. Kraft, "The Use of Risk Analysis in Federal Regulatory Agencies: An Exploration," *Policy Studies Review* 1 (May 1982): 666–675.
11. For a summary of federal activities in this area, *see* Arthur A. Atkisson, Michael E. Kraft, and Lloyd L. Philipson, *Risk Analysis Methods and Their Employment in Governmental Risk Management,* Final report prepared for The National Science Foundation (Redondo Beach, Calif.: J. H. Wiggins, 1985).
12. *See* Robert Field, *Statutory Language and Risk Management,* Report to the Committee on Risk and Decision-Making of the National Academy of Sciences (Washington, D.C.: National Academy of Sciences, 1981).
13. *See* Kenneth J. Meier, *Regulation: Politics, Bureaucracy, and Economics* (New York: St. Martin's Press, 1985); George C. Eads and Michael Fix, *Relief or Reform? Reagan's Regulatory Dilemma* (Washington, D.C.: Urban Institute, 1984); Michael D. Reagan, *Regulation: The Politics of Policy* (Boston: Little, Brown, 1987).
14. U.S. Congress, *Federal Regulation and Regulatory Reform.* Report by the Sub-

committee on Oversight and Investigations of the Committee on Interstate and Foreign Commerce, House of Representatives, 94th Congress, 2d session (Washington, D.C.: U.S. Government Printing Office, 1976); U.S. Congress, *Study on Federal Regulation*, 6 vols. Report by the Committee on Governmental Affairs, United States Senate (Washington, D.C.: U.S. Government Printing Office, 1977).

15. Lester Lave, *The Strategy of Social Regulation: Decision Frameworks for Policy* (Washington, D.C.: Brookings Institution, 1981); Robert E. Litan and William D. Nordhaus, *Reforming Federal Regulation* (New Haven: Yale University Press, 1983).

16. *See,* for example, Eads and Fix, *Relief or Reform?;* V. Kerry Smith, ed., *Environmental Policy under Reagan's Executive Order: The Role of Benefit–Cost Analysis* (Chapel Hill: University of North Carolina Press, 1984).

17. Eugene Bardach and Robert A. Kagan, *Going by the Book: The Problem of Regulatory Unreasonableness* (Philadelphia: Temple University Press, 1982); Litan and Nordhaus, *Reforming Federal Regulation;* Lave, *The Strategy of Social Regulation.*

18. David Okrent, ed., *Risk–Benefit Methodology and Application* (Los Angeles: University of California, 1975); William D. Rowe, *An Anatomy of Risk* (New York: Wiley, 1977); R. W. Kates, *Risk Assessment of Environmental Hazards* (New York: Wiley, 1978); Edmund A. C. Crouch and Richard J. Wilson, *Risk/Benefit Analysis* (Cambridge, Mass.: Ballinger, 1982); Lave, *Quantitative Risk Assessment in Regulation.*

19. Dorothy Nelkin, *Technological Decisions and Democracy* (Beverly Hills, Calif.: Sage, 1977); Kristin Shrader-Frechette, *Nuclear Power and Public Policy,* 2d ed. (Boston: Reidel, 1983).

20. Hadden, *Risk Analysis, Institutions, and Public Policy;* Baruch Fischhoff, Sarah Lichtenstein, Paul Slovic, Steven L. Derby, and Ralph L. Keeney, *Acceptable Risk* (New York: Cambridge University Press, 1981); Kristin Shrader-Frechette, *Risk Analysis and Scientific Method: Methodological and Ethical Problems with Evaluating Societal Hazards* (Boston: Reidel, 1985); idem, *Science Policy, Ethics, and Economic Methodology.*

21. Richard C. Schwing and Walter A. Albers, Jr., eds., *Societal Risk Assessment: How Safe Is Safe Enough?* (New York: Plenum, 1980). *See* U.S. Congress, *Risk/Benefit Analysis in the Legislative Process.* Summary of a Congress/Science Joint Forum, prepared by the Congressional Research Service for the Subcommittee on Science, Research and Technology of the Committee on Science and Technology, U.S. House of Representatives, and the Subcommittee on Science, Technology and Space of the Committee on Commerce, Science, and Transportation, United States Senate, 96th Congress, 2d session (Washington, D.C.: U.S. Government Printing Office, 1980).

22. *See* Lave, *The Strategy of Social Regulation;* idem, *Quantitative Risk Assessment in Regulation.*

23. Michael E. Baram, "Cost–Benefit Analysis: An Inadequate Basis for Health, Safety, and Environmental Regulatory Decisionmaking," *Ecology Law Quarterly* 8 (1980): 473–531; Kenneth T. Bogen, "Public Policy and Technological Risk," *Idea: The Journal of Law and Technology* 21 (1980): 37–74; U.S. Congress, *Risk/Benefit Analysis in the Legislative Process.*

24. Shrader-Frechette, *Risk Analysis and Scientific Method;* idem, *Science Policy, Ethics, and Economic Methodology;* Tong, *Ethics in Policy Analysis.*

25. Rushefsky, "Assuming the Conclusions"; Richard N. L. Andrews, "Economics

and Environmental Decisions, Past and Present,'' in V. Kerry Smith, ed., *Environmental Policy under Reagan's Executive Order: The Role of Benefit–Cost Analysis* (Chapel Hill: University of North Carolina Press, 1984).

26. Shrader-Frechette, *Science Policy, Ethics, and Economic Methodology.*

27. *See* Albert Flores, "Engineering Ethics in Organizational Contexts: A Case Study— National Aeronautics and Space Administration," in Albert Flores, ed., *Designing for Safety* (Troy, N.Y.: Rensselaer Polytechnic Institute, 1982), p. 25.

28. *See* Robert P. Wolff, "Maximization of Expected Utility as a Criterion of Rationality in Military Strategy and Foreign Policy," in Alex C. Michalos, ed., *Philosophical Problems of Science and Technology* (Boston: Allyn and Bacon, 1974); Kenneth A. Sayre, ed., *Values in the Electric Power Industry* (Notre Dame, Ind.: University of Notre Dame Press, 1977). *See also* Tom L. Beauchamp, *Case Studies in Business, Society, and Ethics* (Englewood Cliffs, N.J.: Prentice-Hall, 1983).

29. *See* Richard DeGeorge, "Ethical Responsibilities of Engineers in Large Organizations," *Business and Professional Ethics* 1, no. 1 (Fall 1981): 1–14; Kenneth Kipnis, "Engineers Who Kill," *Business and Professional Ethics* 1, no. 1 (Fall 1981): 77–91.

30. Chauncey Starr, "Social Benefit Versus Technological Risk: What Is Our Society Willing to Pay for Safety," *Science* 165 (1969): 1232–1238.

31. Bernard L. Cohen and I. Sing Lee, "A Catalog of Risks," *Health Physics* 36 (1979): 707–722; Richard Wilson, "Analyzing the Daily Risks of Life," *Technology Review* 81 (1979): 40–46.

32. Chauncey Starr, "Benefit–Cost Studies in Socio-Technical Systems," in *Perspectives on Benefit–Risk Decisionmaking* (Washington, D.C.: National Academy of Engineering, Committee on Public Engineering Policy, 1972).

33. Fischhoff, Lichtenstein, Slovic, Derby, and Keeney, "Weighing the Risks," *Environment* 21 (1979): 17–20, 32–38.

34. Fischhoff, Lichtenstein, Slovic, Derby, and Keeney, *Acceptable Risk,* pp. 86–88.

35. Lloyd L. Philipson, *Risk Assessment Methodologies and Their Uncertainties: Volume II, A Review of Risk Evaluation Approaches* (Redondo Beach, Calif.: J. H. Wiggins, 1982).

36. *See* Ronald Dworkin, *Taking Rights Seriously* (Cambridge, Mass.: Harvard University Press, 1977); Kenneth E. Goodpaster and Kenneth M. Sayre, eds., *Ethics and Problems of the Twenty-first Century* (Notre Dame, Ind.: University of Notre Dame Press, 1979).

37. Baram, "Cost–Benefit Analysis"; Crouch and Wilson, *Risk/Benefit Analysis;* Shrader-Frechette, *Science Policy, Ethics, and Economic Methodology;* Thomas Donaldson, "The Ethics of Risk in a Global Economy," in Albert Flores, ed., *Ethics and Risk Management in Engineering* (Boulder, Colo.: Westview Press, 1988).

38. Shrader-Frechette, *Risk Analysis and Scientific Method,* pp. 205, 207.

39. Rowe, *The Anatomy of Risk,* pp. 312, 344. *See also* Alan L. Porter, Frederick A. Rossini, Stanley R. Carpenter, A. T. Roper, with Ronald W. Larsen, *A Guidebook for Technology Assessment and Environmental Impact Analysis* (New York: North Holland, 1980).

40. Shaul Ben-David, Allen V. Kneese, and William D. Schulze, "A Study of the Ethical Foundations of Benefit–Cost Analysis Techniques," Working paper (Washington, D.C.: National Science Foundation, 1980). *See also* Shrader-Frechette, *Science Policy, Ethics, and Economic Methodology.*

41. American Society for Public Administration, "Code of Ethics and Implementation Guidelines," supplement to the *Public Administration Times*, May 1, 1985.

42. Charles O. Jones, *An Introduction to the Study of Public Policy*, 3d ed. (Monterey, Calif.: Brooks/Cole, 1984). *See also* Douglas MacLean, "Consent and the Justification of Risk Analysis," in Vincent T. Covello, Joshua Menkes, and Jeryl Mumpower, eds., *Risk Evaluation and Management* (New York: Plenum Press, 1986).

43. National Research Council, *Risk and Decision Making*, p. 28.

44. Ibid.

45. *See,* for example, Charles E. Lindblom, *The Policy-Making Process*, 2d ed. (Englewood Cliffs, N.J.: Prentice-Hall, 1980).

46. Atkisson, Kraft, and Philipson, *Risk Analysis Methods and Their Employment in Governmental Risk Management*, p. 239.

47. Rochelle L. Stanfield, "What's the Risk?" *National Journal* 17 (1985): 721.

48. Smith, *Environmental Policy under Reagan's Executive Order;* Eads and Fix, *Relief or Reform?* Judith Havemann, "Here's How You Get the OMB's Attention—Cut Off Its Funds," *Washington Post National Weekly Edition*, 2 June 1986, p. 12.

49. Kraft, "The Use of Risk Analysis in Federal Regulatory Agencies," p. 669.

50. Nelkin, *Technological Decisions and Democracy.*

51. Walter A. Rosenbaum, "The Politics of Public Participation in Hazardous Waste Management," in James P. Lester and Ann O'M. Bowman, eds., *The Politics of Hazardous Waste Management* (Durham, N.C.: Duke University Press, 1983).

52. Mary Douglas, *Risk Acceptability According to the Social Sciences* (New York: Russell Sage Foundation, 1985).

SELECTED BIBLIOGRAPHY

Alcorn, Paul A. *Social Issues in Technology: A Format for Investigation.* Englewood Cliffs, N.J.: Prentice-Hall, 1986.

Baram, Michael E. "Cost–Benefit Analysis: An Inadequate Basis for Health, Safety, and Environmental Regulatory Decisionmaking." *Ecology Law Quarterly* 8 (1980): 473–531.

Berg, George G., and H. David Maillie, eds., *Measurement of Risks.* New York: Plenum Press, 1981.

Conrad, Jobst, ed. *Society, Technology, and Risk Assessment.* London: Academic Press, 1980.

Covello, Vincent T., Joshua Menkes, and Jeryl Mumpower, eds. *Risk Evaluation and Management.* New York: Plenum Press, 1986.

Crandall, Robert W., and Lester B. Lave, eds. *The Scientific Basis of Health and Safety Regulation.* Washington, D.C.: Brookings Institution, 1981.

Crouch, Edmund A. C., and Richard J. Wilson. *Risk/Benefit Analysis.* Cambridge, Mass.: Ballinger, 1982.

Davies, J. Clarence, and Edwin H. Clark II. *Risk Assessment and Risk Control.* Washington, D.C.: Conservation Foundation, 1985.

Douglas, Mary. *Risk Acceptability According to the Social Sciences.* New York: Russell Sage Foundation, 1985.

Douglas, Mary, and Aaron Wildavsky. *Risk and Culture.* Berkeley: University of California Press, 1982.

Fischhoff, Baruch, Sarah Lichtenstein, Paul Slovic, Steven L. Derby, and Ralph L. Keeney. *Acceptable Risk*. New York: Cambridge University Press, 1981.

Gibson, Mary, ed. *To Breathe Freely: Risk, Consent, and Air*. Totowa, N.J.: Rowman and Allanheld, 1985.

Hadden, Susan G., ed. *Risk Analysis, Institutions, and Public Policy*. Port Washington, N.Y.: Associated Faculty Press, 1984.

Keeney, Ralph. "Ethics, Decision Analysis, and Public Risk." *Risk Analysis* 4 (1984): 117–130.

Kunreuther, Howard J., and Joanne Linnerooth, eds. *Risk Analysis and Decision Processes*. New York: Springer-Verlag, 1983.

Lave, Lester, ed. *Quantitative Risk Assessment in Regulation*. Washington, D.C.: Brookings Institution, 1981.

MacLean, Douglas, ed. *Values at Risk*. Totowa, N.J.: Rowman and Allanhald, 1986.

Morone, Joseph G., and Edward J. Woodhouse. *Averting Catastrophe: Strategies for Regulating Risk Technologies*. Berkeley: University of California Press, 1986.

National Research Council. *Risk Assessment in the Federal Government: Managing the Process*. Washington, D.C.: National Academy Press, 1983.

Nelkin, Dorothy, and Michael Pollack. "Problems and Procedures in the Regulation of Technological Risk." In Carol H. Weiss and Allen H. Barton, eds., *Making Bureaucracies Work*. Beverly Hills, Calif.: Sage, 1980, pp. 259–278.

Petak, William, and Arthur A. Atkisson. *Natural Hazards Risk Assessment and Public Policy*. New York: Springer-Verlag, 1982.

Rescher, Nicholas. *Risk: A Philosophical Introduction*. Washington, D.C.: University Press of America, 1983.

Starr, Chauncey and Philip C. Ritterbush. *Science, Technology and the Human Prospect*. New York: Pergamon, 1979.

Tong, Rosemarie. *Ethics in Policy Analysis*. Englewood Cliffs, N.J.: Prentice-Hall, 1986.

6

The Legitimacy of Negotiating Rules and Standards

Lloyd Burton

Toxic pollution of the nation's drinking-water supplies has now become a familiar public policy issue. Ongoing studies by the U.S. Environmental Protection Agency (EPA) and various state governments are finding that the extent and severity of groundwater contamination is much greater than had been formerly assumed, both from "nonpoint sources" such as agricultural runoff and identifiable "point sources" such as manufacturing sites and underground storage tanks.

Several federal statutes have been brought into play in an effort to control the problem, with mixed results. Different statutes delegate implementation authority to different local, state, and federal agencies, creating substantial jurisdictional overlap in some areas, disturbing gaps in others, and causing a considerable amount of confusion overall. Federal statutes include the Clean Water Act, Safe Drinking Water Act, Resource Conservation and Recovery Act, and Comprehensive Environmental Response, Compensation, and Liability Act (the "Superfund" legislation).

Until the early 1980s there was much more public and governmental attention directed toward the issues of *what* groundwater protection policies should be adopted and *who* (i.e., what federal and state agencies) should implement them than on *how* those policies should be carried out. But by the beginning of this decade commentators, critics, and scholars were pointing out the shortcomings of the rigorously adversarial "legal rules" model of implementing environmental policy and were advocating instead the adoption of more consensually oriented negotiation-based strategies for rule-making, standard-setting, and enforcement. Unfortunately, the EPA's wholehearted embrace of negotiation-oriented implementation strategies took place under the administration of officials unaware of the ethical obligations imposed by informal process.

Many of them were eventually forced to resign their posts for actions such as hiring industry consultants to help draft agency regulations, thwarting public involvement in implementation decision-making, and impeding legislative oversight of implementation actions. In the judgment of both Republican and Democratic congressional critics and much of the general public, "negotiation" became synonymous with "caving in to industry" or simple nonenforcement of environmental protection statutes. The legitimacy of negotiation as a decision-making tool was cast into serious doubt.

Yet the negotiated settlement of disputes over the enforcement of state and federal environmental health legislation continues to be a necessary option. Even ardent environmentalists concede that negotiated compliance is critical to the success of environmental policies, in part because regulatory agencies simply lack the resources to take adjudicatory action against all offenders. Likewise, some observers in and out of government contend that the adversarial, legalistic implementation of environmental protection policies inhibits the potential for devising creative solutions to pollution problems, generates inefficiencies in the U.S. economy, and impedes our ability to compete effectively in international markets.

Public confidence in an agency's decision to negotiate a compliance agreement with a toxic groundwater polluter rather than rely on adversarial enforcement action might be measurably enhanced if we knew more about how the agencies make such decisions. What factors do they take into consideration? How are negotiations conducted once that option is chosen? How does an agency determine the point at which an acceptable agreement has been achieved or at which point further negotiation is fruitless? How can legislative overseers and a concerned public evaluate the quality of an agency's adjudicate/negotiate decision-making? These are among the policy issues addressed in this chapter.

It will become evident that a central concern of this work is with the *legitimacy* of an agency's use of power in informal compliance negotiations. This is because—as evidenced by the EPA's initial Superfund implementation problems—when an agency abandons adversarial due process in favor of informal negotiated settlements, it also runs the risk of losing contact with the rich source of legitimacy the due process model provides. Therefore, a necessary goal of this work is also to identify and advocate various means of legitimizing agency bargaining behavior.

The due process model evolved largely as a result of the courts "looking over the agencies' shoulders" as they went about their business and then modifying administrative behaviors the courts thought were incompatible with democratic ideals. If the agencies want to preserve what discretion they have in the area of negotiated compliance with policy mandates, they need to find some means of imbuing informal action with the legitimizing qualities earlier imposed upon them by the courts through traditional due process. This study suggests a means of doing just that.

But in the final analysis, as this chapter concludes, the long-term legitimacy of administrative bargaining may come to rely less on external monitoring of agency performance than on the ethical sensitivity of agency negotiators. This research is grounded on the premise that professionally ethical administrative behavior can be equated with that which enhances—or at least does not detract from—the legitimacy of an agency's use of power (legitimacy as defined below, in terms of constitutionality, efficacy, fairness, and responsiveness).

Chapter nine in this book, by John Burke and Richard Pattenaude, offers three viewpoints on the ethical implications of exercising administrative discretion. The authors' theoretical observations bear directly on the case studies presented here in that when environmental agency personnel negotiate a toxic-substance-decontamination agreement with a polluter, they are explicitly exercising discretion in the application of technical expertise. Among these three models—the "professional/separatist," "ordinary morality," and "political/legal"—the method of analysis of the policy issue described below is clearly most closely associated with the third perspective.

An investigation of the moral reasoning of an individual agency decisionmaker exercising discretion (i.e., what is or should be going on in the mind of the person making the decision, as implied in Burke and Pattenaude's models 1 and 2) is important work, but that is not the task attempted here. Instead, what is suggested is a yardstick for measuring agency bargaining behavior in public health protection from the standpoint of how well it conforms to the democratic ideals on which American bureaucratic authority is based.

BACKGROUND AND LITERATURE REVIEW

There is a very real paradox inherent in the administration of democratic government. On the one hand, we take justifiable pride in being heirs to the world's oldest democracy—to a form of government in which the average citizen is the ultimate source of political authority and (through the choice of elected representatives) the ultimate decisionmaker on questions of what should be the purposes of government and how these purposes should be achieved. On the other hand, we have chosen to assign government the responsibility for performing thousands of tasks considered essential to maintaining health, safety, prosperity, and welfare—tasks requiring discretionary decision-making by public servants *not* elected by the citizens and *not* directly answerable to the citizenry regarding the effects of their decisions. In the federal workforce alone there are nearly 3 million men and women, only 537 of whom are elected by those they will govern.

This 6,000 to 1 ratio between the day-to-day operators of governmental machinery and the authors of the operating manual is not unique to American federal government; nor is it unique to the 79,912 state and local governments in the United States that are ostensibly controlled by elected leaders or even to other Western democratic nations. The prophetic German sociologist Max Weber told us that, like it or not, complex and highly organized bureaucracies

were becoming indispensable mechanisms for the governance of modern indus-
trialized nations.[1] Whether policy is formulated by democratically elected representatives or self-appointed dictators, it must be implemented through bureaucratic organizations.

But Weber also pointed out that simply having the power to act and the
organizational means to exercise that power were not enough to insure that
institutions will govern effectively. Also present must be the perception by
those being governed that their institutions possess the *authority* to govern.
Authority, in turn, rests upon the ability to exercise power combined with the
public's belief that the power of government is being exercised *legitimately*.

The next question is, "how do the governed decide when power is and is
not being legitimately used?" To put it more academically, "what are the sources
of legitimacy from which governmental institutions derive their authority to
act?" An equally academic answer is: "it depends"—on the governmental institution in question, on the cultural and historical context within which the
institution was created, on the attitudes and values of the governed, and on the
task the institution is being called upon to perform.

So we return to the paradox of bureaucratic administration in a democratic
society to focus more specifically on the sources of legitimacy of American
bureaucracy. We have plenty of company. The growth of American bureaucratic government throughout the twentieth century has been paralleled by the
growth of an accompanying body of literature warning of the dangers of delegating too much government authority to unelected officials. Presidents like
Theodore Roosevelt and Franklin Roosevelt expressed great confidence in the
ability of technically expert, apolitical bureaucrats to exercise power rationally,
fairly, and effectively; they urged Congress to keep granting the agencies that
power. Detractors worried (as Weber had earlier) that the federal agencies would
come to dominate and overpower the other two branches of government;[2] a
commission formed by Franklin Roosevelt to study these concerns warned in
1937 that the independent federal regulatory agencies were becoming a "head-
less fourth branch of government" and should be abolished.[3] Instead, Congress
moved to standardize the procedures for discretionary decision-making in the
federal agencies, through adoption of the Administrative Procedure Act. First
enacted in 1946, this statute guarantees a modicum of due process in agency
rule-making, standard setting, and rule enforcement.[4]

But as the breadth of bureaucratic responsibility has continued to grow since
the New Deal, so has public concern over the way the agencies do their work.
Critics charged during the 1960s that the agencies had been "captured" by the
very interest groups they had been established to regulate and that the democratic ideals of informed citizen participation in decisions affecting their interests were being thwarted by arrogant, indifferent bureaucrats who listened only
to the rich and powerful.[5]

Some observers believe that steadily diminishing public confidence in the
legitimacy of American bureaucratic government has reached crisis proportions

and that to remedy the situation we must begin by refocusing attention on the sources of legitimacy of democratic administrative government. The next task is to evaluate agency performance in terms of whether it is honoring these legitimizing values in its day-to-day activities.

In his aptly titled *Crisis and Legitimacy* law professor James Freedman argued that the legitimacy of administrative action in American government is classically dependent on four attributes or characteristics: *constitutionality, accountability, fairness,* and *effectiveness.*[6] Each of these attributes is embodied by one means or another in formal agency decision-making, in the relations between agencies and the legislature, or in court decisions reviewing agency action.

Legal scholarship aside, during the past twenty years it has been the federal judges who have most effectively and articulately addressed the bureaucracy's need to legitimize its decision-making through more meaningful public participation. A host of federal court rulings handed down during the 1960s and 1970s ordered the agencies to make, by one means or another, their processes of deliberation and decision more open to the public. The judges evidently hoped that bureaucratic ills like "agency capture" by powerful regulated interests could be remedied by forcing the agencies to make more of their decisions in public and by inviting more public participation before making them. One commentator has concluded that the federal judiciary forcing the agencies to open up their decision-making is one of the most significant transformations that American public administration has undergone in this century; it has resulted in a new and democratically appealing "interest-group representation" model of administrative law in which no major agency decision may be considered sound unless it is based on a thoughtful consideration of diverse and substantial public input.[7]

By forcing such consideration—whether through public hearings, advisory committees, or other solicitation of a broad range of public views—it is argued that the courts have also enhanced the fairness of agency decision-making. In Freedman's view, a heightened perception of agency fairness further legitimizes the use of bureaucratic power. Interested parties at least have the opportunity for their "day in court," even if administrative decisionmakers do not render a wholly satisfactory "verdict." In mandating more formal and open procedures for making decisions affecting the public interest, the courts have made an important contribution toward shoring up public confidence in bureaucratic authority—or at least slowing down the rate of erosion.

THE TREND TOWARD INFORMAL, NONADVERSARIAL PROCEDURE—THEORY AND PRACTICE

As with anything else of value, the opening up of agency procedure in the interests of fairness and responsiveness has not been cost-free. Since the courts played a major role in the opening process (and later the Congress, by structuring elements of court decisions into Administrative Procedure Act amendments and various environmental statutes), they mandated reforms that have had the effect of "legalizing" agency decision-making, according to subsequent critics. By forcing the agencies to adopt threshold due process standards, they have measurably enhanced the role of lawyers in the bureaucracy and in representing the interests of those affected by bureaucratic decision-making. This in turn has tended to increase the time necessary to reach a decision, the volume of the evidentiary record that must be accumulated before taking significant action, and the content and tone of the decisions themselves.

Thus as procedure became more open in terms of *who* could participate, it also became somewhat more rigid, more complex, and more time consuming in terms of *how* that participation was to be structured. Likewise, the growing necessity of professional representation in agency proceedings and the amassing of ever more elaborate evidentiary records increased the expense of effective participation in agency decision-making as well. Even those who recognized the importance of adequate interest-group representation as a legitimizing influence on bureaucratic behavior perceived the trade-offs at hand. Open, fair, responsive process was also cumbersome, costly, and lengthy. Ironically, the result in some cases was that while procedural barriers were being lowered, economic ones were being raised (i.e., participation costs).

Rise of Negotiated Policy Implementation and Its Ethical Implications

By the late 1970s, critics of the "due process revolution" were arguing that the trade-off was sometimes too great—that better decisions were not emanating from elaborate new processes and that more informality, flexibility, and efficiency were sorely needed.

According to this argument, elaborate traditional processes should be complemented by "alternate decisional processes" such as negotiated standard setting and other decision-making alternatives to formal advocacy (e.g., technical advisory committees for fact verification).[8] By the early 1980s several federal agencies had begun to heed this advice and had brought interested parties together for negotiated rule-making in areas such as occupational safety and health, airline regulation, and fair trade.[9]

However, the concept of negotiated policy implementation evidently meant very different things to different federal agency administrators. In rule-making and standard setting, most administrators have worked with consensus-based methods as an adjunct to, rather than a total replacement of, more traditional processes.[10] But in rule application in the U.S. Environmental Protection Agency from 1981 to 1983 the use of informal negotiation-based methods precipitated a legitimacy crisis of such proportions that the agency's administrator (Ann Gorsuch Burford) and several of her senior subordinates were eventually forced to resign their posts (one of them going from high federal office to internment in a federal correctional facility).[11]

The problem arising in this situation was that when discretionary decision-making was moved "indoors" and out of public view (through dramatic cuts in public participation programs) and industry representatives were allowed unprecedented access to the inner circles of EPA decision-making, the public and Congress began to doubt whether toxic-waste-control programs were being implemented fairly and effectively.[12] When later charges of political manipulation of programs and gross conflict of interest were substantiated in court, the perils of abandoning a formal, open process in favor of private negotiations were made manifest.

In the absence of formal process, then, the ethical sensitivity of program administrators in their exercise of administrative discretion is of paramount importance. In formal adversarial proceedings, Freedman's legitimacy criteria of constitutionality, accountability, effectiveness, and fairness are sought through public and judicial scrutiny of agency decision-making. But in the private, informal exercise of that discretion, Freedman's four criteria became competing values that the public decisionmaker must seek to balance against one another.

As John Worthley put it, the "Hamiltonian" values of expertise, efficiency, and discipline were all structured into American government by the founders in an effort to establish government that could do its job effectively.[13] Yet the framers "also built in the Jeffersonian/Madisonian perspective that included democratic control, accountability, responsiveness, and representativeness as key values."[14] The EPA in the early 1980s evidently sacrificed accountability (public participation and adherence to conflict of interest precepts) with the intent of achieving efficiency and efficacy. As later studies showed that program implementation was also neither efficacious nor efficient, the downfall of senior administrators was insured.

But it is not only competing legitimacy criteria that must be balanced. If we accept as a working definition of administrative ethics "the moral use of power in the public interest," we must also acknowledge competing definitions of "the public interest." Does an administrator best serve that concept through the drafting of elaborate substantive implementation protocols that strive to limit or eliminate the exercise of any independent discretionary authority? Or is a more pluralistic, process-oriented definition in order, in which the administrator best serves the public interest by facilitating participation of rival interest groups in agency decision-making?[15]

Yet another definition is suggested by advocates of the "new public administration," in which serving that interest calls upon the administrator to use his or her influence to redress perceived inequities in the power held by various client groups seeking agency assistance.[16] A fourth model is suggested by public choice theorists, who stress the importance of assessing public preferences and providing alternative, market-modeled choices for attaining those preferences.[17]

Each of these differing definitions of the public interest suggest conflicting means of exercising administrative discretion. Should administrators be merely "traffic cops" in a free-for-all competition for influence over decision-making by rival interest groups, as the pluralist model suggests? Or should administrators seek to represent the underrepresented in their decision-making, as advocated by "new public administration" commentators? Alternatively, perhaps public decisionmakers should leave to the public answers to questions such as how tough environmental regulation should be if it might mean a loss in jobs, as suggested by public choice theorists.

The point is that in instances in which there is a retreat from formal process, there must be an advance in the level of attention and reflection that administrators devote to the questions just raised.[18] These questions are (1) "how are competing criteria for legitimizing my use of power to be balanced and satisfied?" and (2) "how will the public interest best be served by the use of that power?" These questions certainly apply to an agency's use of negotiation no less than to any other form of administrative behavior—and probably more.

CASE ANALYSIS: NEGOTIATING THE CLEAN-UP OF TOXIC GROUNDWATER CONTAMINATION IN CALIFORNIA

Californians had particular cause for concern over the foundering of Superfund implementation and the EPA's legitimacy crisis in the early 1980s. Daily revelations in the national press concerning the EPA's problems were being paralleled by daily revelations in the California press regarding toxic contamination of the state's groundwater. In addition to the threat posed by the notorious Stringfellow Acid Pits to the drinking water in southern California's Riverside County, two sites in populated areas further north were causing growing alarm among regulators and the public alike.

First was the discovery of carcinogenic contamination of groundwater used for drinking on and near the property of the Aerojet General Corporation in Rancho Cordova, a suburb of Sacramento. A major aerospace research and product-development firm, the company is also a significant feature of the Sacramento-area economy. Among contaminants found in groundwater and soil (and some related surface water supplies) were rocket fuels and synthetic organic solvents used in metal cleansing.

Two years later in the San Francisco Bay Area's lower Santa Clara Valley ("Silicone" Valley—birthplace of the state's microelectronics industry) high concentrations of toxic solvents used in microelectronics manufacture began to contaminate drinking water wells in this urban area. In the early days of Superfund implementation, both the Sacramento and Santa Clara Valley area leaks were quickly added to the list of high-priority clean-up sites being created under the federal act. As the failure of closed-door informal negotiated implementation of Superfund was becoming more and more evident at the national level, northern California residents naturally grew concerned regarding the use of such approaches by federal, state, and local officials responding to problems in the Sacramento and Santa Clara Valley areas.

In reading the case studies that follow, it will be helpful to remember that the sort of discretionary decision-making situation faced by the public administrators is by no means unique to the context of California government. A recent in-depth review of the role of negotiation in Superfund implementation nationally has shown that federal, state, and regional bureaucrats across the country are now regularly called upon to engage in the kind of bargaining behavior described in the following case studies.[19] Accordingly, the policy recommendations concluding this chapter are broadly conceived, with applicability to any public administrator with the discretionary authority to set and enforce site-specific environmental health standards.

Case Studies

In examining the use of the federal Superfund legislation and California's water-quality-control legislation to regulate toxic groundwater contamination—particularly the role of negotiation—two core questions must be answered: (1) "How were these laws used to solve the problems at hand?" and (2) "Why were they used this way?" The first question is addressed below, and the second one is discussed in the following section on analysis.

The Aerojet General Case.   Sacramento-area residents first learned of toxic chemical leaks at the Aerojet General plant in Rancho Cordova in mid-1979 through an information leak from a worker at the site.[20] The Central Valley Regional Water Quality Control Board (RWQCB) initiated an investigation, which uncovered five toxic dump sites on Aerojet General's property and pervasive groundwater contamination underlying them.[21] The most prevalent and worrisome contaminants were synthetic organic solvents used as degreasing agents and rocket fuels. The regional board ordered the company to cease polluting the groundwater in June of that year.[22]

Given the enormity of the problem and the responsible party's disinclination to share information freely, the California Attorney General's Office filed suit against Aerojet General Corporation under the state's water-quality-control act (state and federal Superfund legislation not yet having been enacted) on December 27, 1979.[23] However, at the time of filing, then Attorney General George Deukmejian announced that the real purpose of the suit was to elicit information and stimulate clean-up activity. He also expressed faith in the negotiation process, citing the state's desire to "reach agreement on the problem without prolonged and expensive litigation."[24] In addition to the state action, suit was also filed by several Rancho Cordova-area residents as contaminants, allegedly emanating from the Aerojet General site, made their appearance in local drinking-water wells.

During the following year, Aerojet continued its legal resistance to the regional water board's and the attorney general's actions, while reports of worsening water quality in the neighborhood of the plant continued to come forth. Amid these developments and similar cases elsewhere in the country, in 1980 Congress adopted the Comprehensive Environmental Responses, Compensation, and Liability Act ("Superfund").[25] A year later, when the U.S. Environmental Protection Agency compiled its first Superfund-mandated list of the nation's most hazardous toxic-waste sites, it rated the Aerojet General–Rancho Cordova site as the worst in California (thirty-fourth nationally).[26]

About the same time, the state and Aerojet redoubled their negotiation efforts.[27] More active and thorough planning of clean-up activities was also undertaken, although by the end of 1981 the state had still not found the company's decontamination plan adequate.[28]

But in return for cooperating more fully in problem study, clean-up, and negotiated settlement, the company required a significant concession. Aerojet wanted assurances from the attorney general and the regional board that no information it was relinquishing on the nature and extent of contamination at its sites would be given to the public, except for public health warnings required by state law.[29] Both agencies agreed.

Unfortunately, what this meant was that during negotiation only the most alarming information was made public, as more drinking-water contamination was discovered and more wells were capped. Furthermore, all of this was happening while the national press was full of allegations that Rita Lavelle, a former Aerojet executive and current administrator of the federal Superfund program, was manipulating implementation of the law to reward political friends and punish enemies. Meanwhile Aerojet clean-up negotiations in Sacramento proceeded confidentially, while the public was occasionally confronted with facts such as the discovery that volatile organic chemicals in Rancho Cordova-area groundwater were seeping into the surface waters of the American River upstream of the city of Sacramento's drinking water intake. The press also learned at this time that Aerojet may have been aware of (but ignored) its contamination problems as early as 1954.[30]

Rumors of an impending settlement started surfacing in late 1984. But it was not until early 1986—more than six years after the state's original enforcement action was filed—that government officials and the Aerojet General Corporation finally came to agreement. Since the state suit and EPA involvement had been consolidated into one federal civil action, the settlement took the form of a consent decree, filed in U.S. District Court for the Eastern District of California on January 15, 1986.[31]

In return for the state and federal government's agreement to drop their suits, Aerojet General promised to investigate further the extent of toxic environmental contamination, define the most appropriate clean-up technologies, and take all measures necessary to remedy the public health threat at its 8,500-acre Rancho Cordova plant and immediate environs. In addition to the $27 million that Aerojet had already expended in investigation and clean-up and in future expected costs, the company's parent corporation obligated itself to provide up to $45 million more for remedial work if Aerojet went bankrupt.[32] Aerojet also agreed to pay state agencies and the EPA in excess of $7 million in past and future government investigatory and enforcement costs.[33]

Santa Clara Valley.   Located at the southern apex of the San Francisco Bay, the lower Santa Clara Valley was an area devoted to orchards and farm-land until post–World War II urbanization transformed it into a busy commer-cial and industrial center. Its largest city is San Jose, now the most populous in the entire San Francisco Bay region. Farther down the valley are Sunnyvale, Mountain View, and Palo Alto, where invention of the semiconductor and re-lated devices gave birth to the state and the nation's microelectronics industry.

About half of the valley's 1.4 million residents rely directly on groundwater as their primary drinking-water supply, while others are served by systems that import water from the Sierra Nevada Mountains or the Sacramento–San Joa-quin delta. However, these water importers pump much of their incoming sur-face supplies into the aquifer underlying the valley, as a means of low-cost storage and to recharge the water table. About 300 large wells, serving the major water suppliers, provide 86 percent of the groundwater used in the valley for nonagricultural purposes.[34]

Although a variety of commercial and industrial activities support the val-ley's economy, since the late 1960s microelectronics/data processing technol-ogy has been the fastest growing and generally the most profitable. As of 1984 there were several hundred firms in the valley involved in some aspect of re-search, development, or production of devices comprising this technology. One reason that valley residents welcomed such development is that—relative to industrial plants elsewhere in the Bay Area (like oil refineries, metalworks, and chemical manufacturers)—the microelectronics industry was fairly "clean." The only hazardous materials employed in large quantities were synthetic organic solvents used to achieve the high states of cleanliness necessary in microelec-tronics manufacture; they were kept out of public view in large underground storage tanks after use, awaiting final off-site disposal.

The first evidence that the industry might not be as clean as popularly thought came in 1981 with the discovery of high concentrations of one of these solvents in a San Jose-area public well; the chemical involved was 1,1,1 trichloroethane (TCA), a degreasing agent. The state Department of Health Services and U.S. Environmental Protection Agency advise remedial treatment of any drinking water carrying more than 200 parts per billion (ppb) of TCA;[35] the South San Jose well was contaminated with 5,800 ppb—about thirty times the depart-ment's action level.[36]

Public health investigators had suspected drinking-water contamination be-cause of an earlier discovery of a leaking underground solvent-storage tank at the nearby Fairchild Camera and Instrument Company. Soon thereafter, com-pany engineers discovered similar problems at the International Business Ma-chines (IBM) Corporation's South San Jose production facility. Since most microelectronic component manufacturers in the area used solvent-storage techniques similar to Fairchild's and IBM's, county and state health officials initiated a survey of other public water supplies proximal to all of those firms. Meanwhile, the San Francisco Bay Regional Water Quality Control Board began its own underground tank-leak-detection study among South Bay industrial plants and by 1984 had discovered a total of ninety-three contaminated sites in the Santa Clara Valley.[37] Toxic-groundwater pollution at each of these sites was serious enough to trigger regional board jurisdiction under the state water-quality act and EPA authority under the Superfund legislation.

Given the huge regulatory burden the regional board now faced, its staff resolved to adopt one implementation protocol for *all* toxic sites on the Superfund list, rather than making individual decisions on whether to negotiate voluntary compliance or take adjudicatory enforcement action in each case. The protocol adopted by the board staff was embodied in a March 1984 memorandum to the board's executive officer.[38] The protocol first identified the various implementation options available under the Porter–Cologne Act (waste-discharge requirement, cease and desist [C&D] order, clean-up and abatement order [CAO], or referral to attorney general for civil litigation). Then it recommended that as a matter of staff policy, the first action in each case should be the issuance of waste-discharge requirements. The executive officer adopted the recommendation, as did the regional board itself.[39]

This would turn out to be one of the more significant policy decisions made by the regional board. For to take any form of adjudicatory action (C&D order, CAO, or attorney general referral) would be to characterize the responsible party as a violator of environmental law. On the other hand, to issue waste-discharge requirements (WDRs) for each contaminated plant essentially meant treating each of those companies as a lawful applicant for permission to discharge pollutants into the groundwater.

Since at the time of this writing the regional board has not established WDRs for the vast majority of contaminated sites, attention is necessarily focused on the few of those that have progressed at least part way through the administrative process. Among the first sites to have WDRs established, to have clean-up plans approved by the board, and therefore to be relieved of any clean-up responsibilities more extensive than those already undertaken was the IBM plant.

Soon after discovering the underground solvent leakage, IBM on its own initiative sank several monitoring wells at its South San Jose facility to measure the intensity of groundwater pollution and the shape, size, rate of flow, and direction of migration of the contaminant plume seeping into the aquifer. The company also dug several interception wells at locations it considered to be at the leading edge of the plume, to extract the polluted water, cleanse it, and then discharge it into ditches and canals draining in San Francisco Bay.

In December 1984 the regional board issued a waste-discharge requirement ruling on the IBM case that alleviated the company of additional responsibility for defining and containing the contaminant plume beyond those measures IBM was already taking.[40] IBM and Fairchild had already spent close to $40 million in voluntary investigation and clean-up efforts, and the board noted that contaminant residues left in the groundwater—primarily traces of TCA and freon— were much lower than the "action levels" for those chemicals suggested by the California Department of Health Services as requiring remedial treatment.

Just one month later, however, a coalition of environmental organizations, labor leaders, and local governments in Santa Clara County appealed the regional board's WDR ruling on the IBM case to the State Water Resource Control Board. Charging that the regional board had not required IBM to do enough and that the board had resolved complex questions of scientific uncertainty consistently in the company's favor, appellants requested the state board to order the regional board to require more extensive monitoring and possibly to mandate more thorough decontamination of drinking water in the San Jose area.[41]

Analysis of Regional Board Decision-Making

Figure 6.1 depicts the adjudicate/negotiate decision-making situation facing both regional boards. The numbered squares represent "decision points" encountered by the regulator; the circles with uppercase letters are "chance nodes" (actions taken either by the regulated interest or by a court); and the circles within squares are "negotiation end-points" at which negotiations terminate either in agreement or adjudicatory action. The numbered triangles to the far right represent alternative decisional outcomes. The flow of events through time is from left to right.

Central Valley.   Figure 6.2 uses the decision tree to illustrate the Central Valley regional board's decision-making in the Aerojet General case. Decision point 1 occurred in the autumn of 1979. Central Valley board officials said two considerations featured prominently in their decision to refer the case to the attorney general rather than seek negotiated compliance.[42] First, the threat both to the public health (Sacramento-area drinking water) and to other beneficial uses of water was both immediate and serious. Second, the board staff thought that the apparent responsible party (Aerojet General) was not cooperating sufficiently in the provision of information or in emergency containment to constitute compliance with the Porter–Cologne Act.

But after referral to the Attorney General's Office, the state bureaucracy decision-making became more complex. The regional board essentially became the attorney general's client in this case, with the result that the regional board's decontamination strategy and the attorney general's litigation strategy inevitably began to influence each other.

The regional board desperately needed information on the identity of the contaminants, their concentration, and their direction and rate of flow through the groundwater in order to devise an effective clean-up program; the attorney general wanted the same information to prove that Aerojet had violated the law. Moreover, several private citizens and small businesses in the Rancho

Figure 6.1
Toxic-Waste Regulator's Decision Situation

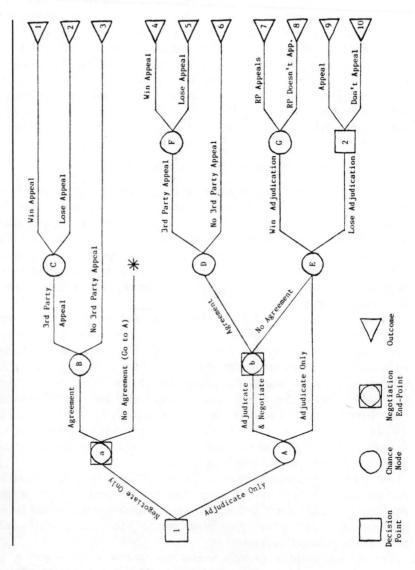

Figure 6.2
State of California and EPA versus Aerojet General Corporation (Central Valley RWQCB)

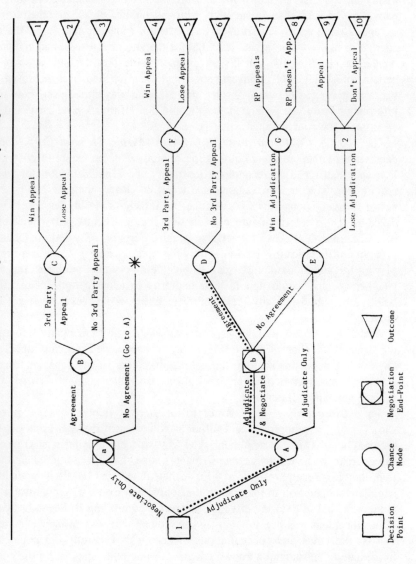

Cordova area that thought they had been harmed by groundwater contamination filed multimillion dollar damages actions against Aerojet, and they wanted access to the same information as the state.

It was within this context that the regional board and the attorney general finally agreed that, in return for the information they wanted from the company, they would share none of it with the public, press, or other litigants except as required by law to avert public health endangerment (e.g., the issuance of drinking-water advisories).[43] Since the attorney general had announced on the day he filed the suit his intention to settle out of court as soon as a certain threshold level of investigation and clean-up had been achieved, the bargaining agenda between Aerojet and the state was already set: how much information had to be generated, how would that information be used, and how clean must the contaminated water be rendered?

The *State of California and U.S. EPA vs. Aerojet General Corp.* consent decree shows that, pending culmination of studies on the extent of contamination and final clean-up technology feasibility, government negotiators would require Aerojet to render contaminated water no cleaner than the 200 ppb suggested standard adopted by EPA and the Department of Health Services.[44] When asked why this interim figure was chosen, regional board staff cited current scientific uncertainty over the adverse health effects of TCA and the technical/ economic difficulties involved in getting the water cleaner.[45] Since Aerojet was playing litigation "hardball," state enforcement personnel were also unsure of whether a court would uphold their authority to adopt a figure substantially below 200 ppb, since adverse health effects below this level have not been proven.[46]

At the time of this writing, it is unclear whether any third party will appeal the terms of the consent decree (Figure 6.2, chance node D) because the decree has not yet been finalized by the court. Since this suit is separate from the dozens of damages actions private citizens have filed against Aerojet, those private suits are still pending.

Santa Clara Valley.   In contrast to the Aerojet General case, Figure 6.3 shows a different approach and different outcomes in the San Francisco Bay regional board's IBM case. When asked why, at decision point 1, staff resolved to negotiate waste-discharge requirements rather than file an adjudicatory action, they had several responses.[47] First, they all stressed IBM's immediate and complete cooperation in identifying the source and extent of groundwater contamination and in devising effective means for controlling it. Second, the public health threat was not as grave as some other situations in their experience; that is, the kinds and concentrations of chemicals generally did not pose as immediate or substantial a known danger as some other sites under the board's jurisdiction. Third, in addition to IBM's having the willingness to do all necessary clean-up, it also had the financial ability to do so; aside from the regional board staff time involved in review of IBM's remedial investigation and

Figure 6.3
In Re IBM, Santa Clara County (San Francisco Bay RWQCB)

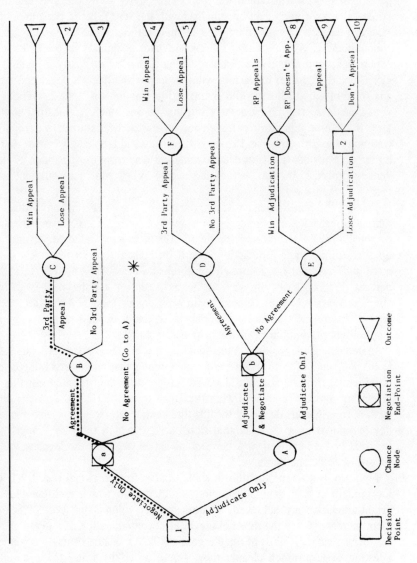

clean-up measures, the clean-up process was being conducted (in the board's view) expeditiously and at little cost to the state.

In further exploring the San Francisco Bay regional board's stated policy preference for regulating *all* Superfund sites through the waste-discharge-requirement process (in which the responsible party's engineers essentially negotiate a site-specific clean-up standard with the staff), board personnel offered several reasons. Overall, they viewed their ultimate goal as getting as much contaminant as possible out of the groundwater as quickly as possible. In their experience, setting a waste-discharge requirement was mostly a matter of regional board engineers interacting with the responsible party's engineers, whereas any form of adjudicatory enforcement action was mostly "our lawyers fighting with their lawyers." They pointed out that just as much engineering staff time goes into an adjudicatory enforcement (research, depositions, interrogatories, testimony) as in setting and reviewing waste-discharge requirements but with no tangible results (i.e., no decontamination occurring during much of the adversary process). In sum, bargaining over a WDR was more efficient and effective in their view.

Finally, the San Francisco Bay regional board staff also acknowledged institutional incapacity insofar as enforcement is concerned. Confronted with the responsibility for overseeing the nearly 100 nationally rated Superfund clean-up sites within their jurisdiction, board officials estimated that their enforcement staff was not large enough to adjudicate effectively more than about 15 percent of those cases anyway. In other words, unless the state is willing to augment massively the regional board enforcement and review staff, the success of the board's clean-up program is critically dependent on the goodwill and voluntary compliance of the responsible parties.

In defense of its position, San Francisco Bay regional board officials referred to the language of both federal and state statutes that authorize taking cost into consideration in site-specific standard setting, and they pointed out that TCA levels are already far below what the Department of Health Services and the EPA currently consider to be health threatening. Reference is also made to a device known as a "cost-degradation curve," which the San Francisco Bay regional board has used as a conceptual aid in deciding the level at which to set site-specific standards.

Figure 6.4 is a reproduction of such a curve from regional board WDR policy guidelines.[48] It generally depicts a situation in which as higher levels of decontamination are achieved, so does the per-volume unit cost of achieving them increase. Once the threshold level of decontamination of a given chemical has been reached (200 ppb in the case of TCA), board officials consider the question of how much cleaner they should order the water to be as entirely within their own discretion. For example, if in the IBM case alternative 3 in Figure 6.4 represented the 200 ppb contamination level, the San Francisco Bay board staff might set a site-specific clean-up standard at any point along the curve to the left of alternative 3. Appellants in the IBM case wanted that stan-

Figure 6.4
Sample Cost/Degradation Curve, San Francisco Bay RWQCB Staff Guidelines (March 1983)

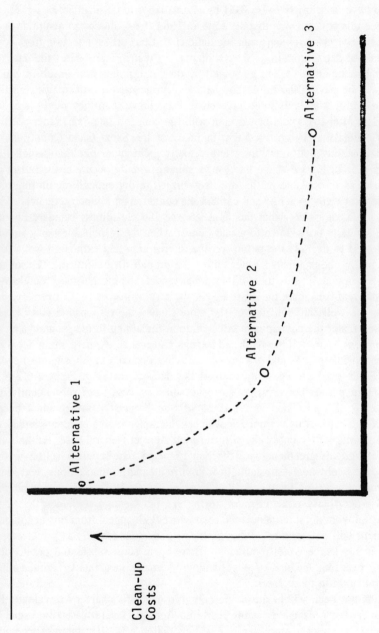

dard set at or near the alternative 1 position; the regional board in this case opted for something between 1 and 3, since they did not consider the costs that would have been imposed on IBM by alternative 1 to be justifiable.

Since this concept was first set forth in 1983 (EPA alluded to a similar construct in its 1984 drinking water regulations,[49] it has drawn attention from supporters and detractors alike. Skeptics point out that in many cases the data on per-unit treatment costs are generated by the toxic polluters themselves; since they will be paying the bills, they have every incentive to make stringent decontamination standards look more costly to achieve than they might actually be. Also, after two years of working with the concept, one San Francisco Bay board official has commented that in many of the Santa Clara County cases they are dealing with now, the curve actually looks more like that depicted in Figure 6.5. In his view, the hardest bargaining usually occurs at the outset of the case, as responsible parties are being urged to dig enough monitoring and interception wells to define and contain the contaminant plume adequately. The other principal issue—what the final site-specific cleanliness standard should be—essentially boils down to a question of when the responsible party should be allowed to turn off the pumps on the interception and extraction wells (the wells pulling contaminated water out of the ground for treatment). The longer the wells operate in this three-dimensional model, the cleaner the groundwater becomes *and* the higher the costs are for the responsible party. Conversely, the sooner the wells are shut down, the more money the responsible party saves and the greater the contaminant concentration remaining in the groundwater.

Comment.   In both the IBM and Aerojet General cases, bargaining between the responsible parties and government officials played a highly significant role in clean-up goal setting along each of the decision paths in Figures 6.2 and 6.3. Third parties not privy to the negotiation process have subsequently attacked the IBM decision as an abuse of San Francisco Bay regional board discretion, but it is as yet unclear whether Sacramento-area residents intend to challenge the settlement of the six-year-long Aerojet General case. Public mistrust of and disagreement with the San Francisco Bay board's action in the IBM case is obviously substantial, or environmental groups, unions, and local governments served by the Santa Clara aquifer would not be appealing the board order. Early press response to the Aerojet General settlement has also not been favorable; it remains to be seen whether an appeal from this negotiated judgment will be mounted, although board personnel see this as a real possibility if the decree is not modified.[50] There is, in sum, substantial public suspicion regarding the use of negotiation to remedy incidents of groundwater contamination in these cases.

It has not been within the scope or purpose of this chapter to evaluate the substance of the decisions in the IBM and Aerojet General cases but rather it has been the intent to study the role of negotiation in settling them. This study was also not designed to second-guess or criticize settlement decision-making by government officials in these cases but to offer criteria that legislative ov-

Figure 6.5
Sample Time/Cost/Degradation Curve, from San Francisco Bay RWQCB Staff Interviews (1986)

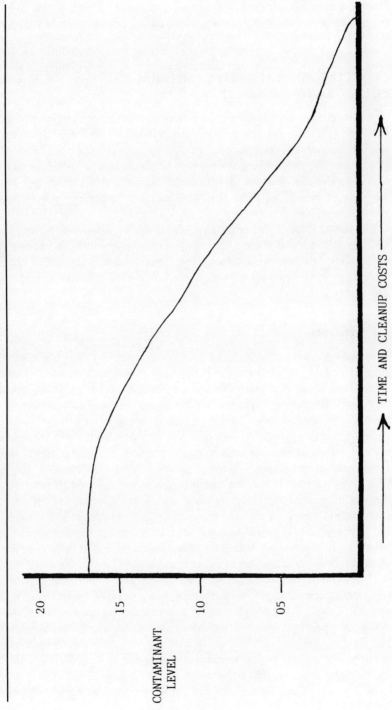

CONTAMINANT
LEVEL

20

15

10

05

TIME AND CLEANUP COSTS

erseers, senior agency personnel, and a concerned public can use to evaluate bargaining behavior by *any* agency responsible for environmental health protection in the future.

CONCLUSION: EVALUATIVE CRITERIA AND POLICY RECOMMENDATIONS

A central concern of this research (and one facing any public official using bargaining in discretionary decision-making) is how to imbue agency actions reached through informal negotiation with some of the same attributes of legitimacy that can usually be acquired only at the cost of lengthy and formalized administrative due process. As discussed earlier in this chapter and based on the work of Freedman, those attributes are constitutionality, effectiveness, responsiveness, and fairness.

The constitutionality of negotiated administrative dispute settlement is a rich and complex enough subject to warrant separate treatment in another forum, such as the law review literature. The concern here is limited to criteria for evaluating when negotiation is or is not being used effectively, responsively, and fairly.

Effectiveness

A starting point in determining whether an agency is or is not using negotiation effectively is to determine if the agency was well advised to undertake negotiation in the first place (Figure 6.1, decision point 1). When asked how they generally decide between adjudication and negotiation once they learn of groundwater contamination, regional board personnel said they take into account factors like (1) past history (if any) of board dealings with the responsible party, (2) magnitude of the contamination problem, (3) promptness of reporting contamination and responsiveness to clean-up suggestions, and (4) the responsible party's intent. If it is the first time the party has caused contamination or if it has fully and voluntarily complied with board directives in the past, if the contamination does not require an immediate and substantial public expenditure for clean-up, if the party promptly and fully reports the contamination and immediately makes a good-faith effort to clean it up, and if there is no evidence of intent to contaminate or to conceal evidence of contamination, the board staff tendency seems to be to negotiate compliance rather than opt for adversarial enforcement. Conversely, if there is a history of enforcement problems with the party, if catastrophic environmental damage is caused, if the party delays in reporting contamination or declines to make good-faith investigation and clean-up efforts, or if the party willfully or negligently contaminated the environment and attempted to conceal the problem, then (in the view of respondents in this research) adjudication is usually indicated.[51]

Ideally, the agency administrator at decision point 1 in Figure 6.1 (the initial adjudicate/negotiate decision juncture) will think through the possible outcomes involved in following either path and, based on answers to questions such as those raised in the preceding paragraph, will be able to assign rough probabilities (at each range node) for the achievement of desired outcomes via the available paths. So one criterion for evaluating an initial adjudicate/negotiate decision is whether there is a rational basis for an agency decisionmaker's judgment that there is a higher probability of achieving a desired level of clean-up through negotiation than through adjudication. Just as lawyers routinely make probabilistic estimations of their chances of winning a case if it goes to trial, so must agency personnel be capable of and ready to make rationally defensible estimations of their chances of achieving desired clean-up objectives through negotiation or adjudication.[52]

Beyond agency action taken at decision point 1 in Figure 6.1 (the initial adjudicate/negotiate decision), it is obvious from the paths traced in Figures 6.2 and 6.3 that negotiation played a significant role in both cases beyond this first juncture. Bargaining in the Aerojet General case commenced *after* an initial decision to adjudicate by the state; it was much more prolonged than in the IBM case, and it ultimately settled the case. Another important efficacy criterion, then, is the length of the time taken to achieve settlement between the agency and the responsible party, if negotiation is attempted. But in addition to a simple measurement of time from the discovery of toxic contamination to the successful conclusion of clean-up negotiations is the question of why a delay in settlement, if any, occurred. Can it be attributed to causes such as the responsible party's recalcitrance, an excessive agency caseload (insufficient personnel), or jurisdictional confusion and lack of interagency coordination?[53] So a second general efficacy criterion involves the three closely related questions of how long clean-up negotiations lasted, why any appreciable delays may have occurred, and what was done about them.

A third significant, quantifiable measurement of the relative effectiveness of agency bargaining is the site-specific clean-up standard for various pollutants achieved through negotiation. For example, there was an approximate fortyfold difference in allowable TCA concentrations at the two sites studied in this research (about 5 ppb at the IBM site and 200 ppb at Aerojet). However, federal and state officials have been careful to point out that the Aerojet figure represents an interim guideline, subject to downward revision after its investigation is completed.[54]

Fairness and Responsiveness

In determining whether an agency has negotiated a decontamination agreement in a manner that is genuinely responsive to public concerns regarding the protection of health and safety, the question of public access to information looms large. Site-specific responsiveness criteria include the answers to questions such as these: "How much was the public told about a toxic contamination incident?'' ''When?'' ''By whom?'' The same questions hold true for public information regarding compliance negotiations with responsible parties.

However, both boards in the cases studied found themselves operating in largely a reactive mode insofar as the flow of public information was concerned. As currently structured and staffed under state budget authority, none of California's regional water-quality control boards has a permanent, full-time public information or community relations officer responsible for fully informing the general public on incidents of toxic-waste exposure.

This reactive bureaucratic stance was in keeping with policy at the EPA during the tenure of administrator Burford, when the agency was making fatal budget cuts in its public participation and information programs.[55] But when William Ruckleshaus briefly reassumed directorship of the agency, one of his first moves was to establish a program to reinstate the ''fullest possible public participation'' in agency decision-making on issues such as Superfund site clean-up.[56]

In part because of this renewed budgetary emphasis, the Region IX EPA offices formulated a detailed community-involvement plan for Santa Clara Valley Superfund sites.[57] Included in this program was a million-dollar grant to the San Francisco Bay regional water-quality-control board; some of these funds were earmarked for the hiring of a temporary public information officer.

In the Sacramento area, the EPA and the state also developed an extensive program for soliciting public comment on the proposed court settlement of the Superfund enforcement suit that the agency and the state filed against Aerojet General. In this case, an additional impetus to inform and consult the public came in part from political leaders bothered by the lack of public participation earlier in the negotiation process. In response to concerns expressed by Sacramento assemblyman Lloyd Connelly to the California attorney general, the state and the EPA wrote a 120-day public comment period into the agreement, to be completed before making final the proposed settlement decree. During this time the EPA and state officials held informational workshops for the public in affected communities. When appropriate, some of these comments may be adopted as substantive modifications to the final settlement, if the state and Aerojet agree and the judge so rules.[58]

One purpose of the EPA community involvement plan was to help the regional boards shift from reactive to proactive modes of action, regarding public access to information on site-specific regulation of toxic environmental contamination.[59] But as important a criterion as the provision of timely, accurate, and unsolicited public information is, agency obligations to enhance the responsiveness and fairness of its negotiating behavior in toxic contamination cases may need to go beyond a proactive public communications effort. When significant questions of public health and safety are at issue, perhaps true responsiveness and fairness connote some form of meaningful public participation in the *making* of bargained settlements, rather than the public simply being informed of the existence of settlement negotiations before, during, or after the fact.

Thus a final criterion for evaluating the legitimacy of agency negotiating behavior concerns the degree to which agency personnel identified interested and concerned parties in the communities affected by decontamination decision-making and then attempted to integrate their participation into the decision-making process.

Exactly how concerned citizens should be involved in agency deliberations is a question that has been stirring considerable controversy and some interesting experimentation lately. In matters concerning not the cleaning up of spilled waste but the siting of new hazardous-waste-treatment facilities, both Massachusetts and California have adopted novel approaches. A recently enacted Massachusetts statute mandates bargaining between state and local government officials and would-be developers of hazardous-waste facilities over questions of plant siting and operations. If negotiations fail, the state has preemptive authority to arbitrate a final siting decision.[60]

Local preemption legislation has so far been viewed as *politically* toxic by the California legislature, and such an approach has not been adopted there—despite the best lobbying efforts of the state's chemical manufacturing and treatment industries.[61] But the state is experimenting seriously with noncoercive multilateral mediation among local and state government officials, would-be facility developers, and concerned citizen groups over new facility siting in southern California.

The supporters and critics of "environmental mediation" seem equally ardent in their views;[62] there is also a growing literature recommending additional cautious experimentation and research with this technique.[63] But Central Valley regional board personnel said Aerojet General was totally resistant to public involvement in negotiations for fear that confidentiality would be breached and sensitive information would find its way to the plaintiffs' future private suits against the company. Board officials also doubted whether most "concerned citizens" had either the technical expertise or the time to devote to a very extensive and involved negotiation process. Furthermore, the board believed that *it* was constitutionally charged with responsibility for protecting the public interest and that direct citizen involvement might well hinder rather than help the negotiation process, especially when there is pending litigation.[64]

But if simple press-release-style public information programs are put at one end of a public involvement spectrum and direct public participation in negotiations at the other, there is still plenty of room for innovative agency action in between. For instance, unless a public agency has made some binding assurance of confidentiality in bilateral compliance negotiations with the responsible party, agency officials can act as "information intermediaries." In addition to disseminating updates on settlement negotiations to the press, agency officials can (1) identify third parties (individuals, community organizations, local government officials) who believe they have the most "at stake" in settlement negotiations; (2) consult with these parties either individually or as a group as negotiations with the responsible party progress; and (3) carry any concerns or suggestions from third parties back to the negotiation process, as a way of structuring those responses into bargaining deliberations without citizens having to be present.

Different observers recommend identifying these "stakeholders" by different means, as well as acknowledging the difficulty of doing so at all.[65] One threshold criterion for consultation is certainly the ability and intent of a disaffected third party effectively to appeal a negotiated settlement if that party did not feel adequately consulted during negotiations.

In review, there are a half-dozen criteria that overseers and observers can use to evaluate the relative legitimacy of administrative bargaining with polluters over toxic-waste decontamination:

1. Based on the responsible party's behavior, was the agency rationally justified in deciding if and when to negotiate compliance rather than adjudicate?

2. How much time elapsed between discovery of toxic contamination and the conclusion of compliance negotiations? If significant delays in compliance occurred, why did they happen and how were they resolved?

3. What site-specific clean-up standards for individual toxic contaminants were adopted and implemented?

4. How thoroughly, when, and by what means did the agency inform the public both of the existence of a toxic contamination threat and of agency intent to remedy the threat through consensual means?

5. Did the agency keep the public apprised of the progress (or lack thereof) of compliance negotiations?

6. Did the agency attempt (1) to identify significant "stakeholders" (e.g., groups of concerned citizens, local government officials, community organizations) with an interest in the outcome of settlement negotiations; (2) to solicit their views and responses regarding compliance talks with polluters; and (3) to integrate those views and responses into the settlement agreement?

Taken together, these questions can provide a useful yardstick for measuring whether an agency has enhanced or detracted from the legitimacy of its use of power in conducting compliance talks with toxic polluters. For these criteria to be used effectively over time, though, requires that a data base of settled cases be established as a starting point in the comparative evaluation of future case handling—a suggestion discussed below.

Policy Recommendations

In the preceding paragraphs I suggested a series of questions, the responses to which can provide useful sources of information in the comparative evaluation of agency bargaining behavior. In conclusion, what remains to be done is to translate these evaluative standards into practical methods for enhancing the legitimacy of that behavior. Although these recommendations are necessarily based on an examination of the California cases described above, extensive research on national Superfund implementation and environmental regulation generally indicates that these recommendations are applicable not just to the specific context of these cases but also to any program implementation situation involving health protection, a certain degree of scientific uncertainty, and substantial administrative discretion in compelling statutory compliance.[66] The comparative data base, media use, and proactive public involvement suggestions made below will by no means solve the legitimacy problems identified at the outset, but they will certainly help. Furthermore, they can provide compelling evidence to the public, to legislative overseers, and—not insignificantly— to the courts that agency administrators do not perceive negotiated compliance as an abandonment of the process values embodied in adversarial enforcement.

Create a data base of cases settled through compliance negotiation. Somewhere in the case files of the agencies responsible for controlling toxic environmental contamination is site-specific information for each incident on (1) when contamination was discovered, (2) the nature and extent of contamination, (3) who the responsible party was, (4) what remedial measures were taken, (5) what site-specific, pollutant-specific clean-up standards were adopted, and (6) the time elapsed from contaminant discovery to achievement of those standards (final clean-up). Unfortunately, although part of the public record, such information is often difficult to come by and is not organized into a standardized, accessible format.

Comparative evaluation of future agency bargaining effectiveness would be made much easier if there existed a standardized reporting format for all settled cases, with data supplied for the six categories listed above. Although the circumstances of each contamination site are to some extent unique, there are likewise many similarities among them. Cooperative examination of factors like extent of contamination, standards adopted, and time needed to achieve them could provide a useful reflection on "how good a deal" an agency was able to make in compliance talks and how efficiently the bargain was monitored, once made. In addition to providing a criterion for external review, such a data base would also provide an invaluable "institutional memory" for an agency to use in monitoring its own performance and the past behavior of responsible parties. If the data show consistently rapid effective compliance by some responsible parties and consistent delay and resistance by others, agency negotiators can use this information in rationally justifying adjudicate/negotiate decisions in the future.

Use a "media report card" to update the public on agency compliance activities. Regional board personnel interviewed for this research reported that one problem with the negotiation process was its use as a delaying tactic by some responsible parties.[67] Polluters would miss deadlines for the submission of needed information and hold off on contracting for clean-up work until the failure of a negotiation seemed imminent and adjudication inevitable. Only then would they reluctantly, half-heartedly respond to agency directives in the hope of achieving weaker standards and more time.

One way for an agency to remedy this behavior without having to resort constantly to the threat of litigation is by regularly informing the public of the comparative bargaining behavior of the responsible parties with which it is working. Perhaps every thirty to sixty days agency personnel could report to local news media on which responsible parties were making good-faith efforts to follow agency clean-up directives and which ones were resisting them. In addition to keeping the public informed of the status of ongoing clean-up efforts, such a technique might persuade otherwise recalcitrant polluters that the public relations liability engendered by "poor grades" in periodic agency reports to the media might not be worth whatever benefits would be achieved through purposeful delays in compliance.

Develop an ongoing, permanent, proactive public involvement capability as an integral component of all compliance activities.   The EPA funding of the San Francisco Bay regional board's community-involvement program has certainly exerted some legitimizing influence on agency action in the Santa Clara Valley. However, the program is also posthoc (established *after* third parties appealed the IBM decision) and temporary (federal funds are running out; no state funds are budgeted). Eventually policymakers must come to grips with the fact that public involvement in informal agency action directly affecting public health and safety is not a public relations luxury to be trimmed away or deleted completely when budgets get tight. As the EPA learned in 1983, some form of effective community participation has become a virtual necessity in establishing the legitimacy of informal agency action. Retreating from the due process model of policy implementation cannot be equated with relieving the agencies of all responsibility for public notice and participation. To do so would be to undercut the very values the due process model has sought to reinforce; it would drastically erode any remaining public confidence in how public agencies use their power. Traditionally, whenever an agency loses that confidence it then finds itself subject to a major legislative overhaul.

Just what kind of public involvement is appropriate to a given agency handling a given case remains an open question. Described earlier was a public involvement continuum, with a proactive public information program at one end, direct "stakeholder" participation in informal compliance talks at the other, and the agency as an "information intermediary" somewhere in between. At the very least, it is incumbent on the agency and its overseers to recognize that *some* form of involvement is necessary and then tailor the specific form to individual cases.

What is being witnessed is a process not of retreating from the due process model but of evolving beyond it—advancing to legitimized informal action when possible and falling back on formal due process when necessary. Some of the authors cited here have discussed this ideal as the evolution from "autonomous" to "responsive" law.[68]

On a more mundane and strategic level, we are also talking about cheaper, simpler, faster ways to achieve policy involvement goals than traditional due process affords. It is clear by now that how well we succeed will depend in large part on how well agency administrators understand the ethical implications of their bargaining behavior. If ethical administrative behavior is equated with that which enhances the legitimacy of an agency's use of power, we may finally come to see that genuinely fair, responsive informal process and cost-effective implementation are not separable or discordant objectives. Ethics and efficiency are and will remain inextricably intertwined.

NOTES

1. H. Gerth and C. Mills, trans. and ed., *From Max Weber: Essays in Sociology* (New York: Oxford University Press, 1946), pp. 232–235.

2. Ibid.

3. President's Committee on Administrative Management, *Report with Special Studies* (Brownlow Report) (Washington, D.C.: U.S. Government Printing Office, 1947).

4. Federal Administrative Procedure Act, 5 U.S.C. 551 *et seq.*

5. Among the more forceful indictments of the "agency capture" phenomenon is that in T. Lowi, *The End of Liberalism* (New York: Norton, 1969).

6. J. Freedman, *Crisis and Legitimacy* (New York: Cambridge University Press, 1978).

7. Stewart, "The Reformation of American Administrative Law," *Harvard Law Review* 88 (1975): 1669.

8. Stewart, "Regulation, Innovation, and Administrative Law," *California Law Review* 69 (1981): 1259, 1338.

9. *See* Sachs, "An Alternative to the Traditional Rulemaking Process: A Case Study in the Development of Regulations," *Villanova Law Review* 29 (1984): 1505–1539; Koch and Martin, "F.T.C. Rulemaking through Negotiation," *North Carolina Law Review* 61 (1983): 175–311; Note, "Rethinking Regulation: Negotiation as an Alternative to Traditional Rulemaking," *Harvard Law Review* 94 (1981): 1871–1891.

10. Ibid.

11. *Congressional Quarterly Almanac* 39 (1983): 332.

12. "Budget Curb on Public Participation," *New York Times,* 15 June 1982, p. 26; Kurtz, "EPA Adviser Participated in Regulatory Meetings Affecting Client," *Washington Post,* 24 February 1983, p. A-3; Russakoff, "EPA Part-timer's Firm Target of Hazards Suite," *Washington Post,* 3 March 1983, p. A-2.

13. Worthley, "Ethics and Public Management: Education and Training," *Public Personnel Management* 10 (1981): 41, 43.

14. Ibid.

15. As suggested in Long, "Power and Administration," *Public Administration Review* (1949): 262.

16. "Symposium on Social Equity and Public Administration," *Public Administration Review* 34 (1974): 1–51. *See also* Miles, "Non Subservient Civil Servants," in F.

Lane, ed., *Current Issues in Public Administration* (New York: St. Martin's Press, 1978), p. 509.

17. V. Ostrum, *The Intellectual Crisis in American Public Administration* (University: University of Alabama Press, 1973). *See also* N. Lovrich et al., *Public Choice Theory in Public Administration: An Annotated Bibliography* (New York: Garland Publishing, 1983); J. Buchanan and R. Tollison, eds., *Theory of Public Choice: Potential Applications of Economics* (Ann Arbor: University of Michigan Press, 1972).

18. These four competing definitions of the public interest are summarized in Lovrich, "Professional Ethics and the Public Interest," *Public Personnel Management* 10 (1981): 87–92.

19. Anderson, "Negotiation and Informal Agency Action: The Case of Superfund," *Duke Law Journal* (1985): 261.

20. "Hundreds Warned Wells May Be Contaminated," *Sacramento Bee*, 23 August 1979, p. A-1; "Worker Tip Led to Cordova Water Pollution Discovery," *Sacramento Bee*, 25 October 1979, p. B-1.

21. "State Seeks Aerojet Toxin Data," *Sacramento Bee*, 11 August 1979, p. B-1; "First Real Proof against Aerojet General," *Sacramento Union*, 18 September 1979, p. A-3; "Study Lists Five Chemical Dumps at Aerojet," *Sacramento Bee*, 25 October 1979, p. A-1.

22. Letter to the author from Tom Pinkos, supervising engineer, Sacramento Valley Regional Water Quality Control Board, August 7, 1986.

23. "Aerojet Silence Criticized," *Sacramento Bee*, 21 November 1979, p. B-1.

24. "California Files Suit on Toxic Wastes in Sacramento County Groundwater," *Los Angeles Times*, 27 December 1979.

25. Comprehensive Environmental Responses, Compensation, and Liability Act of 1980, Pub. L. 96-510, 94 Stat. 2767; codified at 7, 16, 33, 42, and 49 USC, various sections.

26. "Federal Hazardous Waste List Names Aerojet General in First Place," *Sacramento Union*, 24 October 1981, p. A-2.

27. "Aerojet General Settlement with State Is Goal," *Sacramento Bee*, 9 May 1981, p. B-2.

28. "Aerojet Cleanup Plan Is Rejected," *Sacramento Bee*, 14 November 1981, p. B-1.

29. Interview with Tom Pinkos, supervising engineer, Central Valley Regional Water Quality Control Board, Sacramento, Calif., January 21, 1986.

30. "Warning Memos on Aerojet General Waste Disposal Date to '54," *Sacramento Bee*, 25 May 1983, p. A-1.

31. U.S. vs. Aerojet General Corp., California vs. Aerojet General Corp., *Consent Decree*. Filed Jan. 15, 1986.

32. Ibid., 133–134.

33. For a synopsis of the decree, see "EPA, State and Aerojet Settle on an Investigation and Cleanup Plan." *EPA Region IX Bulletin*, January 1986.

34. California Department of Health Services et al., "Ground Water and Drinking Water in the Santa Clara Valley: A White Paper," October 5, 1984, p. 3.

35. "EPA, National Primary Drinking Water Regulations, Volatile Synthetic Organic Chemicals," *Federal Register* 49 (June 12, 1984): 24330.

36. California Department of Health Services et al., "Ground Water."

37. Ibid., p. 9, Table 6.

38. "Regional Board Consideration of Groundwater Contamination Cases," Internal memo from Don Eisenbert and Adam Olivieri, Special Projects Section, to Roger James, executive officer, San Francisco Bay Regional Water Quality Control Board, file No. 1210.39, March 6, 1984.

39. "Waste Discharge Requirements for Hazardous Materials Cleanup: IBM Corporation, San Jose, Santa Clara County," San Francisco Bay Regional Water Quality Control Board, Dec. 18, 1984, finding No. 8.

40. Ibid.

41. Citizens for a Better Environment and Silicon Valley Toxics Coalition vs. San Francisco Bay Regional Water Quality Control Board: Petition for Review of Action and Failure to Act in Re IBM, Before the California State Water Resource Control Board, January 17, 1985.

42. Interviews with William Crook, executive officer; Paul Jepperson, supervising engineer; and Tom Pinkos, supervising engineer, Central Valley Regional Water Quality Board, Sacramento, Calif., January 21, 1986.

43. The information "blackout" did not apply to data the regional board staff gathered on its own initiative, either at or near the plant site. Letter to the author from Tom Pinkos, August 7, 1986.

44. U.S. vs. Aerojet General Corp., California vs. Aerojet General Corp., *Consent Decree*, pp. 32, 110, 118.

45. Interviews with William Crook, Paul Jepperson, and Tom Pinkos, January 21, 1986.

46. Ibid.

47. Interviews with Stephen Morse, senior engineer; Lawrence Kolb, supervising engineer; and Roger James, executive officer, San Francisco Bay Regional Water Quality Control Board, Oakland, Calif., February 25 and 28, March 7, 1986.

48. San Francisco Bay, "Regional Board Staff Guidelines . . . to Identify Water Quality Objectives for Hazardous Material Site Cleanup," March 9, 1983, Appendix, Fig. 2.

49. "EPA, National Primary Drinking Water Regulations, Volatile Synthetic Organic Chemicals."

50. Telephone interview with Tom Pinkos, supervising engineer, Central Valley Regional Water Quality Control Board, Sacramento, Calif., July 1, 1986.

51. Interviews with William Crook, Paul Jepperson, and Tom Pinkos, January 21, 1986; interviews with Stephen Morse, Lawrence Kolb, and Roger James, February 25 and 28, March 7, 1986.

52. *See,* for example, R. Behn and J. Vaupel, *Quick Analysis for Busy Decisionmakers* (New York: Basic Books, 1982), pp. 133–162.

53. Regarding coordination difficulties, *see* "Months after EPA Settlement, Ohio Cleanup Has Yet to Begin," *Washington Post,* 26 February 1983, p. A-11. According to respondents, the state/regional water boards, Department of Health Services and Region IX EPA officials have been experiencing interagency coordination problems of their own. *See* interviews.

54. Letter to the author from Tom Pinkos, August 7, 1986.

55. "Budget Curb," p. 26.

56. Environmental Protection Agency, Region IX, Hazardous Site Control Division, "Community Involvement Plan."

57. U.S. Environmental Protection Agency, Region IX, Hazardous Site Control Di-

vision, "Community Involvement Plan, South Bay Area," Santa Clara County, California, April 15, 1985. *See also* Peterson, "Ruckleshaus Tightens EPA Ethics," *Washington Post,* 20 May 1983, p. A-13.

58. Letter to the author from Tom Pinkos, August 7, 1986; U.S. vs. Aerojet General Corp., California vs. Aerojet General Corp., *Consent Decree.*

59. Ibid.

60. Ch. 508, 1980 Mass. Acts 673 (codified at Mass. Gen. Laws Ann. Chs. 210, 40A). For an explanation and discussion of the law, *see* Bacow and Milkey, "Responding to Local Opposition to Hazardous Waste Facilities: the Massachusetts Approach," *Resolve,* Winter–Spring, 1983.

61. Morell, "The Siting of Hazardous Waste Facilities in California," *Public Affairs Report* 25, no. 5. (Berkeley: University of California, Institute of Government Studies, 1984.

62. A. Talbot, *Settling Things* (Washington, D.C. Conservation Foundation, 1983); Schoenbrod, "Limits and Dangers of Environmental Mediation: A Review Essay," *New York University Law Review* 58 (1983): 1453.

63. Amy, "The Politics of Environmental Mediation," *Ecology Law Quarterly* 11 (1983): 1.

64. Interview with Tom Pinkos, January 21, 1986; letter to the author from Tom Pinkos, August 7, 1986.

65. *See* notes 61–63.

66. Anderson, "Negotiation and Informal Agency Action," p. 261.

67. Interviews with Stephen Morse, Lawrence Kolb, and Roger James, February 25 and 28, March 7, 1986.

68. P. Nonet and P. Selznick, *Law and Society in Transition—Toward Responsive Law* (New York: Harper and Row, 1978).

SELECTED BIBLIOGRAPHY

Breyer, Stephen, and Richard Stewart, *Administrative Law and Regulatory Policy,* 2d ed. Boston: Little, Brown, 1985.

Edwards, Harry, and James White, *The Lawyer as a Negotiator.* St. Paul, Minn.: West Publishing Co., 1977.

Freedman, James, *Crisis and Legitimacy.* New York: Cambridge University Press, 1978.

Lowi, Theodore, *The End of Liberalism.* New York: Norton, 1969.

Nonet, Philippe, and Philip Selznick, *Law and Society in Transition—Toward Responsive Law.* New York: Harper and Row, 1978.

Raiffa, Howard, *The Art and Science of Negotiation.* Cambridge: Harvard University Press, 1982.

Talbot, Allan, *Settling Things.* Washington, D.C.: Conservation Foundation, 1983.

Williams, Gerald, *Legal Negotiation and Settlement.* St. Paul, Minn.: West Publishing Co., 1983.

7

The Role of the Ombudsman in Resolving Conflicts

Jonathan P. West

With the growth of the modern state in this century, government agencies and officials have been given extensive powers and discretion to perform a multitude of functions and provide an increasingly complex array of services. As a result of this increased complexity, the public may experience confusion, frustration, and conflict when dealing with the government. Citizens need protection from governmental errors and misuse of power as well as an avenue for resolving their complaints against government operatives. People (as well as aggrieved civil servants) may become alienated from their government when they feel, rightly or wrongly, that it has treated them in an unreasonable, unjust, or improper manner. Numerous jurisdictions have adopted the ombudsman as an administrative reform designed to resolve grievances, to safeguard individual rights against bureaucratic power, and to aid the legislative branch in its efforts to oversee government agencies and officials.

The term *ombudsman* refers to a legally established office (created by constitution, statute, or local ordinance) led by an independent, high-level staff officer who is responsible to the legislature, who receives complaints and grievances from citizens and employees against government agencies and officials— or who takes action on his own initiative—and who is empowered to investigate and, when complaints are justified, to recommend remedial action.[1] This definition of the traditional legislative office or "classical" ombudsman should be distinguished from the more novel *executive ombudsman*. The latter refers to appointees by the chief executive (e.g., governor) who serve a term no longer than that of the official who appoints them.[2]

The ombudsman has been prescribed as the cure for the "bureaucratic threat," summarized by Larry Hill as follows: "bureaucracy's gargantuan growth dwarfs the individual; bureaucracies are politically unresponsive or inefficient; bureaucratic relationships are inherently dehumanizing; and bureaucracy enjoys strategic power advantages over the traditional governmental control devices."[3] Other "cures" or checks might help insure that public administrators do not violate their public trust. They include both internal and external checks. Ethics are thought to be internal (personal) checks, and accountability is the application of external (legal–institutional) checks on the behavior of public administrators. The ombudsman is an example of a check that is external to the individual client of government and, in its classic form, is also external to the agency providing public services. It is one of several bureaucratic monitoring mechanisms (e.g., courts, legislators, auditors, inspectors general) designed to hold administrators liable for their treatment of citizens.

Hill identified six goals of the ombudsman:

1. To right individual wrongs
2. To make bureaucracy more humane
3. To lessen popular alienation from government
4. To prevent abuses by acting as a bureaucratic watchdog
5. To vindicate civil servants when they are unjustly accused
6. To introduce administrative reform[4]

One reason sometimes given for the ombudsman institution is the inadequacy of existing mechanisms in the legislative, judicial, and executive branches for resolving grievances. The legislator's role in adjusting complaints is limited by the lack of investigative resources (funds, staff, access to information), time devoted primarily to law-making functions, and reliance upon responses from agencies or officials who are the target of the complaints. The court's role, although significant, is limited due to the expense and delay associated with litigation, the formal and adversary nature of judicial proceedings, the infrequent review of administrative acts, and the legal provisions or technicalities that may prevent the courts from hearing appeals. Chief executives (presidents, governors, mayors) or administrative agencies may process complaints, but both suffer from a lack of independence and impartiality.

As a supplement to existing institutions, the ombudsman is a source of expert and impartial aid to citizens. The ombudsman office can act quickly, informally, and inexpensively to investigate citizen complaints against government and, when justified, to recommend remedial action. The mere existence of an ombudsman office may deter bureaucratic wrongdoing and enhance citizen confidence that a watchdog is present to insure government accountability.

This chapter, like others, selectively examines a decision-making tool, in this case the experience with the ombudsman institution in states and localities in the United States. After briefly tracing the history of implementing the concept and reviewing the literature, four brief case studies are presented, two of which illustrate successful ombudsman programs, and two that are examples of programs that were tried and later abandoned. The conclusion highlights lessons learned from the cases and assesses the ombudsman as a mechanism for resolving citizen–government complaints.

BACKGROUND

Before the 1950s the ombudsman institution could be found only in two countries: Sweden, where it originated in 1809, and Finland, where it was adopted in 1919. Military ombudsman were subsequently installed in Sweden (1915), Norway (1952), and Germany (1957). In 1954 Denmark adopted a general ombudsman. The rapid diffusion of the ombudsman innovation began in the late 1950s. Groups like the United Nations Division on Human Rights and the International Commission of Jurists helped the diffusion process by sponsoring international conferences and seminars endorsing the ombudsman idea. Diffusion was also encouraged by the missionary efforts of prominent public officials, academicians, and the ombudsmen themselves. Growth in the office has continued in spurts during the past three decades. Five national ombudsman offices were established in the 1960s (New Zealand, Norway, Guyana, Tanzania, and the United Kingdom). A dozen more started operating in the 1970s: Mauritius, Israel, Fiji, France, Zambia, Papua New Guinea, Portugal, Australia, Austria, Trinidad and Tobago, Jamaica, and the Philippines. Formation of ombudsman offices also occurred during this time in many states, regions, provinces, and local government units. Ombudsmanlike functions were also being performed by a number of more specialized institutions, such as hospitals, schools, and prisons.

These growth patterns have continued into the decade of the eighties.[5] By 1986 there were more than ninety legislative ombudsman offices operating in forty countries (*see* Tables 7.1 and 7.2). The data in Table 7. 2 illustrate a key difference between the United States and other nations in the type of ombudsman offices found. Although nearly three-fourths of the ombudsman offices worldwide are located in the United States, nearly 80 percent of the *legislative* ombudsman offices (patterned after the classic Scandinavian model) are located outside the United States. Indeed, among the 340 ombudsmanlike offices in the United States, only 19 (6 percent) are of the legislative type. By contrast, a majority (56 percent) of ombudsman offices abroad conform to the classical model. The clear pattern in the United States is toward the special ombudsman/complaint handler who concentrates in functional areas (corrections, education, health services) or the general complaint handler/citizen assistance offices. Those legislative ombudsman offices that do exist in America operate exclusively at the state and local level, whereas in many nations overseas, the legislative ombudsman functions exclusively at the national level.

In the United States, four of the nineteen legislative ombudsman offices were created at the state level: in Hawaii (1967), Nebraska (1971), Iowa (1972), and Alaska (1975). Ombudsman-type offices exist in other states, but they differ

Table 7.1
Legislative Ombudsmen: Where Established

Africa	Republic of Ireland	Spain
Australia	Israel	Sri Lanka
Austria	Italy	Sudan
Canada	Jamaica	Swaziland
Cook Islands	Liechtenstein	Sweden
Denmark	Mauritius	Switzerland
Fiji	New Zealand	Tanzania
Finland	Nigeria	Trinidad and Tobago
France	Norway	United Kingdom
Federal Republic	Pakistan	United States
of Germany	Papua New Guinea	Zambia
Ghana	Philippines	Zimbabwe
Guyana	Portugal	
India	Solomon Islands	

Source: Compiled from the International Ombudsman Institute, *Directory of Ombudsmen and International Ombudsman Offices* (Alberta, Canada: University of Alberta, 1986).

considerably from these four, which are based on the Scandinavian model. Legislative ombudsman offices also exist in five U.S. counties (King County, Washington; Cuyahoga County, Ohio; Montgomery County, Maryland; Lexington-Fayette County, Kentucky; and Jackson County, Missouri), in nine municipalities (Anchorage, Alaska; Flint, Lansing, and Detroit, Michigan; New York City and Jamestown, New York; Dayton, Ohio; Wichita, Kansas; Roanoke, Virginia), and in Puerto Rico.

Table 7.3 shows a state-by-state breakdown of the most prevalent types of quasi ombudsmen found in American states and localities. Quasi ombudsmen include executive ombudsmen and ombudsmen-type offices for corrections, education, health services, and general complaint handling.[6] As previously noted, the executive ombudsman is one appointed by and serving at the pleasure of an executive officer of the government. At the local level, such officials would come under the hierarchical authority of the mayor or city manager. Executive ombudsman offices lack subpoena power, have no authorization to conduct *sua sponte* investigations, and receive no funding separate from the executive office.[7]

Purists would not consider any of the offices listed in Table 7.3 to be bona fide ombudsmen. Yet all but four of the fifty states (Alabama, Mississippi, New Hampshire, and Wyoming) have at least one type of the five quasi ombudsmen operating at the state or local level. New York has all five of them. Several states and some localities have multiple "ombudsmen" operating in different functional areas. California, for instance, accounts for 37 percent of

Table 7.2

Ombudsman Offices: Prevalence of Type in United States and Abroad

Type of Office	United States	Other Nations	Total
Legislative Ombudsmen—Federal, State and Municipal	19	72	91
Executive Ombudsmen	8	4	12
Special Ombudsmen and Complaint Handlers			
Agriculture	1	1	2
Antitrust	0	1	1
Business	3	1	4
Children's	2	1	3
Consumer	3	3	6
Corrections	15	1	16
Data	0	1	1
Education	99	2	101
Energy	1	0	1
Health Service	64	1	65
Insurance	0	1	1
Legal	0	3	3
Military	2	4	6
Police	1	5	6
Postal Service	1	0	1
Taxpayer's	1	0	1
Petitions Committees	0	11	11
General Complaint Handlers	84	9	93
Organization of Media Ombudsmen	36	8	44
TOTALS	340	129	469

Source: Compiled from the International Ombudsman Institute, *Directory of Ombudsmen and International Ombudsman Offices* (Alberta, Canada: University of Alberta, 1986).

all complaint-handling offices in the United States dealing with education and health services.

Clearly, widespread acceptance of the ombudsman concept has developed worldwide and throughout the United States in recent decades; however, the application of the concept in America has taken many forms and, in some instances, has departed substantially from patterns elsewhere. The brief litera-

Table 7.3
Distribution of U.S. Ombudsman by States (1986)

STATES	EXECUTIVE OMBUDSMAN	CORRECTIONS OMBUDSMAN	EDUCATION OMBUDSMAN	HEALTH OMBUDSMAN	COMPLAINT-HANDLERS
Alabama					
Alaska				1	
Arizona				1	
Arkansas			1		1
California		1	36	24	5
Colorado	1		4		1
Connecticut		1	1	2	
Delaware				1	
Florida	1		1	1	3
Georgia					1
Hawaii					1
Idaho				1	
Illinois			6	2	3
Indiana		1	2	2	1
Iowa			1		
Kansas		1	3	1	
Kentucky			2	1	4
Louisiana				1	2
Maine					3
Maryland				1	2
Massachusetts			2	1	4
Michigan			5		1
Minnesota		1	2	1	1
Mississippi					
Missouri			1		2
Montana					1
Nebraska			2	1	
Nevada				1	
New Hampshire					
New Jersey		2		1	4
New Mexico	1				
New York	1	2	9	1	4
North Carolina	1	1			7
North Dakota				1	
Ohio			5	2	2
Oklahoma			1		
Oregon	1	1	3		1
Pennsylvania			2	1	7
Rhode Island			1	1	1
South Carolina		1		2	3
South Dakota				1	
Tennessee	1		1	1	
Texas			2		
Utah			1	1	
Vermont				1	1
Virginia		1		1	8
Washington			4		1
West Virginia			1	1	
Wisconsin		2		4	2
Wyoming					
Dist.Columbia				2	7
Panama	1				
TOTAL	8	15	99	64	84

Source: Compiled from the International Ombudsman Institute, *Directory of Ombudsmen and International Ombudsman Offices* (Alberta, Canada: University of Alberta, 1986).

ture review that follows focuses primarily on how the concept has developed in the United States.

LITERATURE REVIEW

There is an extensive literature describing the ombudsman system and the experience of various national and subnational jurisdictions that have adopted this device. It consists of (1) basic works describing worldwide ombudsman developments, (2) important reference works, and (3) general and case-specific studies on the ombudsman in the United States. First, the most up-to-date and useful single published source is the two-volume *International Handbook of the Ombudsman,* edited by Gerald E. Caiden. The thirteen chapters in Volume 1 emphasize accountability and control in public administration with various authors analyzing the ombudsman institution, including its ideological foundations, perspectives on the evolution and role of the ombudsman, complaint-handling procedures, protection of citizen rights, and different substantive areas (information systems, health care, military corrections, higher education, public schools). In Volume 2, country surveys are provided on Australia, Canada, Denmark, West Germany, Finland, France, Hong Kong, India, Israel, Japan, New Zealand, Nigeria, Norway, the Soviet Union, Sweden, the United Kingdom, the United States, selected underdeveloped countries (India, Jamaica, Mauritius), and Western Europe (the Netherlands, Portugal, Spain, Switzerland). The section on the United States discusses American adaptations of the ombudsman concept, summarizing developments in various states, localities, and outlying U.S. areas. A worldwide perspective on the growth of the ombudsman movement is also provided in published works by Walter Gellhorn and Donald Rowat, two noted ombudsman scholars. Gellhorn's research focuses on mechanisms for the redress of citizens' grievances and experiences with the ombudsman in nine countries.[8] His public law emphasis stresses control and bureaucratic accountability. Rowat's analysis of thirteen countries describes the citizen interest served by the ombudsman, highlighting the relationship between the citizen and the state.[9]

Second, numerous bibliographies were compiled in the sixties and seventies containing several pages of references to published works on the ombudsman.[10] Third, there are a number of general articles on the ombudsman in U.S. states and local governments.[11] Descriptive case studies are available on some U.S. ombudsman offices, including those in Hawaii; Iowa; Nebraska; Alaska; Florida; Atlanta; Dayton; Buffalo; New York City; Jackson County, Missouri; Chesapeake, Virginia; and Wichita, Kansas.[12] The best single treatment of the executive ombudsman is that of Alan Wyner.[13]

In the literature on ethics and public administration, there has been a long-standing debate over whether internal or external controls are more effective in insuring ethical behavior and preventing administrative abuse of power. On one side of this debate, Carl Friedrich has argued that administrators must be re-

sponsive to two dominant factors, "technical knowledge" and "popular sentiment," if they are to be "responsible."[14] In assessing administrative responsibility, Friedrich placed little, if any, emphasis on devices that would help
insure compliance with desired standards. Herman Finer took the other side,
criticizing Friedrich's analysis by stressing the latter's neglect of institutionalized safeguards for insuring administrative responsibility. Finer warned that
"sooner or later there is an abuse of power when punitive controls are lacking."[15]

The prevailing view of contemporary analysts seems to be that administrative
responsibility can best be achieved by relying on *both* the internal ethical sensitivity of individual administrators and the external safeguards of political checks
and sanctions.[16] The ombudsman is one of several external safeguards that
seeks to achieve administrative responsibility by subjecting government actions
to the review and redress of independent and impartial authorities. The independence and impartiality of some U.S. quasi ombudsmen might be compromised if they are attached to the administrative agency or executive branch,
rather than the legislature. However, in its traditional legislative form, the ombudsman can provide a useful external check in processing complaints that
would otherwise be dealt with by an agency's own hierarchy.

In the United States, the ombudsman concept had to adapt to a political
system characterized by a federal structure of government and built on principles of separation of powers and the rule of law. Several authors have addressed some of the constitutional, legal, and political issues involved in implementing the institutional framework of the ombudsman in the United States.[17]
Relying on historical and linguistic analysis, Jon Mills asserted that the right
of a citizen to petition for redress of grievances should be seen as a separate
constitutional right distinct from other First Amendment rights and that the
right to petition is inadequately protected under our present legal system. He
contended that the need for some system of complaint handling could be satisfied by creating an ombudsman office.[18] But how should such an office be
superimposed on the existing governmental structure?

In a system that claims to allocate power among three coequal branches,
each operating to check the other, positioning the ombudsman within one particular branch could create imbalances. This dilemma has given rise to competing interpretations of the ombudsman concept in the United States. As noted
previously, the chief executive in many state and local governments has often
appointed a quasi ombudsman; however, the independence of such an official
to critique his or her political and administrative coworkers is restricted. This
weakness led Charles Burbridge to conclude that "the most effective state and
local ombudsmen are the ones most independent of the executive."[19] However, Paul Dolan pointed out that ombudsmen who directly report to the legislature may interfere with executive functions and breach the separation of powers principle when they question the actions of executive-appointed and
empowered administrative officials.[20] Another grey area has to do with the

ombudsman's power vis-à-vis the judiciary, which operates under the rule of law to oversee administrative actions. To implement an ombudsman with the independence suggested by the classical model would be like grafting on a "fourth branch" to our existing three-branch structure.

Harold Gortner observed that no one model of the ombudsman has been applied throughout the United States. Instead, a variety of institutional models exist based on two factors (legal mandate and incumbent's style) and how those factors mesh with organizational characteristics such as leadership style of the chief executive, extent of citizen participation in the public policy process, legislators' attitudes toward constituency casework, and level of government.[21] Gortner contended that applying the ombudsman concept in the American setting led to differences in interpretation because (a) it had to develop in a way that would not threaten other branches of government; (b) it could not adversely affect the powers and duties assigned to other subnational governments; (c) it could not be perceived as inferior in power or jurisdiction or as an obstacle to the efficiency of the administrative units it was investigating; and (d) it had to be installed in a way that was responsive to the needs and demands of a specific political culture.[22]

A key political obstacle inhibiting the introduction of more bona fide ombudsmen into American state and local governments is the diminution of the legislator/councilman role as an intermediary between citizens and the administration. Legislators may feel that they are already performing the ombudsman function and fear the loss of electoral benefits if they should give it up. They would undoubtedly prefer expenditures to increase their own legislative staffs, rather than create a new office to handle citizen complaints. Mills pointed out that although legislators have "clout" with bureaucracies when intervening on behalf of the constituents, they often fail to administer it uniformly by giving undue preference to political supporters over less influential constituents. Furthermore, he contended that legislators are less inclined than ombudsmen to keep a statistical record on agencies that are the frequent target of complaints, to spot trouble areas, and to recommend actions that would rectify inequitable or ineffective agency behavior.[23]

Despite political resistance, there have been, as noted, some bona fide ombudsman offices installed in state and local governments in the United States. Although most existing research on the role of these ombudsman offices focuses on the microlevel (i.e., individual dispute resolution), Hill has conducted research on the macrolevel, focusing on the classical ombudsman's role in stimulating administrative reforms.[24] He defined *administrative reform* as "those situations in which, as a result of the ombudsman's investigation, government departments make policy changes that have consequences reaching into the future beyond the particular decision complained against.[25]

Hill's longitudinally based case study examined reforms stimulated by the Hawaii State ombudsman. He found that reforms addressed the following kinds of problems: licensure, registration, and regulation; employment; prison; education; transportation; business; and taxation. When reforms were categorized as either "procedural" or "substantive," the reforms were nearly evenly split between the two. Most substantive reforms involved adopting, amending, or requiring compliance with laws, regulations, or policies. By contrast, procedural reforms involved providing information or improving convenience to the public; increasing the effectiveness of monitoring, supervising, and record keeping; improving efficiency; and facilitating interdepartmental or intradepartmental coordination.

A few empirical studies have sought to determine whether there are any operational differences between classical ombudsman offices and quasi ombudsman offices in the United States. Although it is difficult to evaluate and compare the different offices, Larry Hill and Samuel Yeager have attempted such analysis.[26]

Hill's comparative survey of the self-perceptions of ombudsmen included respondents from Scandinavian countries, British Commonwealth countries, and the United States.[27] Within the U.S. sample, he reported separately the results for classical ombudsmen and quasi ombudsmen.[28] A distinguishing feature of U.S. vis-à-vis non-U.S. ombudsmen is the content of citizen inquiries, specifically whether such inquiries are requests for provision of government services or information or requests for investigation of grievances against administrative actions. Although most non-U.S. ombudsmen deal mainly with grievances, most U.S. offices (especially classical ombudsmen) are dual purpose: processing requests for services and information as well as investigating grievances. In the U.S. sample, quasi ombudsmen are more inclined than their classical counterparts to receive requests for provision of government services or information about them than to receive requests for investigation of administrative grievances.

Differences were also evident when considering the orientation of complaint-handling offices toward clients. Although classical officials from all countries (including the United States) identified the "impartial investigator" as their primary role model, the U.S. quasi ombudsmen saw their primary role as the "enabler–facilitator." This is consistent with the finding that the intake of quasi ombudsmen is comprised more of requests for information and services than of actual investigations. In general, Hill found that most U.S. offices are reactive, making only moderate efforts to solicit complaints, with access primarily by telephone. However, the quasi ombudsmen were found to be less accessible than U.S. classical officials. Complaints in both types of U.S. offices are registered from a cross-section of society, including those who are traditionally underrepresented (e.g., the elderly, the poor, women, minorities). Few grievances deal with malfeasance; most involve alleged administrative inefficiency, and most grievances arise when citizens desire action by government that it will not approve.

Yeager's research deals with state legislators' perceptions of the ombudsman.[29] Specifically, he is interested in whether state legislators are aware of and use ombudsman offices, whether such offices are perceived to be effective by state legislators, and where state legislators get their information about ombudsmen. Yeager's sample is drawn from states with legislative and executive ombudsmen. His findings show that "legislators in states with traditional ombudsmen believe that these offices are more effective and feel more positively about them" than their counterparts in executive ombudsmen states.[30] He concluded that legislative ombudsmen are assessed more favorably than executive ombudsman because legislators are (a) more likely to be aware that they exist, (b) more likely to refer people to them when they know they exist, and (c) less likely to rely on indirect sources of information about them.

A broader study by William Pearson and Van Wigginton examined state legislators' perceptions of the effectiveness of thirteen administrative controls (including ombudsmen) applied to public bureaucracies and designed to insure administrative accountability.[31] Four of the eight states in their study had executive ombudsmen (Colorado, Florida, New Mexico, Tennessee), one had a legislative ombudsman (Alaska), and three (Alabama, Oklahoma, and Texas) had neither of these offices. The authors found that "innovative controls," such as an ombudsman and sunset requirements, ranked below traditional legislative tools like committee oversight and investigation. In fact, the ombudsman was ranked eleventh out of thirteen controls. Thus although Yeager's research suggests that one type of ombudsman (classical) is perceived by state legislators to be more effective than another (executive), this does not necessarily mean that state legislators perceive either type of ombudsman to be among the most effective of the devices used to control bureaucracies.

The empirical work of Hill and Yeager reinforces Burbridge's contention that the most effective state and local ombudsmen in the United States are the ones most independent of the executive. An oft-repeated argument for the classical approach of establishing an ombudsman office by legislation is that only on such a firm legal footing could an ombudsman be assured the independence and continuity of operation necessary for the office to accomplish its objectives.

Conclusions from the literature highlight both the pros and cons of the ombudsman device. Justifications for this approach cite its advantages as an instrument of human rights, a mechanism of democratic control over bureaucracy, an avenue for redress of grievances against administrative wrongdoing, and an instrument for tackling bureaupathologies. The device has even been referred to as the "institutionalized public conscience—the essence of what government ought to do."[32] Authors have also addressed the difficulties of adapting the ombudsman to a government having the size and complexity of the U.S. federal government, despite successes in implementing it at the subnational level. Although the ombudsman office has done many things its proponents said it would do here and abroad, they have probably oversold its merits and promised more from the device than it can deliver. Less positive observations about the ombudsman stress that the offices are little known, receive few complaints, deal with minor matters, have limited jurisdictions, may conduct superficial investigations, often become too bureaucratic, and lack political muscle.[33] The case studies that follow will help in assessing the validity of some of these claims.

CONCEPTUAL FRAMEWORK AND CASE STUDIES

The four case examples that follow include two from the state level and two from the local level. At each level, one case illustrates the successful implementation of an ombudsman office (Nebraska, 1971–1986; Dayton/Montgomery County, Ohio, 1971–1986) and one describes an instance where an ombudsman office was tried and later dismantled (Florida, 1973–1975; Atlanta, 1974–1976). The Nebraska and Dayton models have been identified as success stories in the literature and among ombudsman professionals. Both offices have a strong support base, a well-documented workload, and a breadth of focus that concentrates on case-by-case and systemic approaches to problem solving. By contrast, the Florida and Atlanta offices are labeled failures in part due to their termination after less than two years' experience. Neither of these offices were able to develop the financial or political support necessary to justify their continued existence. They lacked a firm legal foundation and were unable successfully to differentiate their services from those of other complaint handlers.

The following dimensions are used as a conceptual lens to discuss each case:

—The origins of the office
—The basis for the ombudsman's legitimacy and appropriations
—The organizational characteristics and focal concerns of the office
—The nature of its workload
—The extent of its political support
—Any unique features of the office that provide insights into its operations

Although the four cases vary in the degree to which they conform to the traditional model, they resemble the legislative ombudsman more than the executive ombudsman. Thus the cases illustrate a variety of experiences with the institutional form assessed as most effective in the fragmentary empirical literature. After examination of the cases, common themes and lessons learned from experiences with the ombudsman in these jurisdictions are identified.

Nebraska

Nebraska's ombudsman office is patterned after the original Scandinavian model. This case illustrates the crucial link between legislative support and ombudsman activities, the perceptions of the public and legislators of ombudsman functions, and the vulnerability of even the most successful ombudsman offices to pressures for reduced budgets. Freshman Senator Loran Schmit successfully sponsored ombudsman legislation in the 1969 Nebraska legislature. He was able to overcome objections (e.g., cost, legislators' desire to serve as ombudsmen, concern over agency prerogatives, and uniqueness) by stressing the need for a new channel to redress citizen grievances and humanize government. Legislators with limited staff support were assured by proponents that the ombudsman would reduce their workload by assisting with legislative oversight and citizen complaints.[34]

The Public Counsel Act states that the jurisdiction of the ombudsman covers all state agencies. The ombudsman is nominated by the Executive Board of the Legislative Council and approved by a two-thirds vote of the legislature to serve a term of six years. The public counsel (ombudsman) was envisioned as an independent officer subject to removal, for good cause, only by a two-thirds vote of the legislature. The office has broad investigatory powers that include authority to question state agency officials and employees, access to agency records, and subpoena power. Findings and conclusions related to citizen complaints can be published, action recommendations can be made to agencies, and studies or inquiries unrelated to specific citizen's complaints are authorized.[35]

Two ombudsmen have occupied this office: Murrell McNeil, a former army officer and state tax commissioner, served from June 1971 to July 1980; Marshall Lux, formerly the senior deputy ombudsman, has served since that time. From 1971 to 1979 the office functioned with a very small staff. In 1979 a deputy public counsel for corrections was appointed. Currently, the staff consists of four full-time and three part-time employees.

The Nebraska Ombudsman Office, in contrast to that in Florida, has emphasized the resolution of individual complaints more than formulation of general recommendations about increasing the effectiveness of state government services. The workload of the Nebraska ombudsman from 1971 to 1985 is summarized in the table on page 182.

The increase in the workload in 1979 resulted from implementation of the correctional ombudsman program and installation of a toll-free telephone line.[36] In 1984, caseload statistics were maintained by use of a computer for the first time.

In 1985, 70 percent of total inquiries were complaints; 30 percent were requests for information. Of the complaints, 8 percent were justified, 8 percent were partially justified, 26 percent were unjustified, 14 percent were discontinued, and 4 percent were outside the ombudsman's jurisdiction. The citizens contacting the ombudsman were more likely to be male, residing in the metropolitan areas of Lincoln and Omaha, with family income and education levels exceeding the average statewide. Complainers also differ from the general public in political attitudes with the former showing lower levels of political efficacy and higher levels of cynicism.[37]

Two independent public surveys were conducted in 1981 that provide interesting evidence relating to Nebraska's ombudsman office.[38] The first survey

Year	All Contacts	Complaints	
		Number	*Percent*
1971 (7 mo.)	383	223	58
1972	809	480	59
1973	579	383	66
1974	560	375	67
1975	701	467	67
1976	653	465	71
1977	679	513	76
1978	601	432	72
1979	945	746	79
1980	971	799	82
1981	986	790	80
1982	1,043	780	75
1983	1,008	743	74
1984	1,111	770	69
1985	1,115	852	70

was a statewide telephone poll of 945 people with questions about their awareness of and access to the office. The results were mixed. Six out of ten respondents were not familiar with the term *ombudsman,* and only half of those who claimed familiarity with the word could give a correct or partially accurate explanation of its meaning. Of the 20 percent who were familiar with the term, nearly three-fourths of them knew that Nebraska had an ombudsman. However, a very small percentage (14.4 percent) of the 945 respondents were aware that Nebraska had an ombudsman. This survey did find that 71 percent of those surveyed thought Nebraska needed an ombudsman. The second survey was limited to a sample of persons who had contacted the Nebraska ombudsman with a complaint in 1980. The results were more positive: nine out of ten respondents thought the ombudsman concept was a good idea, and 87 percent thought that Nebraska needed an ombudsman. Although only half of those surveyed agreed with the ultimate decision on their complaint, more than 80 percent of them were satisfied with the treatment they had received from the office.

The two surveys combined show that few Nebraskans are aware of the office but that there is support for the ombudsman concept and a sentiment that Nebraska needs an ombudsman. This opinion is most evident among citizens who have used the office. Thus the office performs functions that are perceived by citizens to be needed and by users to be performed satisfactorily, but the lack of public awareness of the availability of assistance from an ombudsman accounts in part for underuse of these services. Nevertheless, Marshall Lux foresaw increased use and improved operation of the office by pursuit of four broad strategies: (1) intensifying the outreach efforts, that is, increased distribution of pamphlets, public service announcements, and so on; (2) centralizing the information and referral services of Nebraska state government in the ombudsman's office; (3) viewing the ombudsman's office as one component of the legislative oversight apparatus for reviewing the performance of state agencies and programs and conducting extraordinary investigations; and (4) initiating quality-control activities to make follow-up contact with former complainants assessing their satisfaction with the office's disposition of their case and determining whether subsequent problems arose after their case was closed.[39]

In the fall of 1985, the Nebraska legislature faced a financial shortfall requiring a 3 percent cut in the state budget. The Legislative Appropriations Committee recommended completely eliminating the ombudsman's office as a cost-cutting measure. After extensive debate and by a bare majority, the proposal to eliminate the office was defeated. The floor debate on this issue (a forty-five page transcript) provides a legislative perspective on the pros and cons of the ombudsman during its fifteen-year existence.[40] Proponents argued that the ombudsman was a guardian of the public interest, a timesaver for legislators, a repository of expertise, an effective office with an increasing workload, a place where people can go "who have problems with government and don't know where to turn," a source of accurate research on citizen problems and a curb on bureaucratic arrogance. Those opposing continued funding for the office contended that the increased legislative and committee staff made the ombudsman office superfluous. "If there are 49 senators doing our job, why have an ombudsman?" was a subject of recurring debate. One senator cited the low proportion of justified complaints (9 percent in 1984) in support of his contention that this is an office "that we can no longer afford."[41] A key issue was whether the benefits of the program were worth the quarter of a million dollars spent annually to fund the office. Proponents thought it ironic that in an act of "supposed efficiency," they were considering "cutting out an office that helps the entire government to be more efficient."[42] Although the office survived, it did so with no votes to spare, and it was the only state agency that had been recommended for termination. This debate underlines the vulnerability of ombudsman programs during times of budgetary retrenchment.

In summary, Nebraska was a pioneer in creating a state ombudsman office. The public counsel conforms to the classical model with an office created by state law, led by an independent official who is empowered to receive and act upon citizen complaints. The office's well-documented workload is comprised primarily of complaints against government agencies. Complainers are typically urban males who have higher than average education and salary but whose attitudes are more cynical and less politically efficacious than those of the general public. Opinion surveys demonstrated the need for outreach efforts by showing the public to be unfamiliar with the term *ombudsman* and unaware that Nebraska had such an office. However, among users of the office, most favored the ombudsman notion, though that such an office was needed, and expressed satisfaction with their treatment. Legislative budget deliberations highlighted the pros and cons of the ombudsman office from the politician's viewpoint and underlined the need to justify continued funding for such a program and to mobilize political support when cutbacks threatened.

Florida

The Florida case features an alternative to the Scandinavian model where an ombudsmanlike program served the Florida State Senate during a brief eighteen-month period in the early seventies.[43] This innovative rather than traditional approach to the ombudsman function illustrates the use of the computer to aid in the oversight and constituent-service function of the legislature, the importance of establishing long-term political support for the ombudsmanic innovation, the utility to the legislature of an improved ombudsmanic function, and the spin-off effects that can result from such an office.

Mallory Horne, president of the Florida Senate, told his fellow senators in 1973 that the Senate Government Operations Committee would provide a "version of an ombudsman service" to those senators who wanted to participate. He initiated this innovation in June of that year (by proclamation rather than by legislation) because the time-consuming task of dealing with citizen complaints was a concern for senators, and the practice of resolving these problems on a case-by-case basis meant that senators were without crucial data for program evaluation of administrative units. Horne was hoping to increase the policy-making capacity of the legislature and to improve the management of oversight and constituent service. Six months after the Florida Senate ombudsman program was initiated, it was modified significantly so that services could be offered not only through the intervention of a senator but also directly to the public.

Unlike the notion of the traditional ombudsman who serves as a citizen advocate seeking to resolve citizen complaints, the Florida Senate ombudsman program sought to use citizen complaints as a means of identifying problem areas within state government. Such data would enable the Senate to assess the effectiveness of state agencies in responding to justifiable citizen complaints about government services. The ombudsman program acted as a clearinghouse serving both citizens and senators by processing complaints and requests related to state government service delivery.

A staff of five persons responded to inquiries by telephone (two toll-free lines), letters, and personal visits. In resolving problems, the staff made direct contact with the agency in question. Two computerized indices aided their efforts: the first listed the name, position, address, and telephone number of key people in each of the three branches of state government; the second listed the person in charge of each function of state government, the statutory authorization for each function, and the organizational unit charged with responsibility for carrying it out.

The ombudsman staff kept records on agency response time in dealing with citizen complaints and inquiries. The office file systems were computerized enabling the staff to conduct various analyses. Such analyses helped the staff to discern trends and identify areas of administrative inefficiency that could be called to the attention of relevant legislative committees. To identify problem areas in state government and evaluate agency effectiveness in responding to citizen complaints, the staff examined the number of inquiries received, the seriousness of the inquiry, the lag time in processing it, the inability of the agency to carry out its functions, and the accuracy of information provided by the agency.

By processing individual inquiries (microlevel) the office became aware of institutional problems (macrolevel) in the various departments, divisions, and bureaus of state government. For example, dredge and fill permit problems were detected because of the lengthy time elapsed in processing applications. Similarly, motor-vehicle title and license problems were revealed by the high volume of inquiries documenting instances of managerial inefficiency and error. The highest number of inquiries processed by the office were in the areas of mobile homes, energy, welfare and health, insurance, license-tag and refund delays, food-stamp-dispersement problems, unwritten rules for postaudit of financial accounts, staffing problems, and improper procedures for handling claims. Significant problem areas were reported to legislative committees or executive agencies for appropriate action.

In 1974, 5,563 inquiries were received from legislators, their staffs, and citizens. Slightly more than half of these inquiries (2,971) were processed by the ombudsman, whereas others (2,592) did not come under state jurisdiction. On the average, 22 calls were received daily. Of them, 10 fell outside the jurisdiction of state government and the remainder were accepted and sent to the relevant state agency for processing. The direct cost of offering the ombudsman service in 1974 was $56,873, and the direct expense for receiving and responding to the 5,563 inquiries for the year was $10.22 per inquiry.

During the first half year of its existence, the Senate ombudsman program responded to all inquiries through a senator. By serving legislators exclusively, the program enabled elected senators to serve their constituents better. Ironically, the program's initial success led to a change that helped contribute to its eventual demise. In early 1974 a decision was made by the Senate president to alter the program by providing services directly to the public, thereby circumventing individual legislators. However, the legislators lost political benefits when citizens were allowed to go directly to the ombudsman to receive help that senators had previously provided. Thus the ombudsman office may have been viewed by senators as an unwelcome competitor.

The Florida Senate ombudsman program was terminated in January 1975 by the newly elected Senate president. Four reasons were given for this action: (1) the need to reduce the cost of state government and of the legislature; (2) the parallel role of elected state legislators in responding personally to constituent complaints; (3) the establishment of other citizen complaint offices in state agencies formed after the Senate program had begun; and (4) the replacement of the previous Senate president who originated the program with a new solon chief who said, "It isn't my program." The overriding concern in the program's termination was the need for cuts in an austerity budget.

Florida is an example of one state in which executive ombudsmen were created after the formation of a legislative ombudsman. Soon after initiating the state Senate's office, at least three administrative departments created their own ombudsman offices. After the demise of the legislative ombudsman, efforts to reestablish it encountered administrative resistance; however, there was some support for an executive ombudsman in the office of the governor. A few years later, a citizens' assistance office with ombudsmanlike functions was included as part of a massive reorganization package being proposed by the governor's office. The bill was approved in 1979 with the overwhelming support of both houses of the state legislature.[44] The office has maintained a low profile, since then sidestepping conflicts with politically powerful figures in the state and concentrating on its complaint-handling function.

In sum, Florida's short-lived Senate ombudsman office shared some of the classical ombudsman's characteristics but lacked the firm legal footing and broad political support necessary to forestall the budget ax. The focus on macrolevel concerns (administrative performance and reform) took priority over microlevel matters (individual dispute resolution) from the outset. Despite the development of an impressive data base for diagnosing administrative agency problems, the innovative use of computers to aid in processing citizen inquiries, and the support provided to legislators in carrying out their casework function, the office was abandoned after eighteen months in response to strong fiscal pressure, loss of legislative support (due to diminished electoral benefits), overlap in functions with other governmental units, and the close identification of the program with the declining political fortunes of one well-known public official. Eventually, gubernatorial support for the executive ombudsman filled the gap left by the aborted legislative office.

Dayton–Montgomery County

The Dayton ombudsman is in many ways similar to the classical model, but it is not based on a statute; rather, it requires the voluntary support of the city, county, and school board.[45] The Dayton model illustrates the need for a broad funding base, the operation of an ombudsman having multijurisdictional responsibility, and the use of the office to resolve both case-by-case problems and problems that are more systemic.

Graham Watt, city manager in Dayton in the sixties, identified the need for a citizens' appeals officer to work out of his office. His proposal to fund such a project was approved by the U.S. Office of Economic Opportunity (OEO) in 1970 as an "innovative demonstration" grant. Watt left the scene, but his successor as city manager, James Kundle, supported the notion of a complaint office, renaming the citizens' appeals officer as the ombudsman. Instead of having the ombudsman report directly to the city manager, Kundle thought it was more appropriate for the ombudsman to report to a community-based board, thereby strengthening the independence of the office. He also suggested that the ombudsman's jurisdiction be expanded to include not only the city of Dayton but also the Dayton Board of Education and Montgomery County.

Eventually (1972), a nonprofit corporation (Joint Office of Citizen Complaints [JOCC] was formed with a nine-member board—three members each from the county, city, and school board. Four of the nine members are elected public officials. The ombudsman is selected by the board. The independence of this position is strengthened by a management-agreement contract that states the purpose of the office, the ombudsman's functions, and the limitations on interference by the board. If the ombudsman defaults on stated responsibilities, she or he can be terminated by a two-thirds vote of the board.

Grants from the OEO and the Kettering Foundation expired in 1973, leading to some concern about the office's future. But recurring contributions from the city of Dayton, Montgomery County, the Dayton School Board, the United Way, and others insured continuation of the office. Two people have served as ombudsman in the fifteen years of its existence: Ted Bingham, a newspaperman with the *Dayton Journal Herald,* who served from March 1971 to July 1973, and Bonnie Macaulay, vice-mayor of Oakwood and former chairperson of the council of governments, who has served since then. Both people were intimately familiar with the area's problems. In 1979 a nursing-home ombudsman program was instituted as part of the office to help nursing-home residents resolve problems.

The ombudsman budget for 1985 totaled $160,000, with the three sponsoring jurisdictions and the United Way as the principal contributors. The nursing-home ombudsman's 1985 budget totaled $73,601.

Two methods are used by the JOCC in resolving citizen complaints: the individual case method and the systemic approach. In 1985 there were 13,207 inquiries, of which approximately 2,091 were "cases" (i.e., complaints requiring staff investigation and research). The remaining 11,116 inquiries were of the "information and referral" type in which citizens needed to be directed to the appropriate agency.

The JOCC annual report classifies cases into eight main categories: city, county, school board, health district, state government, federal government, miscellaneous, and nursing-home ombudsman. According to the 1985 report, complaints involving housing inspections and inspection services comprised 34 percent of all complaints about city agencies. Five subcategories relating to welfare benefits—emergency assistance, food stamps, aid to families with dependent children, welfare eligibility, and general relief—accounted for 75 percent of all complaints about county agencies. Complaints about the Bureau of Motor Vehicles and the attorney general (consumer) comprised 54 percent of all complaints about state agencies. More than half (52 percent) of all complaints about federal agencies dealt with social security. These caseload data show that a relatively small number of public health and welfare agencies account for most of the complaints handled by the ombudsman and that many of the people contacting the office are in the low- and fixed-income brackets. If such an office did not exist, these citizens' complaints might go unaddressed.

In dealing with macrosystemic problems of the bureaucratic structure rather than individual case resolution, the JOCC seeks results through institutional change. These problems must be researched, their significance must be explained to key agencies and individuals, and recommendations for action must be made. One example of response to a macroproblem occurred as a result of numerous complaints to the Water Department about extraordinarily high water bills. This led to research by the JOCC and three recommendations: (1) to create a Water Review Board of appeal for citizens with high water bills empowered to make adjustments when appropriate; (2) to relocate the Water Revenue Division from the Finance Department to the Water Department; and (3) to have real estate agents take action to insure that new purchasers of property are not responsible for the unpaid water bills of former owners.[46]

The Dayton case illustrates another variation of the classical model in which a management contract approved by the community-based board of a nonprofit corporation grants legitimacy to the office and guarantees its independence. After a shaky start when grants from the federal government and foundations dried up, the office developed a solid and diversified funding base for continued operations. Comprehensive annual reports provide evidence that the office uses both microapproaches and macroapproaches to problem solving. At the microlevel, individual complaints are investigated and resolved, or information and referral inquiries are processed; at the macrolevel, institutional reforms are initiated. The volume and nature of complaints lodged at the city (housing inspections), county (welfare benefits), state (consumer), and federal (social security) levels suggest that the ombudsman is providing valuable assistance to a significant number of needy citizens.

Atlanta

The brief existence of the ombudsman office in Atlanta illustrates the importance of developing a persuasive rationale for the office, the need to establish the office on a sound legal basis, the requirement of well-honed political skills for an ombudsman, and the vulnerability of the office to changing economic and political fortunes.[47]

Under the sponsorship of State Representative William Alexander, a longtime proponent of an ombudsman office for Atlanta, the Georgia General Assembly passed House Bill 85 in 1974 as local legislation, applying exclusively to Fulton County (Atlanta). Subsequently, the validity of this act was questioned by an Atlanta City Council member concerned about "home-rule" provisions. The City Attorney's Office advised that the state act to create a local ombudsman did violate municipal home-rule legislation and that the same objective could be achieved if the Atlanta City Council passed a local ordinance. Such an ordinance was adopted by the council and signed by the mayor, thereby creating the office. However, within two years of its creation, the office was terminated when the City Council voted against appropriating funds to continue Atlanta's ombudsman operation.

Two men served as ombudsman in Atlanta: Calvin O. Carter from May to August 1974; Percy L. Harden from late August 1974 to March 1976. Both men had previous experience on the Atlanta mayor's staff, but they differed in their enthusiasm for the ombudsman job and their skills in carrying out their responsibilities. Despite having many acquaintances in Atlanta government, Harden lacked managerial skills and failed to develop a strong political base for the office.

Assisting the ombudsman was a staff that eventually included a deputy ombudsman, a secretary, two university student interns, and three Comprehensive Employment Training Act (CETA) employees. The office was given a small budget; 1974 expenditures were $35,887 (annual rate = $47,729); 1975, $53,377; and 1976, $14,175 (annual rate = $56,700).

Once staffed and funded, the office began to handle citizen complaints and inquiries. Caseload data are reported below:

Year	All Contacts	Complaints	Information
1974 (May–December)	1,243	461	732
1975	2,026	1,041	985
1976 (January–February)	195	147	48

The office was used by both white and black citizens from all sections of the city. Although both haves and have-nots registered complaints, middle-class complaints predominated.

Several other agencies and offices in city government had powers and duties similar to those of the ombudsman. These units, their functions, and their constituencies are listed in Table 7.4. Furthermore, the small staff of the City Council handled constituency requests and complaints for each council member.

The death of the ombudsman office occurred early in 1976 when the City Council terminated appropriations for it on a ten to eight vote. This followed a previous four to three vote by the Council Finance Committee to terminate the ombudsman office.

Why was the program terminated at this time and in this way? Three public and two private reasons can be identified for the action: (1) the office was an unnecessary duplication of other city agencies; (2) financial cuts were necessary; (3) City Council members and the mayor could handle constituent complaints without aid from an ombudsman. Covert reasons were more crucial to City Council members. They included: (1) the sentiment that the incumbent

Table 7.4
Existing Agencies in Atlanta Performing Functions Similar to Those
of the Ombudsman

Agency/Office	Function	Constituency
Community Relations Commission	investigates civil rights and housing discrimination complaints	civil rights organizations
City Service Coordinator	represents the mayor to neighborhoods troubleshoots on city services for the Mayor	Mayor
Dept. of Public Safety—Bureau of Internal Investigation	investigates complaints against conduct of public safety officers	police officers
Office of Consumer Affairs	deals with consumer complaints	Council members who created it
Department of Administration--Affirmative Action Office	deals with complaints about employment discrimination	public employees

ombudsman had not developed the political support necessary to justify continuation of the ombudsman office; and (2) the four to three vote of the Council Finance Committee to fund the office of consumer affairs but not the office of ombudsman. The ombudsman was the more expendable of the two units because of its lack of strong vocal supporters.

At the Council Finance Committee's final public hearing on the budget, vocal constituencies appeared to lobby for continued funding of other agencies. However, the ombudsman lacked clients with clout willing to speak up for renewed funding. The majority vote refusing appropriation of funds terminated the office. Although the ordinance is still in existence, the office closed on March 1, 1976.

The Atlanta case would seem to confirm one claim of ombudsman critics: that such offices often lack political muscle. Although ombudsman offices in general have a politically weak clientele, Atlanta's office was especially vulnerable at budget-cutting time because of the inability of the incumbent ombudsman to develop a strong cadre of politically influential supporters, the duplication of functions with numerous other agencies, the constituency services provided by elected politicians, and the absence of backing for the office itself. It also shows that without the legitimacy conferred by a strongly worded authorizing statute, a local budget decision (disapproving appropriations) can constitute an important policy decision (to terminate an agency) that can override the relatively weak authorization of a local ordinance.

CONCLUSIONS

Several general observations can be made based on these brief cases.

1. In each case the ombudsman idea was introduced by a single individual who was committed to the concept. In Nebraska a junior senator put the issue on the legislative agenda, and in Florida the idea was advocated by the president of the Senate. In Atlanta the initiative again came from a state representative, and in Dayton it was the city manager who provided the necessary leadership to get things started.

2. Cost concerns were evident in each instance. In Nebraska and Dayton the innovation was made possible, at least in part, by the availability of federal OEO funding. In both Florida and Atlanta, the principal reason cited for the program's termination was the need for budget cuts. Such concerns almost led to the demise of the Nebraska Public Counsel's office in 1985 and threatened the continued existence of the Dayton ombudsman in the early seventies once federal funding ceased.

3. The cases showed that development of political support is crucial if ombudsman-type programs are to survive. Nebraska's ombudsman office was able to survive in 1985 because of its powerful supporters within the state legislature who rallied the necessary support when economy cuts threatened the office's continued existence. Such support was lacking among Florida senators and Atlanta city councilmen when austerity budgets led to termination of both ombudsman programs.

4. The ombudsman is vulnerable to being misunderstood by its potential supporters or being viewed as a threat by other governmental units. Public surveys in Nebraska showed little public awareness of the term *ombudsman* and demonstrated the need for outreach efforts. Additionally, a clear rationale needs to be developed that distinguishes the ombudsman from other existing citizen-grievance mechanisms. This was seen to be especially important in the Atlanta, Florida, and Nebraska cases where the ombudsman functions were perceived as overlapping or duplicating those of other agencies, jurisdictions, or elected officials.

5. The basis for each office's legitimacy and appropriations varied. Nebraska's Public Counsel Office conforms most closely to the traditional Scandinavian-type model based on state legislation. The Florida program was especially vulnerable since it originated as a proclamation issued by a short-term elected official. In Atlanta the office was based on a local ordinance, and in Dayton the office was established by organizing a nonprofit corporation, executing a

management agreement, and securing commitments for multijurisdictional appropriations.

6. Ombudsman offices varied in the emphasis given to case-by-case resolution of individual citizen complaints versus systemic approaches that use citizen complaints as indicators of bureaucratic malfunctions requiring institutional change. The Atlanta ombudsman was more oriented to the former, the Florida program to the latter, and the ombudsman in Nebraska and Dayton have sought to incorporate both approaches.

7. Ombudsman offices receive complaints from citizens who come from a range of socioeconomic backgrounds. In Nebraska, complainers were relatively high in socioeconomic status. In Atlanta, middle-class complaints were most prevalent, and in Dayton, most of the complaints were filed by those in the low- and fixed-income category.

8. The Florida case suggests that creation of executive ombudsman offices can be prompted by experience with a legislative office. The very act of creating a legislative program may stimulate spin-off programs in the executive arena that increase the responsiveness of the government bureaucracy. Although the legislature was considering whether to continue the state Senate office, several agency ombudsmen were being established. Then a few years after the demise of the legislative ombudsman, an executive ombudsman was established in the governor's office. The reverse can also occur. In Iowa, for example, a legislative ombudsman was created to replace an executive ombudsman.

How does this chapter on the ombudsman relate to some of the larger ethical issues covered in this volume? The ethical performance of public administrators refers to more than avoidance of overt financial corruption; it also refers to actions in which the public's welfare, rather than some narrow outlook (e.g., showing favoritism to particular groups, distorting the meaning of laws, formulating confusing regulations, making decisions based on selfish interests), is advanced by public servants. In recent years, public administrators have had a more significant impact on the lives of citizens, and the potential for administrative abuse based on narrow outlooks has increased. As a result, citizens may not be given their due in bureaucratic encounters, and administrative wrongs may need to be made right.

The ombudsman is one mechanism for dispensing administrative justice— insuring fair, equitable, impartial treatment for those harmed by bureaucratic wrongdoing—and stimulating administrative reform. Some writers contend that public maladministration might be reduced as administrators seek to apply ethical principles of behavior (e.g., avoiding conflicts of interest, striving for professional excellence, exercising discretion in the public interest) bolstered by specific guidelines for ethical action (e.g., using regime values, delivering neutral service to elected officials, instilling ethics in organizational arrangements, defining unethical behavior as conflicts of interest).[48] But exclusive reliance upon internal ethical checks on bureaucracy, without simultaneous emphasis on external checks such as "overhead democracy" and the ombudsman, places a great deal of faith in administrators and may reduce the chances for clients to experience administrative justice.

The steady growth of the ombudsman movement here and abroad in recent decades suggests that such offices are more than a passing managerial gimmick and that with some Yankee ingenuity they will likely continue to be successfully adapted in various forms in U.S. state and local governments.[49] Although assessments in the literature indicate that classical ombudsmen differ from executive ombudsmen in important ways—the former being more effective, accessible, and likely to mesh successfully the elements of their dual role as a complaint handler and a satisfier of requests for information and public services—the case examples suggest substantial variation among legislative ombudsmen and the precarious, sometimes wavering support of even the most successful offices. Given firm political backing and the capacity for independent action, the ombudsman can be a useful supplement to existing mechanisms for resolving citizen–government complaints; however, its activities must be buttressed by other control devices if citizen's rights are to be safeguarded and bureaucratic accountability is to be insured.

NOTES

1. Other pertinent definitions, somewhat similar to this, can be found in Donald C. Rowat, ed., *The Ombudsman: Citizens' Defender* (Toronto: Toronto University Press, 1968), p. xxiv; Bernard Frank, "The Growth of the Ombudsman Movement" (Unpublished paper, Allentown, Pa. 1977).

2. *See* Alan J. Wyner, ed., *Executive Ombudsman in the United States* (Berkeley: Institute of Government Studies, University of California, 1973).

3. Larry B. Hill, *The Model Ombudsman: Institutionalizing New Zealand's Democratic Experiment* (Princeton, N.J.: Princeton University Press, 1976), p. 8.

4. Ibid.

5. International Ombudsman Institute, *Directory of Ombudsmen and International Ombudsman Offices* (Alberta, Canada: University of Alberta, 1986); Gerald E. Caiden, ed., *International Handbook of the Ombudsman* (Westport, Conn.: Greenwood Press, 1983), p. 11.

6. Quasi ombudsmen are complaints officials who share many of the classical ombudsman's characteristics but lack one or more structural elements considered essential to the office. *See* Larry B. Hill, "The Citizen Participation–Representation Roles of American Ombudsmen," *Administration and Society* 13, no. 4 (February 1982): 408.

7. *Sua sponte* investigations are those initiated on the ombudsman's own will or motion, without prompting or suggestion from others.

8. Walter Gellhorn, *Ombudsmen and Others: Citizens' Protectors in Nine Countries* (Cambridge, Mass.: Harvard University Press, 1966); idem, *When Americans Complain* (Cambridge, Mass.: Harvard University Press, 1966).

9. Rowat, *The Ombudsman: Citizens' Defender.*

10. Stanley V. Anderson, *Bibliography of Scandinavian and Other Articles on Om-

budsmen (Santa Barbara: University of California, 1964); Carleton W. Kenyon, ed., *The Ombudsman: A Bibliography* (Sacramento: California State Law Library, 1966); Municipal Reference Library Notes, "Ombudsman: A Bibliography of Literature in the Municipal Reference Library," *Municipal Reference Library Notes* 40 (December 1966): 165–175; Charles L. Smith, *Ombudsman, Citizen Defender: A Bibliography* (Pasadena: Friends Committee on Legislation in California, 1966); Robert Sperry, "Ombudsman Bibliography," *New York Law Journal* 155 (February 15, 1966): 1–3; Randy H. Hamilton, *Bibliography on the Ombudsman* (Los Angeles: University of Southern California, School of Public Administration, 1968); Eric L. Swanick, *Ombudsman Bibliography* (Monticello, Ill.: Vance Bibliographies, Public Administration Series, 1978); Manindra K. Mohapatra, *Studies on Ombudsman and Other Complaint-Handling Systems: A Select Bibliography* (Monticello, Ill.: Vance Bibliographies, December 1979).

11. Paul Dolan, "Creating State Ombudsman," *National Civic Review* 63, no. 5 (May 1974): 250–254; idem, "The Ombudsman in the United States: The States," in Gerald E. Caiden, ed., *International Handbook of the Ombudsman* (Westport, Conn.: Greenwood Press, 1983), pp. 217–221; idem, "Pseudo-Ombudsman," *National Civic Review* 58, no. 5 (July 1969): 297–301; Bernard Frank, "The Ombudsman Concept Is Expanding in the U.S.," *National Civic Review* 61, no. 5 (May 1972): 232–235; idem, "State Ombudsman Legislation in the United States," *University of Miami Law Review* 29, no. 3 (1975): 397–445; Samuel Yeager, "State Legislators and the Ombudsman," in Gerald E. Caiden, ed., *International Handbook of the Ombudsman* (Westport, Conn.: Greenwood Press, 1983), pp. 223–230; Jon Mills, "The Ombudsman in the American Constitutional, Legal, and Political Structure," in Gerald E. Caiden, ed., *International Handbook of the Ombudsman* (Westport, Conn.: Greenwood Press, 1983), pp. 209–214; John E. Moore, "State Government and the Ombudsman," in Stanley V. Anderson, ed., *Ombudsman for American Government* (Englewood Cliffs, N.J.: Prentice-Hall 1968), pp. 70–100; Jesse M. Unruh, "The Ombudsman in the States," in Ray V. Peel, ed., *The Ombudsman or Citizen's Defender: A Modern Institution* (Philadelphia: American Academy of Political and Social Science, 1968); William H. Angus and Milton Kaplan, "The Ombudsman and Local Government," in Stanley V. Anderson, ed., *Ombudsman for American Government* (Englewood Cliffs, N.J.: Prentice-Hall, 1968), pp. 101–135.

12. Herman Doi, "The Hawaii Ombudsman Appraises His Office after the First Year," *State Government* 43 (Summer 1970): 138–146; Walter Ikeda, "The Ombudsman in Hawaii," in Gerald E. Caiden, ed., *International Handbook of the Ombudsman* (Westport, Conn.: Greenwood Press, 1983), pp. 241–248; Albert M. Liston, "The Office of the Iowa Citizen's Aide," in Alan J. Wyner, ed., *Executive Ombudsman in the United States* (Berkeley: Institute of Government, University of California, 1973), pp. 151–188; Alan J. Wyner, "Complaint Resolution in Nebraska: Citizens, Bureaucrats, and the Ombudsman," *Nebraska Law Review* 54 (1975): 1–26; idem, *The Nebraska Ombudsman* (Berkeley: Institute of Government Studies, University of California, 1973); Bernard Frank, "The Nebraska Public Counsel—The Ombudsman," *Cumberland–Samford Law Review* 5, no. 1 (Spring 1974): 30–58; Robert Miewald and John C. Comer, "The Nebraska Ombudsman: An American Pioneer," in Gerald E. Caiden, ed., *International Handbook of the Ombudsman* (Westport, Conn.: Greenwood Press, 1983), pp. 231–240; Steven E. Aufrecht and Gregg Brelsford, "The Administrative Impact of the Alaskan Ombudsman," in Gerald E. Caiden, ed., *International Handbook of the Ombudsman* (Westport, Conn.: Greenwood Press, 1983), pp. 231–240; John A. Worthley

and Jack C. Overstreet, "Innovations in the United States: The Florida Senate Ombuds-man Program," *The Bureaucrat* 5 (January 1977): 463–477; idem, "Modern Technol-ogy Applied to Traditional Political Functions: The Florida Senate Ombudsman Pro-gram," *Polity* 11 (Winter 1978): 280–289; Charles H. Moore and Patricia A. Hoban–Moore, "A Death in Atlanta" (Unpublished paper, Atlanta, 1977); idem, "The Design and Implementation of Local Complaint-Handling Processes: Two Experiences—Atlanta and Birmingham" (Paper delivered at the American Society for Public Administration, Anaheim, Calif., April 1986). Theodore L. Bingham, "Ombudsman: 'The Dayton Model,' " *University of Cincinnati Law Review* 41 (1972): 807–822; Jon P. Bormet and Michael R. Shuey, "Dayton/Montgomery County Ombudsman Office," in Gerald E. Caiden, ed., *International Handbook of the Ombudsman* (Westport, Conn.: Greenwood Press, 1983), pp. 269–272; L. Tibbles, "Ombudsman for Local Government? The Buf-falo Experiment," *Urban Lawyer* 2 (1970): 364–370; Rosina K. Abramson, "New York City," in Gerald E. Caiden, ed., *International Handbook of the Ombudsman* (Westport, Conn.: Greenwood Press, 1983), pp. 287–297; Clarence J. Hein, "Jackson County, Missouri," in Gerald E. Caiden, ed., *International Handbook of the Ombudsman* (Westport, Conn.: Greenwood Press, 1983), 273–282; Thomas Wells and Manindra Mohapatra, "Chesapeake," in Gerald E. Caiden, ed., *International Handbook of the Ombudsman* (Westport, Conn.: Greenwood Press, 1983), pp. 283–286; Frederick A. Linde, "Wichita," in Gerald E. Caiden, ed., *International Handbook of the Ombuds-man* (Westport, Conn.: Greenwood Press, 1983), pp. 297–305.

13. Wyner, *Executive Ombudsman.*

14. Carl J. Friedrich, "Public Policy and the Nature of Administrative Responsibil-ity," *Public Policy* 1 (1940): 3–24.

15. Herman Finer, "Administrative Responsibility and Democratic Government," *Public Administration Review* 1, no. 4 (Summer 1941): 335–350.

16. Dewitt C. Armstrong III and George A. Graham, "Ethical Preparation for the Public Service," *The Bureaucrat* 4 (April 1975): 6–23.

17. Charles T. Burbridge, "Problems on Transferring the Ombudsman Plan," *Inter-national Review of the Administrative Sciences* 40 (April–June 1974): 103–108; John M. Capozzola, "An American Ombudsman: Problems and Prospects," *Western Politi-cal Quarterly* 21 (June 1968): 289–301; Dolan, "The Ombudsman in the United States," pp. 217–221; Harold F. Gortner, "The Ombudsman in the U.S.: A Decade After . . .," *Virginia Social Science Journal* 18 (April 1983): 32–38; William B. Gwynn, "Trans-ferring the Ombudsman," in Stanley V. Anderson, ed., *Ombudsman for American Gov-ernment* (Englewood Cliffs, N.J.: Prentice-Hall, 1968), pp. 37–69; and Mills, "The Ombudsman," pp. 209–214.

18. Mills, "The Ombudsman," p. 210.

19. Burbridge, "Problems," p. 104.

20. Dolan, "The Ombudsman in the United States," p. 220.

21. Gortner, "The Ombudsman in the U.S.," pp. 33–34.

22. Ibid., p. 34.

23. Mills, "The Ombudsman," p. 214.

24. Larry B. Hill, "Must Implementation Studies Be Dismal? The Bureaucratic Im-pact of the Ombudsman's Reforms" (Paper delivered at the American Political Science Association, Chicago, September 1983); idem, "The Ombudsman and Bureaucratic Re-form" (Paper delivered at the American Political Science Association, Washington, D.C., August 1986).

25. Hill, "The Ombudsman," p. 2.

26. Hill, "The Citizen Participation–Representation Roles," pp. 405–433; Larry B. Hill, "The Self-Perceptions of Ombudsmen: A Comparative Survey," in Gerald E. Caiden, ed., *International Handbook of the Ombudsman* (Westport, Conn.: Greenwood Press, 1983), pp. 43–58; Yeager, "State Legislators," pp. 223–230. *See also* Brenda Danet, "Toward a Method to Evaluate the Ombudsman's Role," *Administration and Society* 10, no. 3 (November 1978): 335–370.

27. Hill, "The Self-Perceptions," pp. 43–58.

28. Hill, "The Citizen Participation–Representation Roles," pp. 405–433.

29. Yeager, "State Legislators," pp. 223–230.

30. Ibid., p. 228.

31. William M. Pearson and Van A. Wigginton, "Effectiveness of Administrative Controls: Some Perceptions of State Legislators," *Public Administration Review* 46, no. 4 (July–August 1986): 328–331.

32. Caiden, *International Handbook of the Ombudsman*, p. 8; Marshall E. Dimock, "The Ombudsman and Public Administration," *Public Administration Review* 43, no. 5 (September–October 1983): 468.

33. Caiden, *International Handbook of the Ombudsman*, p. 19; Danet, "Toward a Method," pp. 335–370; Dimock, "The Ombudsman," p. 469.

34. For an excellent account of the origins and first twenty-six months of operations in the office, *see* Alan J. Wyner, *The Nebraska Ombudsman* (Berkeley: Institute of Governmental Studies, University of California, 1974).

35. Frank, "The Nebraska Public Counsel," pp. 30–58.

36. Caseload data for recent years were obtained from annual reports and supplemented by data reported by Robert Miewald and John C. Comer, "The Nebraska Ombudsman: An American Pioneer," in Gerald E. Caiden, ed., *International Handbook of the Ombudsman* (Westport, Conn.: Greenwood Press, 1983), p. 252.

37. *See* Robert Miewald and John C. Comer, "Complaining as Participation: The Case of the Ombudsman, *Administration and Society* 17, no. 4 (February 1986): 490.

38. The first survey was part of the Nebraska Annual Social Indicators Survey; the second was conducted by Robert Miewald and John C. Comer of the University of Nebraska–Lincoln, Department of Political Science. Results of both surveys can be found in the *Eleventh Annual Report of the Nebraska Public Counsel* (1981): 7–10, 23–26.

39. Marshall Lux, "Ombudsman's Office: Refinement Potentials" (Report to the Executive Board, Lincoln, Nebraska, March 12, 1986), pp. 1–10.

40. Transcript of Legislative Floor Debate on Legislative Bill 1, Special Session 2 of Nebraska Unicameral Legislature (October 29, 1985), pp. 74–75, 84–85, 88–91, 98.

41. Ibid., p. 81.

42. Ibid., p. 91.

43. This case study is based on two published articles. See Worthley and Overstreet, "Innovation in the United States," pp. 463–477; idem, "Modern Technology Applied," pp. 280–289.

44. 1979 Fla. J. of House of Representatives 1176; 1979 Fla. J. of the Senate 922. Vote in the House was unanimous; vote in the Senate was thirty-three to six.

45. For a more detailed account of the Dayton case, *see* Bingham, "Ombudsman: 'The Dayton Model,' " pp. 807–822; Bormet and Shuey, "Dayton/Montgomery County," pp. 269–272.

46. This example is cited by Bormet and Shuey, "Dayton/Montgomery County," p. 271.

47. This brief analysis of Atlanta's abortive experience with its ombudsman program is based on two papers: Moore and Hobman–Moore, "A Death in Atlanta"; idem, "The Design and Implementation of Local Complaint-Handling Processes."

48. Kenneth J. Meier, *Politics and the Bureaucracy* (Monterey, Calif.: Brooks/Cole, 1987), pp. 172–175.

49. International Ombudsman Institute, *Directory;* Caiden, *International Handbook of the Ombudsman*, p. 11.

SELECTED BIBLIOGRAPHY

Abramson, Rosina K. "New York City." In Gerald E. Caiden, ed., *International Handbook of the Ombudsman*. Westport, Conn.: Greenwood Press, 1983, pp. 287–297.

Anderson, Stanley V. *Bibliography of Scandinavian and Other Articles on Ombudsmen*. Santa Barbara: University of California, 1964.

Angus, William H., and Milton Kaplan. "The Ombudsman and Local Government." In Stanley V. Anderson, ed., *Ombudsman for American Government*. Englewood Cliffs, N.J.: Prentice-Hall, 1968, pp. 1091–1135.

Armstrong, Dewitt C. III, and George A. Graham. "Ethical Preparation for the Public Service." *The Bureaucrat* 4 (April 1975): 6–23.

Aufrecht, Steven E., and Gregg Brelsford. "The Administrative Impact of the Alaskan Ombudsman." In Gerald E. Caiden, ed., *International Handbook of the Ombudsman*. Westport, Conn.: Greenwood Press, 1983, pp. 231–240.

Bingham, Theodore C. "Ombudsman: 'The Dayton Model.' " *University of Cincinnati Law Review* 41 (1972): 807–822.

Bormet, Jon P., and Michael R. Shuey. "Dayton/Montgomery County Ombudsman Office." In Gerald E. Caiden, ed., *International Handbook of the Ombudsman*. Westport, Conn.: Greenwood Press, 1983, pp. 269–272.

Burnbridge, Charles T. "Problems on Transferring the Ombudsman Plan." *International Review of Administrative Science* 40 (April–June 1974): 103–108.

Caiden, Gerald E., ed. *International Handbook of the Ombudsman*. Westport, Conn.: Greenwood Press, 1983.

Capozzola, John M. "An American Ombudsman: Problems and Prospects." *Western Political Quarterly* 21 (June 1968): 289–301.

Danet, Brenda. "Toward a Method to Evaluate the Ombudsman's Role." *Administration and Society* 10 (November 1978): 335–370.

Dimock, Marshall E. "The Ombudsman and Public Administration." *Public Administration Review* 43, no. 5 (September–October 1983): 467–470.

Doi, Herman. "The Hawaii Ombudsman Appraises His Office after the First Year." *State Government* 43 (Summer 1970): 138–146.

Dolan, Paul. "Pseudo-Ombudsman." *National Civic Review* 58, no. 5 (July 1969): 297–301.

———. "Creating State Ombudsman." *National Civic Review* 63, no. 5 (May 1974): 250–254.

———. "The Ombudsman in the United States: The States." In Gerald E. Caiden, ed., *The International Handbook of the Ombudsman.* Westport, Conn.: Green-wood Press, 1983, pp. 217–221.

Eleventh Annual Report of the Nebraska Public Counsel, 1981, pp. 7–10, 23–26.

Finer, Herman. "Administrative Responsibility and Democratic Government." *Public Administration Review* 1, no. 4 (September 1941): 335–350.

Frank, Bernard. "The Ombudsman Concept Is Expanding in the U.S." *National Civic Review* 61, no. 5 (May 1972): 232–235.

————. "The Nebraska Public Counsel—The Ombudsman." *Cumberland Samford Law Review* 5, no. 1 (Spring 1974): 30–58.

————. "The Ombudsman Revisited." *International Bar Association Journal,* May 1975, pp. 48–60.

————. "State Ombudsman Legislation in the United States." *University of Miami Law Review* 29 (1975): 397–445.

————. "The Growth of the Ombudsman Movement." Unpublished paper, Allentown, Pa., 1977.

Friedrich, Carl J. "Public Policy and the Nature of Administrative Responsibility." *Public Policy* 1 (1940): 3–24.

Gellhorn, Walter. *Ombudsmen and Others: Citizens' Protectors in Nine Countries.* Cambridge, Mass.: Harvard University Press, 1966.

————. *When Americans Complain.* Cambridge, Mass.: Harvard University Press, 1966.

Gortner, Harold F. "The Ombudsman in the U.S.: A Decade After . . . ," *Virginia Social Science Journal* 18 (April 1983): 32–38.

Gwynn, William B. "Transferring the Ombudsman." In Stanley V. Anderson, ed., *Ombudsman for American Government.* Englewood Cliffs, N.J.: Prentice-Hall, 1968, pp. 37–69.

Hamilton, Randy H. *Bibliography on the Ombudsman.* Los Angeles: University of Southern California, School of Public Administration, 1968.

Hein, Clarence J. "Jackson County, Missouri." In Gerald E. Caiden, ed., *International Handbook of the Ombudsman.* Westport, Conn.: Greenwood Press, 1983, pp. 273–282.

Hill, Larry B. "Institutionalization, the Ombudsman, and Bureaucracy." *American Political Science Review* 68 (September 1974): 1075–1085.

————. *The Model Ombudsman: Institutionalizing New Zealand's Democratic Experiment.* Princeton, N.J.: Princeton University Press, 1976.

————. "The Citizen Participation-Representation Roles of American Ombudsmen." *Administration and Society* 13, no. 4 (February 1982): 405–433.

————. "Must Implementation Studies Be Dismal? The Bureaucratic Impact of the Ombudsman's Reforms." Paper delivered at The American Political Science Association, Chicago, September 1983.

————. "The Self-Perceptions of Ombudsmen: A Comparative Survey." In Gerald E. Caiden, ed., *International Handbook of the Ombudsman.* Westport, Conn.: Greenwood Press, 1983, pp. 43–58.

————. "The Ombudsman and Bureaucratic Reform." Paper delivered at The American Political Science Association, Washington, D.C., August 1986.

Ikeda, Walter. "The Ombudsman in Hawaii." In Gerald E. Caiden, ed., *International Handbook of the Ombudsman.* Westport, Conn.: Greenwood Press, 1983, pp. 241–248.

International Ombudsman Institute. *Directory of Ombudsmen and International Ombudsman Offices*. Alberta, Canada: University of Alberta, 1986.

Kenyon, Carleton W., ed., *The Ombudsman: A Bibliography*. Sacramento: California State Law Library, 1966.

Linde, Frederick A. "Wichita." In Gerald E. Caiden, ed., *International Handbook of the Ombudsman*. Westport, Conn.: Greenwood Press, 1983, pp. 297–305.

Liston, Albert M. "The Office of the Iowa Citizen's Aide." In Alan J. Wyner, ed., *Executive Ombudsmen in the United States*. Berkeley: Institute of Government, University of California, 1973, pp. 151–188.

Lux, Marshall. "Ombudsman's Office: Refinement Potentials." Report to the Executive Board, Lincoln, Nebraska, March 12, 1986, pp. 1–10.

Meier, Kenneth J. *Politics and the Bureaucracy*. Monterey, Calif.: Brooks/Cole, 1987.

Miewald, Robert, and John C. Comer. "The Nebraska Ombudsman: An American Pioneer." In Gerald E. Caiden, ed., *International Handbook of the Ombudsman*. Westport, Conn.: Greenwood Press, 1983, pp. 249–256.

———. "Complaining as Participation: The Case of the Ombudsman." *Administration and Society* 17, no. 4 (February 1986): 490.

Mills, Jon. "The Ombudsman in the American Constitutional, Legal, and Political Structure." In Gerald E. Caiden, ed., *International Handbook of the Ombudsman*. Westport, Conn.: Greenwood Press, 1983, pp. 209–214.

Mohapatra, Manindra K. *Studies on Ombudsman and Other Complaint-Handling Systems: A Select Bibliography*. Monticello, Ill.: Vance Bibliographies, December 1979.

Moore, Charles H., and Patricia A. Hoban-Moore. "A Death in Atlanta." Unpublished paper, Atlanta, 1977.

———. "The Design and Implementation of Local Complaint-Handling Processes: Two Experiences—Atlanta and Birmingham." Paper delivered at the American Society for Public Administration, Anaheim, Calif., April 1986.

Moore, John E. "State Government and the Ombudsman," in Stanley V. Anderson, ed., *Ombudsman for American Government*. Englewood Cliffs, N.J.: Prentice-Hall, 1968, pp. 70–100.

Municipal Reference Library Notes. "Ombudsman: A Bibliography of Literature in the Municipal Reference Library." *Municipal Reference Library Notes* 40 (December 1966): 165–175.

Pearson, William M., and Van A. Wigginton. "Effectiveness of Administrative Controls: Some Perceptions of State Legislators." *Public Administration Review* 46, no. 4 (July–August 1986): 328–331.

Rowat, Donald C. *The Ombudsman: Citizens' Defender*. Toronto: Toronto University Press, 1968.

———. *The Ombudsman Plan: Essays on the Worldwide Spread of an Idea*. Toronto: McClelland and Stewart, 1973.

Smith, Charles L. *Ombudsman, Citizen Defender: A Bibliography*. Pasadena: Friends Committee on Legislation in California, 1966.

Sperry, Robert. "Ombudsman Bibliography." *New York Law Journal* 155 (February 15, 1966): 1–3.

Swanick, Eric L. *Ombudsman Bibliography*. Monticello, Ill.: Vance Bibliographies, Public Administration Series, 1978, p. 302.

Tibbles, L. "Ombudsman for Local Government? The Buffalo Experiment." *Urban Lawyer* 2 (1970): 364–370.

Unruh, Jesse M. "The Ombudsman in the States." In Ray V. Peel, ed., *The Ombudsman or Citizen's Defender: A Modern Institution.* Philadelphia: American Academy of Political and Social Science, 1968.

Wells, Thomas, and Manindra Mohapatra. "Chesapeake." In Gerald E. Caiden, ed., *International Handbook of the Ombudsman.* Westport, Conn.: Greenwood Press, 1983, pp. 283–286.

Worthley, John A., and Jack C. Overstreet. "Innovation in the United States: The Florida Senate Ombudsman Program." *The Bureaucrat* 5 (January 1977): 463–477.

————. "Modern Technology Applied to Traditional Political Functions: The Florida Senate Ombudsman Program." *Polity* 11 (Winter 1978): 280–289.

Wyner, Alan J. *The Nebraska Ombudsman.* Berkeley: Institute of Government Studies, University of California, 1974.

————. "Complaint Resolution in Nebraska: Citizens, Bureaucrats, and the Ombudsman." *Nebraska Law Review* 54 (1975): 1–26.

————, ed. *Executive Ombudsman in the United States.* Berkeley: Institute of Government Studies, University of California, 1973.

Yeager, Samuel. "State Legislators and the Ombudsman." In Gerald E. Caiden, ed., *International Handbook of the Ombudsman.* Westport, Conn.: Greenwood Press, 1983, pp. 223–230.

8

The Use of Equal Opportunity and Affirmative Action in Employment Decisions

Gary C. Bryner

Equal employment opportunity (EEO) embodies the goal that employment decisions be free of considerations of race, color, national origin, religion, and sex. It rests on the ideal of nondiscrimination—that employees and applicants for employment not be judged on factors other than merit and qualifications. Although the idea of equal employment opportunity has come to enjoy widespread support, many have concluded that affirmative steps must be taken to insure equality of opportunity, that race- and sex-conscious steps be taken so that such considerations can eventually be eliminated.

Affirmative action is defined differently by different people and represents a variety of efforts. It may include special outreach, recruitment, and educational efforts by employers aimed at women and minorities or preferential treatment to women and minorities in hiring and promotion decisions. Affirmative action has been defended as essential to overcome centuries of discriminatory beliefs and practices in public and private institutions and has been attacked by opponents as a violation of constitutional prohibitions against discrimination and a perpetuation of racism and sexism.

The employment decisions of federal, state, and local governments play a critical role in the pursuit of equal employment opportunity. The public service has been a major employer of women and minorities. Government employers are expected by many to serve as exemplars for their private-sector counterparts. Efforts to eliminate discriminatory behavior have been integrated with a number of other policy areas in which compliance with civil rights laws are required before government funds can be received. Public managers must satisfy competing expectations of fairness and equality in determining how equal employment opportunity goals are to be accomplished. Since governments find it increasingly necessary to lay off workers in response to fiscal stress, not only do they have fewer opportunities to hire new female and minority employees, but because of seniority systems, these workers are the first to be fired.

This chapter examines the kinds of ethical and legal choices employers must make every day in employment decisions. It provides a brief historical background of the issues, reviews some of the literature on affirmative action, develops a framework that focuses on the current status of affirmative action law, analyzes the kinds of choices that confront public employers in making reductions in the workforce, and concludes with a discussion of how employers might balance the competing concerns they must confront. The most controversial kind of affirmative action is the giving of preferential treatment, through numerical hiring and promotion goals and ratios, to women and minorities, and the focus here is on preferential treatment and the difficult issues it raises in public employment.

Public managers must make a variety of ethical judgments and decisions in pursuing the policy tasks delegated to them. They must translate general values of justice and fairness into specific decisions concerning when they can (and should) treat their employees differently and when such treatment is unfair and unjust. They must weigh the claims of women and minorities for preferential consideration with those of white males for decisions to be made independent of race and sex.

These and other issues are at the heart of the debate over equal employment opportunity in hiring, promotion, firing, and related employment decisions. A primary concern is that individuals not be treated unfairly: employment decisions made on the basis of race, sex, color, religion, and national origin—except when these attributes are bona fide occupational qualifications—are unjust and unfair. Yet simply requiring that discrimination not take place—that decisions not be made on such criteria—may not be enough. Justice may also require that victims of past discrimination be compensated, "made whole," so that the effects of past discrimination are mitigated or eliminated. Whereas some public employers may find themselves operating under legal obligations to grant preferential treatment, others may decide voluntarily to do so. In both circumstances, preferential treatment requires difficult and controversial ethical choices.

BACKGROUND

The idea of equality of employment opportunity has become widely accepted. It is still occasionally challenged by some who believe that employers have the right to hire whomever they wish or to hire persons who they believe possess characteristics expected or desired by their clients or customers. Although some of these concerns may be legitimate and not motivated by racism, sexism, ageism, or religious bigotry, equal employment opportunity assumes that the rights of individuals to be free from decisions based on these personal characteristics outweigh and must overwhelm the right of employers to hire whomever they wish.

Affirmative action seeks to bring about equality of employment opportunities. Affirmative action encourages, and sometimes requires, employers to develop special programs to recruit women and minority employees. Such efforts include:

1. Recruiting in high schools, colleges, and neighborhoods with high minority populations

2. Publicizing their commitment to equal employment opportunity to combat perceptions of past discrimination

3. Developing remedial educational training programs to assist disadvantaged persons in competing in the job market

4. Giving special consideration to women and minorities on an individualized basis

5. "Making whole" victims of discrimination through back pay or retroactive seniority

Affirmative action obligations were provided for in the Civil Rights Act of 1964, which defined the power of federal judges to order remedies for victims of discrimination, and in Executive Order 11246, issued by President Lyndon Johnson in 1965, which established special obligations for government contractors and federal agencies.[1]

Affirmative action also includes giving preferential treatment to women and minorities through hiring and promotion goals and ratios that set aside certain opportunities available only to members of these groups. This resulted from a number of factors including frustration over the lack of progress in EEO programs, the belief that more than a commitment to nondiscrimination was required to excise guilt from slavery and the history of race relations, the decline of the autonomy of state governments due to the increasing activism of federal judges and bureaucrats, and the synergistic effect of the interaction of courts and agencies that pushed for a more aggressive stance toward equality of opportunity.[2]

Affirmative action policy is also rooted in arguments that discrimination is a result of group characteristics and thus requires group-based rather than individual-based remedies; that enforcement cannot rest on findings of discriminatory intent, because evidence for such motivations is so difficult to uncover, but can be proven by demonstrating statistical disparities; and that recognizing and measuring compliance is so difficult that quantitative measures are needed. Such arguments have led to the establishment of numerical hiring and promotion goals that have been so controversial.

Preferential treatment programs were developed by the Department of Labor (for government contractors), the Civil Service Commission and the Equal Employment Opportunity Commission (for federal agencies), federal courts, and the Justice Department in the late 1960s and the 1970s.[3] The Supreme Court, in a series of cases beginning in the 1970s, permitted employers and unions to create voluntary programs that gave preferential treatment to minority employees in admission to apprenticeship programs, upheld race-conscious relief as a remedy for past discrimination for persons who were not actual victims of discrimination, and decided that lower courts cannot order that seniority systems be abridged in order to maintain hiring ratios resulting from affirmative action efforts.[4] Although legal doctrines are evolving, the Court has clearly upheld the granting of preferential treatment to remedy past discriminatory actions, and ruled that it must be ''narrowly tailored'' but can extend beyond identifiable victims of actual discrimination to women and minorities in general.[5]

The Reagan administration has sought to redirect governmental efforts toward nondiscrimination and away from preferential treatment and numerical hiring and promotion goals. The Justice Department, beginning in 1981, has actively campaigned against affirmative action and has sought to rewrite the executive order that requires goals and timetables in firms that have government contracts.[6] The attorney general has been particularly critical of the rules of the Labor Department Office of Federal Contracts Compliance Programs that require employers to make ''good-faith'' efforts to achieve hiring and promotion goals, but the secretary of labor has defended their use as appropriate.[7] The Equal Employment Opportunity Commission has vacillated in supporting and then rejecting the use of hiring and promotion goals. In 1986 it reaffirmed their use in the wake of key Supreme Court decisions.[8]

The preferential treatment debate has raised questions concerning when employers can voluntarily give or be required to give such treatment and the form that the preference can take. Options range from outreach efforts to attract minority and female applicants to fixed quotas. Public employers must decide how they will respond to this controversy. In part, their decisions will rest on their ethical values and the range of actions they might take within the framework of equal employment opportunity laws, administrative decisions, and judicial rulings. A sample of the broad, philosophical, ethical arguments contained in the literature and the legal requirements employers confront as they make basic choices are examined below.

LITERATURE REVIEW

The Case for Preferential Treatment

Compensatory Justice.   Proponents argue that women and minorities have a right to be compensated for past discrimination. Some kind of preferential treatment is required as recompense for past discrimination. In many cases, government-sponsored discrimination created barriers to members of these groups and served to exclude them from educational, social, and employment opportunities. White males have been artificially advantaged because of the reduced competition for employment benefits.[9]

Hiring and promotion goals and ratios are defended as temporary steps to remedy the effects of past discrimination. Lesser measures have been unable to bring about significant change, and concrete indicators of progress are seen as essential. Proponents believe that race-neutral employment decisions fail to reflect reality: color blindness provides no explanation of "how a society that has inflicted wrongs on a clan of people solely because of race can suddenly become 'race neutral' and still furnish redress to those who have been the victims of discrimination.[10] "Perhaps one day America will be color-blind," William Coleman has argued, but "it takes an extraordinary ignorance of actual life in America to believe that day has come."[11]

Equality and Equal Protection. Preferential treatment is also defended as consistent with equal treatment and the constitutional mandate of equal protection. The equal protection clause does not require that governments treat all persons alike: legislation often makes distinctions, identifies specific groups to be singled out for special treatment, and requires that some people be treated differently. The Constitution itself, in providing that only three-fifths of the slave population be counted for certain purposes, used a form of racial quotas. Victims of discrimination should be treated differently in response to the lack of opportunity from which they have suffered.

The equal protection mandate, it is argued, ought to be understood as applying to groups and not just individuals, since women and minorities have been discriminated against—not because of individual characteristics but because of the group of which they are a part. The concept underlying equal protection is the protection of the rights and concerns of those who are not part of the majority power structure, who do not enjoy power and influence in dominant economic, social, and governmental institutions.

Since governments do not treat all people the same, the key concern is to determine what factors should be relevant in differential treatment. Preferential treatment of women and minorities is required by the idea of equality. Past discrimination has disadvantaged members of certain groups and advantaged others, so that individuals in these groups should not be treated equally. Preferential treatment is defended when its beneficiaries have been clearly disadvantaged, where those who benefited from the discrimination are now required to make some sacrifices, and where the harm resulting from the initial acts are passed on to future generations, even if all current discriminatory practices cease.[12]

Preferential treatment is also defended as necessary since all women and minorities have been at least indirect victims of racism and sexism, the effects of which have been passed on to children from parents or have prevented them from pursuing certain opportunities. Preferential treatment may not be a particularly precise way of responding to past evils, but a failure to remedy past injustices would be a greater wrong than "overcompensating" those who have not been particularly victimized. Yet it also serves to restrict the opportunities of white males who, although they have benefited from discrimination, are

often not themselves perpetuators of discrimination. The choice, then, is between two evils—failing to remedy past discrimination and discriminating against
white males because of their race and sex. Since white males have gained some
benefits from discrimination against women and minorities, they must now sacrifice some of those benefits so that these victims of discrimination can be
compensated.

Such arguments also rest on a particular notion of merit. Although merit is
an appropriate basis for making employment-related decisions, merit-related
decisions that are based on present qualifications fail to recognize the effect of
past discrimination. Current qualifications cannot be the basis of employment
decisions since they are a function of past wrongs. Poor education and skills
that result from discrimination are reflected in less merit and ability, and to fail
to adjust for this is to perpetuate the effects of discrimination. Candidates who
have been victims of past discrimination are not situated the same as beneficiaries of their discrimination, and it would be unfair to treat them the same.
This is especially true when members of groups victimized by discrimination
are competing for jobs or other opportunities with those who have benefited
from those same actions. Preferential treatment is required by justice, since
less qualified candidates may actually be more deserving than the more qualified ones.[13]

Social Welfare.   Preferential treatment is also defended from a utilitarian
perspective. It produces a net increase in opportunity since it reaches those who
have been victims of past discrimination while limiting only to a relatively
minor extent the opportunities of white males. It encourages women and minorities to pursue opportunities that, in the past, have largely been closed to
them. Economic efficiency is enhanced as employment-related decisions are not
limited by discriminatory practices that reduce competitiveness in the labor market
and may result in less than optimal decision-making. For particular professions,
such as medicine, women and minority physicians are believed by some to be
more able to meet the needs of patients of their same sex or race, thus making
the delivery of important social services more effective. Similarly, government
bureaucracies are believed to be more effective if agency officials are representative of the people whom they seek to serve. Preferential treatment may
insure that young people have role models that will encourage them to pursue
careers and opportunities that they might otherwise believe to be closed to
them.

Finally, preferential treatment is defended as producing benefits for all employees and organizations. Special training programs, such as the one created
by Kaiser Aluminum that was the subject of Brian Weber's claim of reverse
discrimination, did not exist before the onset of affirmative action.[14] Some
personnel decisions have become more open and less susceptible to "old-boy
networks," thus improving employee morale and a sense of fairness in employment-related decision-making, although critics of preferential treatment offer counterexamples of how it increases workplace tensions. Selection and pro-

motion criteria that are not job related have been abandoned, and employees argue that they have benefited from a more diverse workforce.[15] Some executives have stated that female and minority employees were a gold mine of talent that would have remained undiscovered were it not for hiring goals imposed on them by court decrees.[16]

Challenges to Preferential Treatment

Equality and Equal Protection.   Critics of hiring and promotion goals argue that they violate the ideal of equality and actually promote inequality. Morris Abram, a Reagan appointee to the U.S. Civil Rights Commission, argued that "equal means equal," that "equal does not mean you have separate lists of blacks and whites for promotions, any more than you have separate accommodations for blacks and whites for eating. Nothing will ultimately divide a society more than this kind of preference and this kind of reverse discrimination."[17] William Bradford Reynolds, assistant attorney general under President Reagan, considers goals and ratios a "social spoils system" that fails to insure that compensation is provided only to actual victims of discrimination.[18] It is much too imprecise, since it gives special benefits to some women and minorities who have not been actual victims of discriminatory employment decisions. It reduces the opportunity for white males, violating their rights and punishing them for wrongs that they did not commit while doing nothing to punish those who were guilty of discriminatory acts. It perpetuates racism and sexism and further divides society.

Central to criticisms of preferential treatment is the equal protection clause. Opponents of goals and ratios argue that equal protection should be understood to protect all persons and not just minorities. Justice Powell, in his Bakke opinion, for example, argued that all social classifications are to be subject to strict judicial scrutiny and that such classifications can only be maintained if there is a demonstrable "compelling state interest." The Supreme Court, he argued, had rightly extended the Fourteenth Amendment protections to all ethnic groups and had rejected the notion that only groups that had been stigmatized were eligible for equal protection. Powell emphasized the "inherent unfairness of, and the perception of mistreatment that accompanies, a system of allocating benefits and privileges on the basis of skin color and ethnic origin."[19]

For Powell, the concept of a preferred status and protection for any minority groups was fundamentally flawed. "The concepts of 'majority' and 'minority' necessarily reflect temporary arrangements and political judgments." Since all of the groups that have suffered discrimination cannot receive preferential treatment, "there is no principled basis for deciding which groups would merit 'heightened judicial solicitude.' . . . The kind of variable sociological and political analysis necessary to produce such rankings simply does not lie within the judicial competence—even if they otherwise were politically feasible and socially desirable.''[20]

Opponents of preferential treatment reason that equal treatment requires that no decisions be made on the basis of race. The Constitution, it is argued, is color blind and views race as a ''suspect classification'' that cannot serve as a legitimate basis for public policy. Although there is some disagreement over whether gender can ever serve as a legitimate basis for the different treatment of individuals, there is general agreement that preferential treatment of women that restricts the opportunities of white males is wrong. Opponents also find in the equal protection clause, as well as in broader constitutional and extraconstitutional imperatives, the principle that individuals must be treated as individuals and not simply as members of groups.

The ''temporary'' basis of preferential treatment is also rejected by its critics. Nathan Glazer has argued that ''if we want a society in which individuals are treated as individuals by public bodies, and as far as possible in private life, without regard to race and ethnicity then we cannot get there by allowing or prescribing public action in the opposite direction, even on a temporary basis.''[21] Such efforts, he argued, are not likely to remain temporary since their beneficiaries will continually demand them, and statistical parity will never be reached.

Others criticize preferential treatment because it merely shifts and does not repair injustices. If the victims and perpetrators of discrimination can be identified, compensation can be made. But compensation cannot be pursued if the calculations are uncertain. Current generations should not be burdened with responsibility for discrimination imposed by previous generations, except to discontinue the discrimination: ''Those who are not responsible for [discrimination] cannot be asked to compensate for the damages.''[22]

Statistical Parity. Preferential treatment relies heavily on statistical comparisons of the representation of women and minorities in employment with relevant populations in identifying discrimination and fashioning remedies. Critics, however, reject the idea that ''relevant aptitudes, talents, and motivations are equally distributable among classes, sexes, nationalities, and races and that such disparities must be eliminated so that employment mirrors the distribution of groups in society.'' Different ethnic and racial groups, Thomas Sowell argued, are not similar in ''age distribution, education, and other crucial variables.''[23] Employment in high-level positions, for example, is usually achieved after years of education and experience, but some groups such as Hispanics have an average age much younger than that for the entire population, so these kinds of positions are not likely to be filled by Hispanics in proportion to their representation in the population as a whole. The performance of members of different groups at work may be a result of cultural and educational background more than employer discrimination.[24]

Preferential treatment may also stigmatize its intended beneficiaries. It may

undermine the achievement of women and minorities by permitting some to
charge that success was due to special treatment and may weaken the self-
image of women and minorities who may come to believe that they cannot
compete in open competition with others.[25]

The Pursuit of Excellence.   Preferential treatment is criticized for threatening the ideal that employment decisions (as well as other decisions, such as
those made by admission officers in institutions of higher education) be made
on considerations of merit and ability. It violates the right of each person to be
compared with other applicants and employees in terms of individual qualifications and abilities by setting up separate lines for hiring and promotion and
giving preference to those with lesser qualifications. Such requirements fail to
encourage or promote excellence and prohibit employers from finding the most
highly qualified candidates for positions, as minimum standards tend to replace
most qualified standards.

Equality in Opportunity or Results.   Preferential treatment, critics contend,
is an attempt to achieve an equality of results rather than opportunity. It goes
beyond what is required to insure equal opportunity and fails to recognize that
individuals should be free to exercise personal choice and maximize the development of their potential. Governmental efforts should be limited to insuring a
formal, legal equality in which employment opportunities are simply open to
those with the requisite talents. Equality of opportunity protects the right of
individuals to enjoy the fruits of their talents and abilities.[26]

Preferential treatment, critics warn, must ultimately be rejected as inconsistent with other values. If it is understood to require equality of results, it threatens the autonomy of the family, since differences in family life are a major
determinant of talents that affect the ability to compete for employment.[27] It
challenges the autonomy of individuals as it threatens intervention by governments into personal lives and decisions.[28]

The debate over preferential treatment also includes an examination of the
consequences of and effectiveness of affirmative action efforts. Empirical studies are not conclusive, although they point to improved opportunities for women
and minorities as a result of requirements for affirmative action by government
contractors and deserve much more attention than can be given here.[29] The
unemployment rate for blacks, for example, has for decades been double that
for whites. The median income of working individuals over the age of fourteen
in 1985 was $17,111 for whites and $10,768 for blacks. In 1970 whites earned
$19,423 and blacks $11,472, as measured in 1985 dollars.[30] The percentage of
blacks in professional and technical occupations grew from 4.7 percent in 1960
to 9.2 percent in 1982 and for managers and administrators from 2.5 to 3.9
percent.[31] Such figures are for some evidence that preferential treatment has
increased opportunities for blacks and should be continued and are for others
the basis for rejecting it as ineffective. As more studies become available, they
can help employers sort out some of the ethical choices that must be made but

will not replace the need for such choices. Employers must also comply with a complex set of legal mandates that are reviewed next as a conceptual framework for such decisions.

CONCEPTUAL FRAMEWORK: LEGAL REQUIREMENTS FOR PREFERENTIAL TREATMENT

Under Executive Order 12246, issued in 1965 and amended in 1968, federal agencies are required to establish an affirmative action plan. They must "take affirmative action to ensure that applicants are employed, and that employees are treated during employment, without regard to their race, color, religion, sex, or national origin."[32] They must provide a review of their workforce to identify any area in which fewer women and minorities are in place than would be reasonably expected by their availability. Goals are to be established in response to this "underutilization" that are not to be inflexible quotas but are to be targets that are attainable by good-faith efforts.[33]

The most important statute affecting equal employment opportunity is Title VII of the Civil Rights Act of 1964, as amended in 1972 and 1978. Title VII applies to the decisions of employers and labor unions that have at least fifteen employees or members and the actions of employment agencies in bringing together employers and prospective employees. Employers are prohibited from hiring or discharging "any individual with respect to his compensation, terms, conditions, or privileges of employment" or to "limit, segregate, or classify . . . employees or applicants for employment in any way which would deprive or tend to deprive any individual of employment opportunities."[34]

The Supreme Court and Equal Employment Opportunity Law

Three kinds of unlawful decisions are recognized: (1) some employment decisions treat employees differently and are violations of the law; (2) some practices result in disparate impacts among different groups of employees; and (3) some kinds of affirmative action violate the rights of white males. Each of these cases has been the subject of a number of important judicial decisions.

1. The Supreme Court has defined, in a series of cases between 1973 and 1981, the burden of proof required in proving disparate treatment. In *McDonnell Douglas Corp. vs. Green,* the Court ruled that the employee must first show that:

(i) he belongs to a racial minority; (ii) that he applied and was qualified for a job for which the employer was seeking applicants; (iii) that, despite his qualifications, he was rejected; and (iv) that, after his rejection, the position remained open and the employer continued to seek applicants from persons of [the employee's] qualifications.[35]

If these conditions are met, the burden then shifts to the employer to "articulate some legitimate, nondiscriminatory reason for the employee's rejection." The employee could then seek to show that the employer's justification was merely a "pretext for discrimination."[36]

2. In *Griggs vs. Duke Power,* the Supreme Court ruled that employment practices resulting in an adverse impact were illegal.[37] At issue was the use by the employer of a general intelligence test and the requirement of a high school diploma in determining promotions. A court of appeals had upheld the use of the test, since it had found no intent to discriminate; the Supreme Court reversed, arguing that "good intent or absence of discriminatory intent does not redeem employment procedures or testing measures that operate as 'built-in headwinds' for minority groups and are unrelated to measuring job capability."

Congress, the justices argued, had authorized in Title VII the use of "any professionally developed ability test" except those that are "designed, intended or used to discriminate because of race."[38] The key word for the Court became *used* since it found that there was an adverse impact on minorities because members of minority groups failed to qualify for employment positions at a greater rate than nonminority applicants. The burden of proof then fell upon the employer to show that the selection devices were reasonably related to job performance and not intended to discriminate. If the employer could demonstrate that tests were job-related, the burden would shift back to the employee to show that the selection devices would be just as useful in insuring the choosing of qualified employees without producing the disparate impact.

In subsequent decisions, courts have failed to agree on how much of a disparity is sufficient proof of a prima facie case of discrimination to be rebutted by employers. In 1978 the Equal Employment Opportunity Commission and the Office of Federal Contracts Compliance Office Programs issued guidelines for the use of selection tests that offered a four-fifths rule: if the passing rate for minorities is less than 80 percent of the rate for nonminorities, a prima facie case of discrimination has been shown, and the burden of proof then falls on the employer to demonstrate that the test measures job-related characteristics.[39] This standard has been used by a number of courts in subsequent cases.[40]

3. Cases brought by white males who charge that they are victims of discrimination provide additional guidance for required and permissible employer actions.[41] In *United Steelworkers of America vs. Weber,* the Supreme Court upheld an affirmative action plan that reserved 50 percent of the openings in a training program for black employees.[42] A white male employee challenged the agreement as a violation of Title VII's prohibition against preferential treatment. The plan in question was upheld for three reasons. First, although Title VII prohibited government from requiring preferential treatment in response to a racial imbalance, it did not, according to the Court, interdict a voluntary effort. Second, the plan was temporary and was "not intended to maintain a racial balance but simply to eliminate a manifest racial imbalance." Third, it did not "unnecessarily trammel the interests of white employees," nor did it

"require the discharge of white workers and their replacement with new black hirees."

In two 1986 opinions the Supreme Court provided guidelines for the use of hiring goals under Title VII. In *Local 28 of the Sheet Metal Workers' International Association vs. EEOC,* the Court upheld race-conscious relief as a remedy for past discrimination and ruled that the remedies need not be limited to actual victims of discrimination.[43] The union had been found guilty of unlawful discrimination in a federal court in 1975 and was subsequently found in contempt for failing to obey court orders. The lower court imposed a membership goal of 29.23 percent by August 1987; the Supreme Court defended the goal as a narrowly tailored and reasonable response to a "history of egregious violation" of Title VII. The remedy was temporary, it did not "unnecessarily trammel the interests of white employees" and, consistent with congressional intent, was not invoked "simply to create a racially balanced work force."

In *Local Number 93, International Association of Firefighters, AFL-CIO, C.L.C. vs. City of Cleveland,* the Court upheld a consent decree adopted by a lower court that set a fixed number for the promotion of minority employees.[44] The city had unsuccessfully defended itself in previous lawsuits, and it negotiated the promotion goals with black and Hispanic firefighters that was then submitted to a federal court as a proposed consent decree. The court approved in 1983, over the objections of the union, which then sued the city. The Supreme Court upheld the plan even though it benefited individuals who were not actual victims of discrimination, arguing that Congress had intended to encourage "voluntary" agreements between unions and employers to eradicate racial discrimination. Consent decrees were characterized by the Court as primarily voluntary, thus exempting them from restrictions placed by Congress on judicial remedies for Title VII violations court orders.

The Court issued two key opinions in early 1987. In *U.S. vs. Paradise,* the Court ruled that federal courts can impose "catch-up" promotion quotas on employers to bring the percentage of qualified minority employees in line with minority representation in the available labor force.[45] A federal judge had ordered the state of Alabama to promote one black state trooper for each white, as long as qualified blacks were available, until either 25 percent of the rank in question was black or the state established an acceptable promotion system. The Court found a long history of discrimination and "resistance to court orders" in Alabama and reiterated earlier cases establishing that "governmental bodies, including courts, may constitutionally employ racial classifications essential to remedy unlawful treatment of racial or ethnic groups subject to discrimination."

In *Johnson vs. Transportation Agency,* the Court ruled that government agencies could respond to an "obvious imbalance" in certain job categories by giving preferential treatment to qualified female employees. The agency's affirmative action plan, according to the Court, did not "unnecessarily trammel the rights of male employees or create an absolute bar to their advancement. . . .

The plan set aside no positions for women. . . . Rather, the plan merely authorizes that consideration be given to affirmative action concerns when evaluating qualified applicants.'' The Court signaled its acceptance of preferential treatment that was a "moderate, flexible, case-by-case approach to effecting a gradual improvement in the representation of minorities and women in the Agency's work force."[46]

In cases related to Title VII and affirmative action, the Supreme Court has provided a variety of hints at what would and would not be acceptable interpretations of affirmative action. In *Fullilove vs. Klutznick,* it upheld a federal works program enacted by Congress that set aside 10 percent of the funds provided for "minority business enterprises."[47] The Court concluded that Congress need not act in a "wholly color-blind fashion" in remedying discrimination but that such action could only be justified under the broad remedial powers of Congress. In *United Jewish Organization vs. Carey,* a case involving the redrawing of voting district lines, the Court ruled that the state legislature could consider the impact of redistricting on racial groups even though there had been no finding of discrimination in previous redistricting decisions.[48] In *Regents of the University of California vs. Bakke,* the Court rejected the university's medical school admission policy that set aside sixteen admissions for minority applicants, arguing that such quotas were appropriate only in response to a clear finding of discrimination.[49] The Court did, however, uphold the consideration of race as one of many factors included in the decision to admit students in order to insure diversity in the school's student body.

In summary, the Supreme Court has generally held that the equal protection clause of the Fourteenth Amendment requires that governmental actions that disadvantage minorities will be considered "suspect," and will be upheld only if they are necessary to achieve a "compelling state interest."[50] It is not clear, however, if the same standard applies to efforts that benefit minorities. In Bakke, Justice Powell argued that there was no distinction to be made between actions that disadvantaged minorities and majorities and that both kinds of efforts were to trigger strict scrutiny. Like the 1986 Title VII cases discussed above, Bakke appears to prohibit the imposition of goals and timetables or quotas on hiring and promotion decisions in the *"absence of judicial, legislative, or administrative findings,"* although such actions, if voluntary, are acceptable. Employers may treat race and sex as "plus factors" in giving preferential treatment to women and minorities on a case-by-case basis without any finding of previous discrimination.

RACE-CONSCIOUS REDUCTIONS IN WORKFORCE

Applying the legal and constitutional strictures for preferential treatment to reduction-in-workforce decisions exemplifies the difficult ethical choices confronting public managers. Decisions concerning layoffs can be especially difficult since they interrupt legitimate employee expectations for employment opportunities and represent uncertainty and fear that can breed tension and competition among fellow workers. Progress made in hiring employees from groups who have suffered discrimination in the past is lost since they are the first to go when payrolls must be reduced. Reduction-in-force decisions confront employers with a choice between responding to the arguments in favor of preferential treatment for a minority of employees and respecting the seniority rights of the majority of them.

In *Memphis Fire Department vs. Stotts,* the Supreme Court maintained that "bona fide" seniority systems could not be interfered with in trying to protect the jobs of minorities that, as last to be hired, were first to be fired or laid off by cities or other employers suffering from financial constraints.[51] That decision was reinforced in *Wygant vs. Jackson Board of Education.*[52] A collective-bargaining agreement between teachers and the school board required that teachers with the most seniority be the last to be laid off, except that a greater percentage of minority teachers could not be laid off than the current percentage of minority personnel employed at the time of the layoffs. The Court reaffirmed the position taken in earlier cases that race-conscious actions must meet three conditions: there must be a "compelling state interest" that requires a response; the action taken must be "narrowly tailored"; and there must be evidence of prior discrimination. In this case, the Court rejected the school board's argument that the value of having minority teachers as role models outweighed the commitment to the seniority system and also noted the absence of a factual finding of discrimination to trigger the preferential treatment.

The arguments of the concurring and dissenting opinions illuminate the kinds of concerns public employers are likely to address when considering affirmative action plans. Justice Powell rejected the lower court's ruling that preferential treatment was justified by the need for more minority teachers to serve as role models for minority students, since the percentage of minority teachers was less than that of minority students. The proper test, according to Powell, was a comparison between the "teaching staff and the racial composition of the qualified public school teacher population in the relevant labor market." Since there are "numerous explanations for a disparity between the percentage of minority students and the percentage of minority faculty, many of them completely unrelated to discrimination of any kind," that disparity could not serve as an appropriate basis for "imposing discriminatory legal remedies that work against innocent people."

A public employer, Powell continued, "must ensure that, before it embarks on an affirmative action program, it has convincing evidence that remedial action is warranted. That is, it must have sufficient evidence to justify the conclusion that there has been prior discrimination." General societal discrimination is not a sufficient basis for granting preferential treatment to minorities but requires "some showing of prior discrimination by the governmental unit involved before allowing limited use of racial classifications in order to remedy such discrimination."[53]

He concluded that if a "limited and properly tailored remedy to cure the effects of prior discrimination" was fashioned, it was permissible for innocent parties to share in that burden. "In cases involving valid hiring goals, the burden to be borne by innocent individuals is diffused to a considerable extent among society generally." But layoffs should be viewed differently:

Though hiring goals may burden some innocent individuals, they simply do not impose the same kind of injury that layoffs impose. Denial of a future employment opportunity is not as intrusive as loss of an existing job. . . . While hiring goals impose a diffuse burden, often foreclosing only one of several opportunities, layoffs impose the entire burden of achieving racial equality on particular individuals often resulting in serious disruption of their lives. That burden is too intrusive.[54]

There appears to be a consensus among the justices that

a public employer, consistent with the Constitution, may undertake an affirmative action program which is designed to further a legitimate remedial purpose and which implements that purpose by means that do not impose disproportionate harm on the interests, or unnecessarily trammel the rights, of innocent individuals, directly and adversely affected by a plan's racial preference.[55]

Indeed, public employers, according to a majority of the Court, have a "constitutional duty to take affirmative steps to eliminate the continuing effects of past unconstitutional discrimination."[56] The problem is in the Court's requirement that public employers have evidence of past discriminatory activity before initiating race-conscious remedies, so that they are clearly remedying their "own unlawful conduct . . . rather than attempting to alleviate the wrongs suffered through general societal discrimination." Such a requirement may undermine the willingness of employers to develop voluntary efforts since employer findings of discrimination can serve as the basis for liability to minorities who claim they are victims of illegal actions.

The idea that voluntary preferential treatment is to be encouraged, while court or agency-imposed efforts are much more likely to be rejected, raises additional problems. The primary concern appears to be that of the rights of the employers to make employment decisions; yet *Weber, Wygant,* and related cases were brought by nonminority employees who argued that their rights were violated. For them, it may not be important whether their employer is acting voluntarily or involuntarily since their rights are threatened in either case. The analysis more appropriately turns on whether the violation of their rights to be treated without regard to their race or sex outweighs the desire to give preferential treatment to their minority and female coworkers and coapplicants.

Most public employers are likely to agree that individuals clearly identifiable as victims of discrimination should be given preferential treatment in order to make them whole. It may be appropriate, however, to go beyond that in arguing that when an employer has engaged in discriminatory practices, it has placed white males in positions of greater seniority than they would have otherwise enjoyed. Although these employees are not responsible for nor guilty of discrimination themselves, they are nevertheless beneficiaries of illegal actions since their seniority is greater than it would have been had there been no discrimination and can be called on to share the burden of rectifying those wrongs. The kind of remedy rejected by the Court in *Wygant* seems to be an appropriate means of responding to past discrimination. The majority's rejection of such efforts (as being insufficiently limited and improperly tailored) defends "less intrusive means of accomplishing similar purposes—such as the adoption of hiring goals." Yet this falls short, since these goals are empty gestures when employers must lay off workers and in no sense constitute remedies to past discrimination.[57]

CONCLUSION

Public employers have a particular responsibility to bring to an end discriminatory employment practices aimed at women and minorities. If they believe they are also obligated to help eradicate the effects of past discrimination on the opportunities of women and minorities—and this is the fundamental question that they must address—they will likely choose to engage in some form of affirmative action. The effects of past discrimination will not be overcome simply by ending discriminatory practices, although the ability of preferential treatment to bring about equality of opportunity is not guaranteed. Preferential treatment has great potential for dividing workers, since it may reinforce the belief that progress made by women and minorities is only due to special treatment. Yet taking steps to insure that discrimination no longer exists, but going no further, may result in lost opportunities to help women and minorities develop employment experience.

Employers can do much to avoid having to pursue the most divisive forms of preferential treatment by expanding educational, training, and outreach efforts that increase the ability of women and minorities to compete in the workplace. When choices do have to be made between applicants and employees for scarce positions, employers should ideally focus on individual situations and give preference to those who have been actual victims of discrimination in education and other areas. This would result in some women and minorities not being given special treatment. Such efforts at individualized justice are more desirable than the gross, imprecise calculations of preferential treatment, but if resources are not available to make such particularized judgments, the goal of eradicating past discrimination may not be satisfied without taking affirmative action in behalf of those who have suffered not because of individual characteristics but because of their collective identity.

For many public employers, every employment decision will be enveloped in ethical, legal, and practical questions. Although there are some legal and administrative restraints and obligations that must be satisfied, many of these decisions will ultimately rest on ethical calculations and considerations. For employers who are optimistic about the ability of government to intervene and engineer employment arrangements that remedy past discrimination and insure equality of opportunity, hiring goals and other initiatives will likely be embraced by them. For employers who believe that a free labor market exists and are optimistic about its ability to generate a fair distribution of opportunities, preferential treatment will be viewed as a mistake.

NOTES

1. Civil Rights Act of 1964, section 7; E.O. 11246, 3 CFR 169.

2. Citizens' Commission on Civil Rights, *Affirmative Action to Open the Doors of Job Opportunity* (Washington, D.C., June 1984).

3. For a history of affirmative action, see U.S. Civil Rights Commission, *Affirmative Action in the 1980s: Dismantling the Process of Discrimination* (Washington, D.C., November 1981).

4. United Steelworkers of America vs. Weber, 443 U.S. 193 (1979); *Local 28 of the Sheet Metal Workers' International Association vs. EEOC,* 106 S. Ct. 3019 (1986); Wygant vs. Jackson Board of Education, 106 S. Ct. 1842 (1986).

5. Local 28 vs. EEOC.

6. Anthony Neely, "Government Role in Rooting Out, Remedying Discrimination Is Shifting," *National Journal,* September 22, 1984, pp. 1772–1775.

7. Robert Pear, "Dispute on Policy on Jobs Continues," *New York Times,* 30 January 1986; "Reagan Weighing Plans to Revise Rules on Hiring Women and Minorities," *New York Times,* 13 February 1986.

8. Howard Kurtz, "What's All This Fuss over Hiring Goals?" *Washington Post National Weekly Edition,* 24 February 1986; "Bias Agency Drops Numerical Goals," *New York Times,* 12 February 1986.

9. *See,* generally, Citizens' Commission on Civil Rights, *Affirmative Action.*

10. William L. Taylor, "Access to Economic Opportunities: Lessons Since Brown," in Leslie Dunbar, ed., *Minority Report* (New York: Pantheon, 1984).

11. Herman Schwartz, "Affirmative Action," in Leslie Dunbar, ed., *Minority Report* (New York: Pantheon, 1984).

12. For an elaboration of these arguments, *see* Louis I. Katzner, "Reverse Discrimination," in Tom Regan and Donald Van Der Veer, eds., *And Justice for All* (Totowa, N.J.: Rowman and Littlefield, 1982).

13. Proponents of preferential treatment also contend that the idea of employment decisions being made exclusively on the basis of objective criteria, such as merit and qualifications, is a chimera. Preferential treatment is sometimes given to candidates or employees because of personal or family relationships rather than merit. Employment decisions are made in response to a number of factors that include conformity to prevailing norms of appearance and personality that are clearly not merit based. The ideal of decision-making on the basis of merit is so rarely satisfied that it cannot serve as the

basis for rejecting preferential treatment. Hardy Jones, "Fairness, Meritocracy, and Reverse Discrimination," in Ellen F. Paul and Philip A. Russo, eds., *Public Policy: Issues, Analysis, and Ideology* (Chatham, N.J.: Chatham House, 1982).

14. *See* United Steelworkers of America vs. Weber.

15. Citizens' Commission on Civil Rights, *Affirmative Action,* chapter four.

16. Douglas Huron, "It's Fashionable to Denigrate Hiring Quotas—But It's Wrong," *Washington Post National Weekly Edition,* 27 August 1984, p. 23.

17. Quoted in Schwartz, "Affirmative Action," p. 63.

18. Ibid. For elaborations of these views, *see* William B. Allen, Drew S. Days III, Benjamin L. Hooks, and William Bradford Reynolds, "Is Affirmative Action Constitutional?" *Regulation,* July–August 1985, pp. 12–18, 39–45; Neely, "Government Role," pp. 1774–1778; Rochelle Stanfield, "Reagan Courting Women, Minorities, but It May Be too Late," *National Journal,* May 28, 1983, pp. 1118–1123; Donna St. George, "Administration May Have to Shelve Its Relaxed Minority Hiring Rules," *National Journal,* October 1983, pp. 2170–2173.

19. *Regents of the University of California vs. Bakke,* 438 U.S. 26 (1978), at 5.

20. Ibid. One would likely believe that Powell overstated the case here, since blacks have arguably had minority status in the United States for more than 300 years.

21. Nathan Glazer, "Why Bakke Won't End Reverse Discrimination," in Ellen F. Paul and Philip A. Russo, eds., *Public Policy: Issues, Analysis, and Ideology* (Chatham, N.J.: Chatham House, 1982), p. 253.

22. Ernest Van den Haag, "Reverse Discrimination: A Brief against It," in Ellen F. Paul and Philip A. Russo, eds., *Public Policy: Issues, Analysis, and Ideology* (Chatham, N.J.: Chatham House, 1982), p. 259.

23. Thomas Sowell, "Are Quotas Good for Blacks?" in Ellen F. Paul and Philip A. Russo, eds., *Public Policy: Issues, Analysis, and Ideology* (Chatham, N.J.: Chatham House, 1982), p. 264.

24. Sowell, *Civil Rights: Rhetoric or Reality?* (New York: Quill/William Morrow, 1984), p. 42.

25. "Is Affirmative Action Constitutional," *Regulation,* July–August 1985, pp. 12–18; Clarence Pendleton, "Equality of Opportunity or Equality of Results?" *Human Rights,* Fall 1985, pp. 19–22.

26. *See* Robert Nozick, *Anarchy, State, and Utopia* (New York: Basic Books, 1974).

27. *See* James S. Fishkin, *Justice, Equal Opportunity, and the Family* (New Haven: Yale University Press, 1983).

28. Robert A. Destro, "Equality, Social Welfare, and Equal Protection," *Harvard Journal of Law and Public Policy* 9, no. 1 (Winter 1986): 51–61.

29. For an introduction to this debate, *see* Paul Burnstein, *Discrimination, Jobs, and Politics: The Struggle for Equal Employment Opportunity in the United States Since the New Deal* (Chicago: University of Chicago Press, 1985); Jonathan Leonard, "The Impact of Affirmative Action," (Washington, D.C.: U.S. Department of Labor, July 1983); idem, "Employment and Occupational Advance under Affirmative Action," *The Review of Economics and Statistics,* August 1984, pp. 377–385.

30. For these and related figures, *see* the *Economic Report of the President* (Washington, D.C.: U.S. Government Printing Office, 1987), pp. 278, 285.

31. *U.S. Statistical Abstract* (Washington, D.C.: U.S. Government Printing Office, 1984), pp. 419–20.

32. Section 202(1).

33. *See,* generally, U.S. Department of Labor, "Employment Patterns of Minorities and Women in Federal Contractor and Noncontractor Establishments, 1974–1980: A Report of The Office of Federal Contract Compliance Programs" (Washington, D.C., June 1984).

34. Title VII also provides several exemptions to this general policy: (1) employment-related decisions can be made on the basis of "religion, sex, or national origin in those certain instances where religion, sex, or national origin is a bona fide occupational qualification reasonably necessary to the normal operation of that particular business or enterprise"; (2) educational institutions may "hire and employ employees of a particular religion" if the institution is "in whole, or in substantial part, owned, supported, controlled, or managed by a particular religion" or if the curriculum "is directed toward the propagation of a particular religion"; (3) employees whose duties and performance are "subject to any requirement imposed in the interest of the national security of the United States" under federal statutes or executive orders are not protected by Title VII; (4) "different standards of compensation, or different terms, conditions, or privileges of employment pursuant to a bona fide seniority or merit system" are permitted, as long as "such differences are not the result of an intention to discriminate" because of the suspect categories; and (5) employers may "give and . . . act upon the results of any professionally developed ability test" that is not "designed, intended or used to discriminate because of race, color, religion, sex or national origin." Section 703(e), (g), (i).

35. 411 U.S. 792 (1973).

36. The Court provided additional guidance for resolving these questions in Furnco Construction Corp. vs. Waters, 438 U.S. 567 (1978); Board of Trustees of Keene State College vs. Sweeny, 439 U.S. 295 (1978); and Texas Department of Community Affairs vs. Burdine, 450 U.S. 248 (1981). According to the Burdine Court, an employer charged with discrimination bears "the burden of explaining clearly the nondiscriminatory reasons for its actions" rather than having to prove "by a preponderance of the evidence the existence of nondiscriminatory reasons."

37. 401 U.S. 424 (1971).

38. Title VII, section 703h.

39. *Federal Register* 43 (1978): 38291.

40. *See* Joel Friedman and George Stricker, Jr., *The Law of Employment Discrimination* (Mineola, N.Y.: Foundation Press, 1983), p. 96.

41. Title VII also provides guidelines for courts and agencies in responding to past discrimination and in fashioning remedies. If a court determines that an employer "has intentionally engaged . . . in an unlawful employment practice," it "may enjoin the [employer] from engaging in such . . . practice, and order such affirmative action, as may be appropriate, which may include, but is not limited to, reinstatement or hiring of employees, with or without back pay . . . or any other equitable relief as the court deems appropriate." Section 703(j), 706(g).

42. 443 U.S. 193 (1979).

43. 106 S. Ct. 3019 (1986).

44. 106 S. Ct. 3063 (1986).

45. 107 S. Ct. 1053 (1987).

46. S. Ct. Dkt. No. 85–1129 (1987).

47. 448 U.S. 448 (1980).

48. 443 U.S. 144 (1978).

49. 438 U.S. 265 (1978).

50. For a general discussion of this issue, *see* Ronald Dworkin, *A Matter of Principle* (Cambridge, Mass.: Harvard University Press, 1985), pp. 311–312.
   51. 104 S. Ct. 2576 (1984).
   52. 106 S. Ct. 1842 (1986).
   53. Ibid., at 1850.
   54. Ibid., at 1850–1852.
   55. Ibid., at 1853–1854.
   56. Ibid., at 1856–1857.
   57. *See* dissenting opinion of Justice Marshall in *Wygant,* 106 S. Ct. 1842, at 1864.

SELECTED BIBLIOGRAPHY

Abram, Morris. "Affirmative Action: Fair Shakers and Social Engineers." *Harvard Law Review* 99 (1986): 1312–1326.
Ackerman, Bruce A. *Social Justice in the Liberal State.* New Haven: Yale University Press, 1980.
Allen, William B., Drew S. Days III, Benjamin L. Hooks, and William Bradford Reynolds. "Is Affirmative Action Constitutional?" *Regulation,* July–August 1985, pp. 12–18, 39–45.
Bureau of National Affairs. "Title VII at 20." *EEOC Compliance Manual,* no. 83 (October 18, 1985): 1–24.
Burnstein, Paul. *Discrimination, Jobs, and Politics: The Struggle for Equal Employment Opportunity in the United States Since the New Deal.* Chicago: University of Chicago Press, 1985.
Citizens' Commission on Civil Rights. *Affirmative Action to Open the Doors of Job Opportunity* (Washington, D.C., June 1984).
Cohen, Marshall, Thomas Nagel, and Thomas Scanlon. *Equality and Preferential Treatment.* Princeton, N.J.: Princeton University Press, 1977.
Destro, Robert. "Equality, Social Welfare, and Equal Protection." *Harvard Journal of Law and Public Policy* 9, no. 1 (Winter 1986): 51–61.
Dunbar, Leslie, ed. *Minority Report.* New York: Pantheon, 1984.
Dworkin, Ronald. *Taking Rights Seriously.* Cambridge, Mass.: Harvard University Press, 1977.
———. "Why Bakke Has No Case." *New York Review of Books,* November 11, 1977.
———. *A Matter of Principle.* Cambridge, Mass.: Harvard University Press, 1985.
Fishkin, James S. *Justice, Equal Opportunity, and the Family.* New Haven: Yale University Press, 1983.
Friedman, Joel William, and George M. Strickler, Jr. *The Law of Employment Discrimination.* Mineola, N.Y.: Foundation Press, 1983.
Fullinwinder, Robert K. *The Reverse Discrimination Controversy: A Moral and Legal Analysis.* Totowa, N.J.: Rowman and Littlefield, 1980.
Glazer, Nathan. *Affirmative Discrimination: Ethnic Inequality and Public Policy.* New York: Basic Books, 1978.
Goldman, Alan. *Justice and Reverse Discrimination.* Princeton, N.J.: Princeton University Press, 1979.
Gross, Barry R. *Discrimination in Reverse: Is Turnabout Fair Play?* New York: New York University Press, 1978.
———, ed. *Reverse Discrimination.* Buffalo: Prometheus, 1977.
Jones, James E. "The Genesis and Present Status of Affirmative Action in Employment:

Economic, Legal, and Political Realities." *Iowa Law Review* 70 (1985): 901–944.

Katzner, Louis I. "Reverse Discrimination." In Tom Regan and Donald Van Der Veer, eds., *And Justice for All*. Totowa, N.J.: Rowman and Littlefield, 1982.

Kennedy, Randall. "Persuasion and Distrust: A Comment on the Affirmative Action Debate." *Harvard Law Review* 99 (1986): 1327–1346.

Leonard, Jonathan S. "The Impact of Affirmative Action." Washington, D.C.: U.S. Department of Labor, July 1983.

———. "Employment and Occupational Advance under Affirmative Action." *The Review of Economics and Statistics* (August 1984): 377–385.

Lucash, Frank S., ed. *Justice and Equality: Here and Now*. Ithaca, N.Y.: Cornell University Press, 1986.

Nozick, Robert. *Anarchy, State, and Utopia*. New York: Basic Books, 1974.

Rawls, John. *A Theory of Justice*. Cambridge, Mass.: Harvard University Press, 1971.

Reynolds, William Bradford. "Civil Rights: Beyond the Conventional Agenda." Speech given at Stanford University, February 17, 1987.

Rodgers, Harrell R., Jr. "Fair Employment Laws for Minorities: An Evaluation of Federal Implementation." In Charles S. Bullock III and Charles M. Lamb, eds., *Implementation of Civil Rights Policy*. Monterey, Calif.: Brooks/Cole, 1984, pp. 93–117.

Rosenbloom, David M. *Federal Equal Employment Opportunity: Politics and Public Administration*. New York: Praeger, 1977.

Sandel, Michael. *Liberalism and the Limits of Justice*. New York: Cambridge University Press, 1984.

Schiller, Bradley R. *The Economics of Poverty and Discrimination*. Englewood Cliffs, N.J.: Prentice-Hall, 1984.

Schwartz, Herman. "Affirmative Action." In Leslie Dunbar, ed., *Minority Report*. New York: Pantheon, 1984.

Sowell, Thomas. *The Economics and Politics of Race*. New York: Morrow, 1983.

———. *Civil Rights: Rhetoric or Reality?* New York: Quill/Morrow, 1984.

Taylor, William L. "Access to Economic Opportunities: Lessons Since Brown." In Leslie Dunbar, ed., *Minority Report*. New York: Pantheon, 1984.

Tribe, Laurence. *Constitutional Choices*. Cambridge, Mass.: Harvard University Press, 1986.

U.S. Civil Rights Commission. *Affirmative Action in the 1980s: Dismantling the Process of Discrimination* (Washington, D.C., 1981).

U.S. Department of Labor. "Employment Patterns of Minorities and Women in Federal Contractor and Noncontractor Establishments, 1974–1980: A Report of the Office of Federal Contract Compliance Programs" (Washington, D.C., June 1984).

U.S. Senate, Labor and Human Resources Committee. "Committee Analysis of Executive Order 11246" (Washington, D.C., 1982).

Van den Haag, Ernest. "Reverse Discrimination: A Brief against It." In Ellen F. Paul and Philip A. Russo, eds., *Public Policy: Issues, Analysis, and Ideology*. Chatham, N.J.: Chatham House, 1982.

Vaughn, Dennis H. "Employment Quotas—Discrimination or Affirmative Action." *Employee Relations Law Journal* 7 (Spring 1982): 552–566.

Weatherspoon, Floyd D. *Equal Employment Opportunity and Affirmative Action: A Sourcebook*. New York: Garland, 1985.

PART FOUR

STUDIES OF SYSTEMIC ISSUES IN GOVERNMENT

9

Professional Expertise in Politics and Administration

John P. Burke and Richard L. Pattenaude

One generalization about the American bureaucracy with which it is difficult to disagree is that bureaucracy has become increasingly professional. Although scholarly analysts of the professions have not settled upon one definition of what constitutes a profession, occupations with general professional characteristics such as a high degree of specialized and systematic knowledge, an orientation to the public interest, a large measure of self and peer control over behavior, and rewards based on relevant standards of work achievement have proliferated in the administrative sphere.[1] At the federal level alone, more than one-third of the employees are presently classified as professional (19.0 percent) or technical (17.0 percent).[2] This is more than three times the rate (10.3 percent) in the private sector.[3]

Not only are the sheer numbers of professionals impressive, particular professions have risen to prominence—dominance in some cases—within particular departments, agencies, and bureaus: for example, public health doctors in the Public Health Service, civil engineers in the Bureau of Reclamation, lawyers in the Department of Justice, natural scientists in the Bureau of Standards, educators in the Department of Education, and foresters in the Forest Service.[4] State and local governments extensively employ social workers, psychiatrists, and civil engineers, as well as those professionals found in all levels of government.[5] Furthermore, government is a primary employer of many of the newly emerging professions: penologists, personnel experts, computer technicians, environmental scientists, and public administrators.[6] As Frederick Mosher concluded in his seminal study of the public service, "For better or worse—or better and worse—much of our government is now in the hands of professionals."[7]

Mosher's comments attest to the increasingly professional character of bureaucracy, but they also point out the mixed consequences of relying upon professional skill and expertise. In its most positive contribution, professional knowledge can offer the most practical and knowledgeable solution to problems of policy design and formulation and the most effective and efficient implementation of policy goals, depending upon the stage in the policy process in which expertise is used. Contributions of this sort would presumably comprise the "better" side, in Mosher's view, of having government increasingly "in the hands of professionals."

But reliance on professional expertise can also create its own problems—Mosher's "worse" outcome. Turning policy problems over to professionals does not guarantee that they will serve the interests of the public or higher political authorities such as legislatures or chief executives; professionals can retard as well as advance public ends and purposes. For example, professional competence can be incorrectly applied, its scope and limits misunderstood. Furthermore, even when correctly matched to the tasks at hand, professional expertise can be tarnished by the self-interested motivation and behavior of practitioners; the label "professional" or "expert" provides no guarantee against venality and other abuses of expertise. Not only is understanding professional expertise in today's bureaucracy descriptively significant—involving the recognition of its growing role in the policy process—but also the increasing reliance upon expertise raises prescriptive questions about its proper and rightful place in policy decisions and outcomes.

It is the latter set of issues that concern us in this chapter. We begin by exploring some of the tensions between democratic rule and professional expertise. Some of the central arguments about the role of professional facility in the policy process, especially as it applies to advising and decision-making, are considered. Drawing on a case study based on an actual interaction between professional experts and political decisionmakers, we offer some suggestions about how professionals and the political elites who turn to them for advice might better conceive of their roles and responsibilities in the policy-making process.

BACKGROUND

Historical Rise of the Professions

The view that professionals have a central and often problematic role in the policy process is well documented, both in the history of American public administration and in scholarly reflection upon it. In the nineteenth century, as political patronage and the spoils system waned, reliance upon the merit system, and hence job-related tests of skill and competence, facilitated the introduction of professional expertise into the bureaucracy. The classic watershed marking this trend is the Civil Service Reform Act of 1883, a "permanent if partial victory," in Leonard White's words, of the administrative reformers over the party bosses and the spoils systems.[8]

Civil service reform began to end some of the abuses that had plagued public management, but it did not smooth all of the tensions between the politics and administration. In his classic essay, "The Study of Administration," published only four years after the Civil Service Reform Act, Woodrow Wilson explored the emerging tension between democratic government and an increasingly professional administrative sphere, noting that it was "getting to be harder to run a constitution than to frame one."[9] Wilson's essay in fact appeared the same year as the Interstate Commerce Act of 1887, another hallmark, as Dwight Waldo has noted, in the

passage of the United States from a simple, agricultural society into a highly complex and interrelated . . . new society based upon a highly advanced division of labor and specialization of skill, a highly developed system of transportation and communication, a vast sprawling technology—all based upon a new method of controlling [the] environment called "scientific method."[10]

These professional and scientific trends in public administration accelerated, in turn, during the twentieth century as government took on new policy functions and tasks—health care, nuclear power, economic management, and environmental protection, for example—where the need for excellence is at its strongest. As Herbert Kaufman noted, in the 100 years following the Civil Service Act of 1883, "despite great political swings, enormous governmental growth, deep depressions, and global wars, the process of neutralizing the civil service and promoting the merit system progressed from hesitant, uncertain beginnings to almost total victory in the federal government."[11]

The Problem of the Professions in a Democracy

Although professionals increasingly employ their expertise in public service, there is no guarantee that what they do or what advice they give will serve the interests and purposes of those who rely upon them, whether the latter are higher authorities in the bureaucracy, legislators, or the public at large. Professionals in the public service generally exercise some measure of discretion, depending on the particular type of expertise or skills they possess. However, the exercise of that discretion requires autonomy of judgment and action that may at times be at odds with the interests and purposes of others legitimately involved in the policy process, as Gerald Pops pointed out in chapter two. Analysis of the role of expertise in the administrative process thus raises issues that are central in understanding the place of bureaucracy within a democratic political system.

A number of problems characteristically crop up that are important in understanding the effects of expertise upon policy choice, the particular problem of using expertise that will concern us here. First, problems that seem to be matters of professional attainment may in fact be political or matters of personal preference. For instance, is the governmental provision of certain kinds of health services a political or properly professional decision? Is the right to die in the case of a terminally ill patient solely a matter of medical knowledge?

Policy issues also may be only partially fit for the application of professional judgment and expertise. Again to use an example from health care, licensing of drugs currently is determined by federal standards that require that drugs be both "safe and efficacious." Assuming that professional standards about safety are adequate, what standards of efficacy should prevail? Should we defer to the stringent, scientific ones of the medical profession, or should we acknowledge other standards, perhaps those of a terminally ill patient who might gain some psychological satisfaction from using a drug that otherwise has no proven medical effects? In cases such as this, simply to leave policy issues wholly to the discretion of professionals ignores competing political or personal claims.

LITERATURE REVIEW

Both the increasing role of professional expertise in the administrative process and the implications, positive and negative, it bears for public policy have been the subject of scholarly speculation and discussion. Frederick Mosher and Herbert Kaufman do not stand alone in observing that the administrative sphere has become increasingly professional and that it bears both positive and negative implications.

The professional—especially scientific—character of public management is a theme resonant in the work of pioneers such as Frank Goodnow, Frederick Taylor, Henri Fayol, Luther Gulick, and Lynall Urwick. In the concluding essay of the seminal volume *Papers on the Science of Administration,* coedited with Urwick, Gulick began by asserting that public administration is a scientific endeavor. He ended the chapter with a series of proposals to enhance the quest of public administration for scientific validity: "All of these factors played their part in the conquest of the natural world by exact science, and may be counted upon again to advance scientific knowledge and control in the world of human affairs."[12] Gulick's optimism, however, belies the scientific character of many administrative activities and fails to recognize the political limits that must sometimes be set upon administrative judgment and advice, whatever the degree of its scientific character.

The dichotomous separation of politics from the "science of administration" present in these early efforts was—rightfully—challenged by the next generation of scholars: luminaries such as Marshall Dimock, Carl Friedrich, John Gaus, Donald Price, Herbert Simon, and Dwight Waldo. However, each retained some notion of the administrative process as professional, even while emphasizing its inherently political character. For example, in an oft-quoted line in an essay in *Public Administration Review,* John Gaus concluded that "a theory of administration means in our time a theory of politics also."[13] But Gaus himself earlier had acknowledged that in "the system of government which is now emerging, one important kind of responsibility will be that which the individual civil servant recognizes as due to the standards and ideals of his profession. This is his 'inner check.' '' [14]

The difficulty in this view is in determining when the professional "inner check" or the dictates of politics ought to prevail. Many like Gaus simply noted the need for both. Similarly, in his famous "debate" with Herman Finer on administrative responsibility, Carl Friedrich was content to propose a "dual standard" of administrative responsibility ("the responsible administrator is one who is responsive to these two dominant factors: technical knowledge and popular sentiment") without any mention of possible conflicts and trade-offs between them. [15]

In more recent scholarship—the "New Public Administration" and the "Critical Theory" approach to management—the professional character of the bureaucratic "experience" continues to loom large. [16] The accent now falls more on the dark side of expertise, such as the effects of self-serving professional interests, false scientism, and a depoliticized, alienating, instrumental rationality, but the significance of professional expertise—albeit now seen in a more critical light—remains central nonetheless. As Frank Fischer observed with respect to a particular professional skill that is widely used in the policy process—policy analysis: "The limitations of a policy science so dominated by the criteria of efficiency emerge dramatically." As Fischer went on to note, the increasing use of such a professional skill is not without its costs: "a growing number of writers attribute the failures that policy evaluation has encountered to its narrowly instrumental focus." [17]

This "instrumental" focus is for Fischer and other proponents of the Critical Theory approach the crux of their criticism of professional expertise. But while alerting us to the dangers and limitations of professional expertise, the New Public Administration and Critical Theory approaches have not given professional expertise its due. Surely in some cases, expertise does at least approach the goal of objectivity; furthermore, political judgments about policy means and goals may be equally if not more flawed when compared to the counsel of professionals.

Clearly, both the claims of politics and of the professions must be subject to critical examination. The goal here is to try to understand more fully the strengths and weaknesses on each side and from this to construct a better understanding of how professional expertise can positively contribute to the policy process.

CONCEPTUAL FRAMEWORK

Although there are undoubtedly a wide range of approaches that might be employed to deal with the problems that professional expertise raises, three in particular stand out: (1) an exclusively professional or "separatist" approach, (2) arguments derived from "ordinary morality," and (3) the claims of politics.

The Separatist Thesis

One way of determining the place of expertise in policy formulation follows from what might be termed the "separatist thesis." The notion here is that professional expertise establishes especially strong claims for autonomous exercise of professional discretion that "trump" other considerations (e.g., the claims of "ordinary" morality or those of politics). As Alan Gewirth summarized, "According to this thesis, professionals, by virtue of their expertise and their consequent roles, have rights and duties that are unique to themselves and that may hence be not only different from, but even contrary to, the rights and duties that are found in other segments of morality." As a result, "the professional's rights may justifiably infringe certain of the moral rights of his clients or of other persons."[18] Arguments of this sort are made by moral philosophers such as Benjamin Freedman and Richard Wasserstrom.[19] They can be found as well in the classic writings of political scientists such as Carl Friedrich and John Gaus.[20]

As a number of critics have pointed out, such a strong view of the primacy of the professional role can lead to the violation of the moral rights of others, which might be equally valued.[21] For example, a doctor's professional rights to some action would always overrule a patient's otherwise rather strong moral rights—to privacy, for example, or freedom of choice—if the separatist thesis is strongly upheld. But this is obviously too extreme a position: surely, there are some moral rights that must be respected whatever the dictates of professional practice.

The way that moral rights sometimes legitimately "hem in" professional practice raises a number of issues that cannot be explored here (e.g., What particular kinds of moral rights limit professional practice? When does professional practice—as a kind of institutional obligation—itself have moral standing?). But at the very least these problems suggest that some limits on professional practice must be established; a strong version of the separatist thesis cannot be maintained.

Furthermore, a strong view of the superiority of the profession's own standards seems overly idealistic, if not naive. The claims to professional status of a particular occupation are often weak. For example, a rough definition of *profession* would probably include characteristics such as collegial determinants of proper service or monitoring of professional practice by some professional body that is empowered to license practitioners and discipline their behavior.[22] Even commonly recognized professions, however, meet these requirements only to some degree.

The absence of many of these criteria is present in many types of expertise employed in a public service context. Studies of city managers, city planners, government-employed engineers, policy analysts, economists, and foreign service personnel, for example, indicate (1) that these occupations do not meet all requirements for professional status; (2) that their professional standards are weak, if they exist at all; and (3) that within these occupations political, rather than professional, considerations are sometimes important in setting policy goals, defining the means to attain them, and regulating ongoing job activity.[23]

Even if these issues about the proper scope of professional expertise—questions relating to whether, in fact, we are dealing with an actual profession—are satisfactorily resolved, questions about the proper application of professional skill and competence remain. One problem concerns the objectivity and neutrality of professional judgment and practice. An implicit assumption in relying upon professional capability to resolve policy matters is that it is somehow superior to "mere politics" and is objective, if not scientific. As Don Price has pointed out, "The professions recognize the extent to which their effective service, and consequently their influence and independence, depend on the objectivity and reliability of scientific data."[24]

In many ways, these claims to objectivity and reliability are unwarranted. Few professions approach the kind of objectivity that even science might claim. Even more telling, few philosophers of science are willing to make such claims about science itself, recognizing the subjectivity that often intrudes into the selection of research projects, organization of research, and the evaluation of research findings.[25] Other analysts have emphasized that science is a community with the same social and collective belief systems and practice as exist in other collectivities.[26] According to Duncan MacRae, "Scientific disciplines may be regarded as largely closed social systems with particular norms and organization structures. . . . [they] favor certain (but not all types) of criticism and innovation."[27] Furthermore, science is a community that may be vulnerable to political pressure and influence, especially through selective governmental support and funding of research projects.[28]

Finally, the professions' claim to autonomy and self-regulation free from political interference are also compromised by the way professions develop self-serving interests. Just as bureaucracies develop "bureaucratic interests," professions can develop their own self-serving pursuits. Interests that serve to maintain or enhance the status, rewards, and power of practitioners or the profession itself can compromise the ability of professionals to work with others in common projects, to serve clients fairly and fully, and to regulate fellow practitioners in the private sphere. Thus not only may the claims to professional status be weak, but the professional practice—even of long established professions—may be rampant with self-interest.[29] To uphold the primacy of the professional role would fail to remedy these imperfections, thereby negatively affecting those policy tasks in which professionals are involved.

The View from Ordinary Morality

At the opposite extreme from the separatist thesis is the view that there is nothing special about professional expertise and that those who make such claims are bound by the same moral considerations that apply in other situations. This view can be found in the writings of Alan Goldman, Robert Veatch, and Bernard Williams.[30] As the discussion of separatist thesis indicates, some weight should obviously be given to the notion that moral rights sometimes trump whatever actions might be dictated by professional norms and values. Yet the difficulty comes in determining precisely what kinds of moral rights should prevail. As Gewirth argued, claims by many proponents of the ordinary morality approach "assume that there is only one set of 'ordinary' ethical beliefs or judgments." But "this overlooks the actual dissensus that exists on many controverted ethical issues, including abortion, welfare provisions, nuclear deterrence, and many others."[31]

Furthermore, professional roles may themselves have some moral standing: they may have the status of "acquired obligations" that could be on a par, morally speaking, with any putative "unacquired" moral rights. As Gewirth concluded, "it is vitally important to recognize that, even when actions are based on morally justified institutions [i.e. a profession], they may justifiably infringe other rationally grounded moral rights."[32]

Finally, there is the problem that ordinary morality is often indifferent to many exercises of professional expertise. Where to locate a highway bridge or how to most efficiently organize the delivery of some service may not raise any moral issues at all. However, such professional decisions may be politically important or they may be subject to some of the problems inherent in professional practice of the sort we have already noted, areas in which ordinary morality is silent but clearly areas in which professional practice might need to be checked or redirected.

The Claims of Politics

The third approach to evaluating the contributions of professional expertise, like that of ordinary morality, denies that there are any special claims to autonomy and discretion to be made on behalf of professionals: politics not professionalism should prevail. Unlike the problems attendant with ordinary morality, this political approach—which essentially leaves it up to political authorities to decide whether and to what extent to heed professional counsel—is not limited to a rather narrow domain. What is politically relevant is generally more encompassing than those policies that are thought to touch upon moral rights. Moreover, political procedures and institutions exist for reconciling conflicts in interests and values; as we have seen, the lack of such agreement weakens the moral approach.

But even with these advantages, a political approach, although perhaps faring a bit better than other alternatives, does not seem fully able to incorporate professional expertise in a sound fashion. Chief executives, legislators, or the public at large are often unable to understand and digest the applicability and limits of expertise in a number of ways.

First, political authorities sometimes undervalue the advice of professionals, deferring to their own judgments. During the 1960s, for example, the drug industry and some members of Congress attempted to pressure professionals in the Food and Drug Administration to place the drug thalidomide on the market despite increasing evidence of the drug's side effects: cases of severe deformities in the infants of mothers who took the drug.[33] Political authorities also can overvalue the claims of professional competence, mistakenly yielding to the advice of professionals. Perhaps the most recent example of this was congressional and legislative acquiescence to professional pressure for a massive, nationwide inoculation program in response to the purported swine flu epidemic that failed to occur.[34]

Finally, political authorities may fail to detect or deal with the self-serving and self-promotional interests that often intrude into professional activities. One study of physicians, while noting that certainly only a minority are culpable, found that "the public dislikes the way physicians seem . . . to have turned means into ends, to have become authoritarian and unresponsive, to care too much about their money income."[35] The same study concluded that a veil of silence enshrouds the profession, protecting "incapacitated, ill, or venal" practitioners: "Those few physicians, nurses or other paramedicals who go against the system and report incompetent physicians may find themselves silenced or punished."[36]

A CASE STUDY OF CONSULTING IN THE PUBLIC SECTOR: ECONOMIC DEVELOPMENT IN OXFORD

To test these various approaches and come to a better understanding of the place of professional expertise and counsel in the policy process, consider a case in which political authorities were in the position of using or not using the advice of experts. The following study is drawn from actual events in a medium-sized northeastern city, although some of the particular names and incidents have been altered.

"Oxford" is a typical declining city in the Northeast: crumbling infrastructure, departing industries, aging population, shrinking tax base, high local tax rate, and competition from its growing suburbs. In an effort to reverse the situation, the voters elected a bright young mayor: "Michele Stevenson."

The mayor threw herself into the job. After three years, with the help of several influential members of the local establishment, she was able to bring about a number of improvements—a hotel complex, a new department store downtown, several light-manufacturing industries, an office building, 200 units of low-income housing, a new sewage-treatment plant, and a proposed bridge across the river to smooth traffic flow into the downtown area. She was particularly pleased when the governor agreed to hold his party's state convention in Oxford to open the new hotel and conference center. At the party convention, there were rumors of a possible Michele Stevenson shot at statewide office.

The mayor believed that Oxford was well on its way to an economic rebound. But much work still remained. The revenue stream was not improving as fast as she had hoped. Furthermore, there was still a lingering image of Oxford as a sleepy backwater. Her economic advisory group, composed of local corporate leaders, especially reminded her of the image problem. In fact, they stressed the negative perceptions of Oxford in the state and region as one of the major roadblocks in drawing talented young professionals to the area.

In her mind, the image problem was simply that: *perceptions* of Oxford, not the reality of living in a city that did have much to offer. But she recognized that all of her economic development projects could be threatened by the lack of cultural resources, one area in which Oxford did lag behind other cities in the region. If she could find some way to solve this problem, Oxford would enjoy a new surge of prosperity.

Accordingly, she asked her chief planner, Carl Ingraham, to ponder the issue. A few days later Ingraham said that his quick research indicated that cities noted for cultural riches had two characteristics: a performing arts facility and a major arts festival in the facility, followed by high-quality programming the rest of the year. Ingraham cautioned her, however, that this was an expensive undertaking. The mayor thanked him for his advice, asking him to keep gathering information. She sensed that this issue was sensitive and too important to be left to the planners' discretion. She would have to get deeply involved.

The mayor became increasingly convinced that Oxford needed the performing arts center to break the log jam on economic development. To do this required two key resources: money and allies. The mayor decided to work first on the allies. If you have the support, she reasoned, money will usually follow. Three potential allies seemed natural: her economic advisory group, her new political friend the governor, and the majority leader in the state House of Representatives.

At the next meeting of the economic advisory group, she raised the issue of the proposed arts center and summer festival. The response was instant and overwhelmingly positive. The mayor warned the group that they might need to raise $250,000 as seed money for the start-up. She asked each person to lobby his or her respective representative on the city council. She also requested that they treat the proposal as confidential; no need to deal with public pressure until there was something actually in the works.

Her new political confidante, the governor, was intrigued by the idea. The mayor was convincing in her arguments about the linkage between economic and cultural development. The governor sensed that the issue might help him politically, especially in overcoming his own image problem as a bright but unsophisticated politician. At the end of their secret meeting, the governor promised his support.

How could she get the crusty, conservative majority leader Johnson to support her proposal? She decided to approach the editor of the local newspaper, who was an old friend of the legislator and a member of her economic advisory group. Within three weeks, the majority leader was on board, albeit in his usual limited way: he would sponsor a bill for a $25,000 feasibility and planning study. More funds would follow, he promised, if the planning study proved positive.

The issue was now too big to contain. Newspaper articles began to appear indicating the possibility of a new cultural facility. It was clearly time to go public with her idea, so the mayor made a personal appeal at the next city council meeting. The council authorized her to arrange for the study. Although he was present at the meeting, Ingraham, the city's in-house planner, sat quietly and watched. No one thought to ask his opinion. If asked, he would have expressed serious misgivings, knowing that Oxford was simply too small for the kind of project the major and the council now envisioned.

When the report arrived some months later, the mayor's initial excitement turned to anger. The consultants supported her basic position that a good-quality performing arts center would add to the image and attractiveness of the city, and there was a clear linkage between image and economic development. They also provided detailed specifications on the size and configuration of an appropriate facility. However, the report indicated that a successful venture into the performing arts was expensive, requiring considerable local support and a large audience base. The report concluded by listing four serious problems:

1. The region, particularly the county, lacked the population base necessary to generate the audience needed for season ticket sales, the financial mainstay of a center.

2. A survey of the public indicated that currently there was only lukewarm interest in fine arts.

3. Within the city, there was no readily available site. It would be necessary to tear down at least one-half of a downtown block or a large section of nearby housing.

4. Parking was inadequate to service the facility. The city would have to build an additional 350 parking spaces in the vicinity of any site they considered.

The report also indicated that the facility would most likely cause a net yearly drain of $100,000 on the city's budget. Although not a catastrophic amount, it would require cutbacks in other areas unless new sources of revenue could be raised. Thus the consultants concluded that there was a strong probability that the capital and operating costs would necessitate a small tax increase.

The mayor clearly had cause for concern. Her reputation and political career were in jeopardy. She wondered if these experts really understood anything about economic development. Besides, coming from outside the region, they probably were wrong about local interest; after all, the economic advisory group was enthusiastic. Also, if the presence of cultural resources added to economic development, the resulting increase in local revenues would pay for the facility.

The mayor realized that she was rationalizing some of the issues, but she had great faith in her ability to make things happen, convince others, and generate the necessary support. She also recognized that her own expertise was

limited; the consultants had done these studies before, and they had been recommended very highly to her.

An additional viewpoint would help. She sent for Ingraham and asked for a
confidential review of the consultants' analysis. After studying the report, Ingraham reported to her that it was essentially accurate, and that the risks listed
in it were real. Yet he was not totally negative. He agreed with the mayor that
there was indeed a slim chance of success. But he also pointed out the dangers
of risking the economic well being of the city on the basis of a personal theory—intuition really—of economic development. He suggested that she distribute copies of the report to the city council.

Until then, the mayor had produced tremendous enthusiasm for the project
without discussing the risks involved or relying on too many facts. She had
done all of this on the basis of her political skills and powers of persuasion,
just as she had done in the case of the other projects, all successful, during her
tenure as mayor. Ingraham realized that the mayor had the political clout to
push the project ahead. They argued for about an hour, with the mayor concluding that he would just have to have faith in her judgment to do what was
best for the city—the same faith the people had when they elected her.

At the next council meeting, the mayor reported on the consultants' findings.
Although the report noted some minor problems and risks, she concluded that
the report was basically supportive and that the city should go ahead. Without
requesting copies of the report, the council instructed the mayor to have
the planning department begin work on the details of the project. The chairman of the council thanked the mayor, noted that the chief planner was in
the room, and suggested that they hear his views as well. Carl Ingraham rose
to speak.

DISCUSSION AND CONCLUSION

The situation in Oxford raises precisely the kinds of issues with which those
who use professional expertise, as well as those who provide it, must wrestle.
In this case, we have a skill—project planning and consulting—that bears some
of the marks of being a profession, for example, systematic knowledge, service
orientation, and use of objective data. But the claims of the consultants' report
to "trump" politics are not wholly decisive: the decision to build an arts facility is also partially political and one that political, not professional, authorities
must ultimately make.

The decision to build the arts facility is thus in a kind of "gray area" between the domains of politics and professional expertise. But given this location, none of the approaches considered seems to provide an adequate way out.

The Professional View

The first view considered—the "separatist thesis"—holds that the professional counsel of the outside consultants should be heeded. But for the mayor

or city council or even Carl Ingraham just to follow the consultants' advice, thereby abandoning the project, does not adequately take into account the limitations of professional expertise that seem present in this case. For example, the cause/effect analysis of the outside experts may be wrong. Instead of acting as a drain on the city's resources, the new arts complex could act as a magnet to attract young professionals to the city, thereby generating the financial resources and revenues that planners feel is absent. Moreover, the "data" in the consultants' report concerning present levels of support could be faulty: no survey is a perfect measure of attitudes. The kinds of empirical measures the "experts" used may not have tapped the enthusiasm and support of key groups.

Treating the decision solely from the perspective of the outside consultants also ignores the nonprofessional considerations that might have an impact upon the decision to build a facility. The mayor, through her past experience—building a hotel complex, attracting new department stores, and bringing in new industries—in fact may possess the skills to generate resources that can make the project work, despite evidence to the contrary.

The Moral View

The mayor's attempted deception of the city council and Ingraham's knowledge of that deception suggest that the case might be viewed with moral considerations in mind. There is, after all, a general moral presumption against lying that a number of philosophers, Saint Augustine and Kant most prominently, as well as more contemporary writers, such as Hannah Arendt and Sissela Bok, have upheld.[37]

One problem with the ordinary morality approach, however, is that many of the features of the case do not directly (even indirectly in most instances) raise moral issues. Whether the consultants have the facts and figures right, whether the mayor's own judgments about the feasibility of the project have merit, and even to what extent the city council has a right to information about the project raise questions of political prudence and institutional rights and responsibilities that are at best only marginally a matter of moral consideration. In fact, they seem to turn more on the political features of the case: the kind of decision-making power the mayor shares with the city council, for example.

Even the more directly moral issues the case raises—the mayor's deception, for example—might require analysis with political and not exclusively moral considerations and principles in mind. Many observers have recognized that the kind of practices deemed impermissible in most situations of personal moral choice may be excusable, even justifiable, for those in public office. Public officials often are forced into "dirty hands" situations in which normally unacceptable means may be necessary to attain legitimate ends.[38]

The Political Perspective

Simply seeing the issue as political—a pattern of "normal" politics in which facts do not count and a competition of ambition and interests prevails—is equally flawed. By mischaracterizing the report, the mayor is misleading the city council. She may believe that her experience should prevail, but in following her own judgment, she is damaging the integrity of the decision-making process of which the city council is a part.

The claims of different participants in what is admittedly a highly political process thus call for further evaluation. The mayor's motives, albeit political, especially call for further examination. For example, her concerns about her own political reputation and future electoral goals seem to intrude too strongly if she decides to deceive the counsel for political reasons. Her judgments about technical matters also go unchallenged. Perhaps the kinds of resources needed to guarantee the success of an arts complex are indeed measurable; what is needed for a successful arts complex may be entirely different from that needed in luring a developer to build a hotel or department store.

Elements of an Alternative Conception

The Oxford case does not allow us easily to choose among the approaches we have considered. Each seems partially flawed. But another lesson of the Oxford case is that each approach has something to offer. Building on this insight, perhaps the best way of reconciling the claims of expertise and the demands of politics should be an interactive approach: one neither wholly political nor wholly professional but attempting to incorporate the insights and strengths of each.

The political nature of the decision, the use of professional expertise in public policy, and the largely political character of the obligations that officeholders have incurred suggest that the political perspective must figure strongly in the evaluation of this case. Ultimately, the choice of heeding the advice of experts must lie in the hands of political authorities. Expertise is not value neutral but value laden, involving substantive value choices and the allocation of scarce goods and resources. If this is true—expertise raises political questions and involves competing political and personal interests, not purely professional matters—the court of final judgment must be political, not solely professional.

Although the various participants should respect the primacy of politics in *ultimately* making decisions that are political and involve differing interests, professional interests included, other responsibilities might dictate intermediate steps and courses of action that can assist political authorities in making better decisions. For example, the various actors in the Oxford case might incur duties and obligations beyond simply furthering the political or professional interests they might favor. Those who hold public office incur broader obligations that relate to upholding the integrity of decision-making processes and institutions of which they are a part. In accepting public office, an individual consents not only to the formally specified duties of his or her office (being mayor, for instance) but also to the more encompassing set of institutions and processes of which they are also a part.[39]

In the Oxford study, this broader conception of official obligation and political duty suggests that the various participants must consider the role of the city council in the decision to build a new facility, not simply their own place and preferences in the decision-making process. Deception of others legitimately involved in decision-making processes violates the integrity of that process. For example, by lying to—or at least deceiving—the council, the mayor has failed to evaluate her obligations and duties correctly. Her insights and judgments may be superior to those of the consultants, but that is not something she alone can determine, especially if it compromises the truth and abridges the rightful participation of others in policy choice. Furthermore, if the mayor is right, her judgments should be able to withstand critical scrutiny and fuller deliberation.

Professionals who are called upon to give policy advice also incur further duties that relate to the process in which they participate. Even though political authorities are ultimately responsible for making the final choice about public policy, professionals still have a critical role to play: they continue to incur the responsibilities of their profession when their skills, knowledge, and expertise are at the disposal of others. For example, when technical expertise is present in policy questions, professionals bear responsibilities for seeing that the technical facets of the problem are properly understood by nonprofessionals and brought to bear in the policy process. Professionals should not accept or passively acquiesce to erroneous uses of professional expertise. If political authorities either give too much (overvaluation) or too little (undervaluation) credence to professional expertise, those professionals involved should take steps to insure that knowledge is not misused in the policy process. The politicians may ultimately decide in ways that professionals find objectionable, but at the very least, their voices should be heard.

The steps a professional might take when he or she finds that expertise is being misunderstood or used improperly by political authorities would vary from situation to situation; the particular circumstances of each case play a large role in defining an effective and responsible course of remedy. In some instances, simply bringing errors to the attention of authorities might suffice; in other cases in which deliberate misuse of expertise occurs, an appeal to a wider audience might be in order, perhaps involving whistleblowing as discussed in chapter three. In the Oxford study, for example, the mayor misrepresented the report of expert consultants to the city council. Ingraham—who possessed the skills and expertise to evaluate the consultants' report—could have brought the full details of the report to the city council's attention. As long as his intentions were not to embarrass the mayor politically (although that surely would be a consequence in this case) but rather to insure that the council's own request for expert judgment was met, he should have spoken out.

Professionals also need to be aware of the limits of their own skills, expertise, and judgments when called upon to give advice in the policy sphere. Few if any judgments by professional experts are wholly value free and objective; many in fact are highly value laden. Professional findings about the feasibility of the Oxford development project serve as a good example of the latter; the mayor might have been right after all, just as she had been right in the past.

Professionals must also be attentive to the self-serving interests of their own professional community. Not only is expertise not wholly objective in the sense of scientific objectivity, but self-serving professional interests and practices—especially involving the prestige of the profession, its power with respect to other service providers, and the monetary rewards for service—can compromise the claims of professionals to provide "expert" advice in the policy process.

Properly bringing to bear the positive contributions of professional expertise, moral judgment, and political skill when controversial political decisions are at stake must ultimately be a critical exercise. Each participant in the policy process has a positive contribution to make, and by checking, challenging, and criticizing the claims of the other, these contributions can most positively enter into policy debate and deliberation. Through critical interaction, based on the responsibilities outlined above, professional expertise can begin to find its proper place in the policy process.

NOTES

1. This definition of profession is taken from Bernard Barber, "Control and Responsibility in the Powerful Professions," *Political Science Quarterly* 93 (1978): 597–612.

2. "Profile of the Typical Federal Non-Postal Employee," *Federal Civilian Workforce Statistics: Employment and Trends as of May 1986* (Washington, D.C.: U.S Office of Personnel Management, 1986), p. 69.

3. "Occupation of the Civilian Labor Force," *Statistical Abstract of the United States, 1986* (Washington, D.C.: U.S. Government Printing Office, 1986), p. 400.

4. Frederick C. Mosher, *Democracy and the Public Service,* 2d ed. (Oxford: Oxford University Press, 1982), p. 115.

5. Frederick C. Mosher and Richard J. Stillman II, "Introduction to Symposium on the Professions in Government," *Public Administration Review* 37 (1977): 631–632.

6. Nicholas Henry, *Public Administration and Public Affairs,* 2d ed. (Englewood Cliffs, N.J.: Prentice-Hall, 1980), p. 249.

7. Mosher, *Democracy and the Public Service,* p. 142.

8. Leonard D. White, *The Republican Era: 1869–1901* (New York: Macmillan, 1963), p. 19.

9. Woodrow Wilson, "The Study of Administration," *Political Science Quarterly* 2 (1887): 200.

10. Dwight Waldo, *The Administrative State* (New York: Ronald Press), p. 4.

11. Herbert Kaufman, "The Growth of the Federal Personnel System," in Wallace

Sayre, ed., *The Federal Government Service* (Englewood Cliffs, N.J.: Prentice-Hall, 1965), p. 56.

12. Luther Gulick, "Science, Values, and Public Administration," in L. Gulick and L. Urwick, eds., *Papers on the Science of Administration* (New York: Institute of Public Administration, 1937), p. 195.

13. John M. Gaus, "Trends in the Theory of Public Administration," *Public Administration Review* 10 (1950): p. 168.

14. John M. Gaus, "The Responsibility of Public Administration," in John M. Gaus, *Frontiers of Public Administration* (Chicago: University of Chicago Press, 1936), p. 40.

15. Carl J. Friedrich, "Public Policy and the Nature of Administrative Responsibility," in E. S. Mason and C. J. Friedrich, eds., *Public Policy, 1940* (Cambridge, Mass.: Harvard University Press, 1940), pp. 12–13.

16. *See,* for example, Frank Marini, *Toward the New Public Administration* (Scranton, Pa.: Chandler, 1971); Dwight Waldo, *Public Administration in a Time of Turbulence* (Scranton, Pa.: Chandler, 1971); Frank Fischer, *Politics, Values, and Public Policy* (Boulder, Colo.: Westview Press, 1980); Michael M. Harmon, *Action Theory for Public Administration* (New York: Longman, 1981).

17. Fischer, *Politics, Values, and Public Policy,* pp. xiii–xiv.

18. Alan Gewirth, "Professional Ethics: The Separatist Thesis," *Ethics,* 96 (1986): 282.

19. Benjamin Freedman, "What Really Makes Professional Morality Different?" *Ethics* 91 (1981): 626–30; Richard Wasserstrom, "Roles and Morality," in D. Luban, ed., *The Good Lawyer* (Totowa, N.J.: Rowman and Allenheld, 1983), pp. 25–37.

20. Carl J. Friedrich, "Public Policy and the Nature of Administrative Responsibility," pp. 3–24; Gaus, "The Responsibility of Public Administration"; idem, "Trends in the Theory of Public Administration."

21. This is Gewith's own view, for example, in his essay "Professional Ethics: The Separatist Thesis." *See also* Alan H. Goldman, *The Moral Foundations of Professional Ethics* (Totowa, N.J.: Rowman and Littlefield, 1980).

22. Note, however, that there is no agreed-upon definition of a profession, a problem that further complicates determining its proper use in the public sphere. For example, W. Goode ("Community within a Community," *American Sociological Review* 22 [1957]: 194–99) emphasized the presence of a "professional community" characterized by a sense of identity among its members, shared values, agreed-upon role definitions, a common language, power of the community over its members, and control over selection, training, and socialization. Harold Wilensky ("The Professionalization of Everyone?" *American Journal of Sociology* 70 [1964]: 137–158) argued that the stages through which the development of a profession progresses are important in determining whether a claim to professional status can be made. According to Wilensky, professionalization begins to emerge when a substantial number of people are engaged in the activity, training institutions are established, professional associations are formed, and political agitation occurs, reaching fruition with the creation of a professional code of ethics.

Bernard Barber ("Some Problems in the Sociology of Professions," in K. Lynn, ed., *The Professions in America* [Boston: Houghton Mifflin, 1965], pp. 15–34) argued that four attributes of a profession must be present: a high degree of generalized and systematic knowledge, orientation to the community interest, a high degree of self-control of behavior, and a system of rewards primarily based on symbols of work achievement. Wilbert Moore *(The Professions: Roles and Rules* [New York: Russell Sage Foundation,

1970], pp. 3–19) claimed that professionalism is measured on a set of continua rather than in terms of a cluster of attributes; for Moore such scales include the practice of a full-time occupation, commitment to a calling, existence of formalized organization, presence of esoteric—but still useful—knowledge and skills, exhibition of a service orientation, and enjoyment of autonomy restrained by responsibility.

Ronald Pavalko *(Sociology of Occupations and Professions* [Itasca, Ill.: Peacock, 1971], pp. 17–30) concluded that professions are marked by intellectual techniques, relevance to basic social values, a training period, motivation, autonomy, a sense of commitment, a sense of community, and a code of ethics. Terence Johnson *(Professions and Power* [London: Macmillan, 1972]) saw professional status simply as a process of successful organizational control over a specific area of expertise: "A profession is not, then, an occupation, but a means of controlling an occupation" (p. 45).

23. Special Symposium on Professions in Government (Part I), *Public Administration Review* 37 (1977): 631–686; Special Symposium on Professions in Government (Part II), *Public Administration Review* 38 (1978): 105–150.

24. Don K. Price, *The Scientific Estate* (Cambridge, Mass.: Harvard University Press, 1965), p. 192.

25. *See,* for example, Thomas Kuhn, *The Structure of Scientific Revolutions* (Chicago: University of Chicago Press, 1970); Paul Feyerbend, *Against Method* (London: New Left Books, 1975).

26. *See* Warren O. Hagstrom, *The Scientific Community* (New York: Basic Books, 1965); Duncan MacRae, *The Social Function of Social Science* (New Haven: Yale University Press, 1976); Joseph Gusfield, *Knowledge Application: The Knowledge System in Society* (Boston: Allyn and Bacon, 1979).

27. MacRae, *The Social Function of Social Science,* p. 14.

28. *See,* for example, Joseph Haberer, *Politics and the Community of Science* (New York: Van Nostrand, 1969); J. J. Salomon, *Science and Politics,* (Cambridge, Mass.: MIT Press, 1973); J. F. Galliher and J. McCartney, "The Influence of Funding Agencies on Juvenile Delinquency Research," *Social Problems* 21 (1973): 78–89; Michael Useem, "Government Patronage of Science and Art in America," *American Behavioral Scientist* 19 (1976): 785–804; Michael Useem, "Government Influence on the Social Science Paradigm," *Sociological Quarterly* 17 (1976): 146–161.

29. *See,* for example, Saul Feldman's discussion of mental health professionals in his article "Conflict and Convergence: The Mental Health Professional in Government," *Public Administration Review* 38 (1978): 137–143.

30. Goldman, *The Moral Foundations of Professional Ethics;* Robert Veatch, "Medical Ethics: Professional or Universal?" *Harvard Theological Review* 65 (1972): 531–559; idem, *A Theory of Medical Ethics* (New York: Basic Books, 1981); Bernard Williams, "Professional Morality and Its Dispositions," in D. Luban, ed., *The Good Lawyer* (Totowa, N.J.: Rowman and Allenheld, 1983), pp. 259–69.

31. Gewirth, "Professional Ethics: The Separatist Thesis," p. 286.

32. Ibid., p. 291.

33. John P. Burke, *Bureaucratic Responsibility* (Baltimore: Johns Hopkins University Press, 1986), p. 152.

34. Richard Neustadt and Harvey Fineberg, *The Epidemic That Never Was: Policy-Making and the Swine Flu Scare* (New York: Random House, 1983).

35. Bernard Barber, "Control and Responsibility in the Powerful Professions," p. 604.

36. Ibid., p. 605.

37. Hannah Arendt, "Truth in Politics," *Between Past and Future* (New York: Wiley, 1968), pp. 227–65; idem, "Lying in Politics," *Crises of the Republic* (New York: Harcourt, 1972), pp. 1–49; Sissela Bok, *Lying: Moral Choice in Public and Private Life* (New York: Random House, Vintage Books, 1979).

38. *See,* for example, Max Weber's classic essay "Politics as a Vocation," in H. Gerth and C. W. Mills, eds., *From Max Weber* (New York: Oxford University Press, 1958); Michael Walzer, "Political Action: The Problem of Dirty Hands," *Philosophy and Public Affairs* 2 (1973): 160–178.

39. For further discussion of this conception of responsibility and obligation, *see* Burke, *Bureaucratic Responsibility,* especially chapter three.

SELECTED BIBLIOGRAPHY

Anderson, Charles W. "The Place of Principles in Policy Analysis." *American Political Science Review* 73 (1979): 711–723.

Barber, Bernard, "Some Problems in the Sociology of Professions." In K. Lynn, ed., *The Professions in America*. Boston: Houghton Mifflin, 1965, pp. 15–34.

———. "Control and Responsibility in the Powerful Professions." *Political Science Quarterly* 93 (1978): 597–612.

Baumrin, Bernard, and Benjamin Freedman, eds. *Moral Responsibility and the Professions*. New York: Haven, 1983.

Bayles, Michael. *Professional Ethics*. Belmont, Calif.: Wadsworth, 1981.

Benveniste, Guy. *The Politics of Expertise*. Berkeley, Calif.: Glendessary Press, 1972.

Bledstein, B. J. *The Culture of Professionalism*. New York: Norton, 1976.

Burke, John P. "Responsibilities of Presidents and Advisers: A Theory and Case Study of Vietnam Decision Making." *Journal of Politics* 46 (1984): 818–845.

———. *Bureaucratic Responsibility*. Baltimore: Johns Hopkins University Press, 1986, pp. 24–31, 142–160.

Camenisch, Paul F. *Grounding Professional Ethics in a Pluralistic Society*. New York: Haven, 1982.

Denhardt, Robert B. *Theories of Public Organization*. Monterey, Calif.: Brooks/Cole, 1984.

Feldman, Saul. "Conflict and Convergence: The Mental Health Professional in Government." *Public Administration Review* 38 (1978): 137–143.

Feyerabend, Paul. *Against Method*. London: New Left Books, 1975.

Finer, Herman. "Administrative Responsibility in Democratic Government." *Public Administration Review* 1 (1941): 335–350.

Freedman, Benjamin. "A Meta-Ethics for Professional Morality." *Ethics* 89 (1978): 1–19.

———. "What Really Makes Professional Morality Different?" *Ethics* 91 (1981): 626–630.

Friedrich, Carl J. "Public Policy and the Nature of Administrative Responsibility." In E. S. Mason and C. J. Friedrich, eds., *Public Policy 1940*. Cambridge, Mass.: Harvard University Press, 1940, pp. 3–24.

Fuchs, James. *Making the Most of Management Consultant Services*. New York: AMACOM, 1975.

Galliher, J. F., and J. McCartney. "The Influence of Funding Agencies on Juvenile Delinquency Research." *Social Problems* 21 (1973): 77–89.

Gaus, Jonn M. The Responsibility of Public Administration." In John M. Gaus, ed., *Frontiers of Public Administration*. Chicago: University of Chicago Press, 1936.

———. "Trends in the Theory of Public Administration." *Public Administration Review* 10 (1950): 161–168.

Gewirth, Alan. "Professional Ethics: The Separatist Thesis." *Ethics* 96 (1986): 282–300.

Goldman, Alan H. *The Moral Foundations of Professional Ethics*. Totowa, N.J.: Rowman and Littlefield, 1980.

Goode, W. "Community within a Community." *American Sociological Review* 22 (1957): 194–199.

Gusfield, Joseph. *Knowledge Application: The Knowledge System in Society*. Boston: Allyn and Bacon, 1979.

Haberer, Joseph. *Politics and the Community of Science*. New York: Van Nostrand, 1969.

Hagstrom, Warren O. *The Scientific Community*. New York: Basic Books, 1965.

Howe, Elizabeth, and Jerome Kaufman. "Social Values in Professional Practice." *Policy Studies Journal* 9 (1980–1981): 622–637.

Johnson, Terence. *Professions and Power*. London: Macmillan, 1972.

Kagi, Herbert. "The Role of Private Consultants in Urban Governing." *Urban Affairs Quarterly* 5 (1969): 45–58.

Kaufman, Herbert. "The Growth of the Federal Personnel System." In Wallace Sayre, ed., *The Federal Government Service*. Englewood Cliffs, N.J.: Prentice-Hall, 1965, pp. 7–69.

Kuhn, Thomas. *The Structure of Scientific Revolutions*. Chicago: University of Chicago Press, 1970.

Lynn, Kenneth, ed. *The Professions in America*. Boston: Houghton Mifflin, 1965.

MacRae, Duncan. *The Social Function of Social Science*. New Haven: Yale University Press, 1976.

Martin, Mike. "Professional and Ordinary Morality: A Reply to Freedman." *Ethics* 91 (1981): 631–633.

———. "Rights and the Meta-Ethics of Ordinary Morality." Ethics 91 (1981): 619–625.

May, William. "Professional Ethics: Setting and Terrain." In D. Callahan and S. Bok, eds., *Ethics Teaching in Higher Education*. New York: Plenum, 1980, pp. 205–241.

Moore, Wilbert. *The Professions: Roles and Rules*. New York: Russell Sage Foundation, 1970.

Mosher, Frederick. *Democracy and the Public Service*. New York: Oxford University Press, 1968.

Neustadt, Richard, and Harvey Fineberg. *The Epidemic That Never Was: Policy-Making and the Swine Flu Scare*. New York: Random House, 1983.

Ostrom, Vincent. *The Intellectual Crisis in American Public Administration*. University: The University of Alabama Press, 1974.

Pattenaude, Richard, ed. "Consultants in the Public Sector." *Public Administration Review* 39 (1979): 203–205.

Pattenaude, Richard, and Larry Landis. "Consultants and Technology Transfer in the Public Sector." *Public Administration Review* 39 (1979): 414–420.

Pavalko, Ronald. *Sociology of Occupations and Professions.* Itasca, Ill.: Peacock, 1971.

Price, Don K. *The Scientific Estate.* Cambridge, Mass.: Harvard University Press, 1965.

Primack, Joel, and Frank von Hippel. *Advice and Dissent: Scientists in the Political Arena.* New York: Basic Books, 1974.

Salomon, J. J. *Science and Politics.* Cambridge, Mass.: MIT Press, 1973.

Thompson, Dennis F. "Moral Responsibility of Public Officials: The Problem of Many Hands." *American Political Science Review* 74 (1980): 905–916.

————. "Ascribing Responsibility to Advisers in Government." *Ethics* 93 (1983): 546–560.

Tong, Rosemarie. "Toward a More Responsive and Responsible Science Advising Policy." *Berkshire Review* 18 (1983): 14–26.

Trapman, John, and Jane McClure. "Social Values in the Policy Process." *Policy Studies Journal* 9 (1980–1981): 585–595.

Useem, Michael. "Government Influence on the Social Science Paradigm." *Sociological Quarterly* 17 (1976): 146–161.

————. "Government Patronage of Science and Art in America." *American Behavioral Scientist* 19 (1976): 785–804.

Veatch, Robert. "Medical Ethics: Professional or Universal?" *Harvard Theological Review* 65 (1972): 531–559.

————. *A Theory of Medical Ethics.* New York: Basic Books, 1981.

Wasserstrom, Richard. "Roles and Morality." In D. Luban, ed., *The Good Lawyer.* Totowa, N.J.: Rowman and Allanheld, 1983, pp. 25–37.

Wilensky, Harold. "The Professionalization of Everyone?" *American Journal of Sociology* 70 (1964): 137–158.

Williams, Bernard. "Professional Morality and Its Dispositions." In D. Luban, ed., *The Good Lawyer.* Totowa, N.J.: Rowman and Allanheld, 1983, pp. 259–269.

10

The Use of Quantitative Analysis in the Public Sector

Jeremy F. Plant

Until the 1970s ethics was not usually considered a core topic in the study of public administration.[1] A number of reasons may be advanced for the paucity of literature on ethics in the field. First, *ethics*—notions of right and wrong human conduct—was heavily influenced by the traditions of legalism in American society. The behavior of public administrators could be regulated by law or binding codes of ethics without requiring explicit tests of belief systems.[2]

A second impediment was the historical importance of ethical discourse for political philosophy.[3] The classical tradition recognized no clear separation between political and individual belief systems, between public and private, or between the overtly "political" and "administrative" facets of governance as it sought to integrate the various aspects of public life and bind them to notions of ethical conduct. A discipline of public administration wed initially to a separation of politics from administration could hardly emulate the classical tradition. Instead, public administration became scientific, pragmatic, oriented to facts and process.

This is not to state that public administration was unconcerned or ignorant of important ethical dilemmas posed by a professional administrative elite in a developed administrative order. But it recognized little need to consider ethics as a separate topic or subfield of study. The prevailing logic was to subsume ethics into accepted topics such as political accountability, efficient management, and professionalism.

Few criticisms were leveled at public administration, either from inside the discipline or from observers of the administrative state for this lack of explicit consideration of ethics. After all, the professionalization of the governance process (*see* chapter nine) ushered in by the discipline had replaced a system of obvious corruption and politicization. A hard-nosed, legalistic approach to monitoring the new public professions seemed to be working. City managers, for example, were an obvious moral improvement over the old machines.[4] Within the system generally, the rising role of professional administration was elevating the level of honesty and defining it positively.[5] The goals of efficiency and accountability were the polestars of normative improvement for the administrative state; perhaps they were never achievable but always the benchmarks for performance. Lacking visible signs of personal corruption or violence, they took on moral connotations that made professional competence and political control the benchmarks of an ethical administration. It worked well, and it did not threaten democratic values and processes.[6]

This chapter looks at one of the factors that in recent years has helped to erode the old faith in an implicit system of public ethics, the increasing use of statistics and probabilistic reasoning in public affairs. As the review of the literature shows, the troubling questions raised by the use of statistics in decision-making reflect the general lack of certainty in the field about ethics. Much has been written during the past two decades, but no single approach to defining the ethical problem or solving ethical dilemmas has found general acceptance. No new orthodoxy has replaced the ruined framework of the politics–administration dichotomy, an ethical as well as an instrumental model of organization and behavior. The scattering of approaches to ethics in the field, discussed in the initial contributions to this volume, now mirrors the uncertainty and flux of the postindustrial order. Only a firm commitment to the search for truth using the best available methods of inquiry seems appropriate for such an order.

BACKGROUND

The orthodox view of ethics for public administration as a balancing of individual and institutional factors was well expressed by Stephen K. Bailey in his famous 1965 essay in memory of Paul H. Appleby. Bailey began by noting the older man's basic assumption: that ethical issues are "centered upon the felicitous interaction of moral institutional arrangements and morally ambiguous man."[7] Bailey examined Appleby's central belief in hierarchy as a moral arrangement. Its force was in referring special or particular interests to a general concern for the public interest. Like the Founding Fathers of the nation, Appleby believed in a system that would allow fallible individuals to function morally, for the general good.

Bailey, by contrast, chose to pursue "a normative theory of personal ethics in the public service" based on mental attitudes and moral qualities. As he noted, "the intermeshing of the mental attitudes and moral qualities of the individual moral actor with the institutional arrangements elaborated by Paul Appleby produces in effect a working definition of the public interest." Taking for granted the role of bureaucracy in modern society, Bailey argued for the *improvement,* not perfection, of the public servant as an agent of the public.[8]

Thus Bailey summed up the thinking of Appleby's generation and provided a transition to a generation of thinkers who have found it more difficult to accept hierarchy and bureaucracy as a moral force. Bailey characterized the belief of prewar public administration in seeing problems of ethics as reconciliation of bureaucracy and democracy, both evolving in pragmatic and utilitarian ways, to meet emerging demands of modern industrial society. As his own contribution, Bailey then sketched for the reader a largely intuitive model of the ethical administrator, unencumbered by reliance upon theories of human behavior, ethical systems, or notions of transcendence.

In the two decades since Bailey's essay appeared, ethics as a topic in public administration has taken his concern for the individual and based theories of personal conduct on the more solid grounding of the social sciences, philosophy, and theology.[9] Specific examples of misconduct in office have shattered the optimism that ethical conduct could be assumed if administrative systems were efficient and accountable to political masters.[10] The misdeeds of the political masters either brought discredit to administrators or showed once again how artificial is the separation of administration from politics. Concern for ethical outcomes from policy, not simply fair or honest procedures, defined good public administration as sensitivity to higher moral and political goals.[11] The writing on ethics had one common theme: the individual public administrator must be self-conscious about the need to bring a sense of right and wrong conduct to every aspect of administrative life.

Current approaches to ethics administration share a set of assumptions about the nature of modern life and governance. Based on Weberian constructs, they can be summarized as a recognition of the central role played by organizations in modern life and the effects on the individual and on groups that result from bureaucratic modes of activity. In the words of Ralph Hummel, a representative of the humanistic school of public ethics, "Bureaucracy gives birth to a new species of inhuman beings. People's social relations are being converted into control relations. Their norms and beliefs concerning human ends are torn from them and replaced with skills affirming the ascendency of technical means, whether of administration or production."[12] This chapter looks at ethical problems of public administration in a society undergoing fundamental, *transforming* change from the industrial and bureaucratic world of Weber to a postindustrial world based on information and communications.[13] Ethical problems must be understood within a society characterized by greater complexity, less certainty in beliefs and institutions, more complicated sorts of social relationships, and accelerated rates of changes.

What will the ethics of the post-Weberian public order be? What can we learn from past discussions of ethics that can guide public administration to an accommodation with the demands of the new order? What new concepts and approaches need to guide a system of public ethics for individuals, organizations, and society?

An old concept, *the disinterested search for truth,* may provide the basis for a new system of public ethics. In a world of uncertainty and flux, it embodies the process of moving from one experiment to another, from one stage of meaning to a higher one. In a decentralized world, it emphasizes less the bureaucratic virtues of accountability and purpose by grand edifices of society and more the learning and teaching opportunities afforded by a looser set of societal arrangements. In a world of uncertainty, it makes an ethic out of self-development and the dissemination of new information. The focus of this chapter is on the ethical problems posed by the increasing use of statistics and probability and the way in which probabilistic thinking can help shape the search for truth.

How the public ethics of the bureaucratic age were analyzed by writers of the bureaucratic age forms the basis for this understanding.

LITERATURE REVIEW

At the time that Stephen Bailey was memorializing Paul Appleby, ethics was not commonly broached by writers in the field (in fact, one wonders if Bailey would have addressed the subject except to underscore the lasting importance of his mentor's earlier contributions to the field). It was occasionally characterized, in highly realistic terms, as either a problem of the politicization of the public service or as corruption resulting from the indistinct boundaries between public and private, specific and general, that characterize a pluralistic system. In both respects, the bureaucratization of the system provided the institutional safeguards needed for the few instances in which a public servant was tempted to betray his or her duties. These instances were seen as scattered, unimportant, and historically irrelevant: they did not challenge the paradigmatic view that bureaucratic institutions could produce ethical behavior if well managed. In fact, mainstream literature of the late 1960s provided a continuation of the belief that democracy was best served by the institutional arrangements of bureaucracy, what Emmette Redford called "overhead democracy."[14]

The acceptance of the administrative state as a benign and fixed reality was shattered, just as the generation of writers who came to age in the prewar period finished their capstone works.[15] Beginning with the new public administration school and continuing to critical theorists such as Ralph Hummel, Michael Harmon, and Robert Denhardt, the Weberian paradigm was challenged as perhaps inefficient and certainly demoralizing and dehumanizing.[16] In the words of Denhardt, "The ethic of the organization suggests itself as a new model for living. We originally sought to construct social institutions that would reflect our beliefs and our values; now there is a danger that our values may reflect our institutions."[17]

The specter of an administered society, bureaucratized through impersonal and inhumane organizational forms and made permanent and static by the inherent conservatism of the administrative state, has become the image of reality animating the various writers on administrative ethics since Bailey. Solutions to the problem are difficult to prescribe, other than various approaches to personal purification or disinvolvement. They range from John Rohr's suggestion of "regime values" enunciated by Supreme Court rulings as a guide to the actions of individual bureaucrats through a variety of intellectual attitudes to deflect the worst effects of the technico-bureaucratic civilization—action theory—or the "reasoned irrationality of our basically spiritual condition" advocated by Denhardt.[18]

The individualistic approaches have paid less attention to the importance of institutions as guides for ethical action. The pendulum swung from the hope of the older generation for a balance of institutional and individual ethics toward one in which the individual search for survival is preeminent. Politics like administration, it was argued, is perverted by the dehumanization of bureaucratic organization. The cleansing grace of a politics that seeks the general, the higher, in life is missing. As Sheldon Wolin observed, the individual confronting the political world of the administrative state is only acting in a way that is reasonable to the conditions: " 'Fragmentation' of the political and its assignment to other associations and organizations are the necessary price for achieving some measure of individual self-determination, freedom, and participation in the modern world. The alternative of reviving the political dimension of existence seems an invitation to totalitarianism." [19]

A related problem has been the bias of the technological society toward power and the use of power based solely on considerations of efficiency, with a means–end rationality. Lewis Mumford warned that the rise of technology was historically related to a lust for power that pointed to the replacement of values based on community by those based upon power.[20] Even gloomier prospects appeared in the writings of Jacques Ellul, who foresaw a civilization dominated by amoral cadres of technicians controlling all aspects of human existence.[21] The technical nature of modern administration, bolstered by the decision-making logic of positivism, destroyed values other than efficiency. In the words of Fred Fischer, "Under the methodological prescriptions of positivism, only technical decisions about the instrumental relationship of means to ends lend themselves to the rules of rational assessment." [22]

Implicit in all of this analysis of the bureaucratic age was the Weberian notion of perfection. Bureaucracy and large-scale organization were the end points of a rationalizing process that made them impervious to criticism for one simple reason: only they could provide the means of rationalizing and controlling modern society. In fact, as we shall see, science and social conditions were changing the entire basis for the organizational society and the administrative state.

By accepting Weber's assumption that bureaucracy was a world force changing the human condition, public administration faced the challenge of building a system of ethics under conditions that were inimical to ethical discourse and action. How to proceed required the field to address three major questions:

1. What constitutes a true system of politics that, as Sheldon Wolin noted, is concerned with common involvements and the general community?[23]

2. What system of organization makes sense according to the needs it addresses and the available knowledge to make it achieve ends?

3. What is the personal involvement that affords the individual an opportunity to seek knowledge and use it ethically for the good of the community?

It is the third question, the ethics of science applied to public administration, that links the understanding of methodology with an appreciation of the human condition. The writings of Herbert Simon and Louis Gawthrop, examined below, provide useful perspectives on the scientific method of public administration.

RETURNING SCIENCE TO PUBLIC ADMINISTRATION

Anyone who has graduated from a curriculum in public administration has no doubt joined in the continuing discussion of whether the field is a science or art form. Can we deduce general and predictive theory for administration, or is it a "craft" we can describe but not consider a science? Typically, the argument fails to consider the ethical implications of the answer. A professional craft is governed by a professional approach to ethics: what are the constraints in applying knowledge to cases? A science searches for truth; its ethical problem is related to the manner in which inquiry is pursued and reported.

Until Herbert Simon's work appeared in the 1940s, the scientific perspective in public administration was given little attention. Science and public administration were no strangers to each other. But the connection was usually seen in institutional arrangements of the sort given us by Don K. Price.[24] This perspective is useful, but more fundamental are the intellectual similarities between the scientists and the administrators at a common point. Are they approaching decisions in a convergent manner, or do they view grounds for action differently? Have they been influenced by a common intellectual reference to the world, or are they "two cultures" alienated from one another and embarked upon divergent patterns of development?

Herbert Simon set as a goal what he has termed "the unity of the arts and sciences."[25] Simon's erudition and his ability to move in directions that foresee major technical and intellectual developments make him unique among modern scholars. At the heart of his understanding of the problem is the need for greater knowledge about the process of cognition. This is the act of thinking, which serves as a common denominator for both descriptive and cognitive processes and has tended to integrate the natural sciences, the social sciences, and technical fields concerned with artificial intelligence and digital computing. In addition, Simon has consciously embraced the philosophy of logical positivism, which he—almost alone among scholars interested in public ethics—has found to be a liberating ethical construct.

Simon's approach diverges from the mainstream of public administration writings in its belief that the phenomenon of administration, or the structure of an administrative state, is in fact not unified. The basic difference is the relative role of facts and values, or factual and ethical statements, in reaching rational decisions. As he noted, "We need to construct not merely a single theory of organization but two bodies of theory—one of them applicable to programmed decision-making, the other applicable to nonprogrammed decision-making. . . . The area of non-programmed decision-making is the principal *terra incognita* of organization theory today."[26] The upshot of this development for public ethics is clear: public officials will increasingly find their roles to consist of higher and higher ratios of "nonprogrammed" decisions, as computers relieve humans of much of the work in situations requiring programmed decisions. Does this mean that science in administration will be the domain of robots and administration increasingly political or nonrational? If so, it elevates the need for a new public ethics and a new politics for the postindustrial world to the level of a crisis.

Simon responded to the sociopolitical implications of the computer age by finding in the concept of "procedural rationality" a functional substitute, perhaps the equivalent, of a system of ethics based on faith, profession, or personal values. Speaking the language of economics, Simon observed in 1978 that " 'reasonable men' reach 'reasonable' conclusions in circumstances where they have no prospect of applying classical models of substantive rationality."[27] That is, under the expected circumstances of complexity and constant change, uncertainty, and severe demands on one's time and attention, reason can still be assumed of decisionmakers.

Simon's belief in the persistence of reasoned human action in the face of modern conditions rests on an understanding of nature, not simply a faith in human virtue. Systems, as he noted, wherever found, have many common properties. One of them is order: "nature loves hierarchies."[28] There is nothing unnatural or perverse about hierarchies per se and by implication nothing dehumanizing about orderly arrangements for the purposes of organized action.

Since writing *Administrative Behavior* Simon has not attempted to construct a theory of administrative ethics that would be effective under the conditions of contemporary administrative decision-making. Such a discussion is the focus of Louis Gawthrop, whose 1984 work *Public Sector Management, Systems, and Ethics* is the first comprehensive effort to integrate the humanistic approach of the 1970s ethics movement with the scientific approach to administration based upon systems theory. He introduced his work in this way:

The basic premise of this brief volume is that if fundamental change in public sector organizations in the United States is needed, then the notions of management, systems, and ethics must themselves be viewed collectively as an integrated metasystem. Management functions, organizational designs, and purposeful ethics may, indeed, be studied as conceptual systems, each unto themselves. Inevitably, though, it must be recognized that these concepts are but subsystems in a broader, all-encompassing system and that the total effectiveness of the overall system is directly related to the effective integration of the management design, and ethical components.[29]

Gawthrop's attempt at a synthesis is unusual in the importance he retains for critical consciousness as the basis for public ethics. One would expect from the title of the volume a functional approach to ethics, creating a mandarinism useful to a system in need of a reintegration of ethics and management but not needful of a critical spirit of inquiry.[30] Such an ethics of prudence has been advocated by Peter Drucker, who in 1979 proposed the construction of an ethics of prudence that is overtly Confucian—focusing on right behavior rather than the avoidance of wrongdoing—and relevant to a pluralistic environment of conflicting claims and organizational actors. As Drucker noted, "prudence makes it an ethical duty for the leader to exemplify the precepts of ethics in his own behavior."[31] What is not likely to appear, however, is an approach to ethics that challenges the basic assumptions of a time period.

The Confucian approach is dismissed by Gawthrop in favor of what he called "the ethics of civility": "The ethics of civility encapsules a closed system by assigning a positive value to the boundary-guarding function. Moreover, it incorporates a situational ethics that stresses the privacy of secular operational values in purely relative terms."[32]

Gawthrop's approach to ethics is an amalgam of insights drawn from systems theory, organization theory, and twentieth-century theology. Structurally, the integration of management with systems theory and ethics is to be effected by the design of a new approach to organization.[33]

Gawthrop said a good deal more about what the new approach will look like, and its ethical challenge, than what it will actually do in practice, what policies it should or will pursue, and which it will avoid. In part this is to avoid the reductionism of a new mandarinism or the determinism of a science of administration in favor of a creativity that will find its own goals:

In the final analysis, a creative ethics is a faithfulness to being critically honest about one's self to one's self. With this as a beginning, individual administrators can start to develop a public management in a systems context that is conducive to and supportive of a critically conscious and mature sense of transcendent purposefulness.[34]

Taken together, Simon's belief in reason and Gawthrop's belief in the possibility of a public ethic that posits creativity as a function of administration would seem to augur well for the postindustrial world that we are told is emerging. As the justification for large-scale organization diminishes and the power of computers removes the need for management to be concerned primarily with programmed, housekeeping functions, management will enter a new stage. Reason will be focused upon issues of values under conditions affording considerable latitude for creative action. That is the promise of the new era, the latest promise of science to liberate humankind from the mindlessness and drudgery of existence so that higher goals and higher values can be pursued. Will it come to pass?

In the next section, one critical ethical problem, the politicization of the bureaucracy, is examined. It, more than any change determined by economic or technological transformation, is standing in the path of evolution to a reunion of individual and institutional ethics for the public sector. To illustrate the politicization of the American bureaucracy in recent years, the area of statistical and informational services will be examined to show how demands for political control may be the barrier between industrial and postindustrial political orders.

Political demands to produce statistical studies that corroborate preset political ideologies and programs, or that satisfy the organizational motives of bureaucratic agencies, are commonplace in the administrative state. What makes them especially troublesome is the compounding of political pressure with ethical dilemmas inherent in the application of statistical analysis to public policy questions.

Stuart Nagel identified a number of dilemmas generic to policy evaluation involving the need to consider the demands of the scientific method, respect individuals involved with testing, and be informed as to the likely impact of analysis on political events and social change.[35] These are, in short, both procedural dilemmas and dilemmas inherent in a disinterested search for truth. As probability-based methodologies become the basis of policy-directed science, the need to consider the ethics of policy-directed statistical activity becomes more and more critical.

STATISTICS, GOVERNANCE, AND POLITICS

Statistical services have a long and honorable tradition in American governance. The federal government in particular has found in the compilation and dissemination of statistical information a logical and legitimate exercise of power. It constituted one of the rare areas in which the federal role was unchallenged, for the most part, and was in keeping with the doctrine of limited national government. It, until recently, did not conflict with the proprietary claims of private business and in fact aided the business community in pursuing its objectives. It augmented the work of other levels of the federal system by providing a national basis for information on the natural environment, the population of the nation, resources, and the economy. The science of data gathering before the computer was labor intensive but not especially threatening to the American ideals of freedom and accountable government.

Data collection has been the basis for the statistical services provided by government, but from the outset statisticians as a recognizable professional group have played a significant role in any such program. Statisticians are needed for three sorts of determination: what data are needed and how they are to be collected, how data are to be interpreted in face of variation, and how others who may need or use the data are to be coached in the proper use of the scientific method.

Traditionally, the ethical problems of the statistical profession were couched in behavioral imperatives, the most fundamental of which was falsifying data or lying about relationships among sets.[36] Since most government statistical services did not lead directly to new policy initiatives but were instead ends in themselves to be used by others in society, no major problems were noted, and no more sophisticated notions were expounded for statisticians in the public service. The American Statistical Association, the major professional association for the profession, came into existence in 1834 but until recently did not seriously investigate the need to establish and promulgate a code of ethics binding on its membership. Speaking to the membership of the American Statistical Society, its president, I. Richard Savage, noted in 1984:

There is not much previous formal experience with ethical issues arising in statistics. Of course, we are familiar with the bad consequences of falsifying data. But we are not familiar with the broad spectrum of ethical issues that would arise in the many forms of statistical practice that now are prevalent. Thus, the effort to form a code of ethics is not yet complete.[37]

The "broad range of issues" noted by Savage includes two roles of government that have arisen to complement the original service function. One is the collection of data, either by its own public employees or by contract, with the purpose of developing new policy and evaluating performance of existing programs. Second is the regulation of the statistical industry, especially that component concerned with surveying and interviewing, which currently conducts more than 20 million interviews in the United States each year.

The heart of the ethical problem for the government statistician is the clash between the value of efficiency, sometimes characterized as the competing goals of "paperwork reduction" and good science in the gathering, interpretation, and dissemination of data. With a more complex society, statistics become more important to effective decision-making by government and business. Coordination of programs and more sophisticated use of statistical data to aid in the policy process is imperative. The most effective means of decision-making is through ongoing data collection, oftentimes without, at a given point in the ongoing process, a clear policy goal or political agenda in place. But does this scientific approach square with the demands for paperwork reduction and the size of the workforce to maintain the data, as well as politicization of the instruments of policy evaluation for "quick and dirty" shortrun analyses of problems?

The problem becomes an ethical issue if one or both of two situations develop. First, the use of statistical evidence is distorted by the user, increasingly the political appointee or politicized career official who sees political demands as more salient than the imperatives of the scientific method. Second, incompetent or politically pressured experts distort the collection and interpretation of data to meet the needs of their program, organization, or superiors.

Professional statisticians are more inclined to understand the ethical problems posed by the latter situation, the distortion of the policy process by statisticians themselves. A petition presented to the American Statistical Association on August 14, 1983, for example, called for action in response to a deterioration in quality of statistical work done by the federal government. The petition called for the profession to "investigate the *actual* quality control, or lack thereof, in the enumeration or interview of respondents in surveys and censuses conducted by the several agencies of the United States Government."

The problem of ethical statisticians is complicated by the organizational demands put upon policy units, the issue noted above. Policy units are typically staff units, and that raises immediate problems: they are expected to be responsive and loyal to their political superiors, to whom they give advice and counsel on a regular basis; and they are expendable under conditions of cutback, since they do not usually implement programs and deliver essential goods and services to clients. To complicate matters further, they often produce greater inefficiency by telling their superiors and the public that things are not as they seem to be, that relations do not exist or are more complex than supposed, that the design of an effective policy is more difficult than the political leadership would suggest. Dealing in probability rather than certainty produces a different view of the world than that held by the action-oriented politician. As one statistician has observed,

It is of little use to society to have a simple yes or no to the question of whether a new treatment is "dangerous" or whether a new treatment "works." We need, instead, to use these studies to identify subsets of patients with specific response patterns and to estimate degrees of effect and the time course of effect.[38]

In fact, the statistician as organizational actor often finds it useful to respond in the clear yes or no mode that plays well in the political system. A typical example is given by a professional statistician at a state statistical analysis center:

My assignment: project the prison population to the year 2000. My data base? End-of-year populations for 1975 and 1976—two years of data to project twenty-three years into the future. I indicated that if I could get that two years converted into twenty-four data points I might take a shot at projecting next month's population. That was O.K., they said; they had already decided to build a 360 bed prison. All they wanted were some statistics to support the decision. It was then that I learned the first law for criminal justice statistics—give them what they want or they'll stop asking. They got a projection; the prison was built, is currently full, and double bunking begins shortly.[39]

Was the analyst unethical in bending to the demands of the political clientele to endorse statistically a political decision already made? Or are the only ethical

Studies of Systemic Issues in Government
systemic >gati

rules related to the methodology used, with the rule being that if the method can pass muster and if no changes are made in data that would falsify them, the statistician can act as if he is innocent to the political demands around him?

It is at this point that the difference between an ethics based on prudence and the avoidance of wrongdoing and one geared to the creative consciousness becomes clear. Should we cater to the organization and political imperatives or push the search for truth in whatever way it wishes to go? As Gawthrop noted, it is at this point that the design of institutions and the ethical sensibility of individuals must be brought into congruence for truth seeking action to replace expediency.

There is no simple prescription for the profound problem of ethics for scientists engaged in the administrative state. Seeking truth through the scientific method is, as D. F. Davis and E. B. Portis have noted, the ethical rule of the scientist *qua* scientist, but "in marketing their expertise to nonscientists, however, scientists accept other responsibilities." The most important of them is the responsibility as citizens not to distort the policy process by using methods and assumptions that are controversial or unproven.[40] To Robert Denhardt and Jay White, it is imperative that scientists consciously serve interests other than the interest in control in the process of knowledge acquisition.[41] Martin Wachs summed up the problem as one of the "inherent dilemma of circularity":

Those who use forecasts, prepare them, or critique them, invariably use the language of technical objectivity. A model used for prediction is assumed to be unbiased, a tool in the hands of a forecaster who is a technical expert rather than a decision maker—a scientist more than a politician. Yet, so many technical assumptions are required to make any forecast that the process can ultimately be quite subjective, while the consequences have great significance.[42]

In the political setting, the ethical dilemma of the quantifier is to meld the absolute prescriptions of the scientific method with the creative consciousness of a political role player involved with major decisions of major consequence in the political system. There is no answer from the pure scientific ethos that can inform decisions about how to act in the more complicated world of politics, but reliance on a search for truth and avoidance of strategies that violate good science is the rock on which to build a creative consciousness. Detachment from the use of power may be needed to maintain not just objectivity but also a tendency to scientific determinism. Relationships in the modern world are complicated, and certainty is rare. Intuition, political brokering, and compromise all may have a taint for the scientist, but they are necessary for decisive political action.

David Salsburg suggested one solution by noting the legal doctrine of statistical proof in three levels of confidence: probable error, with a 50 percent confidence interval; clear and convincing evidence, with an 80 percent interval; and beyond reasonable doubt, with a 99 percent interval. Probable error is enough to bind over a subject for trial, and clear and convincing evidence is enough to convict, but the 99 percent interval is required for execution in capital cases. Similar thresholds could be developed for other types of policy decisions, affording both statisticians and policymakers a clearer understanding of their respective roles.[43]

The use of statistics in jurisprudence and legal decision-making may be an excellent way to clarify the proper use of statistics in situations in which knowledge does not prove certainty but in which it is clearly useful in informing major decisions. As Daniel P. Moynihan perceptively noted, the ground-breaking "Brandeis brief," which showed the importance of statistical evidence for legal doctrine, only pointed out the need to factor statistics into a world of relationships less simple and predetermined than it theretofore had been:

The "Brandeis brief" did not assert that its view of the facts was totally accurate; its purpose was merely to demonstrate that the legislature, in acting as it did, had a reasonable basis, that the facts *might* be accurate in holding, for example, that minimum standards were necessary to protect workers' health.[44]

The judicial forum affords another advantage in its advocacy procedures. Unlike the administrative world and its value of efficiency and economy, the world of law has an element of redundancy built into it by the advocacy nature of litigation. As litigation in areas such as equal opportunity employment, environmental protection, client rights, and other social policy becomes more and more quantitative, it takes the form of statistician versus statistician. Whose statistical proof can compel the jury or judge to decide in favor of one side over the other? Which relationships are more valid to decisionmakers as they try to assay the current meaning of core values and constitutional rights? Disinterestedness comes from the decisionmaker, not simply the scientific expert.

Statistics and statisticians in government seem to be symbols of an emerging social order, because they are useful in developing policies that reasonably and ethically interpret political values into contemporary circumstances. The dangers of politicization of the quantitative work of government are clear and present. They range from questions of competence—which for statisticians as for any professional group is a moral question—through questions of organizational motives to the higher questions of what the state should be doing and by what means.

The importance of statistical evidence for almost any major decision of government is well known. The more than 4,000 professional statisticians in the federal government and the larger body of policy analysts, evaluators, and professional managers who use quantitative methods are asked to be scientists, organizational role players, and citizens. How to be effective and maintain a strong ethical basis for action must rest on a disinterested search for truth and knowledge in ways that respect the need for decisive action but acknowledge the ambiguity of facts and the legitimacy of reasoned discourse by generalists to move society ahead. As Thomas Schelling observed, compromising between opposing values is very different from compromising a principle.[45]

The statistician community, if it hopes to play a useful and ethical role in the new order, must combine understanding of science with awareness of the way decisions are made in government and politics. What is the appropriate role of statistics in public decisions? This role can range from watchdog activities and monitoring the use of statistical arguments in major decisions to educating statisticians on the perils of overreliance on numbers in questions—such as abortion, the death penalty, the allocation of scarce resources among competing programs—that involve an irreducible core of political choice.

Political leadership must recognize the pressures put on quantitative staff units by demands to be responsive, economical in operation, and loyal to political direction. It must understand the process of data collection and interpretation, and respect the expert's quest for knowledge that goes beyond the particular program design or political request of the moment. Actions such as the decision in 1982 to abolish the Statistical Policy Branch of the Office of Management and Budget (OMB) and assign its professional statisticians to OMB's administrator for information and regulatory management—leaving the federal government with no chief statistician and no point at which the voice of the statistical profession could be expressed in federal policy—must be seen in light of values other than simple economy and cost savings.

Perhaps most important is the need for leaders to educate the public on the importance of relationships and probabilities in today's complex world and avoid the language of certainty and ideology that inherited from the industrial epoch. Things are often not as they seem to be, and the leader interested in society's adaptation to long-term change must be a seeker of truth. This may by necessity be in the closet, as the image of leadership remains that of the ethics of prudence, to conform to the model of leadership held by our civilization. But a creative consciousness, a seeking for truth, is not precluded by political involvement, as the classical writers from Plato on have demonstrated. In fact, political leadership now brings access to a dazzling array of informational resources and expert opinions. How disappointing it will be if they are used only to control the system for predetermined ideologically derived truths.

How this will come to pass remains to be seen. Survey research and statistics have become tools in the campaign process, a far cry from the scientific search for truth. Politicians may become cynical by seeing how they can manipulate the electorate through statistics. The statistical profession has never had a position of prominence in society to use in influencing public policy. Leadership, as James Burns has pointed out, is a continuing problem. The change to a postindustrial order seems uncontrolled, unled, by politicians or any other group. It is hard to be optimistic about the odds of creating a new public ethic geared to the emerging order.

he Use of Quantitative Analysis 261

CONCLUSION

Information can either liberate or control. As we begin to assess the meaning of living in an information-based society, the need to find a public ethics that integrates individual and institutional perspectives is fundamental to the operation of the political system. Unless the scientists of the information age are free to search for knowledge that informs the processes of public decision-making, and unless they do this in a hope for truth and not simply personal or organizational advantage, the alternatives will seem to be narrow and demoralizing. We will choose between a politics of ideology that refuses to look at facts or a politics of control that uses information only to maintain centers of power. The result may be a politics of confusion that sees the world in its complexity but can make of it only a pluralism of voices to be answered without a sense of the whole to inform it and make it serve the general interest.

Ethics must, as Stephen Bailey noted a generation ago, speak to the individual needs of public servants. But it must not lose sight of the critical relationship between personal ethical salvation and the life of the community expressed through politics. Because quantitative analysis is a science of relationships and the search for new and exciting ways to see interconnections, it is a good basis for organizing in ways that resemble Gawthrop's network Y approach.[46] Statisticians sensitive to the broader uses and possible abuses of their science may be leaders in informing policymakers of the proper ways to harness their undertakings. Social and policy scientists trained in the application of quantitative methods will provide the body of experts needed to create a political dialogue that is knowledgeable of facts and sensitive to their limitation. It will help in the elevation of the general over the particular and the disinterested over the selfish, which is the proper goal of any public ethics.

NOTES

1. Ethics was usually taught as a sense of political responsibility or operating notion of the public interest. A major breakthrough in approaching ethics as a teachable subject was the publication of John Rohr's *Ethics for Bureaucrats* (New York: Dekker, 1974).

2. It is hard to overestimate the importance of the International City Managers Association Code of Ethics for city managers in proving the efficacy of an explicit behavioral set of guidelines. The experiment in giving great powers to unelected chief executives and requiring those leaders to stay out of partisan politics showed to many the guiding force of professional codes of conduct.

3. An excellent account of the difficulties the classical tradition of political philosophy encountered in the administrative sciences is contained in Sheldon Wolin, *The Politics of Vision* (Boston: Little, Brown, 1960), chapters nine and ten.

4. This statement reflects the bias toward public interestedness and middle-class standards of morality that characterized the Progressive period. Some would argue that machine politics had an ethic of service, if not a defensible system of personal ethics.

5. For a good discussion of the importance of professional systems of ethics in public administration, *see* John Rohr, "Professional Ethics," in Thomas Lynch, ed., *Organization Theory and Management* (New York: Dekker, 1983), pp. 217–248.

6. For example, *see* Frederick C. Mosher, *Democracy and the Public Service* (New York: Oxford University Press, 1968).

7. Stephen K. Bailey, "Ethics and the Public Service," in Roscoe C. Martin, ed., *Public Administration and Democracy* (Syracuse: Syracuse University Press, 1965), p. 283.

8. Ibid., p. 298.

9. Perhaps the best illustration of the interdisciplinary character of recent approaches to public ethics is provided by a review of *Dialogue,* the informal papers distributed by members of the Public Administration Theory Network and partially supported by the section Public Administration Education of the American Society of Public Administration.

10. Watergate is the most significant single example. For understanding the response of the orthodox public administration community to its meaning, *see* National Academy of Public Administration, *Watergate: Its Implications for Responsible Government* (Washington, D.C., 1974).

11. For example, *see* H. George Frederickson, *New Public Administration* (University: University of Alabama Press, 1980).

12. Ralph P. Hummel, *The Bureaucratic Experience,* 2d ed. (New York: St. Martin's Press, 1982), p. 2.

13. For an excellent discussion of the concept of transformation, *see* James MacGregor Burns, *Leadership* (New York: Harper Colophon Books, 1978).

14. Emmette S. Redford, *Democracy in the Administrative State* (New York: Oxford University Press, 1969).

15. Four examples of such works are Mosher, *Democracy and the Public Service;* Redford, *Democracy in the Administrative State;* Harold Seidman, *Politics, Position, and Power* (New York: Oxford University Press, 1980); Dwight Waldo, *The Enterprise of Public Administration* (Novato, Calif.: Chandler and Sharp, 1980).

16. For an understanding of the dynamics of the new public administration school or movement, *see* Frank Marini, ed., *Toward a New Public Administration* (New York: Harper and Row, 1971).

17. Robert B. Denhardt, *In the Shadow of Organization* (Lawrence: University of Kansas Press, 1981), p. 32.

18. Rohr, *Ethics for Bureaucrats,* p. 59; Michael M. Harmon, *Action Theory for Public Administration* (New York: Longman, 1981); Denhardt, *In the Shadow of Organization,* p. 133.

19. Wolin, *Politics and Vision,* p. 433.

20. Lewis Mumford, *The Pentagon of Power* (New York: Harcourt Brace Jovanovich, 1970).

21. Jacques Ellul, *La Technique on L'Enjeu du Siecle* (Paris: Armand Colin, 1954).

22. Fred Fischer, "Ethical Discourse in Public Administration," *Administration and Society* 15 (May 1983): 7.

23. Wolin, *Politics and Vision,* especially chapter ten.

24. Don K. Price, *Government and Science* (New York: Oxford University Press, 1962).

25. Herbert A. Simon, "Unity of the Arts and Sciences: The Psychology of Thought

and Discovery,'' *Bulletin of the American Academy of Arts and Sciences* 35, no. 6 (March 1982): 26–53.

26. Herbert A. Simon, "Recent Advances in Organization Theory," *Research Frontiers in Politics and Government* (Washington, D.C.: Brookings Institution, 1955), p. 41.

27. Herbert A. Simon, "Rationality as Process and as Product of Thought," *American Economic Review* 68 (May 1978): 14.

28. Herbert A. Simon, "Designing Organizations for an Information-Rich World," in Martin Greenberger, ed., *Computers, Communications, and the Public Interest* (Baltimore: The Johns Hopkins University Press, 1971), p. 3.

29. Louis C. Gawthrop, *Public Sector Management, Systems, and Ethics* (Bloomington: Indiana University Press, 1984), p. 7.

30. *Mandarinism* is a closed system of behavioral norms that denotes conduct appropriate to a bureaucratic elite.

31. Peter Drucker, "What Is 'Business Ethics'?" *Public Interest*, no. 63 (Spring 1981): 27.

32. Gawthrop, *Public Sector Management, Systems, and Ethics*, pp. 141–142.

33. *Network Y* is described by Gawthrop as an "orientation" or "ontological value matrix" that has as its most characteristic virtue "its anticipatory response to change." It is summarized by Gawthrop in these terms: teleological, holistic, temporal, horizontal. The contrasting orientation, *Network X,* is ateleological, atomistic, spatial, and vertical and reflects a bureaucratic order. It is up to the reader to determine the similarity of Gawthrop's networks X and Y with the constructs of Douglas MacGregor, theories X and Y.

34. Gawthrop, *Public Sector Management, Systems, and Ethics,* p. 162.

35. Stuart Nagel, *Public Policy: Goals, Means, and Methods* (New York: St. Martin's Press, 1984), chapter eighteen.

36. This is another example of professional behavioral norms as opposed to internalized value structures.

37. I. Richard Savage, "Statistics and Ethics," *Amstat News* 105 (May 1984): 3.

38. David S. Salsburg, "The Religion of Statistics as Practiced in Medical Journals," *The American Statistician* 39, no. 3 (August 1985): 222.

39. Michael H. Rabasca, "Data Analysis Problems at the State Level: Data Problems and Data Collection," *Proceedings of the Second Workshop on Law and Justice Statistics* (Washington, D.C.: U.S. Department of Justice, 1983), p. 46.

40. D. F. Davis and E. B. Portis, "A Categorical Imperative for Social Scientific Policy Evaluation," *Administration and Society* 14, no. 2 (August 1982): 176–177.

41. Robert B. Denhardt and Jay D. White, "Beyond Explanation," *Administration and Society* 14, no. 2 (August 1982): 165.

42. Martin Wachs, "Ethical Dilemmas in Forecasting for Public Policy," *Public Administration Review* 42, no. 6 (November–December 1982): 563.

43. Salsburg, "The Religion of Statistics as Practiced in Medical Journals," pp. 223–224.

44. Daniel P. Moynihan, "Social Science and the Courts," *Public Interest* 54 (Winter 1979): 14.

45. Thomas Schelling, "Economic Reasoning and the Ethics of Policy," *Public Interest* 55 (Spring 1981): 44.

46. *See* note 35.

SELECTED BIBLIOGRAPHY

Anderson, Charles W. "The Place of Principles in Policy Analysis." *American Political Science Review* 73, no. 3 (September 1979): 711–723.

Bailey, Stephen K. "Ethics and the Public Service." In Roscoe C. Martin, ed., *Public Administration and Democracy*. Syracuse: Syracuse University Press, 1965, pp. 283–298.

Davis, D. F., and E. B. Portis. "A Categorical Imperative for Social Scientific Policy Evaluation." *Administration and Society* 14, no. 2 (August 1982): 175–193.

Denhardt, Robert B. *In the Shadow of Organization*. Lawrence: Kansas University Press, 1981.

Denhardt, Robert, and Jay D. White. "Beyond Explanation." *Administration and Society* 14, no. 2 (August 1982): 163–169.

Douglas, Paul. *Ethics in Government*. New York: Greenwood Press, 1952.

Drucker, Peter. "What Is 'Business Ethics'?" *Public Interest,* no. 63 (Spring 1981): 18–36.

Elliston, Frederick A, John Keenan, Paula Lockhart, and Jane Van Schaick. *Whistleblowing: Managing Dissent in the Workplace*. New York: Praeger, 1985.

Ellul, Jacques. *La Technique ou L'Enjeu du Siecle*. Paris: Armand Colin, 1954.

Fischer, Fred. "Ethical Discourse in Public Administration." *Administration and Society* 15, no. 1 (May 1983): 5–42.

Fleishman, J., and B. L. Payne. *Ethical Dilemmas and the Education of Policy Makers*. Hastings-on-Hudson, N.Y.: Hastings Center, 1980.

Gawthrop, Louis C. *Public Sector Management, Systems, and Ethics*. Bloomington: Indiana University Press, 1984.

Hapgood, Fred. "Risk-Benefit Analysis: Putting a Price on Life." *Atlantic Monthly,* January 1979, pp. 33–38.

Harmon, Michael M. *Action Theory for Public Administration*. New York: Longman, 1981.

Hummel, Ralph P. *The Bureaucratic Experience,* 2d ed. New York: St. Martin's Press, 1982.

Kuhns, William. *The Post-Industrial Prophets: Interpretations of Technology*. New York: Harper Colophon Books, 1971.

Latimor, J. "Accountability, Statistics, and Images of Success." *Bureaucrat* 9, (Summer 1980): 53–57.

Lilla, Mark T. "Ethics, 'Ethos,' and Public Service." *Public Interest* 63 (Spring 1981): 3–17.

Marcuse, Peter. "Professional Ethics and Beyond: Values in Planning." *Journal of the American Institute of Planning* 42 (July 1976): 264–274.

Moynihan, Daniel P. "Social Science and the Courts." *Public Interest* 54 (Winter 1979): 12–31.

Rabasca, Michael H. "Data Analysis Problems at the State Level: Data Problems and Data Collection." *Proceedings of the Second Workshop on Law and Justice Statistics*. Washington, D.C.: U.S. Department of Justice, 1983, pp. 46–49.

Redford, Emmette S. *Democracy in the Administrative State*. New York: Oxford University Press, 1969.

Rohr, John A. *Ethics for Bureaucrats*. New York: Dekker, 1974.

Salsburg, David S. "The Religion of Statistics as Practiced in Medical Journals." *The American Statistician* 39, no. 3 (August 1985): 220–224.

Savage, I. Richard. "Statistics and Ethics." *Amstat News*, no. 105 (May 1984): 3.

Schelling, Thomas. "Economic Reasoning and the Ethics of Policy." *Public Interest* 55 (Spring 1981): 49–76.

Simon, Herbert A. *Administrative Behavior*. New York: Free Press, 1947.

————. "Recent Advances in Organization Theory." *Research Frontiers in Politics and Government*. Washington, D.C.: Brookings Institution, 1955, pp. 23–44.

————. "Designing Organizations for an Information-Rich World." In Martin Greenberger, ed., *Computers, Communications, and the Public Interest*. Baltimore: The Johns Hopkins University Press, 1970.

————. "Rational Decision Making in Business Organizations," *American Economic Review* 69 (1979): 493–513.

————. "Are Social Problems Problems That Social Sciences Can Solve?" In William H. Kruskal, ed., *The Social Sciences: Their Nature and Uses*. Chicago: University of Chicago Press, 1982.

————. "Unity of the Arts and Sciences: The Psychology of Thought and Discovery." *Bulletin of the American Academy of Arts and Sciences* 35, no. 6 (March 1982): 26–53.

Tong, Rosemarie. *Ethics in Policy Analysis*. Englewood Cliffs, N.J.: Prentice-Hall, 1986.

Wachs, Martin. "Ethical Dilemmas in Forecasting for Public Policy." *Public Administration Review* 42, no. 6 (November–December 1982): 562–567.

Wolin, Sheldon. *The Politics of Vision*. Boston: Little, Brown, 1960.

11

Fraud, Waste, and Abuse in Government

Jerome B. McKinney

This chapter introduces a topic that has been receiving considerable attention during the past decade because of the growing perception that fraud, waste, and abuse (FWA) are pervasive and that action must be taken to control them. There is widespread belief that FWA exists at all levels of government. Indeed, the crisis of confidence in government during the past two decades has paralleled the rising public concern about FWA. A prevalent view is that significant improvement in the fight against FWA cannot be made in government undertakings without improving the efficacy of most programs. The academic study of FWA, however, has lagged because detailed evidence about fraud, waste, and abuse is difficult to come by and at times cannot be documented publicly.[1]

Fraud, waste, and abuse produce a number of undesirable consequences. They distort public policy, cause a lack of responsiveness and accountability to the public's needs, promote mistrust and a lack of credibility of governmental institutions, and create the perception that "no one is in charge."

The U.S. comptroller general stated that because there is a lack of support in the fight against FWA, efforts to diminish it have been largely ineffectual because of the maintenance of poor internal control systems and the failure of administrators to give priority to the FWA problem.[2] To complicate the problem further, Congress passed many social programs such as the Comprehensive Employment Training Act (CETA) without adequate provisions for monitoring FWA. Where agency incentive systems exist, they are instituted more to promote and enhance the public image of the agency than to identify ways and means of eradicating FWA. With no established internal control management-information system agencies lack the basic data for determining what resources are required to combat FWA.[3]

In an attempt to minimize the FWA problem, inspector generals were insti-

tuted in all federal cabinet agencies and many lesser agencies in 1978. Several
state and local governments have adopted similar actions. The General Accounting Office (GAO) and many counterpart state and local agencies established hot lines to permit citizens to provide tips on possible FWA activities.
Despite these steps, concerns about the misapplication and imprudent use of
public resources remain high. The public outcry has been heightened by revelations such as the Pentagon's $600 toilet seat and the $400 hammer and, more
recently, by the prosecution of many state and local officials for engaging in
FWA activities.

The monetary loss attributable to FWA varies widely among programs. The
GAO estimated in 1978 that monetary losses for all program expenditures range
from 1 to 10 percent. A U.S. Department of Justice official noted in 1979 that
whenever examinations were made of agencies, FWA invariably showed up.[4]
A former inspector general of the U.S. Department of Health, Education, and
Welfare (HEW) estimated that the annual loss due to FWA amounted to between $4 billion and $8 billion. In his book *Fat City,* Donald Lambro suggested that a $100 billion annual savings would be made while the President's
Private Sector Survey on Cost Control (PPSSCC, or the Grace Commission)
proposed cuts and efficiency measures amounting to $424 billion over a three-
year period. These large FWA estimates are taking place when spending out-
paces revenues, creating unprecedented deficits of more than $160 billion yearly.

Fraud, waste, and *abuse* are relatively new terms that have been created to
define better the areas left unclear and undefined by the term *corruption.* To
minimize the problem, the definition of FWA has been made sufficiently inclu-
sive to accommodate the term *corruption*—behavior that violates expectations,
norms, and standards.[5]

Fraud is the violation of civilian and criminal statutes involving intentional,
willful, and conscious (constructive fraud) or unintentional (actual fraud)
wrongdoing or misrepresentation for the purpose of unlawfully obtaining benefits from a public program. It involves acts such as intentional mistakes (including arithmetic or clerical errors), willful misrepresentation of facts, embezzlement, and theft by means of deceit and suppression of truth.[6]

Waste is more a matter of opinion than law, and most waste typically consists of intentional acts that lead to additional cost or reduced benefits to potential recipients. It can be equated with mismanagement.[7]

Abuse is the commission of an act of impropriety that "involves the violation
of an agency's rules, procedures, and regulations, impairing the effective and
efficient implementation of an agency's programs. Acts of abuse typically involve the reduction or denial of goods or services rightfully due to eligible
participants."[8] As with waste, there is an element of ambiguity in defining and
recognizing abuse due to the judgmental factors involved.[9]

BACKGROUND

This section provides a historical overview of FWA by focusing on urban environments because of the influential role that cities play in American politics. In presenting and discussing examples, an effort is made to show the role that FWA has played in creating a crisis of confidence in government.

Although the technical definitions formulated for FWA are relatively new, the phenomena of fraud, waste, and abuse are by no means a recent development. Grecian merchants tried to corner the olive market in 600 B.C. through such methods. In the seventeenth century, the first modern corporation—the British East India Company—negotiated duty-free treatment for its exports by providing the Magai rulers with paintings, carvings, copper, and brass objects.[10] In fact, today FWA is a worldwide problem that has developed a colorful vocabulary. In West Africa it is known as grease or dash, and in parts of India it is referred to as speed money. In Latin America FWA is known as *La Moridia* (the bite), in Italy, as *La bustarella* (the little envelope), and in parts of the Middle East and Asia as *baksheesh*.[11]

Because of the differing objectives of the democratic and aristocratic leaders there may be greater potential for corruption in democratically ruled nations than in those that are aristocratically ruled. Alexis de Tocqueville wrote that democracies were especially susceptible to corruption because their leaders, generally poor, were driven to amass their fortunes. Aristocrats, typically individuals of established wealth, strive to increase their power.[12]

There have been a number of FWA developments that have taken place at state and national levels of government throughout the history of the United States. They include the Credit Mobilier scandal in the 1920s, involving Albert Fall, secretary of the interior under President Harding, who transferred government oil reserves to oil companies for a handsome payoff; Judge Otto Kerner's conviction for accepting bribes from a racetrack owner in the 1960s while governor of Illinois; Watergate and the laundering of money in the early 1970s; government officials convicted in the Abscam cases for accepting bribes by a number of government officials from FBI informers in the late 1970s and early 1980s; and the New York Parking Authority payoffs in 1986.[13]

For the past hundred years or so, corrupt city political machines, with ties to state and national government in places such as New York, San Francisco, and Chicago, have been the target for important reform movements. In his *American Commonwealth*, James Bryce described a pervasiveness of corruption in virtually every American city with more than 200,000 people and to a lesser extent in smaller ones.[14] Speaking about the laxity and imprudence of spending and the control of finances at the national level, Bryce observed in 1891: "Under the system of congressional finance here described, America wastes millions annually. But, her wealth is so great, her revenue so elastic, that she is not sensible of the loss."[15]

Due to the weak national political party structure in the United States, the focal points of power have resided at the state and local levels, especially in the larger cities where powerful political machines emerged. These machines were used to control elected offices and to enrich the political bosses. The operation of New York City Tammany Hall provides a classic example of how a political machine can convert the public interest into self-aggrandizing interest. It was estimated that only 15 cents of each tax dollar collected during Tammany Hall's heyday went to legitimate purposes.

The use of inside information relating to confidential transactions between the city and other parties was regularly used by city officers to reap huge profits. This practice, known as "honest graft," gradually became an acceptable norm indicative of the functionalist approach to FWA.[16] A number of observers believe the honest-graft syndrome (as evidenced by David Levine and Ivan Boesky in the insider trading scandals on Wall Street in 1986) is the prevailing norm due to the basic philosophical foundation on which the American system rests. We live in a society in which private property is enshrined as the maximum good, "the engine of all progress."[17] President Calvin Coolidge expressed it well when he said "the business of America is business."

FWA as a Cause of Crisis of Confidence

Despite the outcry over FWA following the aborted building of the costly TFX plane under Defense Secretary McNamara and the massive cost overrun on the C-5A cargo plane built by Lockheed during the 1960s, there was no sustained concern about FWA during the post–World War II years until the 1970s. Several developments served to raise public consciousness about the exigency and pervasiveness of the problem. The cost of conducting government business continued to increase as did the number of complaints about the quality and quantity of goods and services. There were many reports of bribes, kickbacks, collusion, and widespread corruption among public officials. Yearly estimates of government FWA ranged as high as $140 billion.[18]

When the public was being asked to commit greater and greater resources to the military, experts began questioning its readiness and fighting efficiency. Simultaneously, daily reports were uncovering outrageous prices that the government was paying for materials from no-bid private contractors. Despite the massive rise in the U.S. deficit, managerial performance is still not being evaluated on outputs produced in meeting targeted objectives or on how well agencies have done in developing controls to minimize FWA. "Instead, they (the managers) are rated on such things as how much money they spend, how many program participants they sign up, and how many claims they process."[19] The pace of quiet spending or unappropriated disbursements continued unabated.[20] Through these developments, pressure mounted for government to recognize the problem and the potential harm it inflicts on the country.

Opinion polls taken during the mid to latter part of the 1970s suggest that FWA was a significant factor in creating a crisis of confidence in both public and private sector institutions. The Daniel Yankelovich poll in 1977 indicated a significant rise of public mistrust in national institutions. The 80 percent approval rating that public institutions enjoyed throughout the 1950s fell to a low of 33 percent in 1976, a low that continues. Similar declines were reported for the business sector. The public had concluded that government was ineffective in solving problems and wasteful in spending tax dollars and that officials often engaged in fraudulent practices to enhance their own interests.[21]

On a question posed by Gallup in 1978, 1979, and 1980: "Of every tax dollar that goes to the federal government in Washington, D.C. (the government of this state or your local government) how many cents would you say are wasted?" People thought that the federal waste amounted to a median of 48 cents for the three years. The states wasted 32 cents in 1978 and 29 cents in 1979 and 1980. For the local government, it was 25 cents in 1978 and 23 cents in 1979 as well as 1980.[22] People felt that too much power was concentrated in the hands of too few federal officials and that public officials generally could not be trusted.[23] Despite the waste and misappropriation of government funds, little was being done to eradicate the corruption. When it came to having a say about how things are run, the attitude that "the little guy does not stand a chance" prevailed.[24]

There is a general perception that too many agencies and officials are working at cross purposes with each other. In the area of foreign trade policy, approximately twenty-five agencies have been delegated the responsibility of administering various aspects of international commerce. The overlap of delegated responsibility creates confusion and inefficiency. With so many participants competing for the same policy space, administrative waste inevitably follows, especially when no incentive system is present to encourage bureaucratic efficiency.[25]

The public is bewildered by yet another phenomenon—the presence of federal or state programs carried out by a seemingly endless number of private third-party service deliverers amounting to $200 billion at the federal level in 1981. Decentralization is generally beneficial when effective accountability and monitoring systems are maintained. When such controls are absent, however, the perception arises that "things are out of control."[26] Such a view appeared to be reinforced by the result of a survey assessing federal employees' attitudes toward reporting cases of FWA. The Merit System Protection Board found in 1981 that 53 percent of public servants believed that "nothing would be done" if they brought incidents of fraudulent and wasteful activities to the attention of authorities.[27]

Some extravagant FWA examples appearing in the media and elsewhere have contributed to a widespread attitude that there is inadequate control over the public's purse. Among the outstanding examples are the following:

1. During the past fifteen years, NASA's spendthrift syndrome enabled it to waste more than $3 billion. Millions of dollars of equipment disappeared without audit trails.

Excessively inflated prices were paid to contractors—one of the most disturbing cases related to a building sold to a company for $400,000 and subsequently leased back to NASA for $3.6 million per year.[28]

2. Under minority contracting, white-owned businesses use front minority-owned firms to obtain contracts for which they would otherwise be ineligible.[29]

3. A large number of contractors debarred from doing business with the Defense Department continue to defraud the government of millions, in some cases even from their prison cells. Debarred contractors appealing their penalty are allowed to continue business until the appeal process is exhausted. The Defense Department maintains no monitoring or follow-up system to track these individuals. In the case of a small firm, the contractor may simply change the name of the company to that of his wife or immediate relatives.[30]

4. Between fiscal years 1978 to 1981 and fiscal years 1982 to 1985 the U.S. Air Force and Navy procurement budgets were increased from $69.81 billion to $122.00 billion, representing a 76 percent increase in constant dollars; yet 12 percent fewer planes were purchased.[31]

5. Productivity for many defense-related contractors in some cases is only one-seventeenth of the standards routinely used by contractors to produce similar items for nonmilitary civilian customers.[32]

6. Among the Golden Fleece Awards that Senator William Proxmire (D–Wis.) gave in 1986, one was to the Urban Mass Transit Administration for spending $30 billion over twenty years. The expenditure generated a drop in transit revenue per vehicle mile of 26 percent while increasing costs by 70 percent and causing a subsidy increase from the taxpayer of 1,250 percent. The objectives of decreasing congestion and pollution and lowering energy use were not realized.[33]

7. A Columbia, South Carolina, dentist was convicted for extracting numerous healthy teeth from disadvantaged children to qualify for large payments under the government's special dental plan. A Chicago woman under various aliases drew huge sums of illegal welfare benefits.[34]

FWA, in sum, is not a new phenomenon; the magnitude of it has increased with the growth of government and business. During the 1970s concern about FWA was a major factor in helping to create a crisis of confidence in government, a crisis that continues today.

LITERATURE REVIEW

To show the multifaceted environment and ways in which FWA is discussed in the literature, this section contains four components. The first provides a brief review of the themes that have characterized the professional discussion of FWA. The second shows that FWA occurs not in a vacuum but in a value-laden context, and as such examines the role that ethics may play in influencing actions. The third component shows how one's academic discipline may effect the way that FWA is perceived and interpreted. The fourth summarizes the suggested approaches for analyzing vulnerability to FWA.

Prevention, Apprehension, Enforcement/Prosecution

Prevention, apprehension, and enforcement/prosecution are three main themes that have emerged in the fight against FWA. Prevention offers, perhaps, the greatest long-run payoff because it deters the problem before it occurs. Effective prevention requires, among other things, that a clearly defined set of values, goals, and objectives be understood and accepted by all employees controlling the use of and the maintenance of resources. Indicative of the priority, commitment, and the attention given to prevention are the federal government's publications on the topic, such as the GAO's *Framework for Assessing Job Vulnerability to Ethical Problems;* the *Financial Integrity Act,* mandating internal controls in federal agencies; the Department of Housing and Urban Development's (HUD's) *Fraud Vulnerability Assessment System,* and the Office of Management and Budget's (OMB's) *Internal Control Guidelines.*[35]

Second, apprehension has always been a method that has been used to detect FWA. Recently, however, methods other than financial postauditing have been applied, such as performance auditing, which is concerned with result or accomplishment of a program. For example, Leo Herbert's *Auditing the Performance of Management,* the GAO's *Standard for Audit of Governmental Organizations, Programs, Activities, and Functions,* and Henry Butt's "Value for Money Auditing in Local Government" are suggestive of the available literature.[36]

Finally, enforcement/prosecution has typically received the most attention in the popular press and from politicians as well. Despite the publicity this approach has received, the desired long-term impact of enforcement/prosecution will not be realized until it is integrated as part of the prevention and apprehension system. Nonetheless, laws, ordinances, regulations, and policies pertaining to enforcement are numerous. At the federal level, for example, the Corrupt Practice Act of 1977 prohibits bribe giving to foreign and domestic political parties or government employees, and the Civil Money Penalties Law of 1981 is aimed at minimizing FWA in Medicare and Medicaid and social security.[37]

An understanding of the issues in these three themes found in the extant literature will help administrators in dealing with the ethical problems in the execution of government programs. But what role can ethics play in influencing action?

The Ethical Basis of Government and FWA

Retaining the moral basis of government is indispensable for attaining the good life in a civilized society. Ethics should be "the central feature of good governmental decision-making."[38] Ideally, transgression of the accepted moral norms of a society should galvanize the public against its transgressors. The weight of public opinion, however, does not always operate in this manner as has been exhibited by politicians who were convicted of various charges but continually reelected in the 1960s (e.g., Representatives Adam Clayton Powell and James Flood).

Government officials in a democracy must totally reject the edicts or logical imperatives of Machiavelli.[39] Unlike Machiavelli's prince, who is permitted to act like a fox or a lion as the situation demands, public officials should not seek to uphold or preserve their personal self-interest over community interest. These officials—entrusted with the duties and responsibilities for insuring security, protecting the Constitution, and preserving our way of life—are expected to act in accordance with the moral standards set by society. As either a tacit or explicit condition of employment, public servants have agreed, under threat of penalty, not to violate socially accepted moral behavior.[40]

Peter French suggested that the public servants' official morality should approximate the platonic concept of duty. Plato observed: "They must look upon the Commonwealth as their special concern—the sort of concern that is felt for something closely bound up with oneself that the interest and fortunes for good or ill is held to be *identical* with their own."[41] Thus for Plato's ideally conceived rulers, self-interest and public interest coincide. Justice is pursued for the collective good, not solely to serve the interests of the individual or the needs of a few.

A number of observers have indicated that the ethical basis or philosophical orientation of a community helps to determine the extent of FWA in a given community.[42] In Daniel Elazar's view, communities that espouse the moralistic political culture strongly oppose FWA whereas the individualistic and traditionalistic political cultures display a greater degree of tolerance for FWA. Similarly, middle-class communities exhibit less tolerance for FWA whereas residents of poor communities display the opposite response. Susan Welch and John Peters's findings supported Elazar's hypothesis.[43] A study conducted in Israel on the attitude of new immigrants toward white-collar crime is consistent with the findings conducted in the United States. The Russian immigrants in five out of six offenses such as embezzlement, bribe giving, tax evasion, and consumer fraud were less likely to report infractions. By contrast, the North American immigrants and Israeli citizens exhibited a high degree of likeness in their responses, indicating their willingness to report similar offenses.[44]

By emphasizing the relative response to FWA, the Israeli immigrant findings parallel a functionalist's view. This view suggests that FWA acts should not be evaluated in absolute terms as being either "good" or "bad." Instead, the functionalist attempts to understand FWA within a wider social context. The desired ends or objectives are analyzed and compared with alternative courses of action. The functionalists may want to know whether illegal acts are consistent with prevailing societal norms and whether the acts are functional in facilitating the achievement of the objectives being sought. For example, do FWA acts provide access to people who might otherwise be "shut out" of the economic public decision-making process?[45]

The functionalist, then, does not presuppose absolute moral standards of right or wrong but classifies acts of FWA based upon whether or not they are socially permissible, acceptable, and effective in achieving the organizational or individual goal. Indeed, FWA may be the only means for remedying injustices or problems due to poorly designed programs, rules, and institutional inefficiencies. FWA, thus, acts as a strategic means by which to protect the interests of many and increase the predictability in decision-making.[46]

Opponents of the functionalist school argue that it attempts to rationalize that FWA is a normal part of the process of making public decisions. Critics also charge that the approach suggests that public responses are determined by the amount of money participants can afford. By so doing, the system restricts the positive outcomes of decisions to the "haves" and freezes out the "have nots," thus setting the stage for social resentment, political opposition, and, ultimately, widening of the social inequalities.[47] Like the functionalist approach, however, the discipline perspective discussed below suggests that FWA is subject to relative interpretation.

FWA from the Discipline Perspective

In addition to the explanations for FWA reviewed earlier, another explanation concerns the scholar's academic discipline, which may significantly influence how FWA is interpreted. To the economist, for instance, FWA occurs because of scarcity. When the imbalance between supply and demand of goods or services reaches a critical point, participants are likely to engage in FWA to insure that their interest is protected or enhanced. To the anthropologist, it is viewed predominately as a phenomenon that occurs in an extended system of traditional and informal gift-giving practices. To the sociologist, FWA is a function of power and status relationships. In a system of unequal economic rewards, FWA helps one to adjust and compensate for a defective administrative system in order to make it more responsive. To the political scientist, FWA is a way of exercising institutionalized influence based on wealth and power in the political system.

It cannot be overemphasized that understanding FWA requires the study of an array of actors such as environment, culture, internalized norms, academic discipline, and effective internal control systems. To enhance the ability to predict and deter FWA, recent efforts have focused attention on vulnerability factors contributing to FWA.

Vulnerability Factors for FWA

In an exhaustive two-year study of FWA, attention was focused on three main factors: (1) Situational pressures, typically involving indicators such as high personal debt or losses, gambling, stock market speculations, and expensive habits; (2) opportunities for FWA created due to careless internal controls or "by being the only individual who knows a particular procedure such as modifying the computer program;"[48] and (3) personal integrity related to the code of ethics to which an individual adheres. Ultimately, the decision to commit fraud may depend on the interaction of all three forces.[49]

In their book *Management Principles for Asset Protection*, Phil Kropatkin and Richard Kusserow examined how and why FWA occurs and indicated what managers can do to lessen vulnerability to FWA.[50] They identified four primary motivating factors for FWA: target, motives, access, and opportunity. To minimize these potential problems, the authors evaluated a number of counterstrategies such as internal control, risk analysis, front-end controls, personnel recruiting, management practices, and special security and auditing implications of computers, especially as they relate to the electronic transfer of funds.

The FWA literature embraces many of the trends discussed above, and this chapter contributes to that literature by surveying and integrating the growing publications on the FWA in government. Attention is drawn below to the sources of data and information and how findings may be interpreted in light of existing theory, providing linkages that have so far been missing in the FWA literature.

UNDERSTANDING FWA: A GENERAL FRAMEWORK AND ITS APPLICATION

This section examines a general framework for understanding FWA by exploring three analytical perspectives and indicating how each may be applied: personalistic, institutional, and systemic. The *personalistic approach* indicates that the cause and cure of FWA requires that individuals with defective and unethical qualities be isolated. The identification of such traits permits the removal of those individuals who are unworthy of public trust. Yet since defective attributes may be found in any individual, there is no empirical method that would reasonably identify a specific category of individuals especially prone to committing FWA acts. Without reliable indicators, culpable individuals cannot be easily distinguished in advance from nonculpable individuals. The personalistic approach also ignores defects inherent in institutional structures and social processes that may be responsible for untoward behavior.[51]

In the *institutional approach*, emphasis is placed on imperfections and problems inherent in organizations and laws. Such problems can emerge from maladministration, ineffectual auditing, or poorly conceived structures, such as a weak mayor council form of government. The approach analyzes a number of potential causes of FWA, such as laws, administration, and audit procedures. It requires an examination of the impact that institutions have on individual choices and how certain behavior patterns may lead to FWA. It is insufficient simply to isolate the "bad" individuals; a modification of institutions may be necessary to eradicate problems.

The emphasis on institutional factors, in isolation from the political process and other operating forces in the environment, however, may generate inappropriate responses to FWA.[52] For example, the procedures and laws in a jurisdiction may have been carefully and specifically drawn to permit property-tax-assessment modification only when the facts would so dictate—yet it may have been plagued by corruption. Each time a scandal had occurred, guidelines and penalties were made stricter. Yet problems continued because the permissive political environment and the lack of professional and expert training of their officials were ignored.

The *systemic approach* considers FWA as a result of a multitude of interactions among a number of actors: officials of government agencies, the executive, the legislators, groups, and private citizens. The FWA occurs from the pressures and influences generated from the flux and flow of many forces; individuals and institutions are regarded only as two of the many influencing factors operating in the environment. Individuals participate in FWA for the potential benefits to be gained, laws and public opinion notwithstanding. In fact, it is through the law-making process that influence is exercised and benefits are obtained. Since the systems view encompasses many factors that must be sorted out, it does not provide for easy answers, one-shot solutions or quick "fixes." Instead, it requires a comprehensive analysis of the political system, linkage, and identifiable factions and forces that contribute to FWA.

The three-level perspective, then, permits explanation of FWA in terms of a successively broadening focus of analysis. Because of the assumptions and facts of each perspective, observers may reach different conclusions about the factors producing the problem. As will be seen in the next section, no one focus enjoys a monopoly in explaining corruption. In practice, each approach has been employed in responding to FWA.[53]

Response to Fraud, Waste, and Abuse

To make the personalistic approach operational requires the development of a method that would permit the identification of individuals having defective and unethical qualities. The widely used preaudit and postaudit techniques could be employed. For example, if the apprehension of individuals with defective qualities before FWA acts are committed is stressed, the preaudit technique may be applied.[54] When the stress is placed on apprehending individuals post facto, the postaudit is emphasized.

Internal control, vulnerability assessment, and the single audit are examples of the institutional focus. Internal control has been widely advocated as a basic first step in the fight against FWA. It provides information relating to the protection and security of an agency's assets. It seeks to insure that an agency's transactions are "accurate, complete and procedures for detecting malfunctions are effective."[55]

Vulnerability assessment has also received significant attention. It is a predominantly qualitative technique for measuring a job or an agency's susceptibility to FWA. In 1982 Congress passed the Financial Integrity Act requiring that federal financial managers provide a statement to the president and to Congress about whether the agency has established a system of internal accounting and administrative control in accordance with the standards prescribed by the comptroller general. The latter is required to determine whether the system provides reasonable assurance and properly accounts for all obligations and costs. Additionally, the comptroller general must insure that the system provides adequate and reliable financial statistical reports and that assets are safeguarded against FWA.[56]

The single audit is the final institutional development likely to have a positive impact on reducing FWA. Instead of conducting numerous audits in one agency, each agency conducting an audit is expected to include multiple audit needs. The single audit act requires that the Office of Management and Budget designate a "cognizant agency" (a particular federal department) to monitor the implementation of the audit requirement in a given state receiving federal funds. The cognizant agency has three responsibilities: (1) to see that agencies conduct audits and conform to stipulations of the act; (2) to make certain that audit reports or corrective actions are transmitted to appropriate federal officials; and (3) to coordinate audits done with those required under the act to develop audit continuity and integration.[57]

A number of statutes have been enacted to facilitate the fight against FWA in a systemic manner, the third approach. The Travel Act of 1961 prohibits the interstate distribution of proceeds obtained by illegal activities such as gambling, narcotics, prostitution, extortion, bribery, and arson. The Mail Fraud Act prohibits the use of the U.S. mail to carry out illegal and fraudulent schemes. The Corrupt Practices Act of 1977 prohibits bribe giving to a foreign or domestic political party official or candidate for political office, including other officials or employees. The act requires the maintenance of acceptable standards of record keeping and internal accounting control.[58] Although the Paper Reduction Act of 1980 has been only marginally successful in cutting and minimizing unnecessary procedures, the Civil Money Penalties Law of 1981 is credited with having significant impact in reducing the health-care cost for areas such as Medicare, Medicaid, and social security. Unlike the False Claim Act, which requires criminal prosecution, the Civil Money and Penalties Law permits administrative sanctions for FWA acts.[59] When viewed from a collective standpoint, these acts, then, are indicative of the system perspective.

In addition, the inspector general system, the Civil Service Reform Act, the President's Council on Integrity and Efficiency, zero-base budgeting, and the President's Private Sector Survey on Cost Control represent five major efforts of the systemic focus. The Inspector General Act of 1978 is a major indicator of the government's will to fight FWA; the system is now an integral part of all major federal agencies. The Office of Inspector General consolidates an agency's audit and investigation unit; provides policy direction, making periodic or interim reports as the situation demands; and acts as the ears for "whistle-blowers."[60] The Inspector General's Office, or a variant of it, also has been established in a number of state and local units of government such as New

York City and Massachusetts. Some states have a partial inspector general system. For example, the Pennsylvania Department of Transportation and a number of departments in New York have adopted the inspector general system. Virginia has authorized the creation of an inspector general system, and Montana is considering it.

In many states where the inspector general system has not been established, there is usually a unit identified within the attorney general's office, such as the consumer protection or fraud, fraud/forgery unit, white-collar crime, and economic crime unit.[61] In several states the duties nominally assigned to the inspector general are carried out by the office of the comptroller, such as in Florida.

The Civil Service Reform Act of 1978 (CSRA) recognized the important role that "whistle-blowers" can play in insuring that the integrity of government is preserved. To facilitate whistle-blowers to exchange information with supervisors or responsible authorities, provisions were made to protect the employees making disclosures. The CSRA encouraged employees to report illegal or wasteful activities to their direct supervisor. When this disclosure was not possible, channels outside the formal authority structure, such as the inspector generals, were viewed as an acceptable alternate.[62]

Third, the President's Council on Integrity and Efficiency (PCIE) has been instrumental in fostering cooperation, information sharing, and joint research among the inspector generals of the various federal agencies. Among the research projects that the PCIE has carried out are the "Project to Identify and Verify Significant Underreporting of Income in Federal Assisted Programs," the "Model Prevention Plan," and "The Front-End Operational Controls in the Procurement Process-Contracts." The PCIE issues semiannual and annual reports of its accomplishments on efforts to prevent fraud, waste, and mismanagement.[63]

The zero-base budgeting (ZBB) approach that was ushered in during President Carter's administration initiated a period of decrementalism and shrinking budgets. Although ZBB did perhaps slow down the pace of public spending in those jurisdictions where it was adopted, it lacked the desired impact at the national level. Despite President Reagan's cutback and retrenchment activities, both spending and deficits are increasing.

The President's Private Sector Survey on Cost Control Commission was a major private sector initiative aimed at assisting the government in identifying FWA problems. The commission conducted a comprehensive analysis of all major spending agencies of the federal government. It highlighted many structures and practices that it viewed as factors contributing to corruption.

CONCLUSION

The evolution of fraud, waste, and abuse shows that it is not a new phenomenon. In fact, the history of the United States has been littered with FWA. The economic instability of the 1970s brought with it high inflation, low-quality public services, and steeper taxes. When most national problems seemed impervious to solution, FWA at all levels of government played a significant role in the precipitous decline of confidence in American institutions.

There is a strong ideology that influences policymakers to contract out vast portions of goods and services to the private sector. Because of private-sector pressure to show a profit, contractors have engaged in price gouging and have manufactured shoddy products. Giving bribes to obtain contracts may be viewed as a normal way of doing business in some circles.

A major problem in the allocation of public resources is politics. Most managers see their budget as an indicator of power and success. Budget-review units such as the OMB do not require that agencies prepare budgets based on unit costs. Thus estimates are based on whatever the political winds suggest as feasible. These submissions are aggregated and submitted to the legislature. There is no built-in incentive for budget reduction.

Of the three approaches examined in this chapter, the personalistic and institutional perspectives have problems that seem to outweigh their benefits. The former emphasizes defects in individuals, and the latter restricts itself to the imperfections of laws and institutions.

The systemic approach appears to hold the greatest promise because of its comprehensive and analytical explanation of the forces impacting on FWA. It, too, however, has weaknesses, namely, that it provides few manageable remedies. This may suggest that FWA is inevitable, which it is not. If the systemic approach is followed, it should be sufficiently eclectic to accommodate components of other approaches as the situation demands. The comprehensive approach that is adopted should have great efficacy and be ethically based, that is, consonant with the generally accepted norms of fair play, equity, and justice of the community or society concerned; that is, the usual advocation for laws, regulations, rules, controls, or code of ethics will not be self-executing. They need to be undergirded by a public service that has a well-reasoned, internalized philosophy.

The absence of a public service philosophy is, perhaps, a major impediment in the fight against FWA, especially in a society that exalts profit as the true measure of prosperity and progress. The public interest is supplanted to the pursuit of self-interest, thus creating conflict of interest and also rationalization of kickbacks and bribes as morally permissible behavior. The disregard of public interest permits the infraction of laws, rules, and procedures on the basis that others are doing the same. It encourages unresponsive behavior especially toward the poor and the uneducated. The lack of a public service philosophy not only impedes the pursuit of the public interest as a way of life, but it leaves each individual with the maximum opportunity to amass wealth through FWA.

Despite the pervasiveness of fraud, waste, and abuse in the public sector, strides have been made toward minimizing the problem in the reactive area of enforcement. Such activity is evident from numerous investigations conducted by civil and military agencies and by prosecution and disciplinary actions taken against offenders. A great deal still needs to be done in the preventive, maintenance, and training areas to avoid the debilitating impacts of FWA in American government.

NOTES

1. Jerome B. McKinney, "Concepts and Definitions," in Jerome B. McKinney and Michael Johnston, eds., *Fraud, Waste, and Abuse in Government* (Philadelphia: Philadelphia Institute for the Study of Human Issues, 1986), p. 1.

2. U.S. Congress, House of Representatives, Committee on the Budget, "Task Force on Governmental Efficiency," 96th Congress, first session (Washington, D.C.: U.S. Government Printing Office, 1979), pp. 1–3; Thomas F. Eagleton and Ira S. Shapiro, "Federal Fraud, Waste, and Abuse: Causes and Responses," *Institute of Socioeconomic Studies Journal* 7 (Winter 1982–1983): 34–46.

3. General Accounting Office, *Federal Agencies Can and Should Do More to Combat Fraud in Government Programs* (Washington, D.C., 1978).

4. U.S. Congress, House of Representatives, "Task Force on Governmental Efficiency," p. 17.

5. John A. Gardiner and Theodore Layman, *The Fraud Control Game: State Responses to Fraud and Abuse in AFDC and Medicaid Programs* (Bloomington: Indiana University Press, 1974), chapter one. Public officials are labeled corrupt when they use their positions to serve or enhance their private wealth or ends.

6. *See* McKinney, "Concepts and Definitions"; Robert K. Elliott and J. J. Willingham, *Management Fraud: Detection and Deterrence* (New York: Petrocelli Books, 1980), p. 95.

7. William Roth, Jr., "The 'Malmanagement' Problem: Finding the Roots of Government Fraud, Waste, and Abuse," *Notre Dame Law Review* 58 (1983): 961–984.

8. *See* Jerome B. McKinney, *Effective Financial Management in Public and Nonprofit Agencies* (Westport, Conn.: Quorum Books, 1986), chapter nineteen.

9. Andrea G. Lange et al., *Fraud and Abuse in Government Programs* (Washington, D.C.: U.S. Department of Justice, Law Enforcement Assistance Agency, 1979), p. 8.

10. Mark Green and John Berry, *The Challenge of Hidden Profits: Reducing Corporate Bureaucracy and Waste* (New York: Morrow, 1985), p. 255.

11. Joseph La Palombara, *Politics within Nations* (Englewood Cliffs, N.J.: Prentice-Hall, 1974), p. 403; Michael Johnston, *Political Corruption and Public Policy in America* (Monterey, Calif.: Brooks/Cole, 1982), p. 2.

12. Theodore Lowi, "The Intelligent Persons Guide to Political Corruption," *Public Affairs*, no. 82 (1981): 1.

13. Gerald Caplan and the Police Foundation, *ABSCAM Ethics, Moral Issues, and Deceptions in Law Enforcement* (Cambridge, Mass.: Ballinger, 1983).

14. James Bryce, *The American Commonwealth*, vol. 1 (London: Macmillan, 1891).

15. Ibid., p. 179.

16. William L. Riordan, "Honest Graft," in John Gardner and David Olsen, eds., *The Theft of the City* (Bloomington: Indiana University Press, 1974), p. 7.

17. Jack Newfield and Paul DuBrual, *The Abuse of Power: The Permanent Government and the Fall of New York* (New York: Penguin Books, 1978), p. 84.

18. U.S. Congressional Budget Office/General Accounting Office, *Analysis of the Grace Commission's Major Proposals for Cost Control* (Washington, D.C.: U.S. Government Printing Office, 1984).

19. Eagleton and Shapiro, "Federal Fraud, Waste, and Abuse," pp. 35–46.

20. Herman B. Leonard, *Checks Unbalanced: The Quiet Side of Public Spending* (New York: Basic Books, 1986).

21. Seymour Lipset and William Schneider, *The Confidence Gap: Business, Labor, and Government in the Public Mind* (London: Collier, Macmillan, 1983), pp. 379–398; William Roth, Jr., "The 'Malmanagement' Problem: Finding the Roots of Government Waste, Fraud, and Abuse," *Notre Dame Law Review* 58 (1983): 961–984.

22. Lipset and Schneider, *The Confidence Gap*, p. 343.

23. McKinney, *Effective Financial Management in Government and Nonprofit Agencies*, chapter nineteen.

24. Johnston, *Political Corruption and Public Policy in America*, p. 1.

25. R. Ahearn and D. Driscoll, *Executive Branch Organization to Formulate and Implement U.S. Foreign Trade and Industrial Policy* (Washington, D.C.: Congressional Research Service, 1981).

26. *See* Advisory Commission on Intergovernmental Relations, *The Federal Role in the Federal System: Dynamics of Growth* (Washington, D.C.: U.S. Government Printing Office, 1980).

27. *See* U.S. Merit System Protection Board, *Blowing the Whistle in the Federal Government: A Comparative Analysis of 1980 and 1983 Survey and Fundings* (Washington, D.C., 1983).

28. Stuart Diamond, "NASA Wasted Billions, Federal Audits Disclose," *New York Times*, 23 April 1986, p. 1.

29. Bill Moushey and Bill Carl Remensky, "Fraud Probed in Minority Firms," *Pittsburgh Post-Gazette*, 9 June 1986, p. 1.

30. Eileen White, "Pentagon Dodge: Suspended Contractors Continue to Get More Defense Business," *Wall Street Journal*, 6 May 1986, p. 1.

31. *See* Denny Smith et al., "Should We Accept Defense from Economic Reality? The Need for a Defense Budget Freeze" (Unpublished paper, Washington, D.C., February 7, 1985), p. 7.

32. Ibid., p. 12.

33. William Proxmire, "Golden Fleece Award" (Washington, D.C., 1985).

34. William Webster, "An Examination of FBI Theory and Methodology Regarding White-Collar Crime Investigation," *American Criminal Lawyers* 17 (March 1980): 275–300.

35. General Accounting Office, *Framework for Assessing Job Vulnerability to Ethical Problems* (Washington, D.C., 1981); General Accounting Office, *Financial Integrity Act: Government Faces Serious Internal Control and Accounting Systems Problems* (Washington, D.C., 1985); U.S. Department of Housing and Urban Development, *Fraud Vulnerability Assessment System* (Washington, D.C.: HUD Inspector General's Office, 1982); Office of Management and Budget, *Internal Controls, Guidelines* (Washington, D.C., 1982).

36. Leo Herbert, *Auditing the Performance of Management* (Belmont, Calif.: Lifetime Learning Publications, 1979); General Accounting Office, *Standards for Audit of Government Organizations, Programs, Activities, and Functions* (Washington, D.C.,

1981); Henry A. Butt, "Value for Money Auditing in Local Government," *Public Budgeting and Finance* 5 (Summer 1985): 63–74.

37. General Accounting Office, *Impact of Corrupt Practices Act* (Washington, D.C., 1982); R. P. Kusserow, "Civil Penalties Law, 1981: A New Effort to Confront Fraud and Abuse in Federal Health Care Programs," *Notre Dame Law Review* 58 (June 1983): 985–994.

38. Peter French, *Ethics in Government* (Englewood Cliffs, N.J.: Prentice-Hall, 1983), p. 3.

39. *See* Glen Tender, *Political Thinking* (Boston: Little, Brown, 1970), p. 129; French, *Ethics in Government.*

40. French, *Ethics in Government,* pp. 9–19.

41. Plato, *The Republic,* Crawford translation (New York: Oxford University Press, 1941).

42. Hastings Center, *Ethics of Legislative Life* (Hastings-on-Hudson, N.Y.: Hastings Center, 1985).

43. Daniel Elazar, *The American Federation: A View from the State* (New York: Norton, 1972); David C. Nice, "Political Corruption in American States: Causes 1976–1980," *American Politics Quarterly* 11 (October 1983): 507–517; Michael Johnston, "Corruption and Political Culture in America: An Empirical Perspective," *Journal of Federalism* 13 (Winter 1983): 10–31, John Peters and Susan Welch, "The Effects of Changes of Corruption on Voting Behavior in Congressional Elections," *American Political Science Review* 72 (1978): 974–984.

44. L. Sebba, "Attitudes of New Immigrants toward White Collar Crime: A Cross Cultural Perspective," *Human Relations* 36 (December 1983): 1091–1110.

45. Johnston, *Political Corruption and Public Policy in America,* p. 1.

46. Ibid., p. 13.

47. Ibid., pp. 3, 13.

48. W. Steven Albrecht et al., *How to Detect and Prevent Business Fraud* (Englewood Cliffs, N.J.: Prentice-Hall, 1982), p. 82.

49. Ibid., pp. 38–39.

50. Phil Kropatkin and Richard P. Kusserow, *Management Principles for Asset Protection* (New York: Ronald Press, 1986).

51. *See* Jerome B. McKinney and Michael Johnston, eds., *Fraud, Waste, and Abuse in Government* (Philadelphia: Institute for Study of Human Issues, 1986).

52. Ibid.

53. Johnston, *Political Corruption and Public Policy in America,* p. 13. *See also* Gerald E. Caiden and Naomi J. Caiden, "Administrative Corruption," *Public Administration Review* (1977): 301–308.

54. Preaudit involves determination of the authority, acceptability, and validity of an action before it is undertaken, whereas postaudit is carried out after the action is completed. Vulnerability assessment involves identification of weaknesses in an agency's control system permitting exposure to FWA. *See also* General Accounting Office, *Framework for Assessing Job Vulnerability to Ethical Problems.*

55. New York State Legislative Commission on Economy and Efficiency in Government, *Preventing Fraud, Waste, Abuse, and Error: Internal Control Reform in New York State Government* (Albany, N.Y., June 1982).

56. *See* General Accounting Office, *Financial Integrity Act: Government Faces Serious Internal Control and Accounting Systems Problems.*

57. McKinney, *Effective Financial Management and Nonprofit Agencies,* chapter nineteen.

58. *See* General Accounting Office, *Impact of Corrupt Practices Act on 45 Businesses* (Washington, D.C.: 1981).

59. R. P. Kusserow, "Civil Money Penalties Law of 1981: A New Effort to Confront Fraud and Abuse in Federal Health Care Programs," *Notre Dame Law Review* 58 (June 1983): 985–994.

60. Charles L. Dempsey, "The Inspector General Concept: Where It's Been and Where It's Going," *Public Budgeting and Finance* 5, no. 2 (Summer 1985): 39–51; Gordon W. Harvey and Harold R. Fine, "A Comprehensive Staff Training and Development System for Inspector General Audit Staff," *Government Accountants Journal* 33 (1984): 7–20.

61. Timothy A. Reardon and David A. Peters, "Major Fraud Unit Evaluation and Design Project" (San Francisco: Attorney General's Office, June 23, 1983).

62. U.S. Merit System Protection Board, *Blowing the Whistle in the Federal Government;* Frederick A. Elliston, John Keenan, Paula Lockhart, and Jane Van Schaick. *Whistleblowing Research: Methodological and Moral Issues* (New York: Praeger, 1985); Alan F. Westin, *Whistle Blowing Loyalty and Dissent in American Corporations* (New York: McGraw-Hill, 1981).

63. President's Council on Integrity and Efficiency, *Fraud, Waste, and Abuse: A Summary Report of Inspector General Activities* (Washington, D.C., 1985).

SELECTED BIBLIOGRAPHY

Advisory Commission on Intergovernmental Relations. *The Federal Role in the Federal System: The Dynamics of Growth.* Washington, D.C.: U.S. Government Printing Office, 1980.

Albrecht, W. Steven, Marshall B. Romney, David J. Cherrington, I. Reed Payne, and Allan J. Rowe. *How to Detect and Prevent Business Fraud.* Englewood Cliffs, N.J.: Prentice-Hall, 1982.

Auletta, Ken. *Greed and Glory on Wall Street: The Fall of the House of Lehman.* New York: Random House, 1985.

Benson, George C. S. *Political Corruption in America.* Lexington, Mass.: Lexington Books, 1978.

"Big Trouble at Allegheny." *Business Week,* August 11, 1986, 56–61.

Caiden, Gerald E., and Naomi J. Caiden. "Administrative Corruption." *Public Administrative Review* 37 (1977): 301–308.

Caplan, Gerald, and the Police Foundation. *ABSCAM Ethics, Moral Issues, and Deceptions in Law Enforcement.* Cambridge, Mass.: Ballinger, 1983.

Cressy, Donald R. *The Theft of the Nation: The Structure and Operation of Organized Crime in America.* New York: Harper and Row, 1969.

Defense Contract Audit Agency. *Fraud: Prevention and Detection.* Washington, D.C.: Defense Control Agency, 1980.

Dempsey, Charles L. "The Inspector General Concept: Where It's Been, and Where It's Going." *Public Budgeting and Finance* 5 (Summer 1985): 39–51.

Department of Defense. *Inspector General Semi-Annual Reports* (Washington, D.C., 1983–1986).

Eagleton, Thomas, and Ira S. Shapiro. "Federal Fraud and Waste Abuse: Causes and

Responses." *Institute of Socioeconomic Studies Journal* 7 (Winter 1982–1983): 35–46.

Elazar, Daniel. *The American Federation: A View from the States.* New York: Norton, 1972.

Elliston, Frederick, John Keenan, Paula Lockhart, Jane Van Schaick. *Whistleblowing Research: Methodological and Moral Issues.* New York: Praeger, 1985.

French, Peter. *Ethics in Government.* Englewood Cliffs, N.J.: Prentice-Hall, 1983.

Gardiner, John A., and Theodore Lyman. *Decisions for Sale: Corruption and Reform in Land Use and Building Regulation.* New York: Praeger, 1978.

Gardiner, John A., Theodore Lyman, and David J. Olsen, eds. *Theft of the City: Readings on Corruption in Urban America.* Bloomington: Indiana University Press, 1974.

General Accounting Office. *Framework for Assessing Job Vulnerability to Ethical Problems.* Washington, D.C., 1981.

———. *Fraud in Government Programs: How Extensive Is It? How Can It Be Controlled?* Vols. 1 and 2. Washington, D.C., 1981.

———. *Financial Integrity Act: The Government Faces Serious Internal Control and Accounting Systems and Problems.* Washington, D.C., 1985.

"Government Fraud, Waste, and Abuse: A Practical Guide to Fighting Official Corruption." *Notre Dame Law Review* 58 (June 1983): 1027–1099.

Grace, J. Peter. "The Grace Commission: How Much Waste in Government?" *Public Interest* 78 (Winter 1985): 62–82.

Hastings Center. *Ethics of Legislative Life.* Hastings-on-Hudson, N.Y.: Hastings Center, 1985.

Henriques, Diana B. *The Machinery of Greed.* Lexington, Mass.: Lexington Books, 1986.

Herman, Leonard. *Checks Unbalanced.* New York: Basic Books, 1986.

Inspector Commonwealth of Massachusetts. *Fifth Annual Report.* Boston: Office of Inspector General, 1986.

Johnston, Michael. *Political Corruption and Public Policy in America.* Monterey, Calif.: Brooks/Cole, 1982.

Kelman, Steven. "The Grace Commission Controversy." *Public Interest* 79 (Spring 1985): 111–133.

Kohlmeier, Louis M. "The Bribe Busters." *New York Times Magazine,* September 26, 1976, p. 47.

Kropatkin, Phil, and Richard P. Kusserow. *Management Principles for Asset Protection.* New York: Ronald Press, 1986.

Lange, G. Andrea, Thomas M. Beal, and Robert Bowers. *Fraud and Abuse in Government Benefit Programs.* Washington, D.C.: U.S. Department of Justice, Law Enforcement Assistance Agency, 1979.

Lipset, Seymour, and William Schneider. *The Confidence Gap: Business, Labor, and Government in the Public Mind.* London: Collier, Macmillan, 1983.

Lyman, Theodore, et al. *Prevention, Detection, and Correction of Corruption in Local Government.* Washington, D.C.: U.S. Government Printing Office, 1978.

McKinney, Jerome B., and Michael Johnston. *Fraud and Waste in Government.* Philadelphia: Institute for the Study of Human Issues, 1986.

Nice, David C. "Political Corruption in the American States: Causes, 1976–1980." *American Politics Quarterly* 11 (October 1983): 507–517.

Office of Management and Budget. *Internal Control Guidelines.* Washington, D.C., 1982.

President's Council on Integrity and Efficiency. *Fraud, Waste, and Abuse: A Summary Report of Inspector General Activities* (Washington, D.C., 1985).

President's Private Sector Survey on Cost Control. *Report on Federal Management Systems.* Washington, D.C., 1983.

Sherman, Lawrence W. *Scandal and Reform.* Berkeley: University of California Press, 1978.

Thomas, J. B., Jr. "Addressing Fraud, Waste, and Abuse: The U.S. Department of Education's Office of Inspector General." *American Education* 18 (1982): 24.

Truelson, Judith A. "Blowing the Whistle on Systemic Corruption." Ph.D. dissertation, University of Southern California, 1986.

U.S. Congressional Budget Office/General Accounting Office. *Analysis of the Grace Commission's Major Proposals for Cost Control.* Washington, D.C.: U.S. Government Printing Office, 1984.

U.S. Merit Systems Protection Board. *Blowing the Whistle in the Federal Government: A Comparative Analysis of 1980 and 1983 Survey Findings.* Washington, D.C., 1983.

Weinstein, Allen, and R. Jackson Wilson. *Freedom and Crisis.* New York: Random House, 1974.

Werner, Simcha. "New Directions in the Study of Administrative Corruption." *Public Administration Review* 43 (1983): 146–154.

Westin, Alan F. *Whistle Blowing Loyalty and Dissent in American Corporations.* New York: McGraw-Hill, 1981.

White, Eileen. "Pentagon Dodge: Suspended Contractor's Offer Continue to Get More Defense Business." *Wall Street Journal,* 6 May 1986, p. 1.

Young, J. D. "Reflections on the Root Cause of Fraud, Waste, and Abuse in Federal Social Programs." *Public Administration Review* 43 (July–August 1983): 362–369.

12

Morality in the Making of Foreign Policy

Ralph G. Carter

For those entrusted with political power and held accountable for their actions, moral considerations cannot be avoided. Unfortunately, policy decisions usually involve trade-offs between multiple values, and one option rarely emerges as clearly superior to others. Far from the ideal world of black and white options, the real world of political choice often seems a landscape distinguished only by the remarkable variation in shades of gray.

The difficulties of making moral choices in government are magnified in the foreign policy realm. Foreign policymakers operate in a context in which the moral aspects of both ends and means are judged by two audiences. Internally, foreign policy ends and means must meet existing domestic standards while offering an acceptable likelihood of success. Externally, the success of such actions will be affected by the degree to which the ends and means meet moral standards accepted by other peoples. Consequently, foreign policy actions may be popular at home but prove unacceptable abroad or vice versa. Unlike their domestic counterparts, foreign policymakers are faced with the need to promote policies that are acceptable in both the domestic and external arenas.

During "the war to end all wars," many Americans agreed with President Woodrow Wilson's foreign policy prescription. If nations would adopt democratic forms of government and rely on the "golden rule" in their interactions, global harmony would be advanced. The failure of the world community to preserve the peace through the League of Nations and the rise of fascist regimes glorifying the cleansing role of violence seemed to prove Wilson's notions inappropriate for the chaotic world of international politics. Beginning in the 1930s, however, a number of writers began to explore again the relationship of morality to foreign policy-making. The outbreak of World War II, the development of "crisis diplomacy" between the nuclear superpowers, and the succession of minor conflicts that threaten to escalate into global war have continued to focus attention on the need to define better the relationship of morality to foreign policy-making in the modern era.

After reviewing the relevant literature, this study elaborates three frameworks dealing with moral considerations in foreign policy-making: the realist, idealist, and procedural frameworks. Each one is illustrated by a case study—respectively, the funding of *contra* rebels in Nicaragua, the Panama Canal treaties, and the congressional cut-off of military aid to Turkey. The three frameworks are also evaluated regarding their future utility in foreign policy-making.

BACKGROUND AND LITERATURE REVIEW

Contemporary literature involves the rejection of Wilsonian idealism in the 1930s. Those who saw Wilson's approach to world politics as simplistic and naive called themselves "realists" by comparison. Such realists gained influence and power within the U.S. government after World War II. The consequence of their anti-Communist policies of the 1950s and early 1960s was the increasing identification of the United States with reactionary, repressive, yet anti-Communist authoritarian regimes. The unsavory nature of such regimes, as well as American policies toward them, led others to reject realism as a guide for policy. For such idealists, moral considerations needed to be reintroduced into the foreign policy-making process. For other policymakers, however, choosing among contending moral considerations in making policy was a daunting task. Some elected officials, lacking a solid grounding in foreign-policy expertise, chose to respond to, rather than lead, public opinion regarding what was ultimately right or wrong in specific circumstances. For them, this "procedural" approach, to be described below, was a device to simplify such hard choices.

In the 1930s the attack on Wilsonian idealism was led by Reinhold Niebuhr. In his classic *Moral Man and Immoral Society,* he laid the groundwork for the realists who followed by rejecting the idea that moral considerations appropriate for the individual are also appropriate for society.[1] Groups were far less likely to act in a moral fashion than were individuals since groups tended to be ruled by emotion and force instead of reason. Moreover, the self-criticism required for moral consideration could easily be interpreted as a lack of loyalty to the group. Being emotionally rather than rationally driven, groups would find it difficult or impossible truly to put the needs of outsiders on an equal plane with their own needs.[2] Furthermore, the patriotism promoted by group loyalty had a paradoxical effect regarding morality. Individually, patriotism was a moral act since the individual voluntarily sacrificed his or her needs to those of the group. But as Niebuhr noted, "the sentiment of patriotism achieves a potency in the modern soul, so unqualified, that the nation is given carte blanche to use the power, compounded of the devotion of individuals, for any purpose it desires."[3] Thus the individual moral act of patriotism might produce support for immoral national policies, such as the killing of civilian noncombatants in wartime.

By noting that, according to group morality, the end justifies the means, Niebuhr prepared the way for the realists who followed.[4] The fundamental principles of realism were outlined by Hans Morgenthau. Realists were those who saw politics governed by the laws of human nature. Within the bounds of human frailties, foreign policymakers sought to gain, maintain, or extend their national power. Such realists recognized the dynamic, situational nature of morality and avoided the mistake of equating their own culture's moral views with some broader set of moral laws governing the universe.[5] Morgenthau further argued that the ethics of nationalism had overcome Christian or cosmopolitan ethics in the past 150 years.[6] As a result, leaders who follow their true national interests produced moral national behavior whereas those whose actions were based on their personal moral principles produced moralistic actions. For Morgenthau, moral foreign policy might achieve its goals, but moralistic behavior would surely fail to do so.[7]

Realist stances by foreign policymakers often seemed common because of two advantages to this approach. First, it appeared to mirror the reality of international politics better than did Wilsonian idealism.[8] Second, realism seemed to legitimate the use of immoral means to achieve moral ends.[9] Consequently, Machiavelli and Spinoza could be considered among the earliest realist writers, and the European policy of *realpolitik* was a logical result of such attitudes.[10]

Not surprisingly, critics attacked the realist notion that policymakers could be divorced from the moral consequences of their actions. Such critics noted that policies were made by individuals who were rarely able to keep their own internalized values from affecting their decisions.[11] According to these idealists, those who said morality and politics could be divided were not merely wrong; their dichotomy of idealistic moralists versus amoral realists was simpleminded.[12] As Marshall Cohen said, "some of the actions which simple moralists condemn as immoral and realists defend as, nevertheless, politically necessary are in fact defensible on more complicated moral grounds."[13]

The focal point for idealists was their rejection of the use of immoral means to gain moral ends.[14] John Bennett noted approvingly that Morgenthau agreed with this rejection. Unlike most who believe that realism freed leaders to do whatever was in their short-term power interest, Bennett said a careful reading of Morgenthau's works indicated national interests should be narrowly drawn, free from self-righteousness, and take into account the needs of other nations.[15] Similarly, other alleged realists like Alexander Hamilton, Theodore Roosevelt, and George Kennan endorsed the idealist principle that the pursuit of national interests must be limited by moral considerations.[16]

The broad historical range represented by Hamilton, Roosevelt, and Kennan indicates the continuing impact of moral considerations on American foreign policy. One could assume the public accountability faced by American foreign policymakers forced them to reduce decisions to calculations of right and wrong.[17]

However, this notion begs the question of why the linkage between morality and foreign policy seems more pronounced in the United States than in comparable democracies such as Britain or France. The reason behind such moral considerations in American foreign policy-making probably has to do with the unusual historical isolation within which the United States developed. Blessed by bountiful resources, the lack of hostile neighbors, and protection by the British fleet from European intervention, most Americans in the nineteenth century thought they were God's chosen people, set apart to do great things. Thus American foreign policy could hardly avoid moralistic, self-righteous overtones, and this behavior carried into the twentieth century.[18]

The only major exception to this close linkage between the means of American foreign policy and claims to higher moral values came during the height of the Cold War. From the late 1940s until the mid-1960s, it seemed the evil nature of communism (a totalitarian system that not only enslaved its people but also rejected the fundamental values of Western society and called for that society's violent demise) made any American actions to combat it acceptable. The shattering of this Cold War consensus by the political failure of American involvement in the Vietnam War, aided somewhat by the repugnance of many Americans to Henry Kissinger's policies of *realpolitik,* returned attention to the moral aspect of foreign policy.[19]

No administration since Wilson's was more conspicuously associated with the idea of a moral American foreign policy than that of Jimmy Carter. Carter was not merely content to argue that human rights were important and that the United States would be judged by the company it kept. He also spoke more generally about the need for morality in all foreign policy ends and means:

For too many years we've been willing to adopt the flawed and erroneous principles and tactics of our adversaries, sometimes abandoning our own values for theirs. We've fought fire with fire, never thinking that fire is better quenched with water. . . . Our policy is rooted in our moral values which never change. Our policy is reinforced by our material wealth and our military power. Our policy is designed to serve mankind.[20]

Many critics of the Carter presidency argued that Carter tried to apply moral standards uncritically and too often. For example, his human rights policy publicly castigated right-wing authoritarian leaders in Latin America, causing them to become more recalcitrant, while downplaying similar abuses in China, the Soviet Union, and Eastern Europe. George Kennan offered a more balanced approach. He said American foreign policy must be consistent with American moral standards but that we should not impose our standards on others. We should not object when other states offend our sensibilities but do not hurt our narrowly drawn national interests. Instead, we should try to meet our narrowly drawn national interests with means that do not violate our national moral standards and do not overreach our national capabilities.[21]

Generalizing beyond the American case, there may be broader international agreement on moral issues than many realize. As Niebuhr noted, "enlightened men of all nations have some sense of obligation to their fellow-men, beyond the limits of their nation-state."[22] This sense of obligation may be virtually universal, since most cultures value justice and the equitable treatment of individuals.[23] Many writers have called for policies designed to promote global justice.[24] In their view, foreign policymakers should exercise tolerance in seeking a balance between their narrowly drawn national interests and the legitimate national interests of others.[25]

Unfortunately, universal values are often too general to provide a foreign policymaker with policy guidance in specific real-world cases.[26] In a democracy, one way to avoid the difficult calculation of morally correct national interests, vis-à-vis the legitimate national interests of others, is to fall back on "procedural" attempts to achieve justice. In other words, when the determination of correct moral ends required by realism is difficult and the determination of correct moral means needed by idealism is hard as well, one way of coping with uncertainty is to refocus policy-making attention on procedures that are just per se. In the U.S. Congress, the norm of representation helps facilitate this process. Most members think their first duty is to represent the activist constituencies back home.[27] When foreign matters or other tough issues become highly salient, members try to line up with their perception of constituency opinion.[28] For such issues, presidential leadership may not be enough to override these constituents' directives. More than two-thirds of those in Congress report that they carefully weigh constituency opinion, and more than two-fifths place the needs of their local constituencies over the needs of the nation as a whole.[29] Consequently, this procedural framework can be seen as a mid-range alternative to the realist and idealist approaches. Members of the government can avoid the difficult determination of geopolitical rights and wrongs by using a just decision-making style. They do what the American people want them to do and trust that the outcomes will be judged as moral later.

A careful review of the literature shows three groupings of thought regarding the role to be played by moral considerations in foreign policy. Realist writers focus on the advancement of narrowly drawn national interests while avoiding moralist preaching to other peoples. In practice, many realist political leaders simplify their task by stating that moral ends condone immoral means. Idealists reject this latter interpretation, stating that both ends and means must be moral or long-term foreign policy goals cannot be achieved.[30] Finally, proceduralists in a democracy abdicate their judgmental role by relying on their constituents to make these tough moral choices.

CASE ANALYSIS

Short case examples help to illustrate the three frameworks above. Each one is chosen to reflect the initiating party's perspective on the proper role of moral considerations in the making of foreign policy. President Reagan reveals a realist stance in his appeal to Congress to fund the activities of the *contra* rebels fighting the Sandinista regime in Nicaragua. President Carter's request of the Senate to ratify the Panama Canal treaties, which turned control of the Canal over to the Panamanian regime, is an example of the idealist framework. The congressional cut-off of military aid to Turkey in 1974 demonstrates a procedural approach to questions of morality. Moreover, consideration of these cases suggests that these three approaches to dealing with moral issues, so different in the abstract, may be less different in real-life circumstances. After each case is examined, the moral context within which each occurs is reevaluated to show interrelationships between these three approaches.

Aid to the *Contras:* A Realist Controversy

One of the most dramatic changes associated with the inauguration of the Reagan administration in 1981 was the renewed presidential emphasis on the dire nature of the Soviet threat to American national interests. As both a candidate and president, Ronald Reagan repeatedly described the Soviet Union as "the evil empire" and Soviet communism as "the source of all evil in the world." Given such attitudes, President Reagan was unwilling to allow such a grave threat to establish a beachhead on the American continent in Nicaragua.

The problem began with the 1979 toppling of the repressive, corrupt, but anti-Communist Somoza regime by a broad coalition of both anti-Somoza centrists and representatives of the political Left.[31] However, the presence of some socialists and Marxists in the new regime made it quickly suspect in the eyes of others. During the presidential campaign of 1980, Reagan's future special assistant for national security affairs, Richard Allen, endorsed the use of force to topple what he called a new "Communist" regime.[32] Also in 1980, Congress authorized the suspension of economic aid to the new regime if it became totalitarian or cooperated too freely with Cuba or other Communist states.[33] Upon gaining office, Reagan cited the congressional authorization and suspended Nicaraguan aid.[34]

Ironically, Reagan helped create the "Communist" menace he feared. The cost of the revolution had devastated Nicaragua's financial resources, and the government needed $3 million per day in foreign aid to survive. When Reagan cancelled U.S. aid, the Sandinistas turned to Western Europe, the Soviets, and the Libyans for help. Their assistance was not enough, so the regime tightened economic controls on the free market. When the middle class protested, the regime responded by arresting protesters and pushing moderates out of the coalition government. In this way, the U.S. aid cut-off indirectly resulted in the increasingly Marxist nature of the reformulated Sandinista regime.[35]

By December 1981 the Communist threat appeared severe enough to Reagan to approve a CIA plan to provide training and assistance to an irregular rebel force known as the *contras* battling the Sandinista regime. In 1982 Reagan persuaded Congress to fund the *contras,* stating that their purpose was to prevent the shipment of arms from Cuba to Nicaragua or from Nicaragua to the rebels in El Salvador. However, Democrats were sufficiently uneasy about this force to pass the Boland Amendment, making it illegal to spend funds for the overthrow of the Sandinista regime itself.[36]

In 1983 House Democrats charged Reagan with direct violation of the Boland Amendment. Reagan denied the charge, defended his Central American policy in an address to a joint session of Congress, and urged more funding for the *contras*. Unmoved, Congress responded by cutting Reagan's request for $50 million for the anti-Sandinista rebels to $24 million for fiscal year 1984 (FY1984).[37]

In early 1984 Reagan asked for an additional $21 million for FY1984. However, new reports of direct CIA involvement in the mining of Nicaraguan harbors and the subsequent damage to cargo ships of other nations outraged many on Capitol Hill. Despite Reagan's televised appeal, Congress rejected the $21 million request for FY1984, cut in half a $28 million request for FY1985, and put conditions on the use of the money.[38]

A more severe setback for Reagan's policy occurred in 1985. For the first time, Congress flatly refused to appropriate any money for *contra* military operations and instead appropriated only $27 million for nonlethal, humanitarian aid for the rebels. Nevertheless, Sandinista leader Daniel Ortega's subsequent trip to the USSR and request for Soviet military aid played into Reagan's hands.[39]

With this renewed proof of the Communist nature of the Sandinista regime, Reagan asked for $100 million in *contra* aid in 1986. Seventy million dollars was to be earmarked for military use; $30 million was for nonlethal aid. On March 20 the House rejected the request. Two days later Nicaraguan troops invaded Honduras in search of rebel camps. The Senate responded by approving the $100 million aid request.[40]

By 1988 continued U.S. military support of a rebel force in Nicaragua was uncertain. For his part, Reagan sees in Nicaragua a Communist government serving as a forward base for the extension of Soviet military influence throughout Central America. To protect freedom in Central America, free passage through the Panama Canal, and the United States from thousands of Central American refugees, Reagan said the United States has a "moral duty" to aid the *contras*.[41] For their part, most members of Congress, as well as most Americans, believe a truly democratic Nicaraguan regime would serve the interests of both the American and Nicaraguan peoples.[42]

Unfortunately for the president, many who agree with his basic goal insist on the use of moral means to achieve it. One source of criticism is the presumption that Reagan prefers the use of military force over diplomacy. Citing the public's consistent two-to-one opposition to military aid for the *contras*, many members of Congress have appealed to Reagan to help the "Contadora" nations of Colombia, Mexico, Panama, and Venezuela try to negotiate a solution to the Nicaraguan problem.[43]

A second source of criticism comes from the actions of the rebels themselves. Critics say numerous field commanders are former members of Somoza's National Guard and are guilty of murder, torture, mutilation, and other abuses committed against Nicaraguan civilians.[44] The *contras* have also been accused of cocaine smuggling, gunrunning, terrorist actions including a conspiracy to assassinate the U.S. ambassador to Costa Rica, and the misuse, if not the actual theft, of American foreign aid.[45] According to U.S. intelligence analysts, the *contras* are now so weak that continued military aid is meaningless, and only an American military intervention can force a change in the Sandinista regime.[46]

A final source of congressional opposition has been the use of questionable tactics by Reagan's staff and Reagan himself in the effort to get the most recent aid package approved. Reagan's aides argued that votes against the administration's position were votes for communism. Calling this "Red-baiting" and a return to McCarthyism, both Republican and Democratic members of Congress castigated Reagan for his defense of such offensive remarks that inaccurately oversimplified the aid debate.[47]

Reagan's realist orientation has been the cause of his policy frustration in this case. In his eyes, communism is so evil that virtually any method to prevent the consolidation of power by the Sandinista regime is acceptable. Had more Americans agreed with Reagan's feelings that, in this case, the end justified the means, *contra* funding would not have become so controversial.

The Panama Canal Treaties: An Idealist Initiative

The idea that both means and ends should be morally justified is illustrated in the American return of the Panama Canal and Canal Zone to Panamanian control. As far back as the 1930s, Panamanians resented their loss of control over their territory, and this resentment resulted in the Panamanian decision to break diplomatic relations with the United States in 1964. Following that action, Presidents Johnson, Nixon, and Ford tried to negotiate new treaties to reconcile American and Panamanian interests. It was during the Carter administration that success was achieved.[48]

Previous attempts to deal with the Canal issue had foundered due to the strong negative response by the American public. Since the Panamanian government had agreed to American construction of the Canal in 1903 and was paid $10 million plus an annual fee in return for U.S. control of the Canal, most Americans saw the Canal and Canal Zone as possessions rightfully earned. Consequently, experienced politicians like Johnson, Nixon, and Ford bowed to this public pressure.[49]

However, most Panamanians thought it was wrong to hold them to an agreement, signed when their nation was two weeks old and too weak to object, that deprived them of their greatest resource and split their nation into halves. After campaigning for an American foreign policy as open, honest, and morally upright as the American public, Jimmy Carter was more determined to correct this past injustice than were his predecessors. Thus he negotiated and signed the two treaties that returned the Canal and the Canal Zone to Panamanian control and protected the Canal's neutrality in the future.[50]

Once the treaties were signed, the administration began a vigorous, grass-roots effort to change American public opinion. The administration formed the Committee of Americans for the Canal Treaties (COACT) to serve as an umbrella group to mobilize protreaty forces. These supportive groups included the Americans for Democratic Action, the AFL-CIO, the United Auto Workers, the Democratic National Committee, and New Directions, a liberal interest group. Also strongly protreaty was the Council of the Americas, a business organization representing 90 percent of American investment in Latin America. Finally, religious groups like the National Council of Churches, the Synagogue Council of America, and the U.S. Catholic Conference came out in support of the treaties.[51]

The message pushed by Carter and his allies was straightforward. The Panamanian people saw American control of the Canal and Canal Zone as a past injustice that must be remedied. As Senator Frank Church of the Foreign Relations Committee argued on the Senate floor, "A vote against this treaty represents a vain attempt to preserve the past. It represents a futile effort to perpetuate an American colony in Panama against the wishes of the Panamanian people."[52]

As Carter stressed in his televised address on February 1, 1978, doing "the right thing" represented a course in which the United States had nothing to lose in the long term and everything to gain. Remedying this past injustice would improve U.S.–Panamanian relations, improve the chances of long-term American access to the Canal, and send a powerful signal to the rest of Latin America that the United States was ready to change its historically patronizing and paternalistic attitude toward the region in favor of a new one based on the sovereign equality of nations. Such a change would further protect long-term American business interests in the area and minimize the appeal of communism there as well.[53]

As Carter pressed the issue with the Senate and his allies took the administration's message across the land, public opinion began to shift. By the time of the vote in the Senate, public opinion had moved from three-to-one in opposition to slight margin in favor of the treaties, and Carter went on to win their Senate approval.[54]

Not enough time has elapsed to determine fully whether Carter's gamble with the Canal has promoted progress on the long-term goals mentioned above. However, some tentative observations can be made. A strength of the Carter administration was its ability to look at the changes in Latin America and understand them in a regional context.[55] As a result of such vision, Carter's policies (particularly his emphasis on human rights) contributed to the growing democratization of Latin America.[56] Such developments would normally auger well for continued progress on the long-term U.S. goals noted earlier.

However, the change of the U.S. administration in 1981 cast some doubt on continued progress toward these goals. According to some observers, the Reagan administration responds toward Latin America as have most Republican administrations; what little attention the entire region gets is usually framed in a globalistic East–West context, and military instruments are the preferred foreign policy tools for the area.[57] Although such an approach may limit the short-term growth of communism in the region, it may not be well suited to address other long-term goals. In particular, due to Panama's participation in the Contadora process, Reagan's rejection of Contadora-sponsored negotiations regarding Nicaragua has helped to "cool" U.S.–Panamanian relations. Consequently, Carter's idealist aim of pursuing moral ends by moral means may have been undercut by being followed by a realist administration with dissimilar goals and operating styles.

The Turkish Military Aid Cut-Off: Procedural Morality

Both prior examples have indicated the important role played by the public in a democracy. Jimmy Carter won approval of the Panama Canal treaties because he was able to change public opinion, something Ronald Reagan has been unable to do on the *contra* aid issue. In 1974 Congress showed how, in a circumstance of conflicting moral ends, representing the preferences of the folks back home can offer a way out of such a dilemma.

In July 1974 Turkish military forces invaded the island of Cyprus following the installment of a pro-Greek Cypriot regime. Despite the fact that Turkish Cypriots represented only 20 percent of the island's population, Turkish military forces captured and held 40 percent of the island.[58] Congress responded by passing an amendment to terminate all U.S. military aid to Turkey. The amendment was attached to an emergency funding bill needed to keep the U.S. government running, since FY1975 was nine days old and its budget had not been approved. President Ford vetoed the emergency funding bill due to the inclusion of the military aid cut-off. Congress then attached a new military aid cut-off amendment to the bill. Ford vetoed this second version. Falling only two votes short of the needed two-thirds majority to override his veto in the House, Congress again reattached a Turkish military aid cut-off to the funding bill. The third time the bill came to him, Ford admitted defeat and signed the cut-off into law.[59]

The Ford administration resisted this cut-off because both President Ford and Secretary of State Kissinger believed the cut-off would jeopardize American national interests. Stopping military aid to Turkey would harden Turkish negotiating positions, making a solution to the Cyprus problem harder to attain. More importantly, any real weakening of Turkish military forces and the appearance of U.S.–Turkish discord might weaken NATO's eastern flank and prompt the Soviets to pressure the Turkish regime.[60]

Faced with blatant Turkish aggression on the one hand and a weak response by the White House on the other hand, members of Congress responded by following the dictates of their constituents. In terms of American public opinion, the Greeks were clearly favored.

One reason for the tilt toward Greece was a historical pattern of pro-Greek and anti-Turkish attitudes by the American public. As early as 1821 Americans had sided with the Greeks in Greco-Turkish disputes. American fondness for the Greeks was influenced by Greece's role as a founder of Western civilization and culture, as the birthplace of democracy, and as a Christian nation. Coolness toward the Turks was generated by the image of the anti-Christian Ottoman Empire, past Turkish atrocities committed against Greeks and Armenians, Turkish opposition to the United States in World War I, and Turkey's pro-Axis tilt for much of World War II.[61]

However, the more specific reason for a tilt toward Greece was the strength of the American Greek lobby. Three million Greek Americans cared passionately about the issue and were well organized by the Greek Orthodox Church and the American Hellenic Educational Progressive Association.[62] They worked on members of Congress in two ways. First, they conducted large anti-Turkish demonstrations. Second, and more important, they lobbied hard in the halls of Congress. The relentless pressure of the pro-Greek lobby and the lack of any pro-Turkish lobby proved irresistible on Capitol Hill in the weeks before the general election of 1974, when all House members and one-third of the Senate were up for reelection.[63] Thus when facing a difficult choice between conflicting moral ends, Congress looked for an option to make the decision easier. A procedural approach allowed members of Congress to avoid the agonizing process of choosing between different moral ends; that is, members could claim that the most moral course for them, as the public's representatives, was to follow the public's wishes.

Nonetheless, public wishes can change. In 1978 Congress resumed arms sales to Turkey, despite the lack of a Turkish withdrawal from Cyprus.[64] Pro-Greek pressure on Congress had not ended. Instead, a larger coalition of Americans pressured Congress to end the embargo. The new dominant coalition was composed of two groups. The smaller of the two groups consisted of those who wanted movement in the Greco-Turkish negotiations over Cyprus. Since an embargo on arms sales had not softened the Turkish stance, perhaps resuming arms sales would give the U.S. government additional leverage to force the Turks to negotiate in good faith. The larger group was concerned with the national security disadvantages arising from the American–Turkish dispute. These people stressed that U.S. national security was dangerously weakened by NATO with a soft southeastern flank and, more importantly, by the loss of intelligence on the USSR generated from installations in Turkey.[65]

The 1978 policy reversal suggests the potential interaction of realist and procedural approaches to the role of morality in foreign policy. Like the 1974 arms embargo decision, the 1978 reversal can be seen as procedural in that the Cold War climate had deteriorated, producing larger and more vocal numbers of

Americans endorsing policies seen as either anti-Soviet or prodefense. Viewed from the realist perspective, the 1978 reversal is explained as an indicator of the renewed sense of Soviet threat felt by increasing shares of the American public. With the larger end of protecting the country from Soviet communism again being stressed, means seen as unacceptable in 1974 were seen as acceptable in 1978.

CONCLUSION

In the United States, advocates of the realist and idealist positions have dominated the debate regarding the proper role for moral concerns in the making of American foreign policy. Advocates of the procedural approach have played a significant role in the debate less often, because their approach is more associated with the minority of instances in which Congress tackles controversial foreign policy issues either in the absence of presidential leadership or when public opinion runs strongly against the current administration's position.

The debate between realists and idealists has been neither subtle nor particularly sophisticated. The charges hurled about during the 1980 presidential campaign exemplified how simplistic the debate has often become. Supporters of President Carter charged that, if elected, Ronald Reagan would follow a course that reduced most foreign policy issues to the military containment of Communist expansion. Foreign policy issues that could not be reduced to such basic elements would likely be ignored. Reagan's supporters responded by arguing the "Sunday-school morality" of Jimmy Carter had proven ill suited to the rough-and-tumble world of international politics. Carter, they argued, did not understand that if you played the game by moral rules and your opponent did not, you could not win. Carter's tenure, in their eyes, proved that nice guys finish last.

The way these approaches are usually manifested in practice suggests a linkage to normative philosophy. For example, many practicing realists favor teleological arguments. They see the morality of actions based on the goodness of the goals those actions are meant to achieve, not on attributes of the behavior itself.[66] Moral ends thus allow the use of immoral means. Most idealists favor deontological arguments. In their eyes, actions are either just or unjust, moral or immoral, in their own right. In other words, people have an obligation to act morally, even if moral actions produce unjust outcomes.[67] Thus means *must* be moral, and hopefully ends are as well.

As dramatic as these differences seem in the abstract, a more careful examination shows surprising commonalities between realism and idealism when examining the writings of noted realists rather than the actions of politicians. Two of the most noted early realist writers have underscored this commonality. Hans Morgenthau, the father of modern realism, has called for ends to be narrowly focused and addressed by means that take into account the legitimate national interests of others.[68] George Kennan has been even more explicit. He has also called for ends that address narrowly focused American goals, thereby eschewing the "global policeman" role for the United States so often attributed to him.[69] Furthermore, Kennan has called for the limitation of American foreign policy actions to those acceptable to American moral standards.[70]

Thus there appears to be significant slippage between realism as usually practiced and as strictly defined by Morgenthau and Kennan. Presumably, these two realists would disavow Reagan's funding of the *contras,* applaud Carter's handling of the Panama Canal issue, and support the initial termination of arms sales to Turkey. Whether they would condone the resumption of arms sales to Turkey, based on the premise that the harm to American and European security outweighs the rights of Greek Cypriots to their traditional villages, is uncertain. Nevertheless, there seems to be enough difference between realism as strictly defined and that as usually practiced to clarify these two interpretations of the realist approach as different frameworks: the realist approach as normally conceived to emphasize ends over means in a teleological fashion and a strict realist approach that emphasizes both moral means and ends in a more deontological fashion. Once the notion of strict realism is accepted, its commonalities with idealism are apparent. The foreign policy prescriptions offered by Morgenthau and Kennan are not strikingly dissimilar from those of Jimmy Carter. The only apparent difference regards the scope of foreign policy goals to be pursued. If strict realists prefer a more restricted set of foreign policy ends to be achieved than do idealists, this difference seems to be more a difference of degree than of kind.

The three cases examined here reinforce the important role of moral values regarding foreign policy-making; that is, Reagan has experienced enormous political difficulty in getting large amounts of military aid approved for the *contras* precisely because many Americans believe the rebels commit immoral acts against the Nicaraguan people they are supposed to be saving from a greater evil. Carter was able to prevail in the Panama Canal case because he and his supporters were able to convince many in the Senate and the American public that continued American control of the Canal and Canal Zone were seen as an injustice by Panamanians.

Finally, although the volume, intensity, and unidirectional nature of the lobbying effort by Greek Americans were sufficient by themselves to force a Turkish military aid cut-off in 1974, the moral content of the lobbying message was also important. Greek Americans compared the unprovoked aggression by Turkey with Japan's sneak attack against Pearl Harbor. They also pounded home the theme that the offensive violated U.S. law. Under the Mutual Security Act, U.S.-supplied military aid was to be used only for defensive purposes.[71] Thus the Turkish attack was condemned as both a crime against humanity and a violation of American law. Consequently, each of these cases shows the importance of moral considerations regarding both the ends and means of foreign policy-making in the American context.

Based on the above, the strict realist framework appears to be best suited to achieving long-term foreign policy success. As noted earlier, this modification of realism, as normally practiced, avoids the disadvantages brought on by the acceptance of immoral means to achieve moral ends. Furthermore, by restricting the scope of ends to be pursued from that allowed by idealism, strict realism might lead foreign policymakers to avoid involvement in new quagmires, such as Vietnam. Finally, because of its strictly defined nature, strict realism should produce public majorities in support of policy initiatives, thereby subsuming the procedural approach to morality in foreign policy.

Accepting strict realism as the best guide to follow does not make foreign policy-making any easier. Foreign policy success depends on acceptance of both the ends to be pursued and the means by which to pursue them. At present, there is no consensus among the American public about what our broadest foreign policy goals should be. Recent research shows Americans to be split into three groups of approximately equal size.[72]

The isolationists want an American foreign policy that basically eschews the global policeman role and limits itself to the protection of American territory and the promotion of American business globally. The Cold War internationalists want an American foreign policy that returns to the days of the Truman Doctrine. They believe that the United States has not done enough to meet the Soviet Communist threat and that the United States should make whatever sacrifices necessary to limit, if not roll back, Communist expansion. To them, the goal of limiting Communist expansion overrides all other foreign policy goals. Finally, the humanitarian internationalists want to drop the anti-Communist crusade and instead focus the energies of the U.S. government on meeting global human needs. To them, improving the living conditions of all peoples is more important than the type of regime involved. In other words, repressive totalitarian regimes are to be opposed, whether of the political Left or Right.[73]

In the near term there will be domestic political battles over the appropriate moral ends to be achieved by American foreign policy. Even when there is agreement on the ends, disagreements on the morality of means can still be possible. For example, most Americans find South Africa's apartheid policy unacceptable and want it ended. But how is that to be achieved? Will the divestiture of American investments in South Africa be the necessary prod to force the Afrikaner regime to end apartheid, or will divestiture have counterproductive effects, such as increasing black unemployment and provoking a seige mentality on the part of the Afrikaners? Similarly, most Americans want an end to the kidnappings and assaults on U.S. citizens by those called Mideast terrorists in the Western press. But how can this end be achieved? Is it morally right to launch military attacks against alleged terrorist camps, knowing the high likelihood that such attacks will produce the same kind of nonparticipant civilian deaths? Is it more correct to negotiate and make concessions, since concessions might lead other groups to more readily target U.S. citizens? Should the U.S. government help to force the creation of a Palestinian Arab state, thereby addressing the root cause of much of the violence in the Mideast, even if that new state heightens Israel's national security fears? Given agreement on ends, what means are best?

The adoption of a strict realist approach to the role of moral issues in American foreign policy-making would seem to be an improvement over the status quo, but as the above indicates, reaching agreement on moral ends and means will not be easy in many circumstances.

Many future foreign policy initiatives are going to require a significant degree of marketing by the president, the secretary of state, the secretary of defense, and other top executive and congressional foreign policy officials to convince a majority of Americans that the proposed goal is the most appropriate in the circumstances. Once that considerable hurdle is cleared, the appropriateness of the means must also be successfully defended. All in all, moral considerations are essential in the making of democratic foreign policy, but their explicit consideration will produce more strain, at least in the short run, on a political system already fragmented by the forces of hyperpluralism.

NOTES

1. Reinhold Niebuhr, *Moral Man and Immoral Society: A Study in Ethics and Politics* (1932; reprint, New York: Scribner's, 1955).

2. Ibid., pp. xi–xxiv, 88–89.

3. Ibid., pp. 91–92.

4. Ibid., pp. 174–175, 237–238. *See also* Carl J. Friedrich, *The Pathology of Politics* (New York: Harper and Row, 1972), p. 5; John H. Herz, *Political Realism and Political Idealism* (Chicago: University of Chicago Press, 1951), p. 143.

5. Hans J. Morgenthau, "A Realist Theory of International Politics," in David L. Larson, ed., *The Puritan Ethic in United States Foreign Policy* (Princeton, N.J.: Van Nostrand, 1966), pp. 62–72.

6. Hans J. Morgenthau, *Politics among Nations* (New York: Knopf, 1951), p. 191.

7. Hans J. Morgenthau, "The Mainsprings of American Foreign Policy," in James M. McCormick, ed., *A Reader in American Foreign Policy* (Itasca, Ill.: Peacock, 1986), pp. 48–50.

8. Percy E. Corbett, *Morals, Laws, and Power in International Relations* (Los Angeles: The John Randolph Haynes and Dora Haynes Foundation, 1956); J.D.B. Miller, "Morality, Interests, and Rationalisation," in Ralph Pettman, ed., *Moral Claims in World Affairs* (New York: St. Martin's Press, 1979), pp. 45–47.

9. Herz, *Political Realism and Political Idealism*, pp. 135–142.

10. Niccolo Machiavelli, *The Prince* and *The Discourses,* with an introduction by Max Lerner (New York: Modern Library, 1940); Benedictus de Spinoza, *The Political Works,* ed. and trans. A. G. Wernham (Oxford: Clarendon Press, 1958); Ralph Pettman, "Moral Claims in World Politics," in Ralph Pettman, ed., *Moral Claims in World Affairs* (New York: St. Martin's Press, 1979), p. 22.

11. *See,* for example, Herbert Butterfield, *International Conflict in the Twentieth Century* (New York: Harper and Row, 1960), p. 16; Paul Ramsey, "Force and Political Responsibility," in Ernest W. Lefever, ed., *Ethics and World Politics* (Baltimore: Johns Hopkins University Press, 1972), pp. 51–52; Kenneth W. Thompson, "Ethics and In-

302   Studies of Systemic Issues in Government

ternational Relations: The Problem," in Kenneth W. Thompson, ed., *Ethics and International Relations* (New Brunswick, N.J.: Transaction/Council on Religion and International Affairs, 1985), p. 1.

12. Edward H. Carr, "The Limitations of Realism," in David L. Larson, ed., *The Puritan Ethic in United States Foreign Policy* (Princeton, N.J.: Van Nostrand, 1966), pp. 105, 108; Kenneth W. Thompson, *Christian Ethics and the Dilemmas of Foreign Policy* (Durham, N.C.: Duke University Press, 1959), p. 37.

13. Marshall Cohen, "Moral Skepticism and International Relations," in Charles R. Beitz et al., eds., *International Ethics* (Princeton, N.J.: Princeton University Press, 1985), p. 21.

14. John C. Bennett, *Foreign Policy in Christian Perspective* (New York: Scribner's, 1966), p. 19; John C. Bennett and Harvey Seifert, *U.S. Foreign Policy and Christian Ethics* (Philadelphia: Westminster Press, 1977), p. 30; Peter Singer, "Famine, Affluence, and Morality," in Charles R. Beitz et al., eds., *International Ethics* (Princeton, N.J.: Princeton University Press, 1985), pp. 249–250; Michael Joseph Smith, "Moral Responsibility in International Affairs," in Kenneth W. Thompson, ed., *Ethics and International Relations* (New Brunswick, N.J.: Transaction/Council on Religion and International Affairs, 1985), p. 36.

15. Bennett, *Foreign Policy in Christian Perspective,* pp. 60–61.

16. Arthur Schlesinger, Jr., "National Interests and Moral Absolutes," in Ernest W. Lefever, ed., *Ethics and World Politics* (Baltimore: Johns Hopkins University Press, 1972), p. 31; George F. Kennan, "Morality and Foreign Policy," *Foreign Affairs* 64 (Winter 1985): 205–218.

17. Dexter Perkins, "The Moralistic Interpretation of American Foreign Policy," in James M. McCormick, ed., *A Reader in American Foreign Policy* (Itasca, Ill.: Peacock, 1986), pp. 20–21.

18. Thompson, *Christian Ethics and the Dilemmas of Foreign Policy,* pp. 55–57.

19. Mark O. Hatfield, "Vietnam and American Values," in Ernest W. Lefever, ed., *Ethics and World Politics* (Baltimore: Johns Hopkins University Press, 1972), p. 79; Smith, "Moral Responsibility," pp. 36–37.

20. "Commencement address at the University of Notre Dame," in James M. McCormick, ed., *A Reader in American Foreign Policy* (Itasca, Ill.: Peacock, 1986), pp. 151, 155.

21. Kennan, "Morality and Foreign Policy."

22. Reinhold Niebuhr, *Christian Realism and Political Problems* (New York: Scribner's, 1953), p. 28.

23. Paul A. Freund, "Philosophy, Moral Reasoning, and Law," in Kenneth W. Thompson, ed., *Ethics and International Relations* (New Brunswick, N.J.: Transaction/Council on Religion and International Affairs, 1985); Daniel S. Robinson, *Political Ethics* (New York: Crowell, 1935), pp. 174–179.

24. Robert Gordis, *Religion and International Responsibility* (New York: The Church Peace Union, 1959); W. H. Smith, "Justice: National, International, or Global?" in Ralph Pettman, ed., *Moral Claims in World Affairs* (New York: St. Martin's Press, 1979), p. 98; Ramsey, "Force and Political Responsibility," pp. 70–72.

25. Thompson, *Christian Ethics and the Dilemmas of Foreign Policy,* pp. 126–131; Kenneth W. Thompson, *Political Realism and the Crisis of World Politics: An American Approach to Foreign Policy* (Princeton, N.J.: Princeton University Press, 1960), pp. 169–170.

26. Niebuhr, *Christian Realism and Political Problems*, p. 28.

27. William J. Keefe and Morris S. Ogul, *The American Legislative Process*, 5th ed. (Englewood Cliffs, N.J.: Prentice-Hall, 1981), p. 63.

28. Barbara Hinkley, *Stability and Change in Congress*, 3d ed. (New York: Harper and Row, 1983), p. 87.

29. Roger H. Davidson and Walter J. Oleszek, *Congress and Its Members* (Washington, D.C.: Congressional Quarterly Press, 1981), pp. 113–114.

30. A recent statement by singer/activist Joan Baez incorporates these "idealist" ideas. Criticizing the American bombing of Libya and the terrorist actions that prompted it, she noted that the logical result of a policy of "an eye for an eye" is a blind world.

31. Walter LaFeber, "The Reagan Administration and Revolutions in Central America," in James M. McCormick, ed., *A Reader in American Foreign Policy* (Itasca, Ill.: Peacock, 1986).

32. Ibid., p. 196.

33. *Congressional Quarterly Almanac, 1980* (Washington, D.C.: Congressional Quarterly, 1980), p. 331.

34. *Congressional Quarterly Almanac, 1981* (Washington, D.C.: Congressional Quarterly, 1981), p. 171.

35. LeFeber, "The Reagan Administration," pp. 210–211.

36. *Congress and the Nation, 1981–1984*, vol. 6 (Washington, D.C.: Congressional Quarterly, 1985), p. 184.

37. Ibid.

38. Ibid.

39. *Congressional Quarterly Almanac, 1985* (Washington, D.C.: Congressional Quarterly, 1985), p. 61.

40. *Congressional Quarterly Weekly Report, March 29, 1986* (Washington, D.C.: Congressional Quarterly, 1986), pp. 695–698.

41. *Congressional Quarterly Weekly Report, March 22, 1986* (Washington, D.C.: Congressional Quarterly, 1986), pp. 671–673.

42. *Congressional Quarterly Weekly Report, March 29, 1986*, pp. 695–698.

43. *Congressional Quarterly Weekly Report, March 22, 1986*, p. 672.

44. *New York Times*, 20 January 1986, p. 31; 12 February 1986, p. 6; 20 February 1986, p. 7; 6 March 1986, p. 27.

45. *Dallas Morning News*, 12 April 1986, p. 18A; 23 April 1986, p. 15A; 2 May 1986, p. 16A.

46. *Dallas Morning News*, 13 March 1986, p. 13A.

47. *New York Times*, 24 February 1986, p. 15; 8 March 1986, p. 4; 15 March 1986, p. 27.

48. *Congressional Quarterly Almanac, 1978* (Washington, D.C.: Congressional Quarterly, 1978), pp. 379–397.

49. Ibid.

50. Ibid.

51. David Farnsworth and James McKenney, *U.S.–Panamanian Relations, 1903–1978: A Study in Linkage Politics* (Boulder, Colo.: Westview Press, 1983).

52. *Congressional Quarterly Almanac, 1978*, p. 380.

53. Ibid., pp. 379–397.

54. Ibid.

55. Viron P. Vakey, "Hemispheric Relations: 'Everything Is Part of Everything Else.' " *Foreign Affairs* 59, no. 3 (1981): 646–647.

56. Alfred Stepan, "The United States and Latin America: Vital Interests and the Instruments of Power." *Foreign Affairs* 58, no. 3 (1980): 691–692.

57. *See*, for example, Vakey, "Hemispheric Relations," pp. 646–647; Paul E. Sigmund, "Latin America: Change or Continuity?" *Foreign Affairs* 60, no. 3 (1982): pp. 629–630.

58. *Congressional Quarterly Almanac, 1974* (Washington, D.C.: Congressional Quarterly, 1974), p. 515.

59. Ibid., pp. 547–553.

60. Ibid.

61. Thomas A. Bailey, *A Diplomatic History of the American People* (Englewood Cliffs, N.J.: Prentice-Hall, 1974), pp. 181, 444, 455, 563, 757.

62. *New York Times,* 12 October 1974, p. 3; *Columbus (Ohio) Dispatch,* 19 July 1978, p. A6.

63. *New York Times,* 29 August 1974, p. 12; 12 October 1974, p. 3.

64. *Congressional Quarterly Almanac, 1978,* pp. 419, 421.

65. Ibid.

66. *See*, for example, Richard B. Brandt, *Ethical Theory* (Englewood Cliffs, N.J.: Prentice-Hall, 1959); John Plamenatz, *The English Utilitarians* (Oxford: Basil Blackwell, 1958).

67. *See*, for example, Alfred C. Ewing, *The Definition of Good* (1947; reprint, Westport, Conn.: Hyperion Press, 1979); Alfred C. Ewing, *Ethics* (New York: Free Press, 1965); Harold A. Prichard, *Moral Obligation and Duty and Interest* (London: Oxford University Press, 1968); William D. Ross, *Foundations of Ethics* (New York: Oxford University Press, 1939); idem, *Kant's Ethical Theory* (1954; reprint, Westport, Conn.: Greenwood Press, 1978).

68. *See* Morgenthau, "The Mainsprings of American Foreign Policy."

69. Kennan, "Morality and Foreign Policy," pp. 209–210.

70. Ibid.

71. *Congressional Quarterly Almanac, 1974,* pp. 547–553.

72. Ole R. Holsti and James N. Rosenau, *American Leadership in World Affairs: Vietnam and the Breakdown of Consensus* (Winchester, Mass.: Allen and Unwin, 1984).

73. Ibid.

SELECTED BIBLIOGRAPHY

Beitz, Charles R., Marshall Cohen, Thomas Scanlon, A. John Simmons, eds., *International Ethics*. Princeton, N.J.: Princeton University Press, 1985.

Bennett, John C. *Foreign Policy in Christian Perspective*. New York: Scribner's, 1966.

Bennett, John C., and Harvey Seifert. *U.S. Foreign Policy and Christian Ethics*. Philadelphia: Westminster Press, 1977.

Falk, Richard A. *Law, Morality, and War in the Contemporary World*. New York: Center for International Studies, Princeton University/Praeger, 1963.

Girvetz, Harry K., ed. *Contemporary Moral Issues*. Belmont, Calif.: Wadsworth, 1963.

Gordis, Robert. *Religion and International Responsibility*. New York: The Church Peace Union, 1959.

Herz, John H. *Political Realism and Political Idealism*. Chicago: University of Chicago Press, 1951.

Kennan, George F. "Morality and Foreign Policy." *Foreign Affairs* 64 (Winter 1985): 205–218.

Larson, David L., ed. *The Puritan Ethic in United States Foreign Policy*. Princeton, N.J.: Van Nostrand, 1966.

Lefever, Ernest W. *Ethics and United States Foreign Policy*. New York: Living Age Books/Meridian Books, 1957.

Lefever, Ernest W., ed. *Ethics and World Politics*. Baltimore: Johns Hopkins University Press, 1972.

Mowat, R. B. *Public and Private Morality*. Bristol, Eng.: Arrowsmith, 1933.

Morgenthau, Hans J. *Politics among Nations*. New York: Knopf, 1951.

———. *In Defense of the National Interest*. New York: Knopf, 1952.

Niebuhr, Reinhold. *Moral Man and Immoral Society: A Study in Ethics and Politics*. 1932. Reprint. New York: Scribner's, 1932.

———. *Christianity and Power Politics*. New York: Scribner's, 1940.

———. *Christian Realism and Political Problems*. New York: Scribner's, 1953.

Pettman, Ralph, ed. *Moral Claims in World Affairs*. New York: St. Martin's Press, 1979.

Robinson, Daniel S. *Political Ethics*. New York: Crowell, 1935.

Thompson, Kenneth W. *Christian Ethics and the Dilemmas of Foreign Policy*. Durham, N.C.: Duke University Press, 1959.

———. *Political Realism and the Crisis of World Politics: An American Approach to Foreign Policy*. Princeton, N.J.: Princeton University Press, 1960.

———. *The Moral Issue in Statecraft*. Baton Rouge: Louisiana State University Press, 1966.

———. ed. *Ethics and International Relations*. New Brunswick, N.J.: Transaction/ Council on Religion and International Affairs, 1985.

Walzer, Michael. *Just and Unjust Wars*. New York: Basic Books, 1977.

Conclusion: A Comparative Analysis of Ethics, Public Policy, and the Public Service

O. P. Dwivedi

I agree with Hegel that the state exists for the realization of the moral ideals and protection of freedoms.[1] As such, the state is more than an entity or a legal activity. Actually, roots of all legal activity by and for the state are based on ethical principles. The state provides a person freedom of action (within some limitations) and a chance to self-realization. Thus it is a moral reality. Hence all state actions (i.e., public policies and programs) are moral actions, and those who formulate and implement such policies and programs are morally as well as legally accountable. It is widely acknowledged that the modern state is, and ought to be, legally as well as morally responsible for its actions. But this assertion creates a dilemma: although the legality of state action can be challenged in a court of law, how does one hold the state morally accountable? The dilemma emanates from the difficulty in assigning moral responsibility only to individual human beings, because usually we do not attribute such a responsibility either to animals or things. As long as the state falls into the category of "things," or in the domain of an entity that has no separate and distinct existence to commit purposive actions, how can one hold the state morally responsible for its action?

The argument does not end here because it is also claimed that the state exists only because it is so acknowledged and accepted by people and, more importantly, because its actions are those of individuals who govern in its name and on authority, and such individuals do undertake "purposive" actions. Such purposive actions are called public policies; individuals making and implementing those policies are public officials and bureaucrats. Thus purposive actions by them become the actions for the state. Hence all actions committed by governments on behalf of the state are, and ought to be, moral actions. It follows, then, that in this chapter we discuss ethical issues in public policy;

bureaucratic morality, with special emphasis on issues confronting Western and Third World countries; and finally, a plea for an "administrative theology" as a means to enhance ethical standards.

ETHICAL ISSUES IN PUBLIC POLICY: AN OVERVIEW

Many of the ethical norms suitable for interpersonal relationships are not necessarily applicable in the public sector. For example, murder is by definition immoral, but killing any enemy soldier during war is not called murder and is widely, though not universally, considered justifiable. Sometimes government officials are ordered into unethical and illegal activities, and in order to protect the "good" name of that agency, the government tries to cover up. There is, therefore, a great danger in accepting blindly the official versions of certain administrative actions.[2]

Since public policy is an authoritative allocation of public resources, it perforce becomes related to moral issues; similarly, the implementation of a policy is not devoid of ethical implications. Various ethical concerns arise when public policies and programs are administered. Earlier in the book, ethical issues in legislative affairs, employment decisions, risk assessment, quantification, administrative policy-making, toxic waste disposal, foreign policy-making, and fraud and waste in government were discussed. It is an awesome task to examine all social and political problems that are, in fundamental respects, ethical issues. But within the focus of this book, it is desirable to discuss briefly those issues that are not examined here and that have enduring importance and contemporary relevance. Thus the following discussion broadens the range of various ethical issues and emphasizes the necessary connection between the issues and their impact on the role of public servants in a comparative context.

These issues are (1) human rights and civil liberties, (2) biomedical technology and the practice of medicine, (3) abortion and family planning, (4) environmental crimes, (5) inmate rights, and (6) secrecy and deception in government.[3] All are examples of fundamental social and political issues that pose serious ethical problems to public officials and the society they serve.

Human rights and civil liberties are based on the ideals of equality of all people, regardless of race, creed, religion, sex, color, and national origin. These ideals have been given legal force of law so that the dignity and worth of human beings could be protected. The concept of equality is among the oldest of ethical standards; however, people have created barriers (all legally enforced) to keep the concept from being properly applied in society. Equality includes a whole range of fundamental rights (such as freedom of thought and religion, freedom of expression, freedom of peaceful assembly and of association, freedom of press) and certain rights such as equality before the law and the right to equal protection of the law, the right to own property, and the right to liberty and security.

Among these fundamental freedoms and rights, the most abused has been the right to equal treatment by all public bodies and in all public places. Any public policy that discriminates against any person for whatever reason must be considered an immoral policy. Any policy and the means used to administer it that falls short of showing primary concern for the dignity of individuals will produce, as has happened in the past, an environment that degrades and demeans.

Consequently, efforts made by government to enact laws that protect and enhance human dignity should be considered as having a salutory impact on the populace. It should be noted, however, that discrimination cannot be completely eradicated in a society. At the same time, efforts have been made to provide compensation to the disadvantaged and underprivileged groups by enforcing a quota system in educational and employment opportunities or by providing financial help in the form of grants and allowances. This policy has raised the issue of "reverse" discrimination. People who object to such a quota system claim that the fundamental right of equality before law is watered down by such practices. Whenever any group is singled out by the government for special treatment, be it the old, the sick, the mothers, or others, moral issues are raised by those who are excluded. The irony in society is that only those who are excluded complain, but those who receive benefits never bother to think whether by receiving such treatment they are depriving others from their natural rights and expectations.

Scientists tell us that the technology in the biomedical field, the second issue, is so developed that we are capable not only of prolonging life by intervening in the course of human development in ways never dreamt of in the past but also of prolonging life by genetically engineering the species itself. These research strides have created predicaments for policymakers. Ethical issues in medicine also cover subjects such as the nature of death, restrictions on population growth, sterilization under duress, pharmacological alteration of personality, psychosurgery, health-care delivery, experimentation with human subjects, and the allocation of scarce medical resources.[4] All involve ethical questions concerning whether medical practitioners and researchers should be permitted to develop control of the human mind and body. Since governments are involved in these ventures either as promoters or as conductors of research, some people are asking on what moral grounds the government permits such activities. On the other hand, the government is responsible for providing facilities that can further the frontiers of knowledge. Similarly, there are arguments against and for euthanasia, genetic engineering, and neurological and psychological manipulations. The major issue is whether government should protect human dignity at all costs or limit those experiments that might lead to dehumanization. So far no accepted body of moral and legal rules have been developed to establish guidelines in regulating these experiments. The practice of Medicare and payment for services rendered by medical practitioners created public controversy in Canada because doctors were unable to charge more than what was permitted under the governmental Medicare policy. Should the doctors be permitted to charge more than the official fee and still conduct business under the system?

Abortion and family planning are the third area where effect of public policy is difficult to measure. In the case of abortion, many believe that a fetus acquires the status of a human life and hence has at least some rights after conception. As such, abortion becomes "murder" or "justified homicide," and killing of the innocent fetus can never be permitted under a democratic system. Contrary arguments are that a woman has a right to defend her own life against a threat posed by her unborn child even though the fetus may have acquired some claim to life, that a very early abortion is surely not the killing of a person, and that abortion is one means of controlling population and extricating a woman from a psychological trauma caused from rape. Family planning, particularly through vasectomy, has been used as a means to control population. In India, during the 1975–1977 emergency rule, government force was used to perform these operations without consent on protesting males. Through such experimentation, the conduct of public policy on population control became, in the eyes of many, immoral.

The fourth issue relates to the application of the criminal code to pollution offenses. Most pollution cases do not *directly* inflict physical harm and danger to individuals or group of individuals, and whatever harms there may be, they are generally caused by corporate bodies rather than individuals; such acts are considered not as real crimes but mostly as regulatory offenses. For pollution activity to be a criminal offense, it is not enough that the act was committed; the judicial system requires that it must have been done intentionally, recklessly, or with criminal negligence. Although not a sufficient condition, it is a necessary condition that one of these three characteristics be established for securing a successful prosecution. But these factors (which derive from the attitudes at the time of committing such an activity) are difficult to establish beyond a reasonable doubt if the polluter claims that he or she was unaware of the causes and impacts of spills (both accidental and willful if proven). The ethics of environmental damage has been recognized in many societies as a necessary aspect of corporate responsibility. However, the legality of pollution activity still remains beyond the ambit of criminal code, although some offenses have been designated as quasi criminal. The main reason for this ambivalence is that in terms of harm done, risks caused, degree of intent, and values threatened, environmental problems span a continuum from minor to catastrophic, from what appears to be harmless to what is tolerable to what is intolerable and deserving social denunciation, and from what is only accidental or careless or even negligent to what is grossly negligent.[5]

This wide range of environmental harm requires an equally similar range of prohibitions, deterrence, and legal controls. This also calls for a number of legal, regulatory, and administrative approaches, controls, incentives, and enforcement mechanisms. But of particular importance are the attitudes of regulatory, monitoring, and enforcement officials who seek compliance. That mental attitude depends on the values and ethics of those officials and particularly on the importance they place on protecting the environment and how vigilant they wish to remain. Unless the state recognizes that environmental quality is a fundamental value, unique and easily threatened, and that any harm or danger to it must be dealt with all necessary legal authority under its command, crimes against the environment will continue to be committed. That recognition by the state is a moral imperative.

The function of criminal law is to enforce society's values by responding appropriately when these values are violated. The trial and the humiliation of imprisonment, the fifth issue, dramatizes the importance of the violated values. This morality, as enforced by the judicial system, not only punishes the offender but also supposedly conditions others to avoid similar antisocial acts. However, issues have been raised about prisoner rights, capital punishment, sentences imposed against young and socially deprived groups, and punishment for one crime (which does not necessarily deter the offender from another).

Some people in the judicial field believe that the law does not have a moral function; hence its primary aim should be to protect society as efficiently as possible. Law, however, should articulate society's values within a judicial system that is both effective and fair—but effective in what ways and fair to whom, the offender or the victim? Does the public have authority to take away inalienable human rights? Related questions of inmate rights include activities and the use of authority by the law-enforcement agencies. For example, in Canada, the testimony presented at the Macdonald Royal Commission into the Royal Canadian Mounted Police (RCMP) wrongdoings revealed that officers had planted wiretaps, broken into offices, used confidential medical information to disrupt organizations, burned barns, stolen dynamite, and opened mail. Whatever might have been the compelling reasons for such activities, the fact remains that they were criminal acts. It is necessary that those who enforce public policies should not be above the law, unless we desire a double standard of morality.

Finally, deception and lying have been used as instruments of public policy during war and peace. It seems that certain acts that a government orders its employees to commit, in the name of the state or patriotism, would be considered criminal if done by individuals outside the protective arm of government. Why should the government get involved in immoral activities whether during peacetime or wartime? At the same time, why is it considered unethical and criminal for a conscientious objector either to oppose war or to leak certain confidential government documents? Leaks in government have become a common phenomena.

The major policy question is, should there be government secrets in a democracy, and should government indulge in deception and other immoral acts at any time? It seems that the security of the country might demand such an action, but (as happened during the Nixon Administration) when the regime equates itself with the nation, moral problems arise. To give another example from Canada, when it was revealed that the Atomic Energy of Canada Limited and Polysor Limited (both federal government Crown Corporations) were involved in kickbacks on the sale of their products, then Prime Minister Trudeau rationalized their behavior by stating that as long as these agencies did not break any Canadian laws, any unethical activity beyond the borders of Canada were acceptable if done for commercial purposes. A double standard was given tacit approval. But an unethical act committed inside or beyond the borders of a nation remains immoral; distance does not absolve it.

Similarly, in the Iran–Contra affair, Admiral John Poindexter (a former national security adviser) absolved the president from any direct blame by distancing the head of the state from direct responsibility for the sale of arms to Iran in order to finance the Nicaraguan *contras* by providing him a means of "plausible deniability." However, the president could not distance himself from the ultimate responsibility to be accountable to the nation. The ethics of this affair has left much to be desired in terms of the moral responsibility of public officials as the situation remained shrouded in a web of lies, deception, and half-truths. At the same time, the incident created a moral dilemma about what a head of state should do if he or she feels constrained by legislative direction in attempting to fulfill his or her constitutional responsibility to govern the nation. In such a dilemma, the temptation to use power and authority to achieve certain political objectives becomes sometimes overwhelming, while the wider ramifications of morality of such an action are ignored.

The six topics briefly discussed above, and other chapters in this book, share a fundamental concern that the basis of moral, legitimate, and effective government is public trust and confidence. Such confidence is predicated on two sets of ideals. The first set is based on the belief that the state is a moral entity whose actions and policies are, and should be, liable to ethical and moral judgment. The second set of ideals holds that government is a public trust, and public service is a noble calling for persons who should know how to behave morally. But this assertion has certain implications. Are public officials aware of the ethical implications of the power they exercise? What values should they choose in the exercise of their responsibilities?

THE BUREAUCRATIC MORALITY

Bureaucratic morality in the context of the public sector includes two terms. The first is *bureaucrat,* which means an official who is appointed, promoted, and retired or removed from government through a merit system. Thus an elected politician, as well as one who is politically appointed, does not belong to this category. The second is *morality,* which includes wider connotations than the term *ethics,* which has a narrower concern usually associated with unethical activities and codes of conduct. Morality includes both the positive and negative values and attributes of holding an office.

Often *ethics* is defined as a "set of standards by which human actions are determined to be right or wrong.''[6] Ethical behavior in the public service is considered as a blend of moral qualities and mental attitudes. The requisite moral qualities include not only the willingness to serve the public but also the willingness to behave competently, efficiently, honestly, loyally, responsibly, objectively, fairly, and accountably. Mental attitudes include awareness of moral dilemmas inherent in policies and of conflicting claims on the substantive and procedural aspects of policy, an empathy for divergent views held not only by some members of the public but also by professional colleagues, and a sensitivity for paradoxes of rules that may lead to frustrating and unkind actions.

Bureaucratic morality, thus, includes not only the ethical behavior, the accomplishment of a job in a most professional manner, but also positive attributes such as trust, fairness, conduct beyond the call of duty, and goodwill. Hence standards and requisites of performance should include what a public servant ''ought not to do'' as well as an equal emphasis on the positive side of what he or she ''ought to do.'' Rectitude and ''duty to serve the public'' both are the requisite part of expected standards of the public servant. That part also includes an acknowledgment of the moral implications of public policy and administrative action.

It should be noted that there is a difference between a ''legal'' action and the ''right'' action. ''Doing right'' requires more than a legally justified action; it means doing something that is more positive, looking at both sides of the case so that one can make a *fair* decision that may require one to go beyond the legality of a case. Many a public servant would not venture beyond the legal requirement of a case irrespective of moral implications or the problem of fairness. But the public expectation about bureaucratic morality can be very high, akin to what one expects from a member of the clergy, a nurse, or parents. The public still believes that those who work for the state are there primarily to honor the call to serve the nation. Consequently, when public servants go on strike to demand better working conditions or higher wages, the public is generally unwilling to change its perception. Also, whenever there is a report in the media about some unethical activity by a government official, the public responds as if the event should not have occurred.

Some people who have recently joined the ranks of civil services, however, view their employment as a job. They would rather not accept the traditional roles of public servants wherein duty, patriotism, serving the community at all times, and sacrificing one's personal life for higher values are considered more important than the union approach to work ethics. Thus a conflict exists between the traditional public expectation from those who serve the state and those modern-day employees who believe that their obligations to serve are restricted to those duties that are part of their job classification and for which they can be held *legally,* and not necessarily morally, responsible. Thus the meaning of professional standards has acquired, in recent years, less of a moral and more of a legalistic connotation.

ETHICS AND THE PUBLIC SERVICE:
A COMPARATIVE ANALYSIS

The 1970s has been described as "the ethics decade" as information about ethical problems in government was highlighted by the worldwide publicity given to the Watergate affair. About the same time, similar revelations of unethical activities by officials in other countries were also reported. Although the examples of blatant corruption among politicians and public servants of some Third World countries have been known to exist, the recent instances of official misconduct in high places of Western democratic nations were especially shocking. It seems that no nation or culture is immune from immoralities among public officials. Continued revelations in the 1980s have confirmed the perception that "ethical standards are too low and a suspicion that many ethical infractions are never uncovered."[7]

Ethics and the Public Service in Western Nations

In countries such as Australia, Great Britain, France, Canada, and the United States, civil service reforms were introduced in the late nineteenth and early twentieth centuries to reduce patronage, nepotism, and the use of political power for private gain. An era of responsible and objective administration began that was based on the foundation of civil service neutrality, ministerial responsibility and noninterference in day-to-day operations of departments, civil service anonymity, and the merit principle in personnel management. Today, in these countries, these traditions are generally taken for granted.

These same governments, however, suffer from persistent preoccupation with procedures and functions to the exclusion of ethical values and standards. In any country, and particularly in the West, where efforts to instill rationality and efficiency in the management of public programs have been made, the administrative structure gets cumbersome, complex, rule bound, too elaborate, too slow, and too expensive. In such a system, the locus of responsibility and accountability becomes diffused, eroded, and blurred. Massive production of paperwork leaves less time for decisionmakers to reflect on the basic purposes of the activity at hand.

It is not surprising, then, to see public servants viewing their domain as rational, objective, and value free, where expediency and technical considerations may dominate the policy decisions. Consequently, ethical issues do not enter into such functional rationality. At the same time, ethical dilemmas continue to crowd public servants' vision. These dilemmas include many issues; for example, if there is a conflict between an individual's privately held convictions and publicly held obligations, what should that person do? Should the individual interpret government policies according to a personal sense of right and wrong? Or when a public servant believes there is a clear-cut conflict between what he or she is required to do and what the person really thinks is right, where should the individual's loyalty lie? Is a public servant committed to keeping information secret that might be embarrassing to the government of the day? What should an employee do when he or she finds deliberate inefficiency, protection of incompetence, extravagant and unreasonable expenditure of public funds, use of government equipment and machinery for personal purposes, or subjective criteria used in recruitment or in the award of government grants or licenses?

To what extent should a public servant support the political ideology practiced by the current political head of the government? Or when a person accepts government employment, how much should the individual subordinate or abdicate his or her claims to private life, property, and values? These and other questions need to be considered, debated, and resolved according to each country's culture, tradition, and values. However, the most important requisite for any public servant is to develop an inner sense of professional responsibility. It should be realized that public responsibility and morality are multidimensional; they flow upward and downward as well as outward and inward. Such a complex notion is bound to create dilemmas; consequently, a responsible administrator would be well advised to be on guard against forces that might attempt to influence the person to act otherwise.[8] Public servants in the West may have a more difficult task ahead than their colleagues in the Third World as they try to balance different and various demands imposed by the society to act responsibly and morally.

Third World Public Service Ethics and Responsibility

Public service ethics and responsibility, particularly as they relate to Third World countries, should be examined in the context of their historical development. Many of these countries inherited the tradition of an apolitical bureaucracy operating under a hierarchy, merit system, and a strict chain of command. Government officers were there to maintain law and order and to protect the interest of the colonial power. After independence, however, the services were expected to be responsive and oriented to the needs and aspirations of the citizenry. The first generation of political leadership took care to see that the public services responded to the new and existing chain of command. The rhythm and balance of the two command systems in administration and politics were, therefore, hardly disturbed. Later, however, continued political interference in the normal functioning of the administrative apparatus generated suspicion between the bureaucrats and the political leaders. This interference disrupted the balance in the politico-administrative systems and created, at the same time, a debilitating nexus between politicians and administrators. This development called into question the fundamental neutrality of the bureaucracy and brought into sharp focus other problems such as the limits of political control, the issue of public interest and morality government, and public service accountability. Such a situation has continued particularly in those nations where a democratic system of government operates.

In the realm of public policy, administrative accountability connotes the government's obligation to justify its actions to the legislature and afford opportunities for its members to comment, repudiate, modify, or initiate new policy measures. Accountability is real if the legislature is able to initiate programs and to oversee government actions with a view to satisfying itself that they remain in accordance with the aspirations of the people. However, clear indications are that in recent years the central legislatures in Third World countries have not played discernible roles in the preparation of policy proposals. For instance, the capacity of India's Parliament to modify proposals initiated by the executive has been moderate if not weak. Its efficacy has been much more in evidence in implementation rather than in other stages of policy development. Its competence to initiate policy measures is extremely limited irrespective of their nature. It has performed a more active role as policy influencer rather than either policymaker or policy transformer. The influence of legislatures in the policy-making process in other Third World countries has been even less crucial.

In the pursuance of development goals, not only have the powers of bureaucracy increased, but also the changing emphasis on the theory, ideology, and nature of economic development has further confused the already bewildered beneficiary: the common people or the rural poor, who find the administrative labyrinth extremely complicated. Consequently, it should be stressed that formulation of development goals alone, or making the government development oriented, does not serve any purpose unless those who administer these programs are responsive, effective, and prompt in satisfying the needs of those who are to be the beneficiaries of such development.

Regarding the role of the bureaucracy in the development process, it appears that bureaucratic values inherited from the colonial past have not by themselves stood in the way of development. But later, elected politicians found that these characteristics make the system dysfunctional when administrators place greater emphasis on using these inherited values as tools for accomplishing development goals. To politicians, a responsible developmental bureaucracy should have provided a framework that was flexible and pragmatic and encouraged open client-oriented decision-making laden with human values of service and compassion. This could be possible only by requiring administrators to reduce the number of levels in the decision-making structure, vest district and regional administrators with adequate authority commensurate with their performance, and encourage teamwork to achieve fixed goals with a determined leadership.[9]

CONCLUSION

Public policies or governmental actions are full of moral ambiguities. Circumstances of history that may justify one set of policies may prove them morally reprehensible actions at a later date. Slavery is one such example.

Moral ambiguities are going to remain because no one can formulate policies that are morally justified under all circumstances. It is important, therefore, that those formulating, implementing, and evaluating policies be made aware of these ambiguities and be ethically sensitive so as to act in a responsible manner. Ambiguity does not diminish the importance of the issue; the moral dimension of governance represents a concern for the quality of public service and governmental conduct. Otherwise, how can citizens trust that their affairs are fairly managed and that they have not surrendered rights and freedoms to an irresponsible administrative state?

Both developed and developing countries have exemplified the need to nurture a sense of moral obligation and personal responsibility for making public policies. It is the elected and appointed officials in these countries who wield the authority and use it in the name of the state. It is they who are liable to misuse the power entrusted to them. It is they who, by their own volition, may cross the limits of legal norms and moral standards. Consequently, it is they who are to be held answerable for acts undertaken and not undertaken. The state cannot be a shield for unethical, illegal, or improper activities of public officials.

Ethics in the public service does not only mean that one should exhibit negative obligations such as to do no harm, to avoid injury, or to keep out of trouble; on the contrary, the notion of governmental ethics suggests that administrators actively undertake acts that are socially just. Only by proactively pursuing social justice can the official and the government be moral and just. Unlike in the past when negative obligations and admonitions warned public officials to avoid waste, injustices, and abuses of authority, today the administrators need personally to exercise positive moral judgment in their duties. By demonstrating the highest standards of personal integrity, honesty, fairness, and justice, public officials can inspire confidence and trust, which are the key ingredients of a moral government.

Morality has been a guiding force in the history of humankind, particularly in statecraft, that is, how we are governed, our relationship with others both individually and collectively, and our understanding of the nature and destiny of humankind. Although the emphasis on secular government and democracy may have relegated the place of morality to individual conduct, it has, nevertheless, maintained a continuing tension between the requisites of public policy and the moral standards by which they can be measured. But in the recent past, a healthy tension has not been adequately maintained as we have witnessed an increase of unethical activities in public places all over the world. If justice, equality, equity, and freedom are to be protected, proximate political and administrative acts must have moral standards by which they can be judged. As I have advocated elsewhere:

All governmental acts, if they are to serve the present and future generations well, must be measured against some higher law. That law can not be a secular law because it is limited in vision as it is framed by imperfect people in their limited capacities and therefore limited in vision. That law has to be, perforce, based on the principles of higher spiritual and philosophical foundations. Administrative theology is one such foundation which can provide an important base to a moral and responsible statecraft.[10]

"Administrative theology" as a concept is based on the ideal of service to others, particularly to the community. That ideal draws upon self-sacrifice, a concept that rises above individualism and hedonism to create an environment of public duty among government officials and bureaucrats. In modern times, however, it does not mean that public servants must take a vow of poverty. Rather, it means they must adhere to the principle of serving others by setting a high standard of moral conduct and by considering their jobs as vocations akin to a religious calling. Thus administrative theology emphasizes the *service* dimensions in public employment. It involves a notion of duty and service *to* members of the public, as well as the responsibility *for* their welfare. It is not to be equated, however, with bureaucratic ideology or even theocracy because it is reconciliated with the higher values of democratic secularism and morality.

Furthermore, the morality that determines political and administrative action is multidimensional. It is rooted in the civilization of humankind and derives from its nobler foundations. It draws from the community of nations and various cultures and influences the universe that we know. The confidence and trust in the democracy can be safeguarded only when the governing process exhibits a higher moral tone, deriving from the breadth of morality. This calls for a commitment on the part of elected and appointed public officials to moral government and administration. Actually, we get a moral government by creating those conditions within which a moral government can operate. This is done by making it possible for officials to acquire the necessary traits and by the practice of the same. An exemplary public servant, to be specific, is not simply one who obeys the laws and behaves within the confines of bureaucratic values but is also one who strives for a moral government. Such is the duty for those who wish to be involved in the difficult and complex world of government. This is the essence and basis of a moral state and its public policies. Only by demonstrating the highest standards of personal integrity and morality can public officials inspire public confidence and trust, the true hallmarks of moral government.

NOTES

1. I originally developed part of this argument in "Moral Dimensions of Statecraft: A Plea for an Administrative Theology" (Presidential address delivered at the annual meeting of the Canadian Political Science Association, Hamilton, Ontario, June 1987). The address is published in the *Canadian Journal of Political Science* 20 (December 1987): 699–706.

2. Wayne A. R. Leys elaborated on this point in his book *Ethics for Policy Decisions: The Art of Asking Deliberate Questions* (New York: Prentice-Hall, 1952).

3. Discussion on some of these issues has been drawn from the author's essay,

"Ethics, the Public Service and Public Policy: Some Comparative Reflections," *International Journal of Public Administration* 10, no. 1 (1987): 32–37. (Reprinted by courtesy of Marcel Dekker, Inc.)

4. *See,* for further information, Tom L. Beauchamp, ed., *Ethics and Public Policy* (Englewood Cliffs, N.J.: Prentice-Hall, 1975), especially part seven, "Biomedical Technology," pp. 361–441.

5. Law Reform Commission of Canada, *Crimes against the Environment* (Ottawa, 1985), pp. 3–4.

6. James S. Bowman, "The Management of Ethics," *Public Personnel Management* 10 (April 1981): 61.

7. W. D. Kenneth Kernaghan and O. P. Dwivedi, eds., *Ethics in the Public Service: Comparative Perspectives* (Brussels: International Institute of Administrative Sciences, 1983), p. 2.

8. Comment by O. P. Dwivedi on *The Responsible Administrator: An Approach to Ethics for the Administrative Role,* by Terry L. Cooper (Port Washington, N.Y.; Kennikat Press, 1982), published in *Public Administration and Development* (1983): 384.

9. For further details, *see* O. P. Dwivedi and R. B. Jain, *India's Administrative State* (New Delhi: Gitanjali Publishing, 1985); O. P. Dwivedi and Nelson E. Paulias, eds., *The Public Service of Papua New Guinea* (Boroko: Administrative College, 1986).

10. Dwivedi, "Moral Dimensions of Statecraft," p. 705.

SELECTED BIBLIOGRAPHY

Appleby, Paul H. *Morality and Administration in Democratic Government.* Baton Rouge: Louisiana State University, 1952.

Australia, Government of. *Guidelines on Official Conduct of Commonwealth Public Servants.* Canberra: Australian Government Publishing Service, 1976.

Bowman, James S. "The Management of Ethics." *Public Personnel Management* 10 (1981): 59–66.

Brady, N. F. "Feeling and Understanding: A Moral Psychology for Public Servants." *Public Administration Quarterly* 7 (1983): 220–240.

Canada, Government of. *Ethical Conduct in the Public Sector.* Ottawa: Supply and Services, 1984.

Chapman, L. *Your Disobedient Servant: The Continuing Story of Whitehall's Overspending.* London: Chatto and Windus, 1978.

Cooper, Terry L. *The Responsible Administrator: An Approach to Ethics for the Administrative Role.* Port Washington, N.Y.: Kennikat Press, 1982.

Doig, Alan. *Corruption and Misconduct in Contemporary British Politics.* Harmondsworth, Eng.: Penguin Books, 1984.

Dwivedi, O. P. "Bureaucratic Corruption in Developing Countries." *Asian Survey* 7 (1967): 245–253.

———. *Public Service Ethics.* Brussels: International Institute of Administrative Sciences, 1978.

———. "Ethics and Values of Public Responsibility and Accountability." *International Review of Administrative Sciences* 51 (1985): 61–66.

———. "Moral Dimensions of Statecraft: A Plea for an Administrative Theology." *Canadian Journal of Political Science* 20 (December 1987): 699–706.

Dwivedi, O. P., and E. Engelbert. "Education and Training for Values and Ethics in the Public Service." *Public Personnel Management* 10 (1981): 140–145.

Ekpo, M. U., ed. *Bureaucratic Corruption in Sub-Saharan Africa*. Washington, D.C.: University Press, 1979.

Fitzwalter, R., and D. Taylor. *Web of Corruption*. London: Granada, 1981.

Foster, G. D. "Law, Morality, and the Public Servant." *Public Administration Review* 41 (1981): 29–34.

Gould, David J. *Bureaucratic Corruption and Underdevelopment in the Third World: The Case of Zaire*. New York: Pergamon Press, 1980.

Gould, David J., and Jose A. Amaso-Reyes. *The Effects of Corruption on Administrative Performance: Illustrations from Developing Countries*. Washington, D.C.: World Bank Staff Working Papers, 1985.

Heclo, Hugh, and Aaron Wildavsky. *The Private Government of Public Money*. London: Macmillan, 1974.

Heidenheimer, Arnold J., ed. *Political Corruption: Readings in Comparative Analysis*. New York: Holt, Rinehart and Winston, 1970.

Hill, M. J. *The State, Administration, and the Individual*. Glasgow: Fontana/Collins, 1976.

Hope, Kemp R. "The Administration of Development in Emergent Nations: The Problems in the Caribbean." *Public Administration and Development* 3 (1983): 49–60.

Jackson, M. S. "Eichmann, Bureaucracy, and Ethics." *Australian Journal of Public Administration* 43 (1984): 301–307.

Johnston, M. *Political Corruption and Public Policy in America*. Monterey, Calif.: Brooks/Cole, 1982.

Kernaghan, W. D. Kenneth, and O. P. Dwivedi, eds. *Ethics in the Public Service: Comparative Perspectives*. Brussels: International Institute of Administrative Sciences, 1983.

Leigh, D. *The Frontiers of Secrecy: Closed Government in Britain*. London: Junction Books, 1980.

Lilla, Mark T. "Ethos, 'Ethics,' and Public Service. *Public Interest,* no. 63 (1981): 3–17.

Linklater, M., and D. Leigh. *Not with Honour*. London: Sphere Books, 1986.

Olowu, Dele. "The Nature of Bureaucratic Corruption in Nigeria." *International Review of Administrative Sciences* 69 (1983): 70–76.

———. "Bureaucratic Performance in Developed and Developing Countries." *Public Administration Review* 44 (1984): 453–458.

Quah, Jon. S. T. "Bureaucratic Corruption in the ASEAN Countries: A Comparative Analysis of their Anti-Corruption Strategies." *Journal of South-East Asian Studies* 13 (1982): 153–177.

Rohr, John A. *Ethics for Bureaucrats: An Essay on Law and Values*. New York: Dekker, 1978.

———. "Ethics for the Senior Executive Service: Suggestions for Management Training." *Administration and Society* 12 (1980): 203–216.

Scott, James C. *Comparative Political Corruption*. Englewood Cliffs, N.J.: Prentice-Hall, 1972.

Thomas, Rosamund M. *The British Philosophy of Administration*. London, 1978.

Thompson, Dennis F. "Moral Responsibility of Public Officials: The Problem of Many Hands." *American Political Science Review* 74 (1980): 905–916.

United Kingdom, Government of. *Royal Commission on Standards of Conduct in Public Life*. London: Her Majesty's Stationery Office, 1976.

Waldo, Dwight. *The Enterprise of Public Administration: A Summary View*. Novato, Calif.: Chandler and Sharp, 1980.

Young, H., and A. Sloman. *No, Minister: An Inquiry into the Civil Service*. London: British Broadcasting Corporation, 1982.

Selected Bibliography

Alcorn, Paul A. *Social Issues in Technology*. Englewood Cliffs, N.J.: Prentice-Hall, 1986.

Barber, Bernard. *The Logic and Limits of Trust*. New Brunswick, N.J.: Rutgers University Press, 1983.

Bayles, Michael. *Professional Ethics*. Belmont, Calif.: Wadsworth, 1981.

Beauchamp, Tom. *Ethics and Public Policy*. Englewood Cliffs, N.J.: Prentice-Hall, 1975.

Bergerson, Peter. *Ethics and Public Policy: An Annotated Bibliography*. New York: Garland, 1988.

Bernard, Baumrin, and Benjamin Freedman, eds. *Moral Responsibility and the Professions*. New York: Haven, 1983.

Bok, Sissela. *Lying: Moral Choice in Public and Private Life*. New York: Pantheon, 1978.

Bowie, Norman, ed. *Ethical Issues in Government*. Washington, D.C.: Urban Institute Press, 1981.

Bowman, James S. "Ethical Issues for the Public Manager." In William B. Eddy, ed., *Handbook on Public Organization Management*. New York: Dekker, 1983, pp. 69–102.

————, ed. "Special Issue on Ethics in Government." *Public Personnel Management* 10, no. 1 (1981).

————, ed. *Essentials of Management: Ethical Values, Attitudes, and Action*. Port Washington, N.Y.: Associated Faculty Press, 1983.

Bowman, James S., Frederick A. Elliston, and Paula Lockhart. *Professional Dissent: An Annotated Bibliography and Resource Guide*. New York: Garland, 1984.

Burnstein, Paul. *Discrimination, Jobs, and Politics*. Chicago: University of Chicago Press, 1985.

Caiden, Gerald E., ed. *International Handbook of the Ombudsman*. Westport, Conn.: Greenwood Press, 1983.

Cooper, Terry. *The Responsible Administrator*. 2d ed. New York: Associated Faculty Press, 1986.

Covello, Vincent T., Joshua Menkes, and Jeryl Mumpower, eds. *Risk Evaluation and Management*. New York: Plenum, 1986.

Denhardt, Kathryn G. *Toward a More Ethical Public Administration*. Westport, Conn.: Greenwood Press, 1988.

Dunn, William N., ed. "Symposium on Social Values and Public Policy." *Policy Studies Journal* 9, no. 4 (1981).

Elliston, Frederick, John Kennan, Paula Lockhart, and June Van Schaick. *Whistleblowing: Managing Dissent in the Workplace*. New York: Praeger, 1985.

Ewing, David W. *"Do It My Way or You're Fired": Employee Rights and the Changing Role of Management Prerogatives*. New York: Wiley, 1981.

Fleishman, Joel, Lance Liebman, and Mark Moore. *Public Duties: The Moral Obligations of Public Officials*. Cambridge, Mass.: Harvard University Press, 1981.

French, Peter. *Government Ethics*. Englewood Cliffs, N.J.: Prentice-Hall, 1983.

Gawthrop, Louis. *Public Sector Management, Systems, and Ethics*. Bloomington: Indiana University Press, 1984.

Glenn, James R., Jr. *Ethics in Decision Making*. New York: Wiley, 1986.

Goldman, Alan. *The Moral Foundations of Professional Ethics*. Totowa, N.J.: Rowman and Littlefield, 1980.

Gutmann, Amy, and Dennis Thompson, eds. *Ethics and Politics: Cases and Comments*. Chicago: Nelson Hall, 1984.

Hampshire, Stuart. *Public and Private Morality*. New York: Cambridge University Press, 1978.

Heidenheimer, Arnold J., Michael Johnston, and Victor T. LeVine, eds. *Political Corruption: New Perspectives in Comparative Analysis*. New Brunswick, N.J.: Transaction, 1986.

Jennings, Bruce, and Daniel Callahan, eds. *Representation and Responsibility: Exploring Legislative Ethics*. New York: Plenum Press, 1985.

Johnston, Michael. *Political Corruption and Public Policy in America*. Monterey, Calif.: Brooks/Cole, 1982.

Kernaghan, W. D. Kenneth, and O. P. Dwivedi, eds. *Ethics in the Public Service: Comparative Perspectives*. Brussels: International Institute of Administrative Sciences, 1983.

Lucash, Frank S., ed. *Justice and Equality*. Ithaca, N.Y.: Cornell University Press, 1986.

Mertins, Herman, Jr., and Patrick J. Hennigan, eds. *Applying Professional Standards and Ethics in 1980's: A Workbook and Study Guide for Public Administrators*. 2d ed. Washington, D.C.: American Society for Public Administration, 1982.

Moore, Christopher. *The Mediation Process*. San Francisco: Jossey-Bass, 1986.

Mosher, Frederick C. *Democracy and the Public Service*. 2d ed. New York: Oxford University Press, 1981.

Pastin, Mark. *The Hard Problems of Management*. San Francisco: Jossey-Bass, 1986.

Rohr, John. *Ethics for Bureaucrats*. 2d ed. New York: Dekker, 1986.

Thompson, Kenneth W., ed. *Ethics and International Relations*. New Brunswick, N.J.: Transaction/Council on Religion and International Affairs, 1985.

Tong, Rosemarie. *Ethics in Policy Analysis*. Englewood Cliffs, N.J.: Prentice-Hall, 1986.

U.S. General Accounting Office. *Fraud in Government Programs.* 2 vols. Washington, D.C.: U.S. Government Printing Office, 1981.

U.S. Merit Systems Protection Board. *Whistle Blowing and the Federal Employee.* Washington, D.C., 1981.

Index

About the Editors
and Contributors

LARRY A. BAKKEN is a professor of law at Hamline University and a faculty member in the Graduate Program in Public Administration. He is an elected city council member and has served as a consultant to the Minnesota legislature, the Administrative Conference of the United States, and the Document Design Center of Washington, D.C. He is also president of the Minnesota Chapter of the American Society for Public Administration and the Urban, State, and Local Government Section of the Minnesota Bar Association. Bakken has had articles published on government regulation and is the author of *Justice in the Wilderness* and *Minnesota Administrative Practice*. He holds the following degrees: B.A., Concordia College; M.S., North Dakota State University; J.D., University of North Dakota; LL.M., University of Manitoba.

JAMES S. BOWMAN is professor of public administration at Florida State University. His articles on professionalism, ethics, Japanese-style management, the behavioral sciences, the meaning of work, and trends in the discipline have been published by leading business and public management journals. Bowman is the contributing editor of *Essentials of Management: Ethical Values, Attitudes, and Actions* and *Professional Dissent*. He is a member of the editorial board of *Public Administration Quarterly*, the *Review of Public Personnel Administration*, and *Public Productivity Review*. Bowman has been a National Association of Schools of Public Affairs and Administration Faculty Fellow as well as a Kellogg Foundation Fellow.

GARY C. BRYNER teaches in the Department of Political Science at Brigham Young University. His teaching and research interests are in public policy and public law. He received the Ph.D. from Cornell University and was a research fellow at the Brookings Institution. Bryner is the author of *Bureaucratic Discretion.*

JOHN P. BURKE is assistant professor of political science at the University of Vermont. He is the author of *Bureaucratic Responsibility* and articles about executive decision-making and ethical problems in public affairs. Burke has taught at Williams College and Princeton University, where he received the Ph.D.

LLOYD BURTON is an assistant professor in the Graduate School of Public Affairs at the University of Colorado, Denver. He holds a teaching law degree from Boalt Hall School of Law, at the University of California, Berkeley. Burton has taught environmental law and conflict management on the Berkeley and Davis campuses of the University of California. He is a registered mediator and arbitrator with the American Arbitration Association.

ANTHONY G. CAHILL is assistant professor of public administration in the Department of Public Administration, Pennsylvania State University. His interests focus on the application of scientific and technical information by policymakers, the design and evaluation of information systems, and program evaluation. He is associate editor and member of the Editorial Board of the journal *Knowledge: Creation, Diffusion, Utilization* and is the senior research consultant to the Legislative Office for Research of the Commonwealth of Pennsylvania.

RALPH G. CARTER is an assistant professor of political science at Texas Christian University. He received the B.A. from Midwestern State University in Wichita Falls, Texas, and the M.A. and Ph.D. from Ohio State University. Previously, he taught at Wichita State University in Wichita, Kansas. Carter's primary research area concerns the role of Congress, and other domestic inputs, in the making of American foreign policy.

O. P. DWIVEDI is professor of political science and chairman, Department of Political Studies, University of Guelph, Canada. He has been policy consultant to the government of Canada. His international assignments include work for the United Nations, the government of Papua New Guinea, and the World Health Organization. Dwivedi has had ten books published including *Governments as Employers, Protecting the Environment, Resources and the Environment, Public Service Ethics, Administrative State in Canada,* and *India's Administrative State,* and articles in professional journals. He is a past president of the Canadian Political Science Association.

FREDERICK A. ELLISTON was a visiting professor of philosophy at the University of Hawaii at the time of his death in 1987. He received his Ph.D. in

Philosophy from the University of Toronto in 1974. His areas of specialization included ethics, social philosophy, and phenomenology. The author of numerous books and articles, his most recent works were *Moral Issues in Public Work, Whistleblowing, Conflicting Loyalties in the Workplace,* and *Ethics and the Legal Profession.*

ALBERT FLORES is professor of philosophy at California State University, Fullerton. His research and teaching has focused on examining ethical problems created by modern technology for the practice of business and the professions. Among the books he has edited, the most recent is *Professional Ideals.*

MYRON PERETZ GLAZER holds a B.A. from City College of New York, an M.A. from Rutgers University, and a Ph.D. from Princeton University. He is currently professor of sociology and anthropology at Smith College. His published works include *Student Politics in Chile, Latin American University Students: A Six Nation Study,* and *The Research Adventure: Promise and Problems of Field Research.* With Penina Migdal Glazer, he is the coauthor of *The Courage of Their Convictions: The Fate of Whistle Blowers in Government and Industry.*

PENINA MIGDAL GLAZER received the B.A. in history from Douglass College and the M.A. and Ph.D. degrees from Rutgers University. She is professor of history and dean of the faculty at Hampshire College. Her fields of specialization include American social history and the history of professionalization. Glazer recently had a book published (with Miriam Slater) entitled *Unequal Colleagues: The Entrance of Women into the Professions, 1890–1940.*

MICHAEL E. KRAFT is a professor of political science and public administration at the University of Wisconsin–Green Bay. He had taught previously at Vassar College and Oberlin College and was recently a visiting professor at the Robert M. La Follette Institute of Public Affairs at the University of Wisconsin–Madison. Kraft is the coeditor of *Environmental Policy in the 1980s: Reagan's New Agenda* and *Technology and Politics,* and he has written extensively on environmental policy and politics. His current research focuses on management of technological risks in a democratic polity, with special attention to issues of nuclear-waste disposal.

JEROME B. MCKINNEY is professor at the Graduate School of Public and International Affairs, University of Pittsburgh. He is coauthor of *Planning and Budgeting in Four Commonwealth Caribbean States, Introduction to Public Administration, Introduction to Organization Theory, Public Administration: Balancing Power and Accountability,* and *Understanding ZBB: Promise and Reality.*

E. SAM OVERMAN is an associate professor at the Graduate School of Public Affairs, University of Colorado, at Denver. He has conducted research and has written articles on topics such as information policy and management, decision theory, ethics, and public policy. His most recent book, *Methodology and Epistemology in Social Science,* is an edited volume of selected papers by Donald Campbell.

RICHARD L. PATTENAUDE is vice-president for academic affairs at Central Connecticut State University. He received the Ph.D. in political science from the University of Colorado. Pattenaude has had works published and has consulted in the fields of decision-making, organizational analysis, and public sector management.

JEREMY F. PLANT is associate professor of public affairs and director of the doctoral program in public administration at George Mason University. A graduate of Colgate University, he received the Ph.D. in government from the University of Virginia. Plant has taught at North Carolina State, SUNY–Albany, and the University of Virginia. His current research includes work on transportation policy in suburban regions, the history and development of public administration between 1940 and 1970, and the role of public organizations in public policy.

GERALD M. POPS works in the areas of administrative law, justice, ethics, conflict resolution, and public sector labor relations. Currently professor of public administration at West Virginia University, his career includes legislative staff work in California state government, trial work as an air force lawyer, and teaching in public administration and political science. Pops is the author of *Emergence of the Public Sector Arbitrator* and the coauthor of *Conflict Resolution in the Policy Process.*

VERA VOGELSANG-COOMBS is the director of Hamline University's Graduate Public Administration Program. She has taught political science and public administration at the University of Missouri–St. Louis, Washington University, and the University of Maryland's extension division in Bicester, England. Active in the American Society for Public Administration, Vogelsang-Coombs is a past president of the Minnesota Chapter and is currently serving a three-year term on the National Council. A Phi Beta Kappa graduate of the City College of New York, she holds M.A. and Ph.D. degrees from Washington University in St. Louis.

JONATHAN P. WEST is professor and chair of the Department of Politics and Public Affairs at the University of Miami. His teaching and research are in the areas of public personnel management, collective bargaining, and productivity in government. He has recently authored or coauthored articles appearing in *Review of Public Personnel Administration, Polity, Public Productivity Review, Journal of Collective Negotiations in the Public Sector, Industrial and Labor Relations Review,* and other scholarly journals.